CLASSICAL PRESENCES

General Editors

LORNA HARDWICK   JAMES I. PORTER

CLASSICAL PRESENCES

Attempts to receive the texts, images, and material culture of ancient Greece and Rome inevitably run the risk of appropriating the past in order to authenticate the present. Exploring the ways in which the classical past has been mapped over the centuries allows us to trace the avowal and disavowal of values and identities, old and new. Classical Presences brings the latest scholarship to bear on the contexts, theory, and practice of such use, and abuse, of the classical past.

Milton, Longinus, and the Sublime in the Seventeenth Century

THOMAS MATTHEW VOZAR

Great Clarendon Street, Oxford, OX2 6DP,
United Kingdom

Oxford University Press is a department of the University of Oxford.
It furthers the University's objective of excellence in research, scholarship,
and education by publishing worldwide. Oxford is a registered trade mark of
Oxford University Press in the UK and in certain other countries

© Thomas Matthew Vozar 2023

The moral rights of the author have been asserted

All rights reserved. No part of this publication may be reproduced, stored in
a retrieval system, or transmitted, in any form or by any means, without the
prior permission in writing of Oxford University Press, or as expressly permitted
by law, by licence or under terms agreed with the appropriate reprographics
rights organization. Enquiries concerning reproduction outside the scope of the
above should be sent to the Rights Department, Oxford University Press, at the
address above

You must not circulate this work in any other form
and you must impose this same condition on any acquirer

Published in the United States of America by Oxford University Press
198 Madison Avenue, New York, NY 10016, United States of America

British Library Cataloguing in Publication Data
Data available

Library of Congress Control Number: 2023942434

ISBN 978–0–19–887594–9

DOI: 10.1093/oso/9780198875949.001.0001

Printed and bound in the UK by
Clays Ltd, Elcograf S.p.A.

Links to third party websites are provided by Oxford in good faith and
for information only. Oxford disclaims any responsibility for the materials
contained in any third party website referenced in this work.

Contents

Acknowledgments vii
Abbreviations and References ix
Figures and Tables xi

   Introduction 1
   The Philology of the Sublime 4
   The Plan of This Study 10

1. The Sublime from Antiquity to the Renaissance 13
   Longinus and Greek Rhetorical Theory 13
   Longinus and the Sublime in the Renaissance 23
   The Physical Species of the Sublime 32
   The Theological Species of the Sublime 37

2. Milton and the "Stile of Lofty" 43
   Milton's Education in the Sublime 43
   Biblical Sublimity of Style and Milton's Soaring 54
   Sublime Style and the Problem of Enthusiasm 64
   Republicanism, Liberty, and Sublime Rhetoric 72

3. Sublime Physics in *Paradise Lost* 85
   Etna, Typhon, and Satan 86
   Milton's Hyperbolic Similes 93
   Astronomy and the Sublimities of Space 101

4. Milton and the Theological Sublime 120
   The "Sublime Notion" of Virginity 120
   The War in Heaven as Sublime Theomachy 125
   Milton's Sublime God 132
      Timor Dei and *Timor Idololatricus* 140

   Conclusion 147

   Bibliographical Appendix 149
      Longinus in English Private Libraries to 1674 149

   Textual Appendix 155
      The Lansdowne Longinus 155

Works Cited 169
Index 205

Acknowledgments

This book took shape as a PhD thesis at the University of Exeter, and I am principally indebted to my supervisor, Karen Edwards, a Miltonist whose learning, generosity, and confidence in this project were essential to its completion. I was also very fortunate to have been able to benefit from the expertise and guidance of Matthew Wright, my secondary supervisor in Classics, in matters ranging from ancient literary criticism to Renaissance Greek palaeography. I am immensely grateful as well to my examiners, two masterful scholars of Milton and seventeenth-century intellectual history who provided helpful comments for turning my thesis into a book: Will Poole, whose *Milton and the Making of Paradise Lost* was constantly on my desk, and Nick McDowell, whose *Poet of Revolution: The Making of John Milton* appeared just after the completion of my research. While I was unable to take the latter work into account in this book, I find its emphasis on Neoplatonism and the daemonic in Milton's early thought to be congruent to a great extent with my own interpretations of Miltonic inspiration and enthusiasm.

For their observations and encouragement I would also like to thank Hugh Adlington, Colin Burrow, Hannah Crawforth, Martin Jay, Sarah Knight, and Sylvana Tomaselli, as well as audiences at the 2018 Graduate Conference in Political Thought and Intellectual History in Cambridge, the 2019 International Milton Symposium in Strasbourg, and the autumn 2019 British Milton Seminar in Birmingham. I am especially grateful to John Hale, who read and commented on several chapters, and to Richard Serjeantson, who provided invaluable advice for my work on the Lansdowne Longinus. Wieneke Jansen, Micha Lazarus, and Eugenio Refini graciously shared their important work on the early modern reception of Longinus.

In the course of writing this book I had the pleasure of spending time with early modern books and manuscripts at the Bodleian Library, the British Library, and the Cambridge University Library. Alex Hailey at the British Library was especially helpful in facilitating my work on the Lansdowne Longinus. In preparing the bibliographical appendix I contacted a number of institutions asking for information on their collections, and I would like to thank the librarians who responded to these queries: Sandra Bailey (Wadham College Library, Oxford), John Boneham (Rare Books and Music, British Library), Ken Gibb (Rare Books, Lambeth Palace Library), Jo Maddocks (Special Collections, Bodleian Library), Liam Sims (Rare Books, Cambridge University Library), Danielle Westerhof

(Rare Books, Durham University Library), and Peter Whidden (Special Collections, Stanford University Libraries).

I am also grateful to have been funded by an International Excellence Scholarship from the University of Exeter Doctoral College, without which this project could not have been undertaken. A small grant for an additional research visit to the British Library was provided by the Thomas Wiedemann Memorial Fund. Final revisions were completed at the University of Hamburg, where I have begun work on a second book on scholarship and politics in the English Revolution as an Excellence Strategy Postdoctoral Fellow.

Finally, I would like to thank the Classical Presences series editors, Lorna Hardwick and Jim Porter; the Commissioning Editor, Charlotte Loveridge; the two anonymous readers; and the Oxford University Press staff who helped bring this publication to fruition.

Several articles incorporate or expand on parts of this book: "Sir Henry Wotton's Copy of Portus' *Aphthonius, Hermogenes, & Dionysius Longinus*," in *Notes & Queries* 66.3 (2019): 473–4; "An English Translation of Longinus in the Lansdowne Collection at the British Library," in *The Seventeenth Century* 35.5 (2020): 625–50; "*Timor Dei* and *Timor Idololatricus* from Reformed Theology to Milton," in *Reformation* 26.1 (2021): 62–72; "Milton, Sublime Style, and the Problem of Enthusiasm," in *Milton in Strasbourg: A Collection of IMS12 Essays*, eds. Christophe Tournu, Neil Forsyth, and John K. Hale (Bern: Peter Lang, 2022), 137–60; and "Ps.-Longinus, Dionysius Cassius. Addenda et Corrigenda," forthcoming in *Catalogus Translationum et Commentariorum: Mediaeval and Renaissance Latin Translations and Commentaries*, eds. Greti Dinkova-Bruun, Julia Haig Gaisser, and James Hankins (Toronto: Pontifical Institute of Mediaeval Studies).

My wife, my mother, my sister, my grandmother, and the rest of my family have sustained me throughout and beyond my work on this book with their constant love and support. I dedicate this book to my father, Thomas Joseph Vozar (1955–2018), who passed away before its completion.

> At tibi, chare pater, postquam non aequa merenti
> posse referre datur, nec dona rependere factis,
> sit memorasse satis, repetitaque munera grato
> percensere animo, fidaeque reponere menti.

Abbreviations and References

In-text citations are used for Milton's works, classical texts, and the Bible. Classical and patristic texts and books of the Bible are abbreviated according to standard conventions. Additionally, the following abbreviations appear in the text and notes:

BAV	Bibliotheca Apostolica Vaticana
BL	British Library
BnF	Bibliothèque nationale de France
Bod.	Bodleian Library
CPW	Yale *Complete Prose Works of John Milton*
CSP Dom.	*Calendar of State Papers, Domestic*
CUL	Cambridge University Library
CW	Oxford *Complete Works of John Milton*
EF	Milton's *Epistolae Familiares*
HP	Hartlib Papers, Sheffield University Library
KJV	King James Version
L&S	Lewis and Short's *Latin Dictionary*
Maske	*A Maske Presented at Ludlow Castle, 1634*
ODNB	*Oxford Dictionary of National Biography*
OED	*Oxford English Dictionary*
PL	*Paradise Lost*
PR	*Paradise Regain'd*
SA	*Samson Agonistes*
WJM	Columbia *Works of John Milton*

The question of which edition of Milton's writings to use is not an uncomplicated one. Scholars of Milton now have, in addition to myriad publications of individual and selected works, three monumental series of scholarly editions to choose from: the Columbia *Works*, the Yale *Complete Prose Works*, and the Oxford *Complete Works*, of which five of a projected eleven volumes have been published to date. It is not superfluous to repeat here the observation that there is no such thing as a definitive edition: these three series differ from one another in content, priorities, and much else besides. Each has its virtues and its vices. The Yale series, for example, has for decades been established as the standard reference edition for Milton's prose, but it omits his original Latin entirely.[1] The Oxford *Complete Works*, which will provide, once completed, annotated texts of all of Milton's poetry and prose, including both original texts and new translations of his Latin works (and which is conveniently accessible, to those with access to a subscription, through Oxford

---

[1] Hale 1997b: 82 calls this "a terrible editorial blunder." See also Corns 1984.

Scholarly Editions Online), promises to become the standard reference series for the foreseeable future. Yet while most of the volumes in this series to have appeared thus far have been of a very high quality, not all have escaped criticism: in particular, the Oxford volume of Milton's shorter poems provoked a harsh review from Paul Hammond, which prompted the press to quietly publish a corrected impression.[2]

In this study the currently available volumes of the Oxford *Complete Works* are the preferred sources for quotations of Milton, encompassing the shorter poems, the 1671 poems, the commonplace book, the vernacular regicide and republican prose, and *De Doctrina Christiana*. References to Milton's letters are from the 2019 edition of Haan. Otherwise I cite from the Yale *Complete Prose Works* for the English prose and the Columbia *Works* for the Latin prose. Quotations of *Paradise Lost* are from Barbara Lewalski's 2007 Blackwell edition.

For Longinus I have relied primarily upon Donald Russell's 1964 Greek text and commentary as well as his 1999 revision of W. H. Fyfe's English translation for the Loeb Classical Library. I have also regularly consulted the 1992 Greek-Italian edition and commentary of Carlo Mazzucchi. The new text and commentary by Stephen Halliwell, published in Italian in 2021 and in English in 2022, unfortunately appeared too late for its insights to be fully incorporated into this study, and though I have added a few pertinent citations the reader is advised to turn to it for the latest major treatment of Longinus.

Translations of primary sources in Greek, Latin, Italian, and French are my own except where otherwise indicated. In each instance the source text is also provided. Greek is transliterated when it is deemed helpful or necessary to follow the use of particular words or phrases. Hebrew is always transliterated.

---

[2] Hammond 2013; see also Herman 2015.

Figures and Tables

Figures

1. Detail of a Byzantine manuscript of Longinus, Parisinus Graecus 2036, fol. 1v, courtesy of the Bibliothèque nationale de France — 14
2. Title page of Portus' *Aphthonius, Hermogenes, and Dionysius Longinus* (1569/1570) with the autograph of Henry Wotton, RBC KB1570.A6, courtesy of the Department of Special Collections, Stanford University Libraries — 29
3. Detail of Wotton's copy of Portus (1569/1570), p. 12, RBC KB1570.A6, courtesy of the Department of Special Collections, Stanford University Libraries — 30
4. Title page of Gerard Langbaine's edition of Longinus (1638), STC 16789, used by permission of the Folger Shakespeare Library — 61
5. Illustration from Athanasius Kircher's *Mundus Subterraneus* (1678), vol. 1, between p. 200 and p. 201, BSB-ID 2166670, courtesy of the Bayerische Staatsbibliothek and the Munich Digitization Center — 87
6. Title page of John Wilkins' *A Discourse Concerning a New World & Another Planet* (1640), STC 25641, used by permission of the Folger Shakespeare Library — 103
7. Title page of Galileo's *Dialogus de Systemate Mundi* (1635), BSB-ID 14444526, courtesy of the Bayerische Staatsbibliothek and the Munich Digitization Center — 104
8. Title page of Galileo's *Dialogo sopra i due massimi sistemi del mondo* (1632), BSB-ID 11799516, courtesy of the Bayerische Staatsbibliothek and the Munich Digitization Center — 105
9. Detail of William Marshall's title page for Langbaine's Longinus (1638), STC 16789, used by permission of the Folger Shakespeare Library — 106
10. Detail of William Marshall's title page for John Wilkins' *Discourse* (1640), STC 25641, used by permission of the Folger Shakespeare Library — 107
11. Frontispiece to Bernard le Bovier de Fontenelle's *Entretiens sur la pluralité des mondes* (1686), 228–339q, used by permission of the Folger Shakespeare Library — 115

12. Title page of the Lansdowne Longinus, MS Lansdowne 1045, fol. 166v, © The British Library Board   156
13. First page of the Lansdowne Longinus, MS Lansdowne 1045, fol. 167r, © The British Library Board   157

Tables

1. Manuscript translations of Longinus before 1674   25
2. Printed editions and translations of Longinus before 1674   27

Introduction

Many years ago the writer in company with an accidental party of travellers was gazing on a cataract of great height, breadth, and impetuosity, the summit of which appeared to blend with the sky and clouds, while the lower part was hidden by rocks and trees; and on his observing, that it was in the strictest sense of the word, a sublime object, a lady present assented with warmth to the remark, adding—"Yes! and it is not only sublime, but beautiful and absolutely pretty."[1]

—Samuel Taylor Coleridge, *Essays on the Principles of Genial Criticism* (1814)

Ever since his death in 1674 the works of John Milton have been accorded the epithet *sublime*—so much so that just over a century later Mary Wollstonecraft complained that she was "sick of hearing of the sublimity of Milton," which she compared to the cliché of "the original, untaught genius of Shakespear."[2] If the sublimity of Milton is to mean anything more than a banal affirmation of literary greatness, the sublime must be considered as a concept grounded within a particular context, that of European cultural and intellectual history. The conventional historiography of the sublime, as represented most recently by Robert Doran's *The Theory of the Sublime from Longinus to Kant* (2015), begins with the Greek treatise entitled *Peri hupsous*, usually translated into English as *On the Sublime* and traditionally ascribed to a certain Dionysius Longinus;[3] resumes with the 1674 translation of Longinus by the French poet-critic Nicolas Boileau; and then proceeds to eighteenth-century writings on the sublime by the likes of Edmund Burke and Immanuel Kant with the advent of philosophical aesthetics.[4] There remains here, it will be noticed, a discontinuity of some fifteen hundred years: the impression is that Longinus was the sole and anomalous inventor of the

---

[1] Coleridge 1995: 362. [2] Wollstonecraft 1787: 52.
[3] On the date and authorship of this treatise see Chapter 1. I use the name Longinus alone (or Dionysius Longinus) to refer to the author of this work; the third-century philologist and philosopher Cassius Longinus is referred to by his full name.
[4] Though Doran 2015, to be fair, does not purport to present a comprehensive history of the sublime, but more specifically a history of the "theory" of the sublime, I consider the stages of his narrative representative of the conventional view. The same leap from Longinus to Boileau is made by Shaw 2006 and Fritz 2011. On Burke's use of Milton, esp. in relation to Lucretius, see Bullard 2012; on Kant and Milton see Tisch 1968; Budick 2010; Shore 2014.

idea of the sublime, and that his treatise was all but unknown until diffused throughout the European republic of letters by Boileau, thereby enabling the development of the philosophical theory of the sublime in the Enlightenment.

If this picture is right, it becomes difficult to see how Milton himself could have had any notion of the sublime. Milton mentions Longinus only once, recommending "a gracefull and ornate Rhetorick taught out of the rule of *Plato, Aristotle, Phalereus, Cicero, Hermogenes, Longinus*" (CPW 2: 402–3) in his tract *Of Education*, and for a long time scholars have mostly yielded to the view Samuel Monk pronounced almost a century ago, that Milton "seems not to have felt Longinus's charm."[5] If Longinus was just a name Milton tacked onto a list of classical authorities and the idea of the sublime was not otherwise developed until after his lifetime, Milton could not have had any conception of the sublime. It is perhaps not surprising then that, aside from the occasional passing reference to Longinus, scholarship on the subject, when it has not strayed into anachronism, has been limited almost entirely to the study of Milton's reception.[6] Once a commonplace, Milton's sublimity has now been so thoroughly eclipsed that a recent monograph on Milton and the ineffable—which one might expect to provoke at least a perfunctory allusion to the idea of the sublime—makes no mention of it,[7] nor do any of the various Miltonic companions, reading guides, and subject encyclopedias in current use.[8] Given this state of affairs, one would seem to have good cause to surrender to the judgment that the Miltonic sublime is, in the words of Leslie Moore, "a fiction of eighteenth-century criticism."[9]

Advances in scholarship, however, have rendered obsolete the conventional view of the history of the sublime upon which this judgment depends. While Longinus was certainly less familiar to Renaissance readers than some other Greek authors, evidence has steadily accumulated that his treatise attracted the attention of a number of humanists, poets, clergymen, artists, and many others in the sixteenth and seventeenth centuries, even, to a much lesser extent, before the

---

[5] Monk 1935: 20. See recently Hale 2016a: 206 (but cf. Hale 2022, citing my research); Martindale 2012a: 89 n.93; Martindale 2012b: 854.

[6] For passing references to Longinus see Burrow 1999: 496–7; Shore 2012: 102–3; Dobranski 2015 passim; Goldstein 2017: 175, 205 n.81. As Sedley 2005: 158 n.20 observes: "Theoretically advanced discussions of the sublime that do consider authors prior to Boileau (e.g., Milton) still look through the lens of eighteenth-century discussions." Sedley cites Knapp 1985 and Kahn 1992 as examples of such anachronism, to which one may add for example Teskey 2015: 409–35. Cheney 2018b: 9 n.16 declares: "Alone among early modern authors, Milton's sublimity has been much discussed." Nearly all the examples he gives, however, and others he does not, are studies of the sublime in relation to Milton's reception. These indeed are legion, including, but not limited to, Nelson 1963: 39–73; Morris 1972 passim; Moore 1990; von Maltzahn 2001; Budick 2010; Crawford 2011; Martindale 2012a: 71–8; Leonard 2013 passim; Sugimura 2014a; Gigante 2016; Hoxby 2016.

[7] Reisner 2009. I am thinking here for example of Long. *Subl.* 9.2, on the sublimity of Ajax's silence in the underworld of the *Odyssey*.

[8] In my survey of these materials I have found only passing mentions of the sublime, and then strictly as it relates to Milton's reception, in Danielson 1999: 161, 245, 247; Corns 2012a: 80–1; Schwartz 2014: 198, 201; Corns 2016: 552–3, 576; and none at all in Reisner 2011.

[9] Moore 1990: 2.

1554 *editio princeps* of Francesco Robortello.[10] Moreover, though the *Peri hupsous* is the only surviving ancient work of rhetoric devoted to the sublime, it is increasingly appreciated that the idea of the sublime in rhetoric was not limited to Longinus but was instead much more widespread in both the classical rhetorical tradition and its later reception.[11] Lastly, and perhaps most crucially, the ancient idea of the sublime, as James Porter's magisterial *The Sublime in Antiquity* (2016) has shown, was not restricted to rhetoric but extended into various discourses and domains of inquiry, including natural history and philosophy.[12]

When all of this is taken into account, the notion that Milton would have had an idea of the sublime begins to seem less like a chronological impossibility than a near certainty. Thus far, however, Miltonic scholarship has not fully assimilated this emerging new understanding of the history of the sublime as a pre-aesthetic concept (i.e. as a concept predating eighteenth-century aesthetics).[13] Despite some important studies by the likes of Annabel Patterson and David Norbrook, who have argued that the political resonances of Longinus in the seventeenth century would have appealed to the republican Milton, the subject of Milton and the sublime in a seventeenth-century context has not yet received the comprehensive treatment it deserves.[14] It is the task of the present study to ameliorate this status

---

[10] Following the bibliographical research of Weinberg 1950, 1962, and 1971, a number of studies have appeared concerned with the dissemination of Longinus and the influence of Longinian ideas before Boileau in Italy (Costa 1984a, 1984b, 1985, 1987a, 1987b, 1994, 2003; Mazzucchi 1989; Lehtonen 2016 and 2019; Refini 2012 and 2016), in France (Fumaroli 1986; Gabe 1991; Gilby 2006; Gilby 2016), in the Netherlands (Bussels 2016; Nativel 2016; van Oostveldt and Bussels 2016; Jansen 2016 and 2019), and in England (Ringler 1938; Spencer 1957; Cheney 2009a, 2011, 2018a, 2018b; Lehtonen 2016; McDowell 2008: Ch. 5 passim; and Lazarus 2021); see also the papers collected in van Eck et al. 2012.

[11] Fumaroli 2002; Shuger 1988; Goyet 1996; Hendrix 2005.

[12] Porter 2016 is the most thorough and significant, but studies specifically of the Lucretian natural-philosophical sublime have been fruitful as well, including e.g. Conte 1966 and 1994: 9–52; Hardie 2009; and Porter 2003, 2007. See also the papers collected in Jaeger 2010a on the medieval conception of the sublime.

[13] On the sublime as a concept that developed concomitantly with aesthetics itself in the eighteenth century see de Bolla 1989, esp. 27–102.

[14] Patterson 1993: 258–72 first drew attention to the political aspect of the Longinian sublime in relation to Milton, which Norbrook 1999: 137 later dubbed its "republican accent." Stark 2003 detects Longinus' concept of *psuchrotēs* ("false grandeur," literally "frigidity") in the rhetoric of Satan and other fallen angels in *PL*. Feinstein 1998 considers Milton's use of the word *sublime*, including its alchemical sense. Sedley 2005, in a comparative study of sublimity and skepticism in Montaigne and Milton, offers chapters on "*Comus* and the Invention of Milton's Grand Style" (82–107) and "*Paradise Lost* and How (Not) to Be Sublime" (108–33), but both are predominantly concerned with Miltonic skepticism rather than sublimity; one could also argue that the aporetic quality of the sublime, which underpins Sedley's thematic connection of sublimity and skepticism, is part of the distinctively aesthetic concept of the sublime which did not develop until after Milton, but that would require more space than is available here. Cheney 2009b considers Milton's sublimity in relation to Marlowe and republicanism; see also Cheney 2018b passim. Machacek 2011: 121–35 argues generally for the potential impact of Longinus on Milton, in particular by drawing attention to Longinus' Homeric exempla. Norbrook 2013 provides an important first step toward an extra-Longinian understanding of the Miltonic sublime by considering *Paradise Lost* in relation to the Lucretian sublime. Prompted by Porter 2016 and others, Shaw 2017 (the second edition of Shaw 2006) includes a chapter on "Early Modern Sublimity" (41–66), with a short section on Milton (45–8). Most recently, Lehtonen 2019 sees the sublimity of Milton's Satan as a response to a Tassoan model of heroic charisma.

quo. More than a comparative study of Milton and Longinus—though that lies within its purview—this requires a historical exposition of ideas of the sublime, Longinian and otherwise, as these existed in Milton's lifetime, which can then inform a historically grounded exegesis of the sublime in Milton.

The Philology of the Sublime

The first chapter of this study will consider the history of various conceptions of the sublime from antiquity to the Renaissance. But how is the sublime to be defined? Patrick Cheney, in the most recent of his several studies of the sublime in English Renaissance literature, characterizes it as nothing more than "literary greatness."[15] Yet this definition seems to me inadequate, being at once too specific and too general, for the sublime is not limited to literature, nor is it quite so vague as a quality of "greatness." I submit that the question of definition instead needs to be approached philologically. Given its post-classical importance, I shall begin by treating the root of the English word *sublime*—Latin *sublimis* and its derivatives—before turning to the more expansive Greek vocabulary of Longinus and its implications for the philology of the sublime.

As my own usage suggests, the most obvious words for the concept of the sublime are the Latin *sublimis* and its derivatives in English and other languages. The Roman grammarian Festus glosses the Latin word as "Sublime means lifted on high" (*Sublimem est in altitudinem elatum*, Festus *Gloss. Lat.* 306.17–18) and speculates that it derives from "a higher threshold, because it is above us" (*limine superiore, quia supra nos est*, Festus *Gloss. Lat.* 306.26–27 Lindsay). Alfred Ernout and Antoine Meillet dismiss this as a *calembour* such as ancient etymologists were wont to make.[16] The first element of *sublimis* most likely does not derive from *super* ("over, above") but instead from *sub*, meaning "under, beneath," and hence also "movement from below, reaching upward."[17] The origin of the second element (*-lim-*) is less clear. Festus' *limen* could be correct, giving *sub* + *limen* ("up to the threshold"). But the etymological dictionaries of Ernout-Meillet and Michiel de Vaan both agree in preferring *limus* ("oblique, transverse"), from the Proto-Italic root **limo-*: the compound **sub-lim-i* would thus signify "that which ascends in an oblique line, that which rises on an incline" or "transverse from below upward."[18]

---

[15] See Cheney 2018b passim, esp. 36: "*Literary greatness* is my working definition of the sublime."
[16] Ernout and Meillet 2001 s.v. sublimis.
[17] Ibid.; de Vaan 2008 s.v. sub, su(b)s notes: "The meaning 'movement upwards' can be seen e.g. in *suspicio, sublevo, surgo, sublatus*."
[18] Ernout and Meillet 2001 s.v. sublimis; De Vaan 2008 s.v. limus 2.

The Latin word is first attested in early Roman drama of the late third and early second centuries BC.[19] Its earliest appearance is in a fragment from Naevius' tragedy *Lycurgus*: the text is corrupt, but it seems to represent the titular character's instruction to "lure" (*inlicite*) and trap the maenads, here called "two-footed birds" (*bipedes volucres*) or "flying bipeds" (*bipedes volantes*), "on high" (*sublime*, Naev. *Trag.* 18 Schauer). The use of *sublimis* in relation to flight in general, particularly in the phrase *sublime volans* ("flying high"), is found in such authors as Accius (Acc. *Trag.* 390, 576 Ribbeck), Lucretius (Lucr. 2.206, 6.97), and Vergil (Verg. *Aen.* 10.664), but here in Naevius the inhibited flight of the maenads on high (*sublime*) may also refer to the mystical notion of the dying soul as a fluttering bird.[20] More legible are the several places in the tragedies of Ennius in which the word *sublimis* is used for various phenomena above the earth, meteorological, astronomical, and divine: in one instance he applies it to clouds (*sublimas subices* [= *nubes*], Enn. *Trag.* 3-4 Jocelyn; cf. Lucr. 4.135, 6.97), while the phrase *sublime iter* ("sublime journey") is used both for the heavenly path of the horses of Helios and for the movement of the constellation Boötes (Enn. *Trag.* 169, 190 Jocelyn). Elsewhere Ennius uses *sublimis* to describe the sun "on high" (*sublime*), identified as Jupiter (*quem vocant omnes Iovem*, Enn. *Trag.* 301 Jocelyn),[21] and provides the earliest attestation of the verb *sublimare* ("to elevate, raise up") when he says that the sun "lifts up its glowing torch in the sky" (*candentem in caelo sublimat facem*, Enn. *Trag.* 243 Jocelyn). H. D. Jocelyn notes that *sublimis*, "a word of some dignity," appears "not at all in comedy except in the set phrases *sublimem rapere* (*arripere*) and *sublimem ferre* (*auferre*)."[22] It is not difficult to see how the upward movement denoted by the first element of *sublimis* could have led to the word being applied to the general act of lifting someone off their feet, as is the case in Roman comedy, but later usage of *sublimem rapere* for abduction by the gods or assumption into the heavens suggests the possibility that the original sense of the phrase may have been more numinous than humorous, as later in the *Aeneid* (Verg. *Aen.* 1.259, 5.255).[23] Rudolf Ehwald in 1892 even proposed that Livy's description of the apotheosis of Romulus as a *sublime raptum* (Liv. *Ab Urb. Cond.* 1.16.2) was taken from Ennius' epic *Annales*, a hypothesis that has been accepted by a number of scholars since.[24]

---

[19] The most extensive overview of the early use of *sublimis* remains Haffter 1935, reprinted in Lefèvre 1973: 110–21.

[20] See Seaford 2009: 410–11.

[21] Possibly inspired by Eur. fr. 941 Snell ὁρᾷς τὸν ὑψοῦ τόνδ' ἄπειρον αἰθέρα, in which case Ennius' *sublime* would be translating ὑψοῦ; see the discussion in Jocelyn 1969: 423–4.

[22] Jocelyn 1969: 169. See Plaut. *Asin.* 868; *Men.* 992, 995, 1002, 1052; *Mil.* 1394; and Ter. *Ad.* 316, *An.* 861.

[23] The word *rapere* in general is strongly associated with divine abduction, like the rape of Persephone, as in Ovid; see Hinds 1987: 151 n. 20.

[24] Ehwald 1892: 12. Cf. Enn. *Ann.* 54–55, 105–11 Skutsch and see Norden 1957 on Verg. *Aen.* 6.719f., Meister 1925: 35; Haffter 1935: 252; Hardie 2009: 200.

These early attestations suggest some of the ways that *sublimis* would continue to be used throughout the history of Roman literature: it could simply mean "high," and hence something as mundane as lifting someone up (*sublimem ferre*); it could describe anything in the air or sky, including clouds, stars, meteors, or the movement of celestial bodies and heavenly figures above (*sublime iter*); and it could be used in relation to flight (*sublime volans*), especially for modes of divine transport such as abduction or apotheosis (*sublime raptum*). It is only in the first century BC that we find evidence of the semantic development of *sublimis* into the sense "great, distinguished, eminent," as applied for example to persons—of which the first instance is in Varro (Varr. *Rust.* 2.4.9)—and the sense "grand, noble, lofty" as a literary-critical term, first found in Ovid (Ov. *Am.* 1.15.23, 3.1.39–40). Columella in the first century AD provides the earliest witness for the substantive *sublimitas* ("sublimity"), here used simply with regard to the physical height of a building (Colum. *De Re Rust.* 8.3.3).

In post-classical Latin *sublimis*, *sublimare*, and *sublimitas* spawned a number of new words. The deverbal noun *sublimatio* ("elevation") is first attested in the late antique author Avitus of Vienne with a sense of theological deliverance (Alc. Avit. *Contra Eutych. Haer.* 20.6 Peiper), but later becomes the standard Latin term for the process of alchemical sublimation, so called because the extract rises to the top of the vessel. Renaissance authors produced such coinages as *sublimamentum* ("cloudiness"), *sublimaticus* ("distilled"), *sublimipeta* ("one who aspires to heights"), and *sublimivagus* ("striving to heights").[25] Derivatives from the Latin begin to appear in vernacular languages from the fourteenth century onward. Perhaps the earliest instance is in the often highly Latinate Italian of Dante's *Commedia*, in which the angels circling around God strive "to make themselves like the point [i.e. God] as much as they are able, / and are able as much they are sublime [*soblimi*] in their vision" (*per somigliarsi al punto quanto ponno, / e posson quanto a veder son soblimi, Paradiso* 28.101-102). French *sublime* and Occitan *sublimatiu* are first attested around the same time, in fourteenth-century translations of medieval Latin encyclopedic works.[26]

In English, *sublime* is first found as an alchemical term, after Latin *sublimatio*, referring to the process of sublimation: in *The Canterbury Tales* Chaucer has the Canon's Yeoman describe "his science" with reference to the process of "sublymyng," the product "sublymed mercurie," and the vessels in which sublimation takes place, "sublymatories."[27] Before the end of the fifteenth century there appears the verb *sublime* in the sense "to elevate, exalt, or purify" as well as the noun *sublimity*, which like Latin *sublimitas* is not used in relation to alchemy but

---

[25] See Ramminger 2020 s.v. sublimamentum, sublimaticus, sublimipeta, sublimivagus.
[26] See Godefroy 1902 s.v. sublime and Raynouard 1843 s.v. sublimatiu.
[27] Chaucer 2008: VIII G 721, 770, 774, 793. Cf. the quotation of the roughly contemporary English translation of the *Chirurgia Magna* of Lanfranc of Milan in *OED* s.v. sublime, *v.* I.1.

rather signifies nobility, greatness, height, as in "hevenly sublimitee."[28] The adjective *sublime* is first attested in the 1567 English psalter of Matthew Parker, Archbishop of Canterbury, who in his verse proem "To the Reader" recommends the elevating power of music because "flat verse it reysth sublime."[29]

Milton's usage of *sublime* is largely consistent with early modern English practice more generally, but with the alchemical sense predominating.[30] From this one might surmise that Milton had no special conception of the sublime at all, at least in the sense with which I am concerned. But the significance of this one word, *sublime*, should not be overstated. After all, it is a word that the great ancient authority on the subject, Longinus, as a writer of Greek, does not use at all.

Longinus opens his treatise by noting his disappointment with a work that Caecilius of Calacte wrote "about the sublime" (*peri hupsous*, Long. *Subl*. 1.1) and responding to his addressee's appeal to write "something about the sublime" (*ti peri hupsous*, Long. *Subl*. 1.2) himself. It was presumably from these statements that the work was given the title *Peri hupsous*, if the author did not devise it himself. The noun *hupsos* is simply the most basic word for "height" in the Greek language, derived from *hupsi* ("up, above").[31] Longinus uses this and related words like *hupsēlos* ("high," Long. *Subl*. 40.2), *hupsēgoria* ("lofty expression," Long. *Subl*. 8.1), and *hupsēlophanēs* ("lofty-seeming," Long. *Subl*. 24.1) throughout his treatise. But *hupsos*-words are hardly the only terms in which Longinus discusses his subject: as James Porter has noted, the text's "indifference to terminology can be breathtaking—and a bane to modern philology."[32] If, as Porter has claimed, the obsolete historiography of the sublime depends in part on a "narrow *Wortphilologie*" which takes for granted that only the words *hupsos*, *sublimitas*, and the like can signify the sublime, attention to the range and variety of Longinus' vocabulary should serve as a corrective.[33]

Longinus once even appears to treat *bathos* ("depth"), seemingly the semantic opposite of *hupsos*, as a virtual synonym, when he wonders "if there is some technique [*technē*] of loftiness [*hupsous*] or depth [*bathous*]" (εἰ ἔστιν ὕψους τις ἢ βάθους τέχνη, Long. *Subl*. 2.1). I say "appears" because the Byzantine archetype of the manuscript tradition has the reading *bathous*,[34] although a number of scholars have thought that the text required emendation: the best conjecture is *pathous* ("passion, emotion"), first intuited by Giovanni di Niccolò da Falgano in his Italian translation dedicated in 1575.[35] This reading has been adopted by many editors since, including Carlo Mazzucchi, who proposes in his 1992 edition that

---

[28] See *OED* s.v. sublime, v. II.5.a.(a) and s.v. sublimity, n.
[29] Parker 1567: sig. A2r. See *OED* s.v. sublime, adj. and n. A.1.a.(a). [30] Feinstein 1998.
[31] See Beekes 2010 s.v. ὕψι. [32] Porter 2016: 182.
[33] Ibid. 49; see 7ff. Ibid. 180–2 provides a comprehensive list of Longinian terms for the sublime which forms the basis of my discussion here.
[34] BnF Codex Parisinus Graecus 2036, fol. 179v.
[35] Biblioteca Nazionale Centrale di Firenze, MS Magl. VI.33, fol. 5v (*affetto*); see the app. crit. in Mazzucchi 1992 ad loc. On Giovanni da Falgano's translation see Cardillo 2010.

the pairing of heights and depths in biblical imagery prompted "the error of the Byzantine scribe."[36] The pairing of heights and depths, however, is as classical as it is biblical, and the imagery of sublime depths even appears elsewhere in the *Peri hupsous*.[37] Moreover, the emendation *pathous* is problematic in itself, as Longinus later criticizes Caecilius for implying that sublimity and passion are identical (Long. *Subl*. 8.2). To name his subject both loftiness and profundity would have been no contradiction for Longinus, who had a multitude of words for the sublime at his disposal.

Longinus speaks of the sublime in terms of size, greatness, or magnitude, many of which are formed from the root *mega-*, including *megas* ("great, large"), *megethos* ("greatness, size"), *megalophuēs* ("great-natured"), *megalophrosunē* ("greatness of mind"). He speaks of the sublime as *ogkos* ("mass, bulk, swelling") and as *hadrotēs*, which means "strength, vigor, ripeness, thickness, abundance," from the adverb *hadēn* ("to one's fill, to satiety, unceasingly").[38] He uses words with the prefix *huper-*, which have the sense of going over, above, and beyond: these include, among others, *huperphuēs*, literally "over-natured" or "overgrown," used to mean "extraordinary, strange, monstrous;" *huperbolē* ("excess"), literally "overshooting;" and *to huperairon*, from the verb *huperairein* ("to go beyond, to raise above"), which for Longinus signifies something like transcendence: "One seeks in statues the likeness of a human, but in literature, as I was saying, the transcendence [*to huperairon*] of humanity" (κἀπὶ μὲν ἀνδριάντων ζητεῖται τὸ ὅμοιον ἀνθρώπῳ, ἐπὶ δὲ τοῦ λόγου τὸ ὑπεραῖρον, ὡς ἔφην, τὰ ἀνθρώπινα, Long. *Subl*. 36.3). Words with the prefix *ek-* ("out") have a sense of displacement, such as *ekphulos*, literally outside of (*ek*) the tribe (*phulē*), hence "strange, alien, horrible;" *ekstasis* ("ecstasy"), literally out of (*ek*) place (*stasis*), displacement; and *ekplēxis*, from *ek* and *plēxis* ("blow, strike")—glossed by D. A. Russell in his commentary on Longinus as "surprise or fear which 'knocks you out.'"[39] He also uses the word *deinos*, as well as derivatives like *deinotēs*, which in rhetorical writings often has the sense "forceful" or "intense" but whose basic meaning, from the Proto-Indo-European root **duei-no-*, is "fearful, dreaded, terrible."[40] The fearful aspect of the sublime is not limited to *ekplēxis* and *deinos* but found also in Longinus' use of words with the root *phobos* or "fear" (e.g., Long. *Subl*. 10.6). Longinus also speaks of the sublime in terms of divine inspiration and possession: *pneuma* ("inspiration,") *enthousiasmos* ("divine possession"), *mania* ("madness"), *Korubantiasmos* ("Corybantic frenzy"), *Bakcheia* ("Bacchic possession"), *Phoibolēptos* ("seized by Apollo"). The sublime is *semnotēs* ("solemnity, majesty") as well as *sphodrotēs*

---

[36] Mazzucchi 1992: 135.
[37] See Grube 1957: 360–2, Capizzi 1983, and Porter 2016: 530–1, with reference to Long. *Subl*. 9.6, 35.4.
[38] See Beekes 2010 s.v. ἄδην.
[39] Russell 1964: 122. On the dislocating power of Longinian rhetoric see Too 1998: 187–217.
[40] See Beekes 2010 s.v. δεινός.

("violence, vehemence"). In one place the sublime is "ambitiousness [*to*... *hadrepēbolon*] in ideas" (τὸ περὶ τὰς νοήσεις ἁδρεπήβολον, Long. *Subl.* 8.1), the dis legomenon *hadrepēbolon* literally meaning "aiming at vigor [*hadrotēs*];"[41] in another it is simply *kallos* ("beauty").

The extensive vocabulary of Longinus not only shows the impoverishment of any historical study of the sublime which does not take into account any terms beyond *sublimis* or *hupsos* but also suggests the wide semantic field of the sublime: loftiness, elevation, and exaltation; depth and profundity; vastness; magnitude; mass or bulk; fear, terror, and dread; divine inspiration and possession; excess, going beyond, exceeding limits, transcendence; vehemence, violence, and force; flight, transport, rapture; shock, displacement, and ecstasy.[42] There are therefore a number of words that could be used to signify the sublime, whether in classical or vernacular languages.

In Latin, for instance, some other terms besides *sublimitas* are indicated by the different ways that the title of Longinus' treatise was translated in the early modern period. Most follow the pattern of the *editio princeps*, which has the title *De grandi sive sublimi orationis genere*, identifying the subject as a form of speaking (*genus orationis/genus dicendi*) that is grand (*grandis*) or sublime (*sublimis*): *sublimis* translates the literal sense of height in *hupsos*, while *grandis* connects this quality with the grand style (*genus grande*) in rhetoric and with a more general kind of grandeur (*granditas*).[43] The manuscript of the earliest extant Latin translation, on the other hand, is entitled *De altitudine et granditate orationis*, likewise naming the subject as "grandeur of speech" (*granditate orationis*) but here translating *hupsos* with *altitudo*—a word which can equally signify height or depth, and thus perfectly encapsulates the Longinian conjunction of *hupsos* and *bathos*.[44] In a section of his 1630 rhetorical treatise treating "the various names of the sublime style" (*variis sublimis styli nominibus*) the Dutch classical scholar Gerardus Vossius illustrates some of the possible lexical breadth involved when he records the alternative adjectives *magnificus* ("magnificent"), *magniloquus* ("magniloquent"), *altiloquus* ("high-speaking"), *magnus* ("great"), *altus* ("high"), *summus* ("supreme"), *plenus* ("full"), *uber* ("rich"), *gravis* ("grave"), *copiosus* ("copious"), *ornatus* ("ornamented").[45] Samuel Hartlib, to whom Milton addressed his essay *Of Education*, offers *sublimitas* as a synonym of *magnitudo* ("greatness, magnitude"), the Latin cognate of the Longinian Greek term *megethos*, together with *infinitas* ("boundlessness, infinity"), *amplitudo* ("extent, abundance"), and *sufficientia* ("sufficiency, plenitude").[46]

---

[41] The only other appearance of *hadrepēbolon* in all of extant Greek literature is at Vett. Val. 43.2.
[42] Cf. the respective lists of Hardie 2009: 81ff. and Porter 2016: 51–3.
[43] Robortello 1554; Manutius 1555; Portus 1569/70; de Petra 1612; Langbaine 1636, 1638, 1650; Manolessi 1644.
[44] BAV MS Vat. Lat. 3441.   [45] Vossius 1630: II 432.   [46] HP 38/7/11A.

Many more words in Greek and Latin could be added, not to mention the vernaculars, an exhaustive list of which would itself warrant a Longinian label such as *mania* or *huperbolē*. But it suffices to have intimated the great variety of terms that can be used to signify the sublime, and having concluded this brief philological investigation I am now prepared to offer a working definition of the sublime, imperfect though it certainly is, as I think Milton and his contemporaries might have understood it. It is this: the sublime is a rhetoric, and a thematics, of loftiness, grandeur, power, and scale, which effects ravishment, astonishment, awe, and often terror. Milton himself may never have formulated such a definition of the sublime, but the confluence of these elements in his writings and thought, as shall become apparent, suggests that he would have recognized it.

The Plan of This Study

Boileau's popular French translation of Longinus was published in July 1674, within days of the appearance of the second edition of *Paradise Lost* and less than half a year before Milton's death,[47] and it was over the following decades, partly under the influence of Boileau's Longinus, that Milton's sublimity became entrenched as a critical commonplace among writers including John Dryden, John Dennis, and Joseph Addison.[48] But, crucially, it is not only after Boileau that such comments were made. As early as 1669 Edward Phillips, Milton's nephew and former pupil, commends *Paradise Lost* for its "sublimity of argument" (*sublimitatem Argumenti*), its "majesty of style" (*Majestatem Styli*), and its "sublimity of invention" (*sublimitatem Inventionis*).[49] In their dedicatory poems included in the second edition of *Paradise Lost*, both Samuel Barrow and Andrew Marvell praise Milton as a poet of the sublime: Barrow in his Latin verses lauds Milton's *grandia carmina* ("sublime cantos"), while Marvell more pointedly uses the English word *sublime* in the line "Thy verse created like thy Theme sublime."[50] These early responses identify in Milton some of the aspects of the pre-aesthetic sublime that will be considered in this study.

Chapter 1 outlines the diachronic development of various notions of the sublime in European thought from classical antiquity to the early seventeenth century. I begin with an overview of the *Peri hupsous* and its context in Greek

---

[47] See Brody 1958, Cronk 2002, and Doran 2015: 97–123.
[48] See esp. Moore 1990. On the influence of Boileau's Longinus see inter alia Clark 1925: 361–79; Huntley 1947; Gelber 2002: 161–5; and Delehanty 2007. Boileau's Longinus was translated from French into English at least twice (Pulteney 1680; [Anon.] 1698). Additionally, a 1679 advertisement records the existence of an otherwise unknown volume printed by Jacob Tonson under the title "A Treatise of Sublimity: Translated out of *Longin*, by H. Watson, of the *Inner Temple*, Gent." (Hall 1679: sig. Ttt4r); the use of the French form *Longin* and the date both suggest that this too was translated from Boileau.
[49] Phillips 1669: 399. See McDowell 2019 and Chapter 2.
[50] Lewalski 2007: 5, Marvell 1971: I 138. See von Maltzahn 2001: 166ff. and Miner 2004: 35–40. Lieb 1985 recognizes Barrow's verses as constituting a "sublime commentary" on *PL*. On Barrow see also von Maltzahn 1995.

rhetorical theory, which is followed by an examination of the reception of Longinus and the Longinian sublime in early modern Europe. This provides the necessary background to the rhetorical species of sublimity, or a certain notion of lofty style, as it would have been understood by Milton and his contemporaries. I then provide sketches of the other two species of the sublime, the physical and the theological. The sublime in natural-philosophical discourse is traced from classical authors such as Lucretius to the seventeenth-century Jesuit polymath Athanasius Kircher, while a tradition of the sublime in theological discourse is shown to extend from biblical commentators such as Philo of Alexandria to theologians of the Reformation. The historical exposition furnished here prepares the ground for the subsequent chapters on Milton, each of which takes as its focus one of the three species of the sublime.

Chapter 2 argues for the importance of a conception of sublime rhetoric in Milton's poetry and prose. I first speculate on when and in which edition Milton might have first encountered Longinus. Milton's education in rhetoric more broadly is also considered, as is the evidence from his tract *Of Education* and from the writings of Edward Phillips that Milton himself may have taught the *Peri hupsous* to his nephews. I then show, with reference to Isaac Casaubon and Hugo Grotius, that Milton possessed a sense of biblical sublimity of style which deeply informed his soaring prophetic poetry. The potentially dangerous association of such sublimity with enthusiasm or religious fanaticism, as touched on by John Spencer and especially Meric Casaubon, is also explored. Finally I turn to the political import of Longinus for Milton. I discuss what David Norbrook has called the "distinctively republican accent" of the sublime in the period of the English Civil Wars,[51] agreeing with this general characterization but with the qualification that sometimes, as for John Aubrey, Longinian *hupsos* did not always align with revolutionary politics. The chapter concludes with an analysis of Satan in *Paradise Lost* as a republican orator whose enslavement by his passions, as Longinus warns, prevents him from achieving true sublimity.

Chapter 3 contends that in *Paradise Lost* in particular Milton makes use of a physics of sublime magnitudes in his attempt to render adequately the unimaginable sizes and spaces of the poem, inspired both by classical authors and by the technologies and discoveries of the new science. I begin with a focus on Mount Etna, an object of physical sublimity for both Longinus and Athanasius Kircher, as it appears in Milton's early work *In Quintum Novembis* and especially in *Paradise Lost*. I then consider what I call Milton's "hyperbolic similes" in *Paradise Lost*, which I posit can be understood logically as quantitative comparisons developed in a process of Ramist *inventio*. These similes are shown to magnify Satan and his ilk to sublime dimensions, though not unproblematically, and I propose that the simile of the diminishing demons at the end of Book 1 in particular may bear the

---

[51] Norbrook 1999: 137.

influence of a passage of Longinus regarding pygmy slaves. The last part of this chapter is concerned with the new astronomy and the vastness of space. Looking to early modern scientists such as Galileo and John Wilkins, I examine Milton's attempts to depict the impossibly huge sublimities of the universe—indeed the *multiverse*—in the poem, ranging from the seemingly incalculable span of the finite created universe to the infinite expanse of Chaos.

Chapter 4 asserts that a notion of the sublime also pervaded Milton's theological thought. I first attend to *A Maske Presented at Ludlow Castle, 1634*, which Sir Henry Wotton describes in terms of rapture, as a work in which virgin purity so sublimes the soul that the threat of God's wrath is invoked against its enemies. This speaks to a notion of divine sublimity which, as the Reformed theologian Daniel Chamier writes, inheres not in rhetorical style but in holy matter. Next I consider the war in heaven in *Paradise Lost*, arguing that this episode should not be interpreted wholly or predominantly as farce or comedy but rather as a sublime theomachy which closely follows the Homeric pattern praised by Longinus. After this I turn to the contentious topic of Milton's God. Briefly considering the views of Pseudo-Dionysius the Areopagite and John Colet on the representation of the divine, I endeavor to demonstrate that in *Paradise Lost* and in the theological treatise *De Doctrina Christiana* Milton portrays a deity whose obscurity and wrath suggest the ultimately incomprehensible sublimity of the divine. Milton's sublime God is to be met with the right Christian practice of *timor Dei* ("fear of God"), which stands in opposition to *timor idololatricus* ("idolatrous fear"): the final part of the chapter considers this neglected theological notion, which Milton inherited from the Reformed theologians Amandus Polanus and Johannes Wollebius, in *De Doctrina*, *Paradise Lost*, and *Samson Agonistes*.

The conclusion of this study briefly reviews its contributions. Two appendices follow, which offer additional evidence for the reception of Longinus in seventeenth-century England. The first is a bibliographical study of copies of Longinus that I have been able to place in English private libraries before 1674. The second provides an edition of the Lansdowne Longinus, a previously unknown seventeenth-century English translation of the *Peri hupsous* that I discovered in the Lansdowne collection at the British Library.[52]

Milton's sublimity, as I hope to show, is no "fiction of eighteenth-century criticism."[53] On the contrary, notions of the sublime touch on almost every aspect of Milton's career, from rhetoric to politics, from science to theology. Making contributions to literary scholarship, classical reception studies, and the history of ideas, this study seeks to return the sublime to its proper place at the forefront of Milton criticism, to reevaluate the diffusion of Longinian texts and notions in early modern Europe, and to record a crucial missing chapter in the history of the sublime.

---

[52] See Vozar 2020.   [53] In the words of Moore 1990: 2.

1
The Sublime from Antiquity to the Renaissance

The aim of this chapter is to offer a genealogy of the sublime from antiquity to the Renaissance. I take genealogy in this sense to signify a kind of historical inquiry into the evolution and development of some concept or institution which emphasizes its contingency.[1] This chapter, accordingly, is concerned with tracing the development of various historical notions of the sublime from their ancient origins to the seventeenth century. It first considers Longinus and the notion of rhetorical sublimity in Greco-Roman antiquity, then treats the reception of Longinus in the Renaissance. After this I turn to two other modes of sublimity, adapted from James Porter's concepts of the material and the immaterial sublime: physical sublimity, or the sublime as it relates to nature and matter, and theological sublimity, or the sublime as it relates to divinity.[2] These three lineages of the sublime—the rhetorical, the physical, and the theological—provide the template for the subsequent three chapters, as each type of sublimity is considered in relation to Milton. This tripartite division must be understood as a mere heuristic device or organizational principle: the sublime can easily transgress such artificial limitations. Nevertheless, this tripartite division has the advantage of allowing the rhetorical idea of the sublime to be treated with due attention on its own, while also giving space to consider the more expansive reach of the sublime into both the physical or natural realm and the metaphysical or theological one. I begin, then, with Longinus.

Longinus and Greek Rhetorical Theory

As noted earlier, Longinus does not claim to have discovered something new, but rather frames his work as a response to a "little treatise" (*sungrammation*) that Caecilius of Calacte wrote "about sublimity" (*peri hupsous*, Long. *Subl.* 1.1), which

---

[1] Nietzsche 2006, with his genealogy of morality, was the first to use the word in this sense; on his conception of genealogy see Geuss 1994. Foucault 1995 genealogized the institution of the prison; see Foucault 1977 for his own thoughts on genealogy. Bevir 2008: 266 identifies "nominalism, contingency, and contestability" as features of genealogy; for its function as a form of critique see Geuss 2002.

[2] For what I call "physical" and "theological" sublimity cf. the concepts of "material" and "immaterial" sublimity in Porter 2016.

Longinus and his Roman addressee, a certain Postumius Florus Terentianus,[3] found defective. But how the *Peri hupsous* should be situated within this larger conversation about the sublime in antiquity is not straightforward. Neither Caecilius' nor any other ancient work devoted to the sublime survives, and the date and authorship of the *Peri hupsous* are matters of continuing speculation and debate. Internal references to authors of the first century BC restrict its earliest possible date to the Augustan period. In the earliest witness of the text, a Constantinopolitan manuscript in a hand dated to the second half of the tenth century AD now at the Bibliothèque nationale de France in Paris, the author is listed in the table of contents as "Dionysius or Longinus" (*Dionusion ē Longinon*), while the heading at the beginning of the *Peri hupsous* itself attributes it to a "Dionysius Longinus" (*Dionusiou Longinou*).[4] The scribe, or his predecessor, seems to have been suggesting the Augustan rhetorician and historian Dionysius of Halicarnassus and the third-century AD philosopher Cassius Longinus as possible authors, or suggesting one in addition to the name that he found in his source, only to conflate the two later. Alternatively, it is possible that Dionysius Longinus was the form that was transmitted, and that the scribe later added the eta (*ē*) as an afterthought to indicate some measure of doubt, as appears possible from the spacing of the line (Figure 1).[5] In any case, the manuscript's Dionysius Longinus, identified with Cassius Longinus (Dionysius usually being interpreted as the philosopher's *praenomen*), became the name under which the text circulated in the Renaissance. Occasional attempts have been made to salvage the traditional attribution of the text to Cassius Longinus, but most scholars today date the work earlier, to the late first century BC or to the first century AD, making him a contemporary or near contemporary of Caecilius.[6]

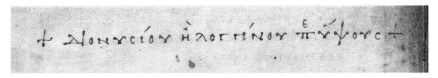

Figure 1 Detail of a Byzantine manuscript of Longinus, Parisinus Graecus 2036, fol. 1v, courtesy of the Bibliothèque nationale de France.

---

[3] On the emendation of the name see Mazzucchi 1992 and Halliwell 2022 at Long. *Subl.* 1.1.
[4] BnF Codex Parisinus Graecus 2036, fol. 1v, fol. 178v. [5] Mazzucchi 1992: xxx.
[6] The traditional attribution to Cassius Longinus has been defended most notably by Heath 1999; see also Heath 2012a: 15–16 and 2012b: 169–79. Grube 1965 finds a "first-century date [...] improbable" (342). Among others, Goold 1961: 168–78 and Mazzucchi 1992: xxxi–xxxiv argue for an Augustan date, tentatively supported by de Jonge 2012 and 2014; Russell 1990 writes that "convincing arguments against an Augustan date are difficult to find" (309). Crossett and Arieti 1975, on the other hand, posit a Neronian date. See also the discussion in Martano 1984: 365–70. See most recently Halliwell 2022: x–xix, who notes that problems of dating derive in part from the text's pursuit of a "timeless" Greek ideal.

In establishing the context of the *Peri hupsous* in ancient criticism, Caecilius would seem to be a crucial author, but the very little that is known of his work on the sublime is from Longinus himself.[7] Caecilius, Longinus objects, though he provided many examples of the sublime, omitted "by what means we might be able to advance our natures to some increase of greatness [*megethous*]" (δι' ὅτου τρόπου τὰς ἑαυτῶν φύσεις προάγειν ἰσχύοιμεν ἂν εἰς ποσὴν μεγέθους ἐπίδοσιν, Long. *Subl.* 1.1). Later, in treating the rhetorical vice of "frigidity" (*psuchrotēs*) in the historian Timaeus,[8] Longinus says: "I shall cite just one or two passages of the man, since Caecilius seized upon most of them before me" (παραθήσομαι δὲ τἀνδρὸς ἓν ἢ δύο, ἐπειδὴ τὰ πλείω προέλαβεν ὁ Κεκίλιος, Long. *Subl.* 4.2). Elsewhere Longinus claims that Caecilius misunderstood the relationship between sublimity (*hupsos*) and passion (*pathos*): if Caecilius understood passion and sublimity as identical, he erred, for passion need not be lofty, and sublimity need not be passionate; if, on the other hand, Caecilius did not consider passion something that contributes to the sublime, he was also mistaken, since "there is nothing so magniloquent as intense passion [*pathos*] right where it is needed" (οὐδὲν οὕτως ὡς τὸ γενναῖον πάθος, ἔνθα χρή, μεγαλήγορον, Long. *Subl.* 8.4). While Longinus, given his dissatisfaction with Caecilius' work, must be considered a somewhat prejudiced source, it seems fair to deduce from these comments that Caecilius' work on the sublime was probably more descriptive than analytical, not so much concerned with providing a theory of the sublime as listing illustrations of it, an approach paralleled in some extant fragments of Caecilius' other rhetorical works.[9]

Before Caecilius there are intimations of a notion of the sublime in rhetoric as far back as the sophists, as when Gorgias writes about how poetry can produce a "fearful shudder" (*phrikē periphobos*, Gorg. *Hel.* 9) in its auditors.[10] Aristotle remarks in the *Rhetoric* on how an audience is made "enthused" or "god-possessed" (*enthousiasai*) by orators who are themselves "in a state of enthusiasm" (*enthousiazontes*, Arist. *Rh.* 3.7.11) and declares that speech requires both a measure of "solemnity" (*semnotēta*) and the ecstatic capacity "to take one out of oneself" (*ekstēsai*, Arist. *Rh.* 3.8.4).[11] His disciple Theophrastus, as far as can be gleaned from the extant testimonia, seems to have written about "the magnificent" (*to megaloprepes*, Simplic. *Cat.* 10.30 Diels), the orator's power to "shock" (*ekplēxai*) and "overpower" (*cheirōthenta*) an audience (Ammon. *Int.* 66.6-7 Diels), and the reading of poetry as an aid to the orator in achieving "sublimity in words" (*in verbis sublimitas*, Quint. *Inst.* 10.1.27), in Quintilian's phrase.[12] These authors, and others besides, seem to anticipate the language in which Longinus would later describe the sublime.

---

[7] On ancient criticism generally see esp. Russell 1981 and Too 1998.
[8] On rhetorical *psuchrotēs* see Wright 2012: 108–10.
[9] See Innes 2002 and Porter 2016: 184–94.   [10] See Porter 2016: 314–19.
[11] See ibid. 289–303.   [12] See ibid. 283–9.

Before the Augustan period, however, perhaps the clearest predecessor of Caecilius and Longinus is Demetrius, the author of a work entitled *Peri hermēneias*, which most likely dates to the second or early first century BC.[13] Rather than the tripartite schema of styles—grand, middle, and plain—familiar from works like the *Rhetorica ad Herennium*, Demetrius presents a fourfold division consisting of the magnificent (*megaloprepēs*), the elegant (*glaphuros*), the plain (*ischnos*), and the vehement (*deinos*). Most relevant for our purposes are the first and the last of these, the great (*megaloprepēs*) and the forceful (*deinos*), both of which, as shown in the previous chapter, are Longinian terms for the sublime. For Demetrius, rhetorical grandeur or magnificence (*megaloprepeia*) is equally discernible at the most elemental level of language—"the long syllable is grand in nature" (φύσει γὰρ μεγαλεῖον ἡ μακρά, Demetr. *Eloc*. 39), he writes at one point—and at the general level of subject matter, as when the theme is a battle on land or sea, or something about heaven or earth (Demetr. *Eloc*. 75). Aberrant magnificence devolves into the fault of *psuchrotēs* (Demetr. *Eloc*. 75), the same quality that for Longinus results from a failure to achieve sublimity (Long. *Subl*. 3–4). Forcefulness or vehemence (*deinotēs*), on the other hand, can be expressed through compression, "for length loosens intensity [*sphodrotēta*], and much meaning displayed in a few words is more forceful [*deinoteron*]" (τὸ γὰρ μῆκος ἐκλύει τὴν σφοδρότητα, τὸ δὲ ἐν ὀλίγῳ πολὺ ἐμφαινόμενον δεινότερον, Demetr. *Eloc*. 241).[14] As with grandeur, some subjects are "forceful" (*deinos*) in themselves, specifically subjects of moral invective like prostitution (Demetr. *Eloc*. 240). Neither of these two styles, the grand (*megaloprepēs*) and the vehement (*deinos*), exactly corresponds on its own to the sublime in the Longinian sense. For Demetrius, however, any of the four styles, besides the contrary pairing of the grand and the plain, can be combined with any other—"all mixing with all" (πάντας μιγνυμένους πᾶσιν, Demetr. *Eloc*. 37)—notably including the combination of the grand and the vehement. Demetrius in fact makes this point in response to those who claim there are only two styles, "rather attributing the elegant [*glaphuron*] to the plain [*ischnō*], and the vehement [*deinon*] to the magnificent [*megaloprepei*]" (τὸν μὲν γλαφυρὸν τῷ ἰσχνῷ προσνέμοντες μᾶλλον, τῷ δὲ μεγαλοπρεπεῖ τὸν δεινόν, Demetr. *Eloc*. 36). The combination of grandeur (*megaloprepeia*) and forcefulness (*deinotēs*) in Demetrius looks very much like a prefiguration of Longinian sublimity.[15]

The word *hupsos*, in particular, seems to have been first employed as a literary-critical term by the previously mentioned Augustan critic Dionysius of

---

[13] The oldest MS, the tenth-century BnF Codex Parisinus Graecus 1741, in one place identifies the author as Demetrius of Phaleron (c.350–c.280 BC), an attribution which became conventional but is now generally considered erroneous; on the date of the *Peri hermēneias* see e.g. Grube 1961: 39–46; Chiron 1993: xiii–xl; Innes 1999: 310–19; Marini 2007: 8ff.; de Jonge 2009.
[14] On the sense of *deinotēs* see Grube 1961: 136–7 and Chiron 1993: cii–ciii.
[15] See Chiron 1993: c–cii and Porter 2016: 246–82.

Halicarnassus, who could call Caecilius a "dear friend" (*philtatō*, Dion. Hal. *Pomp.* 3). Dionysius wrote no treatise of the sublime himself, but throughout his rhetorical works he evinces a clear interest in sublimity, which he often calls *hupsos*. For Dionysius the sublime (*hupsēlon*), together with the intermediate (*metaxu*) and the plain (*ischnon*), constitutes one of the familiar three styles, but sublimity (*hupsos*) is also one of the virtuous qualities (*aretai*) of speech in general.[16] Throughout his rhetorical oeuvre sublimity is a recurring topic of interest. Dionysius best defines it by antithesis. When he claims that Lysias' style is not *hupsēlon*, he clarifies what this lack of sublimity means, illustrating by negation what he takes sublimity to be:

ὑψηλὴ δὲ καὶ μεγαλοπρεπὴς οὐκ ἔστιν ἡ Λυσίου λέξις οὐδὲ καταπληκτικὴ μὰ Δία καὶ θαυμαστὴ οὐδὲ τὸ πικρὸν ἢ τὸ δεινὸν ἢ τὸ φοβερὸν ἐπιφαίνουσα οὐδὲ ἀφὰς ἔχει καὶ τόνους ἰσχυροὺς οὐδὲ θυμοῦ καὶ πνεύματός ἐστι μεστή οὐδ', ὥσπερ ἐν τοῖς ἤθεσίν ἐστι πιθανή, οὕτως ἐν τοῖς πάθεσιν ἰσχυρά οὐδ' ὡς ἡδῦναι καὶ πεῖσαι καὶ χαριεντίσασθαι δύναται, οὕτω βιάσασθαί τε καὶ προσαναγκάσαι. ἀσφαλής τε μᾶλλόν ἐστιν ἢ παρακεκινδυνευμένη. (Dion. Hal. *Lys.* 13)

The style of Lysias is neither lofty [*hupselē*] nor magnificent [*megaloprepēs*]; not astonishing [*kataplēktikē*], by Zeus, nor wonderful [*thaumastē*]; not displaying sharpness [*to pikron*] nor forcefulness [*to deinon*] nor fear [*to phoberon*]; nor does it have a gripping quality and strong notes; nor is it full of spirit [*thumou*] and inspiration [*pneumatos*]; nor is it as powerful in its emotions [*pathesin*], as it is persuasive in its morals; nor is it as able to force [*biasasthai*] and compel, as it is to please and persuade and charm. It is safe [*asphalēs*] rather than daring [*parakekinduneumenē*].

Similarly, in a passage concerned with "sublimity of speech" (*to hupsos tēs lexeōs*), Dionysius writes that "one who aspires to great things [*megalois*] sometimes fails" (τὸν ἐπιβαλλόμενον μεγάλοις καὶ σφάλλεσθαί ποτε) like Plato "aiming at lofty [*hupsēlēs*] and magnificent [*megaloprepous*] and daring [*parakekindyneumenēs*] expression" (τῆς ὑψηλῆς καὶ μεγαλοπρεποῦς καὶ παρακεκινδυνευμένης φράσεως ἐφιέμενον, Dion. Hal. *Pomp.* 2). He declares that "the sublimity [*hupsos*] of Isocratean artistry is a great [*mega*] and wonderful [*thaumaston*] thing, belonging more to a semi-divine [*hērōikēs*] nature than to a human one" (θαυμαστὸν γὰρ δὴ καὶ μέγα τὸ τῆς Ἰσοκράτους κατασκευῆς ὕψος, ἡρωϊκῆς μᾶλλον ἢ ἀνθρωπίνης φύσεως οἰκεῖον, Dion. Hal. *Isoc.* 3); that the speeches of Demosthenes provoke a state of enthusiasm (*enthousiō*) or divine possession and evoke the experience of Corybantic dances (*ta Korubantika*, Dion. Hal. *Dem.* 22). Dionysius' language and

---

[16] Dion. Hal. *Dem.* 33, *Thuc.* 23.

conceptualization of the sublime seems to represent perhaps the closest parallel to Longinus that survives from antiquity.[17] It is also in this same period, when Dionysius wrote extensively of *hupsos* as a rhetorical quality and Caecilius devoted a work to the sublime, that *sublimis*, as noted in the previous chapter, seems to first enter the literary-critical vocabulary of Latin, as when Ovid writes of the "sublime songs" (*sublimia carmina*, Ov. Am. 3.1.39) of tragedy. The interest in sublime rhetoric and poetics apparently developing at this time makes an Augustan date for Longinus look highly plausible.[18]

Lastly, before turning to Longinus himself, there remains one other rhetorician who should not be overlooked, Hermogenes of Tarsus. If the *Peri hupsous* is correctly assigned to the Augustan period or soon after, then Hermogenes, who flourished during the reign of Marcus Aurelius, in fact postdates Longinus. As the third-century philosopher Cassius Longinus, however, was credited with the authorship of the *Peri hupsous* in the Renaissance, Hermogenes may as well be considered here as Longinus' predecessor, since this is how he would have been understood in the seventeenth century, though the issue of precedence is irrelevant to my purposes. Several works were passed down as part of the Hermogenic corpus, some of which are presumed to be spurious, but of these the longest, the most influential, and the most pertinent to this discussion is the work entitled *Peri ideōn*, concerned with the "ideas" (*ideai*) of style.[19] As with Demetrius, these are not strictly delineated categories into which works are to be sorted, but abstracted qualities of which the writer or orator partakes in different measures and combinations: Hermogenes describes how these various ideas in Demosthenes' oratory are "interwoven" (*sumpeplegmena*, Hermog. Id. 1.1.16). Not content with the traditional three *genera dicendi* or even the four styles of Demetrius, Hermogenes enumerates seven different types, several of which include their own subtypes. Much of his terminology should by now be quite familiar as a kind of vocabulary of rhetorical sublimity: *megethos* ("grandeur"), *semnotēs* ("majesty"), *sphodrotēs* ("vehemence"), *deinotēs* ("forcefulness"). In his treatment of the last of these, there is even a Longinian sort of "profundity" (*bathos*) in Hermogenes' statement that a speech "requires depth and grandeur" (*bathutētos dei kai megethous*, Hermog. Id. 2.9.33).

Now for Longinus himself. While a comprehensive treatment of the *Peri hupsous* need not be ventured here, I would at least like to consider the general structure of the treatise and touch on some of its most salient points. Longinus offers his work as a *technologia* (Long. Subl. 1.1), a technical work or systematic treatise, intended to be "useful to political men" (ἀνδράσι πολιτικοῖς... χρήσιμον, Long. Subl. 1.2)—that is, those involved in political affairs, or more generally those

---

[17] See de Jonge 2012 and Porter 2016: 213–39.   [18] A point made by de Jonge 2012: 273.
[19] See e.g. Patillon 2012: VII and Lindberg 1997: 2005–53.

THE SUBLIME FROM ANTIQUITY TO THE RENAISSANCE 19

who speak in public.[20] In the first section of the work Longinus offers a definition of his subject that is worth quoting at length:

ἀκρότης καὶ ἐξοχή τις λόγων ἐστὶ τὰ ὕψη, καὶ ποιητῶν τε οἱ μέγιστοι καὶ συγγραφέων οὐκ ἄλλοθεν ἢ ἐνθένδε ποθὲν ἐπρώτευσαν καὶ ταῖς ἑαυτῶν περιέβαλον εὐκλείαις τὸν αἰῶνα. οὐ γὰρ εἰς πειθὼ τοὺς ἀκροωμένους ἀλλ' εἰς ἔκστασιν ἄγει τὰ ὑπερφυᾶ· πάντῃ δέ γε σὺν ἐκπλήξει τοῦ πιθανοῦ καὶ τοῦ πρὸς χάριν ἀεὶ κρατεῖ τὸ θαυμάσιον, εἴγε τὸ μὲν πιθανὸν ὡς τὰ πολλὰ ἐφ' ἡμῖν, ταῦτα δὲ δυναστείαν καὶ βίαν ἄμαχον προσφέροντα παντὸς ἐπάνω τοῦ ἀκροωμένου καθίσταται. καὶ τὴν μὲν ἐμπειρίαν τῆς εὑρέσεως καὶ τὴν τῶν πραγμάτων τάξιν καὶ οἰκονομίαν οὐκ ἐξ ἑνὸς οὐδ' ἐκ δυεῖν, ἐκ δὲ τοῦ ὅλου τῶν λόγων ὕφους μόλις ἐκφαινομένην ὁρῶμεν, ὕψος δέ που καιρίως ἐξενεχθὲν τά τε πράγματα δίκην σκηπτοῦ πάντα διεφόρησεν καὶ τὴν τοῦ ῥήτορος εὐθὺς ἀθρόαν ἐνεδείξατο δύναμιν.
(Long. Subl. 1.3–4)

The sublime [*ta hupsē*] is a certain pinnacle and preeminence of discourse, and not from anything otherwise than this have the greatest of poets and writers claimed the first rank and wrapped their glories with eternity. Extraordinariness [*ta huperphua*] leads the audience not into a state of persuasion but into one of ecstasy [*ekstasin*], and awe [*to thaumasion*] with its power of astonishment [*ekplēxei*] always in every way triumphs over the merely persuasive and charming. Persuasion is for the most part within our own control, but this, bringing to bear domination [*dunasteian*] and irresistible force [*bian amachon*], establishes control over everyone experiencing it. We perceive craft in invention [*heureseōs*], and the design [*taxin*] and management [*oikonomian*] of material, not in one or two places, but appearing only in the whole texture of the work; yet sublimity [*hupsos*], brought forth at the right time, shatters everything like a thunderbolt [*skēptou*] and displays the overwhelming power [*dunamin*] of the orator in a single moment.

Here, in the first section of the *Peri hupsous*, is the Longinian sublime, *hupsos*, in précis: it is the extraordinary (*huperphuēs*) sine qua non of the best poets and prose-writers, not a persuasive manner of speech but a discourse that transports you outside of yourself (*ekstasis*), a quality of shock (*ekplēxis*) and awe (*thauma*), of raw, dominating force (*bia*). In contrast to invention (*heuresis*) and design (*taxis, oikonomia*) in the overall structure of a composition, which, as *inventio* and *dispositio* in Latin, constitute two of the familiar canons of classical rhetoric,[21] sublimity is a momentary flash of lightning (*skēptos*). The *fulmen eloquentiae* or lightning bolt of eloquence, perhaps Longinus' most vivid and memorable—one

---

[20] On the sense of πολιτικοῖς here see Russell 1964 ad loc.   [21] See Russell 1964: ad loc.

might say emblematic—image of the sublime, appears to originate with Pericles, who was pictured bearing bolts of lightning like Zeus when he spoke: Aristophanes writes that "Pericles, an Olympian, hurled lightning, thundered" (Περικλέης οὐλύμπιος / ἤστραπτ', ἐβρόντα, Ar. *Ach.* 530–531), while Plutarch later recalls that the orator was said to "bear a dreaded [*deinon*] thunderbolt on his tongue" (δεινὸν δὲ κεραυνὸν ἐν γλώσσῃ φέρειν, Plut. *Per.* 8.4).[22] Longinus, like Cicero, applies the metaphor to Demosthenes, one of his favorite exemplars of sublimity (Long. *Subl.* 12.4, 34.4; cf. Cic. *Orat.* 234), but its Periclean origin only makes the thunderbolt even more fitting as an emblem of sublimity, so that it not only signifies the fearsome power and singularity of the sublime but points to the kind of individual capable of it, those orators whose powers make them "equal to the gods" (ἰσόθεοι, Long. *Subl.* 35.2). Throughout the treatise, as adumbrated in the previous chapter, Longinus envisions the sublime speaker as one divinely inspired or possessed, as when he writes of Archilochus' "outburst of divine inspiration" (τῆς ἐκβολῆς τοῦ δαιμονίου πνεύματος, Long. *Subl.* 33.5), or of Demosthenes' "terrible [*deina*] heaven-sent gifts" (θεόπεμπτα δεινὰ δωρήματα, Long. *Subl.* 34.4).[23] Such descriptions are prefigured, as noted above, in Aristotle and in Dionysius of Halicarnassus among others, and indeed go back to Plato's treatment in the *Ion* of the inspired madness of poets, or *furor poeticus*.[24]

This understanding of the sublime as inspired and lightning-like may suggest that, unlike the rhetorical canons of *inventio* and *dispositio*, sublimity is something that cannot be taught.[25] Longinus maintains that this is only partially true, as sublimity is a matter of nature (*phusis*) but also of art (*techne*): "grandeur [*ta megala*]," he insists, "runs the greatest risk [*epikindunotera*] when on its own, without proper knowledge [*epistēmēs*], left by itself unsupported and unballasted, abandoned to impulse alone and to untutored [*amathei*] boldness" (ἐπικινδυνότερα, αὐτὰ ἐφ' αὑτῶν δίχα ἐπιστήμης, ἀστήρικτα καὶ ἀνερμάτιστα ἐαθέντα τὰ μεγάλα, ἐπὶ μόνῃ τῇ φορᾷ καὶ ἀμαθεῖ τόλμῃ λειπόμενα, Long. *Subl.* 2.2). Yet sublimity does require one who can take risks, for "great things, by their very greatness, are perilous [*episphalē*]" (τὰ δὲ μεγάλα ἐπισφαλῆ δι' αὐτὸ γίνεσθαι τὸ μέγεθος, Long. *Subl.* 33.2). Excessive artifice can lead to failed attempts at sublimity, as when "over-elaboration" (*periergasia*) results in "frigidity" (*psuchrotēs*, Long. *Subl.* 3.4)—which, as noted above, was a Demetrian demerit,

---

[22] See Russell 1964: xxxix and Porter 2016: 385.
[23] Most editors emend δεινὰ to τινα, following Manutius 1555, as δεινὰ could have been a scribal error motivated by the preceding δεινότητα, but the transmitted reading is not obviously ungrammatical, and it serves to emphasize Longinus' point, signifying that Demosthenes' powers are both rhetorically "forceful" and divinely "fearsome."
[24] Similarly, de Jonge 2012 remarks that Longinus' "sublime author...sometimes reminds us of the inspired poet of Plato's *Ion*" (279).
[25] On nature and art in relation to sublimity in Long. *Subl.* see especially Porter 2016: 60–83.

a blunder in the pursuit of grandeur (*megaloprepeia*). Sublimity, then, requires a certain nature, namely what Longinus calls "greatness of soul" (*megalopsuchia*, Long. *Subl.* 7.1) or "greatness of mind" (*megalophrosunē*, Long. *Subl.* 7.3), which in turn must be trained by art—though not overmuch. That both nature and art are necessary is apparent from the five founts or sources of sublimity that Longinus enumerates: the first two, "ambitiousness [*to . . . hadrepēbolon*] in ideas" (τὸ περὶ τὰς νοήσεις ἁδρεπήβολον) and "vehement and enthusiastic [*enthousiastikon*] passion" (τὸ σφοδρὸν καὶ ἐνθουσιαστικὸν πάθος), are "mostly inborn" (τὸ πλέον αὐθιγενεῖς), matters of natural genius and inborn ability; the other three—figures of speech (*schemata*), diction (*phrasis*), and composition (*sunthesis*)—are achieved through art (*technē*, Long. *Subl.* 8.1).

These five sources of the sublime provide the general framework for the remainder of the *Peri hupsous* as each is treated in succession, with the notable exception of the second source, *pathos*, which Longinus promises to consider in a separate work (Long. *Subl.* 3.5, 44.12).[26] Since the three sources that are matters of technique (*technē*) are de rigueur for ancient rhetorical treatises, I shall confine myself here to the first source of sublimity, what Longinus first calls "aiming at vigor in thoughts" (τὸ περὶ τὰς νοήσεις ἁδρεπήβολον). Sublimity of thoughts emerges through magnanimity (*megalophrosunē*), imitation (*mimēsis*), and imagination (*phantasia*, Long. *Subl.* 9–15). "Sublimity [*hupsos*] is the echo of magnanimity" (ὕψος μεγαλοφροσύνης ἀπήχημα, Long. *Subl.* 9.2), Longinus writes in perhaps his most quotable line. Sublimity cannot be achieved by those of a "slavish" (*douloprepēs*) character, but only those with the spiritual and intellectual quality of magnanimity (*megalophrosunē*): "their words are grand, it seems, whose thoughts are weighty" (μεγάλοι δὲ οἱ λόγοι τούτων, κατὰ τὸ εἰκός, ὧν ἂν ἐμβριθεῖς ὦσιν αἱ ἔννοιαι, Long. *Subl.* 9.3). Imitation (*mimēsis*) of great authors offers another means of attaining the sublime. Imitation or mimesis is of course a commonplace of ancient criticism going back to Plato and Aristotle, but Longinus seems to invest it here with a higher significance, understanding it as something more like the communing of spirits, or even metempsychosis: just as the Pythia is inspired by the "god-filled vapor" (*atmon entheon*) rising up from the earth at Delphi, "so from the great natures [*megalophuias*] of the ancients some effluences, as from the sacred vaults, are borne into the souls of their emulators" (οὕτως ἀπὸ τῆς τῶν ἀρχαίων μεγαλοφυίας εἰς τὰς τῶν ζηλούντων ἐκείνους ψυχὰς ὡς ἀπὸ ἱερῶν στομίων ἀπόρροιαί τινες φέρονται, Long. *Subl.* 13.2).[27] Finally, sublimity of thought can also be produced by "imagination" (*phantasia*) or "image-making" (*eidōlopoiia*), "when through enthusiasm [*enthousiasmou*] and passion [*pathous*]

---

[26] On the structure of Long. *Subl.* see the outlines in Russell 1964: x–xxii and Fyfe and Russell 1999: 148–52 and in Mazzucchi 1992: lxi–lxiii.
[27] On Longinian imitation see Russell 1964 at Long. *Subl.* 13.2 and Walsh 1988: 264ff.

you seem to see what you speak of and you set it before the eyes of the audience" (ὅταν ἃ λέγεις ὑπ' ἐνθουσιασμοῦ καὶ πάθους βλέπειν δοκῇς καὶ ὑπ' ὄψιν τιθῇς τοῖς ἀκούουσιν, Long. *Subl.* 15.1).

It is not necessary to dwell too much longer on this overview of the *Peri hupsous* itself, but some attention should be paid here to its final chapter, in which Longinus presents his conversation with "a certain one among the philosophers" (τις τῶν φιλοσόφων) concerning the "sterility of letters" (λόγων... ἀφορία, Long. *Subl.* 44.1) in his time.[28] The philosopher rehearses the opinion "that democracy [*dēmokratia*] is a good nurse of the great [*tōn megalōn*], and that, generally speaking, those who were fearsome [*deinoi*] in speech flourished with it alone, and perished with it" (ὡς ἡ δημοκρατία τῶν μεγάλων ἀγαθὴ τιθηνός, ᾗ μόνῃ σχεδὸν καὶ συνήκμασαν οἱ περὶ λόγους δεινοὶ καὶ συναπέθανον, Long. *Subl.* 44.2). Under the Empire, the philosopher says, "we seem to be taught a justified slavery [*douleias*] in childhood" (Ἐοίκαμεν... παιδομαθεῖς εἶναι δουλείας δικαίας),[29] instead of "freedom [*eleutherian*], the most beautiful and fertile spring of letters" (καλλίστου καὶ γονιμωτάτου λόγων νάματος, τὴν ἐλευθερίαν, Long. *Subl.* 44.3). Longinus in his own voice counters that the dire state of letters should not be attributed to the current political dispensation, with its "world peace" (*hē tēs oikoumenēs eirēnē*), but rather to the passions (*pathē*), such as "love of money" (*philochrēmatia*) and "love of pleasure" (*philēdonia*), which "enslave" (*doulagōgousi*) the soul (Long. *Subl.* 44.6). The "world peace" (*hē tēs oikoumenēs eirēnē*) referred to here is certainly the Pax Romana of the Principate, which has superseded the "democracy" (*dēmokratia*) of the Republic. Exactly when within this period the *Peri hupsous* was written is, again, a matter of speculation: it suffices to mention that the decadence of oratory is a topic treated among others by Seneca the Elder, who laments that "eloquence has gone into decline" (*eloquentia se retro tulerit*, Sen. *Contr.* 1 *praef.* 6), and Tacitus, in whose *Dialogus de oratoribus* the character Maternus supposes that orators in the days of the Republic could achieve greater heights "when everything was confused and there was no single ruler" (*mixtis omnibus et moderatore uno carentibus*, Tac. *Dial.* 36.2).[30] Whether Longinus makes his unnamed philosopher's case so persuasive that he should be credited with that opinion, which it might have been unwise for him to claim openly, is unclear. Superficially, at least, his rather Stoic resolution of the question—inner liberty, freedom from the passions, is the true requisite of greatness—seems to

---

[28] On the interpretation of Long. *Subl.* 44 and its position in the treatise see e.g. Segal 1959 and Boot 1980.

[29] The exact sense of δικαίας here, which I have translated as "justified," is unclear. Russell 1964 ad loc. asks: "'Justified' or 'justly exercised'? More probably the former; our moral degeneration deserves political subjection." Fyfe and Russell 1999: 299 translate δουλείας δικαίας as "an equitable slavery." Mazzucchi 1992: 119 offers "a fair slavery" (*un'equa schiavitù*); in the commentary he clarifies that this should be understood "not so much as 'deserved' but 'imposed by a just authority'" (*non tanto come «meritata»... ma «imposta da un'autorità equa,»* Mazzucchi 1992: 294), i.e. that of a lawful monarch.

[30] See Russell 1964 at Long. *Subl.* 44 and Russell 1990: 309–10.

follow from his earlier emphasis on the importance of magnanimity (*megalophrosunē*) and his statement that sublimity cannot be achieved by those with a "slavish" (*douloprepēs*) cast of mind.

Longinus and the Sublime in the Renaissance

For all the interest that it would later generate in early modern Europe, it is remarkable that the *Peri hupsous* is neither quoted nor cited anywhere in the extant writings of Greco-Roman antiquity. In this respect Longinus seems to belong more to posterity than to his own time. The earliest reference to the *Peri hupsous* may be that of a certain John of Sicily active in Constantinople during the reign of Basil II (976–1025), around the same time that the previously mentioned Constantinopolitan manuscript was written.[31] At one point in his voluminous commentary on Hermogenes' *Peri ideōn* John writes that Moses was revered not only by Christians but also by Longinus, in apparent reference to a passage of the *Peri hupsous* to which I shall return in the final section of this chapter.[32] One wonders just how well known the *Peri hupsous* was among the learned in the Greek East before the Fall of Constantinople: tantalizingly, if somewhat tenuously, one Byzantinist has recently raised the possibility that Michael Psellos, writing half a century or so after John of Sicily, was familiar with the text.[33] What is known is that the Constantinopolitan manuscript had made its way to the Latin West by 1468, when the Greek émigré Cardinal Bessarion commissioned a copy of it, which he donated along with the rest of his library to the Republic of Venice as the founding bequest of the Biblioteca Marciana.[34] The Constantinopolitan manuscript itself passed through the hands of Bessarion's fellow expatriate Janus Lascaris, whose own copy bears annotations in his hand.[35] Further copies and copies of copies soon began to circulate in Italy and beyond.[36] Yet when the press of Aldus Manutius printed the *Rhetores Graeci* (1508), an influential collection of Greek rhetorical works—specifically those of Aphthonius, Hermogenes, and Aristotle—the *Peri hupsous* was not included among them: Longinus had apparently missed his chance at becoming part of the early Renaissance canon of Greek rhetoric. Why this is so is uncertain. The *Rhetores Graeci* is dedicated to Lascaris, who apparently provided manuscripts and aid to Manutius in the process of the book's composition.[37] As Lascaris not only possessed a copy of the *Peri hupsous*

---

[31] BnF Codex Parisinus Graecus 2036. On John of Sicily see e.g. Roilos 2018.
[32] Walz 1832–6: VI 211; see Mazzucchi 1990. [33] Papaioannou 2013: 81 n.89.
[34] Biblioteca Nazionale Marciana, MS Marcianus Graecus 522.
[35] BnF Codex Parisinus Graecus 2974.
[36] For more detail on the manuscript tradition see Mazzucchi 1989 and Mazzucchi 1992: xxxv–xxxviii.
[37] Manutius 1508: sig. Iv.

but had studied it too, as his annotations show, it hard to believe that Manutius would not have been made aware of this work.[38] In any case, the *Peri hupsous* remained unpublished for several decades, though it continued to circulate in manuscript: Conrad Gessner in his 1545 *Bibliotheca Universalis* notes the existence of copies of Longinus' "brief work concerning grandeur of oratory" (*opuscula de magnitudine orationis*) both in Rome and in the possession of Diego Hurtado de Mendoza, the Spanish ambassador in Venice.[39]

The first printed editions of Longinus appeared in the wake of the controversy over Ciceronianism reignited by Erasmus' *Ciceronianus* (1528), which made space for new stylistic and rhetorical resources that could contribute to "a rhetorical *aggiornamento* of Italian humanism," in the words of Marc Fumaroli.[40] By the 1550s Paulus Manutius, Aldus' son and successor, was seeking to add Longinus to the canon, and had asked the French scholar Muretus to prepare a Latin translation.[41] But he was preempted by Johannes Oporinus in Basel, who in 1554 published the lean *editio princeps*, featuring the Greek text and a few marginal notes in Latin, produced by Francesco Robortello.[42] The younger Manutius rushed to bring out his own edition the following year, in 1555, but did not include Muretus' translation, which is now lost, if it ever was completed.[43] The Hungarian humanist Andreas Dudith was apparently writing his own translation around this time, though no trace of this survives either.[44] The Vatican holds an early manuscript translation into Latin that has been ascribed to Fulvio Orsini, librarian to the influential Farnese family, and which may well even predate the *editio princeps*.[45] This is the earliest of several extant manuscript translations into Latin and the vernacular (Table 1).

In 1570 Jean Crespin in Geneva published Franciscus Portus' volume of Greek rhetorical writings, a collection not dissimilar to the earlier Aldine *Rhetores Graeci*, but adding to the more familiar names of Aphthonius and Hermogenes that of Longinus. In his dedication of this collection to Theodore Beza, John Calvin's successor as leader of the Reformed community in Geneva, Portus praises Longinus as "the most discerning [*kritikōtaton*] man among all the rhetoricians,

---

[38] See Steppich 2006: 62–3.
[39] Gessner 1545: sig. 212v. See also Steppich 2006, who argues that, based on a parallel understanding of *imitatio* as *furor* in his *De Poetica* (Vadian 1518), the Swiss humanist Joachim Vadian was familiar with Longinus several decades before the publication of the *editio princeps*.
[40] Fumaroli 1986: 42; see 41ff.   [41] See Muretus 1554: 57r–57v, noted in Weinberg 1950: 145.
[42] Robortello 1554. Elsewhere Robortello writes: *Dionysium Longinum Περὶ ὕψους et Aelianum de exercitu instruendo more Graecorum edidi, et in Latinum verti* (Robortello 1975: 53–4, cited in Costa 1985: 235). Costa 1985: 228 concludes from this that "Robortello not only edited, but also translated Longinus, a fact that has hitherto escaped the attention of scholars." But in the absence of any other evidence it is simpler to understand the phrase *in Latinum verti* as referring only to Aelian, whom Robortello did translate into Latin (Robortello 1552).
[43] Manutius 1555.
[44] Dudith 1560: sigg. B2v–B3r, noted in Weinberg 1950: 145–6. On Dudith see Costil 1935, and on his Longinus translation see also Jansen 2019: 34–5.
[45] BAV MS Vat. Lat. 3441; see Costa 1985: 225–8. On Orsini see de Nolhac 1887.

Table 1 Manuscript translations of Longinus before 1674

Date (est.)	Manuscript	Translator	Language
1550s?	Vatican City, Bibliotheca Apostolica Vaticana, MS Vat. Lat. 3441	Fulvio Orsini	Latin
Dedicated 1575	Florence, Biblioteca Nazionale Centrale di Firenze, MS Magl. VI.33	Giovanni di Niccolò da Falgano	Italian
Before 1631	Rome, Biblioteca Vallicelliana, MS Allacci XXIX.1-8	Leo Allatius	Latin
c. 1640s	London, British Library, MS Lansdowne 1045, fols. 166–172	[Unknown]	English
c. 1645	Paris, Bibliothèque nationale de France, MS Italien 2028	[Unknown]	French

whom the ancients in admiration used to call a living library [*bibliothēkēn empsuchon*] and a walking museum [*mouseion peripatoun*]" (ἄνδρα συμπάντων τεχνογράφων κριτικώτατον, ὃν βιβλιοθήκην ἔμψυχον, καὶ μουσεῖον περιπατοῦν οἱ παλαιοὶ θαυμάζοντες ἐκάλουν)[46]—clearly identifying the author with the philosopher Cassius Longinus, who was praised in the same terms by Porphyry (*kritikōtatou*, Porph. *Plot.* 20) and Eunapius (*bibliothēkē...empsuchos kai peripatoun mouseion*, Eunap. *Vit. Soph.* 4.1.3). The dedication to Beza hints at what John Logan has called the text's "early associations with heterodoxy," following from the fact that so many of Longinus' early editors, translators, and printers were Protestants, even including, in the case of Dudith, a Socinian.[47] Portus' text formed the basis for subsequent editions through the seventeenth century. From the 1554 *editio princeps* to the 1663 edition of Tanneguy Le Fèvre, a total of twelve different editions of Longinus appeared before Boileau's in 1674, including three different Latin versions as well as translations into Italian and English (Table 2).[48] It is worth noting here that the dedications of all five printed translations affiliate the text with republican polities, a connection that will be further explored later: Domenico Pizzimenti's and Pietro Pagano's respective dedications of their 1566 and 1572 Latin translations to Aldus Manutius the Younger and Doge Alvise I Mocenigo both pay prominent tribute to the glory of the Republic of Venice,[49] as

---

[46] Portus 1569/70: sig. *iiiir. The Greek text of Portus' preface, together with a French translation and notes by Bertrand Bouvier, is available in Aubert et al. 1980: 254–9.
[47] Logan 1999: 533.
[48] The Latin translations of Pizzimenti 1566, Pagano 1572, and de Petra 1612 were all reprinted in Manolessi 1644; that of de Petra 1612 was reprinted in Langbaine 1636, Aromatari 1643, and Le Fèvre 1663.
[49] Pizzimenti 1566; Pagano 1572. See Costa 1985: 230–1.

does Niccolò Pinelli's dedication of his 1639 Italian version to Benedetto Erizzo, nephew of Doge Francesco Erizzo and *primicerio* of the Basilica of San Marco; Gabriel de Petra, a professor of Greek at the Academy of Lausanne, dedicated his Greek-Latin edition to Albert Manuel, a magistrate of the city-republic of Bern, and Abraham Sturler, treasurer of the Swiss county of Vaud, which was then under Bernese control;[50] and John Hall, then in the employ of the revolutionary government, dedicated his 1652 English translation to Bulstrode Whitelocke, a member of the fledgling English Commonwealth's Council of State.[51]

From the mid-sixteenth century onward the *Peri hupsous* attracted increasing attention from Continental humanists and was gradually incorporated into the canon of late Renaissance rhetorical theory.[52] On the title page of his copy of Robortello's *editio princeps*, now at the British Library, Isaac Casaubon, who had studied Greek under Portus, wrote that it was a "golden book" (*liber aureus*), and other scholarly luminaries such as Joseph Scaliger, Henri Estienne, Daniel Heinsius, and Gerardus Vossius looked to Longinus as an authority on matters of rhetoric.[53] Longinian *enthousiasmos* was identified with the Neoplatonic notion of *furor poeticus*, as expounded by the likes of Marsilio Ficino, as early as the *editio princeps*: where Longinus compares the emanations that transmigrate from writers of the past to the divine vapors that inspire the Pythia, Robortello's marginal note labels this *furor*.[54] The Venetian philosopher Francesco Patrizi in his 1587 treatise *Della Poetica* used Longinus to formulate his notion of the *ammirabile* ("marvelous"),[55] while Lorenzo Giacomini in his *Discorso del furor poetico*, presented that same year before the Accademia degli Alterati in Florence, drew from Longinus' conception of *phantasia* in his discussions of *fantasia* and *imaginazione*.[56] Francesco Benci, a student of Muretus, turned to Longinus in lecturing on the sublime style at the Jesuit-founded Collegium Romanum.[57] Torquato Tasso, the great Italian poet, was familiar with Longinus from the numerous references in Pietro Vettori's 1562 commentary on Demetrius and may have read the Latin translation of Pagano.[58] The quality of *meraviglia* that Tasso extolled in his *Discorsi del poema eroico* owes much to the idea of rhetorical sublimity as found

---

[50] De Petra 1612. On the Academy of Lausanne in this period, with references to de Petra passim, see Heubi 1916.
[51] Hall 1652.
[52] On Italian Renaissance criticism, with references to Longinus passim, see Weinberg 1961 and Hathaway 1962; on Renaissance rhetoric generally see esp. Mack 2011.
[53] BL shelfmark 1088.m.2; Scaliger 1577: 247 (in the separately numbered *Castigationes*); Estienne 1587: 18, 296; Heinsius 1627: 230; Vossius 1630: 432-3. On Longinus among seventeenth-century Dutch scholars in particular see Jansen 2019.
[54] Robortello 1554: 26, noted by Steppich 2006: 52. On *furor poeticus* in Renaissance thought see esp. Allen 1984: 41-67.
[55] Text in Patrizi 1969-71; see Platt 1992 and Prins 2014: 385-6.
[56] Giacomini 1597: 53-73, edited in Weinberg 1972: III 423-44. See Refini 2012: 37ff.
[57] See Fumaroli 2002: 177-8.
[58] Vettori 1562; Pagano 1572. See Costa 1987a and Graziani 1996: 122 n.9.

Table 2 Printed editions and translations of Longinus before 1674

Year	Place	Editor/Translator	Printer/Publisher	Language
1554	Basel	Francesco Robortello	Johannes Oporinus	Greek
1555	Venice	Paulus Manutius	Paulus Manutius	Greek
1566	Naples	Domenico Pizzimenti	Giovanni Maria Scoto	Latin
1569/70	Geneva	Franciscus Portus	Jean Crespin	Greek
1572	Venice	Pietro Pagano	Vincentius Valgrisius	Latin
1612	Geneva	Gabriel de Petra	Jean de Tournes	Greek/Latin
1636/38, 1650	Oxford	Gerard Langbaine	William Turner/William Webb	Greek/Latin
1639	Padua	Niccolò Pinelli	Giulio Crivellari	Italian
1643	Venice	Giuseppe Aromatari	Giuseppe Aromatari	Latin
1644	Bologna	Carlo Manolessi	Carlo Manolessi	Greek/Latin
1652	London	John Hall	Roger Daniel/Francis Eaglesfield	English
1663	Saumur	Tanneguy Le Fèvre	Jean Lesnier	Greek/Latin

in Longinus, Hermogenes, Demetrius, and others.[59] Like Portus, who in his commentary on the *Peri hupsous* identified Longinus' *hupsos* with Hermogenes' *megethos*,[60] Tasso understood the ancient rhetoricians to be writing about essentially the same thing, observing that that "which is called magnificent by Demetrius, grand by Hermogenes, and sublime by Cicero are one and the same" (*che magnifica da Demetrio, grande da Ermogene, e sublime da Cicerone vien detta, è una medesima*).[61] "Terms like *meraviglia*, *stupore* and *estasi*," Eugenio Refini notes, "became the keywords of an idea of artistic and poetic creation which perfectly fits in with the Longinian notion of the sublime."[62] In Paris, Denys Lambin, editor of Lucretius and other classical authors, procured and annotated a copy of the *editio princeps* sometime between 1555 and his death in 1572.[63] Several passages in the *Essais* suggest that Montaigne, a friend and former student of Muretus, may have been familiar with the *Peri hupsous*, as when he writes of Vergil and Lucretius: "This is not a soft and inoffensive eloquence: it is vigorous

---
[59] Tasso 1594, English translation Tasso 1973.
[60] Pearce 1733a: 279; Portus' commentary survives in MS as Biblioteca Estense, Campori App. 432 but was first printed in Pearce 1733a: 279–360.
[61] Tasso 1823: 42–60, at 45; noted in Porter 2016: 17 n.44.   [62] Refini 2012: 37.
[63] BnF shelfmark X.3074; see Gabe 1991.

and solid, one which does not so much please as it fills and ravishes [*ravit*]; and it ravishes [*ravit*] the strongest spirits most" (*Ce n'est pas une eloquence molle, & seulement sans offence: elle est nerveuse & solide, qui ne plaist pas tant, comme elle remplit & ravit: & ravit, le plus, les plus forts espris*)—twice using the same word (*ravit*) that Boileau would use in his own description of the sublime a century later.[64] Throughout Europe Longinus, together with Hellenistic rhetoricians like Hermogenes, became assimilated into the late Renaissance notion of what Debora Shuger has called "the Christian grand style."[65]

In England the diffusion of the *Peri hupsous* seems to have been more gradual, and when the Oxford scholar John Rainolds praises Longinus as a "distinguished rhetorician" (*rhetor insignis*) in an oration delivered shortly after Christmas 1573 he seems to be a lone voice.[66] Portus' volume of Hermogenes, Aphthonius, and Longinus was for sale in Cambridge in the 1570s,[67] but if the surviving copy of Bartholomew Dodington, Cambridge's Regius Professor of Greek, is any indication, Longinus was hardly the focus of most readers' attention: Dodington's copy, which he inscribed in 1573, contains only Portus' text of Hermogenes, then an item on the Cambridge syllabus, Aphthonius and Longinus having been removed to make space for Dodington's interleaved annotations.[68] Nevertheless, Portus' volume was probably the first place that English readers encountered Longinus: some few, at least, of those who acquired it for the more familiar works of Aphthonius and Hermogenes must have been intrigued by this hitherto unknown work on *hupsos* appended to them. And indeed there exists some relatively early evidence of this in a copy of Portus' volume with the autograph of Sir Henry Wotton (Figure 2).[69] Predictably, the text of Hermogenes has been extensively marked in places, but in this case Longinus has not been neglected. Wotton—if it is, as it seems, his hand—has underlined just two words, but they are well chosen: *hadrepēbolon* and *enthousiastikon* (Long. *Subl*. 8.1), describing the two sources of the sublime that come from nature, "ambitiousness" (*to hadrepēbolon*) in thought and "enthusiastic" (*enthousiastikon*) passion (Figure 3).[70] Generally speaking, however, the evidence does not suggest that Longinus was widely read in Elizabethan and Jacobean England: besides that of Rainolds, the only direct references from this period are apparently those of George Chapman in the

---

[64] Montaigne 1588: 382v (in the essay "Surs des Vers de Virgille"). Montaigne's acquaintance with Longinus was suggested in passing by Moore 1967: 110–11 and elaborated by Logan 1983 and Coleman 1985; see also Logan 1999: 535–7. On Montaigne's relationship with Muretus see Boutcher 2017: I 277.
[65] Shuger 1988.
[66] Rainolds 1619: 327–8, quoted from Ringler 1938: 23. Shuger 1988: 80 n.87 notes that "Longinus is mentioned but not discussed" in Thorne 1592: 5.
[67] See Leedham-Green 1986: II 29.
[68] CUL shelfmark Adv.d.4.4, signed and dated "B. Dodingtonus 1573" on the title page. See Leedham-Green 2004: 618.
[69] Stanford UL RBC KB1570.A6; see Vozar 2019.
[70] Stanford UL RBC KB1570.A6, p. 12 (in the separately numbered text of Longinus).

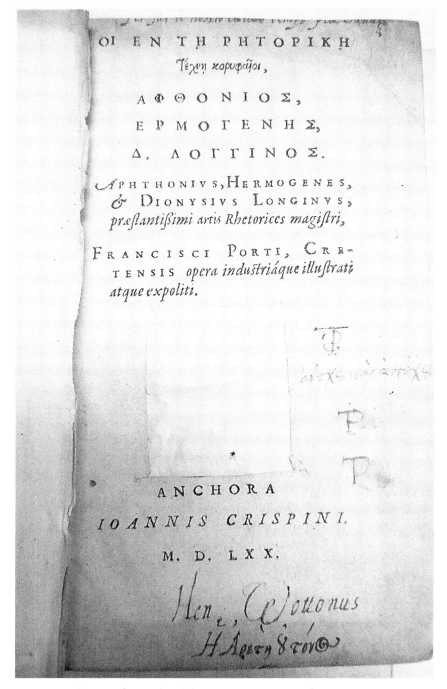

Figure 2 Title page of Portus' *Aphthonius, Hermogenes, and Dionysius Longinus* (1569/1570) with the autograph of Henry Wotton, RBC KB1570.A6, courtesy of the Department of Special Collections, Stanford University Libraries.

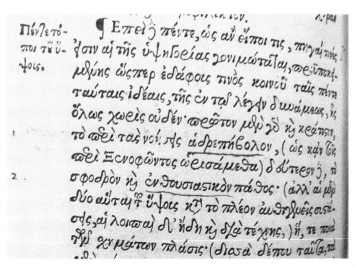

Figure 3 Detail of Wotton's copy of Portus (1569/1570), p. 12, RBC KB1570.A6, courtesy of the Department of Special Collections, Stanford University Libraries.

dedicatory epistle to his 1614 translation of the *Odyssey*, in which he remarks on "the Censure of Dionysius Longimus [sic]" that the poem is like the setting sun, the product of Homer's old age (*Subl.* 9.13), and Thomas Farnaby in his *Index Rhetoricus* (1625), in which Longinus is cited with reference to rhetorical *amplificatio* and sublime style.[71] Nevertheless, even without Longinus a notion of literary sublimity was certainly current: Roger Ascham writes of the need "to make trew difference betwixt *Sublime, et Tumidum*" and "in *Genere sublimi*, to avoide *Nimium*," while Thomas Newton remarks that Seneca's tragedies were "penned with a peerelesse sublimity and loftinesse of Style."[72] Patrick Cheney, in particular, has drawn attention over the past decade to the conjunction of rhetorical sublimity and a newly emerging model of authorship, as well as to a lesser extent political republicanism, in Elizabethan and Jacobean literature.[73]

The first edition of Longinus to be printed in England was published in Oxford in 1636.[74] As was the case for a number of other classical editions produced by

---

[71] Chapman 1614: sig. A4r; Farnaby 1625: 14, 30, also mentioned at sig. A2r. Both are noted in Spencer 1957: 137–8. Wolfe 2015: 491 n.92 calls into question the importance of this reference, however, suggesting that Chapman may have known this indirectly—"the passage of the *Peri Hupsous* cited by Chapman in his epistle to Somerset also appears in the general introductory remarks of Eustathius's commentary on *Od.*, a more likely source for Chapman, since he cites this text elsewhere in his commentary"—though I have not been able to locate the reference in Eustathius to which she refers.

[72] Ascham 1570: M1r, M1v; Newton 1581: sig. A3v.

[73] See Cheney 2009a, 2009b, 2011, 2018a, 2018b.   [74] Langbaine 1636.

English presses at this time,⁷⁵ the facing Greek and Latin texts were reprinted from a Continental edition, in this instance specifically the 1612 Geneva edition of Gabriel de Petra, but added to the bilingual text was a series of *Notae* by the young Oxford scholar Gerard Langbaine, later Provost of Queen's College. Langbaine had been persuaded to undertake this task by his tutor Thomas Wethereld,⁷⁶ possibly before taking his MA in June 1633: some years later Thomas Smith, the future Bishop of Carlisle who overlapped with Langbaine at Queen's College, recalled that "those Notes were writt by him when hee was but a Bachelour of Arts, and should therefore be read *cum excusatione aetatis*."⁷⁷ Patrick Young, the royal librarian, lent Langbaine a copy of Robortello's edition—possibly even Casaubon's annotated copy⁷⁸—as well as a Greek manuscript with Italian notes in Portus' hand.⁷⁹ Judging from the number of copies that can be traced to private owners in this period,⁸⁰ and taking into account the fact that Langbaine's edition was reissued twice—in 1638 and, without the engraved title page, again in 1650—it appears that Langbaine's edition was moderately successful, and indeed it is only in the years following its first publication that one begins to find references to Longinus with some regularity in England. In the 1640s alone, besides Milton's reference in *Of Education*, Longinus is cited in sermons by Laudians and Puritans, theological and exegetical works, a treatise on "Erotique Melancholy," and a poem on Charles I published shortly after his execution.⁸¹ Given this increasing interest in Longinus, it is not surprising that the text was soon translated into English, with John Hall's vernacular version published in 1652.⁸² This may not have even been the first English translation. The Lansdowne collection at the British Library contains an anonymous manuscript with the title "Of Sublimity of Stile Or The Raptures of Eloquence From Dionysius Longinus Περὶ Ὕψους Done from the Greek in to English For the Improvement of Oratory," the composition of which

---

⁷⁵ See Binns 1990: 238–9.
⁷⁶ Langbaine 1636: *Notae* 117. Cheney 2018b: 14 errs in stating that "[John] Rainolds was […] the tutor of Gerard Langbaine"—an impossibility, given that Rainolds died (1607) before Langbaine was born (1609); he has apparently mistaken Rainolds as the referent of "[Langbaine's] old Oxford tutor" in Anderson 2008: 384 n.42 (see Cheney 2018a: 623 n.10).
⁷⁷ National Archives, SP 18/155, fol. 131. Smith does not name Langbaine here, but it is an obvious inference. The letter is addressed to Joseph Williamson, who corresponded with Le Fèvre and visited Saumur several times in the 1650s; on his correspondence from 1660, including with Le Fèvre, see Tessier 2015. This raises the possibility that Williamson brought Langbaine's work, which Le Fèvre cites throughout his commentary, to the attention of the French scholar. On Le Fèvre see Ribard 2008.
⁷⁸ My own speculation; Casaubon's annotated copy (BL shelfmark 1088.m.2) passed into the royal library at his death in 1614, so it is possible that this was the copy Young lent Langbaine.
⁷⁹ Langbaine 1636: *Notae* 115. Rhys Roberts 1898 identified CUL KK.VI.34 (previously called the Codex Eliensis, because it derived from the collection of John Moore, Bishop of Ely) as the manuscript in question and found Langbaine's supposition that it was Dudith's copy probable, while Costil 1935: 278–84 proposed Portus as a more likely candidate.
⁸⁰ See the bibliographical appendix.
⁸¹ Stoughton 1640: 53, 75, Farindon 1647: 504, and Hughes 1647: sig. A2r; Casaubon 1646: 73, Gregory 1646: sig. *3r, and Leigh 1646: 22; Ferrand 1640: 113; Pierce 1649: 2. Some of these are noted by Lazarus 2021.
⁸² Hall 1652.

I have tentatively dated to the period between the first publication of Langbaine's edition in 1636 and the first appearance of Boileau's translation in 1674.[83] Given that the Lansdowne translator evinces no awareness of the existence of Hall's translation, it is quite possible that it preceded Hall's, though a date in the early Restoration is also plausible. An edition of the Lansdowne translation is provided in the textual appendix.

The Physical Species of the Sublime

The rhetorical, however, is not the only species of sublimity. Failure to recognize this is one of the many reasons that so much of the history of the sublime has been neglected. Hermogenes, Longinus' fellow theorist of the sublime, speaks not only of styles but of what he calls "majestic thoughts" (*ennoiai... semnai*), which are concerned with nature (*phusis*) and inquiries into the causes of natural phenomena such as earthquakes or celestial motions (Hermog. *Id.* 1.6.4–1.6.6.), or with "the gods spoken about as gods" (θεῶν ὡς περὶ θεῶν λεγόμεναι, Hermog. *Id.* 1.6.1). These two kinds of sublime ideas provide the respective subjects for this section and the next. I shall begin here with the physical or natural species of the sublime.

Though the *Peri hupsous* is concerned primarily with rhetoric, Longinus also points to another kind of sublimity, that of *phusis* or nature. It is implicit in the Longinian term *huperphuēs*, which signifies the overgrown, the over-natured, or literally that which goes beyond (*huper*) nature (*phusis*): hyper-nature, an excess of nature, nature in the extreme. It is apparent in Longinus' concern with physical excess, massive size, and vast distances, as when, commenting on the lines of the *Iliad* which say that as far as one can see "looking out over the wine-dark sea, / so far do the high-necked horses of the gods leap" (λεύσσων ἐπὶ οἴνοπα πόντον, / τόσσον ἐπιθρῴσκουσι θεῶν ὑψαύχενες ἵπποι, *Il.* 5.771–772),[84] Longinus writes that the poet "measures their motion with a cosmic interval [*kosmikō diastēmati*]: truly anyone would say after this, because of the excess of greatness [*tēn huperbolēn tou megethous*], that if the horses of the gods take but two steps in succession, they will find no more space left in the universe" (τὴν ὁρμὴν αὐτῶν κοσμικῷ διαστήματι καταμετρεῖ. τίς οὖν οὐκ ἂν εἰκότως διὰ τὴν ὑπερβολὴν τοῦ μεγέθους ἐπιφθέγξαιτο, ὅτι ἂν δὶς ἑξῆς ἐφορμήσωσιν οἱ τῶν θεῶν ἵπποι, οὐκέθ᾽ εὑρήσουσιν ἐν κόσμῳ τόπον, Long. *Subl.* 9.5). But there is one passage in particular that epitomizes Longinus' understanding of physical sublimity, and which therefore deserves to be presented in full:

---

[83] BL MS Lansdowne 1045, fols. 166–172; see Vozar 2020.
[84] I adopt here and translate Paulus Manutius' conjecture ὑψαύχενες for ὑψηχέες, which is featured in subsequent early modern editions of Longinus; on this lemma see Porter 2016: 523 n.413.

διόπερ τῇ θεωρίᾳ καὶ διανοίᾳ τῆς ἀνθρωπίνης ἐπιβολῆς οὐδ' ὁ σύμπας κόσμος ἀρκεῖ, ἀλλὰ καὶ τοὺς τοῦ περιέχοντος πολλάκις ὅρους ἐκβαίνουσιν αἱ ἐπίνοιαι, καὶ εἴ τις περιβλέψαιτο ἐν κύκλῳ τὸν βίον, ὅσῳ πλέον ἔχει τὸ περιττὸν ἐν πᾶσι καὶ μέγα καὶ καλόν, ταχέως εἴσεται πρὸς ἃ γεγόναμεν. ἔνθεν φυσικῶς πως ἀγόμενοι μὰ Δί' οὐ τὰ μικρὰ ῥεῖθρα θαυμάζομεν, εἰ καὶ διαυγῆ καὶ χρήσιμα, ἀλλὰ τὸν Νεῖλον καὶ Ἴστρον ἢ Ῥῆνον, πολὺ δ' ἔτι μᾶλλον τὸν Ὠκεανόν· οὐδέ γε τὸ ὑφ' ἡμῶν τουτὶ φλογίον ἀνακαιόμενον, ἐπεὶ καθαρὸν σῴζει τὸ φέγγος, ἐκπληττόμεθα τῶν οὐρανίων μᾶλλον, καίτοι πολλάκις ἐπισκοτουμένων, οὐδὲ τῶν τῆς Αἴτνης κρατήρων ἀξιοθαυμαστότερον νομίζομεν, ἧς αἱ ἀναχοαὶ πέτρους τε ἐκ βυθοῦ καὶ ὅλους ὄχθους ἀναφέρουσι καὶ ποταμοὺς ἐνίοτε τοῦ γηγενοῦς ἐκείνου καὶ αὐτομάτου προχέουσιν πυρός. ἀλλ' ἐπὶ τῶν τοιούτων ἁπάντων ἐκεῖν' ἂν εἴποιμεν, ὡς εὐπόριστον μὲν ἀνθρώποις τὸ χρειῶδες ἢ καὶ ἀναγκαῖον, θαυμαστὸν δ' ὅμως ἀεὶ τὸ παράδοξον. (Long. Subl. 35.3–5)

The whole universe is not enough for the vision and thought of human understanding, but our ideas often pass beyond the limits that confine us, and if one looks at life in the round, how much it holds in all things the extraordinary and the great and the beautiful, that which we came into being for will immediately become apparent. So somehow led by nature [*phusikōs*] we marvel at [*thaumazomen*] not, by Zeus, the small streams, even if they are clear and useful, but at the Nile, the Danube, the Rhine, and still more so the Ocean: we are not struck with awe [*ekplēttometha*] by the little fire we kindle ourselves, when it keeps clear and bright, more than we are by the heavens, though indeed they are often darkened, nor do we think it more wonder-worthy [*axiothaumastoteron*] than the craters of Etna, the eruptions of which throw up rocks and whole hills from the depths and sometimes pour forth rivers of that earthborn and spontaneous fire. Yet of all such things as these I would say this, that that which is necessary or indispensable is easily obtained by humans, but nevertheless it is always that which is beyond belief [*to paradoxon*] that is wonderful [*thaumaston*].

Here Longinus indicates how sublimity is found when the human mind exceeds limits, transcends boundaries, as when images of great physical size, magnitude, and extent are contemplated: small things do not move the soul, but a sense of wonder and awe (*thauma*)—of the sublime—is felt before those things that are vast or massive, like the great rivers of the world, and even more so the seemingly infinite stretches of Ocean and the earth-shattering eruptions of the Sicilian volcano Etna, into which the philosopher Empedocles famously leapt. Such physically sublime features convey an impression of the incredible (*to paradoxon*), or literally that which is beyond (*para*) belief (*doxa*), which overwhelms human capacities of perception and cogitation.

Like rhetorical sublimity, however, the physical species of the sublime is hardly exclusive to the *Peri hupsous*. Another key figure in this tradition is Lucretius, to whom Ovid gave the epithet *sublimis*, (Ov. *Am.* 1.15.23), author of the philosophical poem *De rerum natura*, which is concerned with, among other things, the "majesty" or "sublimity" (*maiestas*) of things (Lucr. 5.2, 5.7).[85] For Lucretius, contemplation of the natural world provokes a combination of a sensation of intense passion (*divina voluptas*) and a shudder of terrible awe (*horror*) that can only be identified as "the signs of the sublime in action,"[86] as when he addresses his philosophical hero Epicurus: "So from these things a certain divine pleasure and horror seizes me, because nature thus by your power lies manifestly open and is uncovered in every part" (*his ibi me rebus quaedam divina voluptas/percipit atque horror, quod sic natura tua vi/tam manifesta patens ex omni parte retecta est*, Lucr. 3.28–30). Democritus famously declared that there are only atoms and the void; the atomist Lucretius finds sublimity in minuscule atoms and the magnitude of matter formed from them—"the small thing can give analogy of great things" (*rerum magnarum parva potest res/exemplare dare*, Lucr. 2.123-124)—but also in the infinite space between atoms, which the poet calls *inane* ("emptiness")—"a sublime of the void," in Philip Hardie's words.[87] This puts one in mind of "the space [*diastēma*] between heaven and earth" (τὸ ἐπ' οὐρανὸν ἀπὸ γῆς διάστημα, Long. *Subl.* 9.4) in Longinus. Indeed, the similarity between Lucretius and Longinus is sometimes striking: compare the passage of the *Peri hupsous* on physical sublimity quoted above with Lucretius when he writes that Epicurus "advanced far beyond the flaming walls of the world and passed through the immeasurable universe in mind and spirit" (*et extra/processit longe flammantia moenia mundi/atque omne immensum peragravit mente animoque*, Lucr. 1.72-74) or when he describes in Book 6 of his epic the same physically sublime images—the universe, the Ocean, the Nile, Etna.[88]

This similarity is probably not due to direct influence, but rather to common sources in a long tradition: notions of physical sublimity can be traced all the way back to the Archaic dawn of Greek thought, to the Presocratic philosophers or *phusiologoi* ("natural philosophers") who in exploring the limits of matter developed the concept of the *apeiron*, the infinite.[89] The use of the Longinian term *hupsos* can be observed in such contexts later: in a papyrus from Herculaneum usually dated to around 100 BC, natural philosophy (*phusiologia*) is said to elevate the mind through the "sublimity [*hupsos*] of its discourses" (ὕψος τούτων τῶν λόγων);[90] the pseudo-Aristotelian treatise *Peri kosmou*, of uncertain date, opens

---

[85] On the Lucretian sublime see Conte 1994: 1–34, Hardie 2009 passim, Porter 2003 and 2007.
[86] Conte 1994: 22.   [87] Hardie 2009: 95.
[88] Noted in Russell 1964 at Long. *Subl.* 35.1; Porter 2016: 452.
[89] See Sedley 1998: 157–60 as well as Porter 2016: 454–7 and Ch. 5 passim. On the Presocratics and the sublime see Porter 2010: 144–5, 158–65.
[90] Biblioteca Nazionale di Napoli, Papyri Herculanenses 831, col. 8.7-13 N f. 75, cited in Porter 2016: 458 n.220, including the revised readings of Kirk Sanders.

noting that "the contemplation of the universe" (τὴν τῶν ὄντων θέαν) is not undertaken by other sciences "on account of the sublimity [*hupsos*] and grandeur [*megethos*]" (διὰ τὸ ὕψος καὶ τὸ μέγεθος) of the subject (Arist. *Mund*. 391a).[91] Seneca evinces a clear conception of physical sublimity in the *Naturales Quaestiones*. He recounts how the discoverers of a huge underground chamber with "massive rivers and vast reservoirs of still water" (*flumina ingentia et conceptus aquarum inertium vastos*) beheld this sight "not without a shudder of awe" (*non sine horrore*, Sen. *Nat. Quaest.* 5.15.1): even if Seneca had not made this into an allusion to Lucretius' *horror ac divina voluptas* by adding that he read about this "with great pleasure" (*cum magna...voluptate*, Sen. *Nat. Quaest.* 5.15.2) his *horror* could still be recognized as the shudder of sublime awe.[92] Etna, which Seneca elsewhere calls "this customary subject for all the poets" (*hunc sollemnem omnibus poetis locum*, Sen. *Ep*. 79.5), inspired one author, probably Neronian, to devote a poem of several hundred Latin hexameters to the subject: entitled simply the *Aetna*, it foregrounds the sublimely destructive powers of the volcano, "the fires that erupt from its deep furnaces" (*ruptique cavis fornacibus ignes*, *Aet*. 1) and the "chaos and ruin without end" (*chaos ac sine fine ruinae*, *Aet*. 139) that these produce.[93]

Notions of physical sublimity were passed down to the Renaissance through such classical sources. In 1417 Poggio Bracciolini discovered the sole surviving manuscript of the *De rerum natura* in a German monastery, thus beginning the reintroduction of Lucretius into Latin European culture. The poet's materialism and atheism may have posed problems for his new Christian readers, but his sublimity was apparent. In a dialogue written in the late 1490s entitled *Actius* the Italian humanist and poet Giovanni Pontano identifies this quality in the poet directly when he writes that Lucretius, with his "magnitude" (*magnitudo*) and "wonder" (*admiratio*), transports his reader in rapture (*rapit*).[94] A number of Lucretian poems were written in Latin in sixteenth-century Italy, among which there are a number of suggestions that Renaissance readers recognized the same form of physical sublimity.[95] In his *Zodiacus vitae* Marcellus Palingenius declares that he follows the example of Lucretius, a truth-seeker "desiring to break through the secret gates of nature" (*abdita naturae cupiens irrumpere claustra*), one of those ancient poets who writes "sublime songs" (*sublimia carmina*).[96] Giordano Bruno remarks on the "sublime nature" (*sublime ingenium*)

---

[91] Noted in Porter 2016: 474. The text reads simply τῶν ἄλλων ("the others"), usually translated as something like "the other sciences," as in Thom 2014: 21; see Thom 2014: 3–8 for a discussion of its date.

[92] The allusion to Lucretius is noted in Porter 2016: 455. On the Senecan sublime see also Williams 2016: Ch. 6.

[93] On the sublime in the *Aetna* see Porter 2016: 508–17.

[94] Pontano 1943: 238–9, quoted from Haskell 1998: 503. On the reception of Lucretius in the Renaissance see Brown 2010; Passannante 2011; Palmer 2014; Norbrook et al. 2016.

[95] See Haskell 2016.   [96] Palingenius 1548: sigs. A3r-v, quoted from Haskell 2016: 98–9.

expressed in Palingenius' poem, with its "marvels" (*mira*).[97] Aonio Paleario, in *De animorum immortalitate*, extols that "power" (*vis*) which, as he quotes Lucretius, "advances far beyond the flaming walls of the world" (*extra/procedit longe flammantia moenia mundi*).[98] Lodovico Parisetti, author of the Lucretian poem *De immortalitate animae*, writes in a letter to his friend Francesco Martelli that "our mind is a Daedalus" (*Dedalus ergo/est intellectus noster*) which "while it is an explorer of the sublime causes of things" (*dum speculator/sublimes rerum causas*) soars "on high in flight" (*volatu...in altum*).[99] The same author wrote to Pietro Bembo that the poet of nature is able to "drive the four-horse chariot from the prison it has broken out of to the sublime end of space" (*rupto de carcere currum/quadriiugum ad spacii sublimem impellere metam*).[100] Bembo himself wrote a work, first printed by the Aldine press in 1496, about his ascent of the sublime Mount Etna, whose destructive effects he describes as "a truly awful spectacle" (*horrendum sane spectaculum*).[101] The famous seventeenth-century polymath Athanasius Kircher also had a sense of sublime Lucretian *horror*. In a section of his geological work *Mundus Subterraneus* devoted to Etna Kircher describes the volcano's "terrifying appearance" (*horrenda facies*) and ends with a quotation of Lucretius: *extruditque simul mirando pondere saxa* ("and at the same time it shoots out rocks of wondrous weight").[102] In his later work on the environs of Rome entitled *Latium*, Kircher writes of a "most profound chasm" (*profundissima voragine*) created by the falls of the Aniene in Tivoli, "which, from the awful spectacle, you might call the jaws of hell" (*quam ex horrendo spectaculo inferni fauces diceres*).[103] The Italian artist Salvator Rosa, who painted among other subjects the sublime figure of Empedocles falling into Etna, once remarked on the *horrida bellezza* ("dreadful beauty") of the sight of "a river that falls from the precipice of a mountain of half a mile and raises foam just as high" (*un fiume che precipita da un monte di mezzo miglio di precipizio et inalza la schiuma altrettanto*).[104]

Many of Lucretius' Renaissance readers, admiring his adventuring beyond the limits of the universe and exploring the sublime causes of nature, found in him a model of physical sublimity. For a Puritan poet like Lucy Hutchinson, however,

---

[97] Bruno 1879: 17.   [98] Paleario 1992, quoted from Haskell 2016: 115.
[99] Parisetti 1541b: *Ep.* 5.6, quoted from Haskell 2016: 120. The Lucretian poem was published as Parisetti 1541a.
[100] Parisetti 1541b: *Ep.* 1.3, quoted from Haskell 2016: 120. The phrase *spacii...metam* means literally "the turning post of the track," as in a chariot race, but I translate the possible sense "end of space" to suggest a more cosmic and sublime sense, which may be intended here given the Lucretian dimension.
[101] Quoted from Williams 2017: 344, which features a study, text, and translation of Bembo 1496.
[102] Kircher 1664–5: I 186, quoting Lucr. 6.692. The connection between Kircher and the Lucretian sublime is made by Porter 2007: 177.
[103] Kircher 1671: 140.
[104] Quoted from Langdon et al. 2010. On Rosa and the sublime see Porter 2007: 177 and Langdon 2012.

who translated Lucretius into English in the 1650s, this natural-philosophical species of the sublime was not easily assimilable. Like John Evelyn, who undertook his translation of Lucretius in the same decade, Hutchinson does not seem to have been entirely comfortable with the natural sublimity offered by Lucretius, taming his *divina voluptas atque horror* into "sweete delight and wonder."[105] In her poem *Order and Disorder* Hutchinson asks:

> was it not sublime
> Enough, above the lower world to climb,
> And in Angelick converse to delight,
> Although it could not reach the supreme height?[106]

"No," she answers back, emphasizing the distance between humble humanity and sublime divinity.[107] In this question ("was it not sublime") Hutchinson points to another kind of sublimity, one which Lucretius would have accounted among the superstitious "fears of the mind" (*animi terrores*, Lucr. 3.16) that reason puts to flight: the sublimity of the divine.

The Theological Species of the Sublime

Thus far I have not mentioned what is surely one of the most remarkable passages in the *Peri hupsous*, one which marks the domain of sublime divinity:

ταύτῃ καὶ ὁ τῶν Ἰουδαίων θεσμοθέτης, οὐχ ὁ τυχὼν ἀνήρ, ἐπειδὴ τὴν τοῦ θείου δύναμιν κατὰ τὴν ἀξίαν ἐχώρησε κἀξέφηνεν, εὐθὺς ἐν τῇ εἰσβολῇ γράψας τῶν νόμων 'εἶπεν ὁ Θεός' φησί· τί; 'γενέσθω φῶς, καὶ ἐγένετο· γενέσθω γῆ, καὶ ἐγένετο.' (Long. Subl. 9.9)

So too the lawgiver of the Jews, no ordinary man, for he understood [*echōrēse*] and exhibited [*kaxephēnen*] the power of God as it deserved, when he wrote in the very beginning of the Laws: "God said," he says—what? "Let there be light, and there was light; let there be earth, and there was."

This quotation of Genesis—perhaps it would more accurately be termed a paraphrase, given its differences with the text of the Septuagint—is so rare in classical literature that it has sometimes been considered an interpolation, beginning with

---

[105] Hutchinson 2011: 157 (l. 3.32); see Norbrook 2013; Hutchinson 2011: 583; Hardy 2016: 215. Evelyn's translation of the first book of *De rerum natura* was published in his lifetime as Evelyn 1656, while translations of books 3–6 survive in MS (BL Evelyn MSS 34 and 34a, commentary in MS 33); all five extant books were edited together as Evelyn 2000. There also exists an anonymous English prose translation dating to around the same time (Bod. MS Rawl. D.314), on which see Barbour 2010.
[106] Hutchinson 2001: 41 (3.291–294).   [107] See Norbrook 2013.

Franciscus Portus, who suspected that the marginal annotation of "some monk" (*aliquem Monachum*) had been copied into the text by an "inept scribe" (*librarium...imperitum*).[108] Alternatively, some scholars have suggested that Longinus borrowed the quotation from Caecilius' work on the sublime, since according to the *Suda*, the Byzantine encyclopedia, Caecilius was "Jewish in belief" (τὴν δὲ δόξαν Ἰουδαῖος), though the biographer adds: "I am rather surprised that he is Jewish—a Jew who knows about Greek things" (πῶς δὲ Ἰουδαῖος τοῦτο θαυμάζω: Ἰουδαῖος σοφὸς τὰ Ἑλληνικά, *Suda* κ 1165 s.v. Κεκίλιος. Theodor Mommsen proposed that the author of the *Peri hupsous* was himself a Hellenized Jew.[109] Setting these questions aside, what pertains here is the way that this passage reveals a conception of divine sublimity. For Longinus does not only commend how Moses "exhibited [*kaxephēnen*] the power of divinity"—with a play on words, in that the verb *kaxephēnen* means literally brought to light (*phōs*)—but how he *echōrēse*, made space for it, or—as the conjecture proposed by Paulus Manutius and adopted into the early modern editorial tradition reads—*egnōrise*, became acquainted with it: the sublimity of Genesis derives partly from its manner of expression, but also from its conception of the divine. This is reinforced by the fact that Longinus' paraphrase of Genesis is just the last in a sequence of passages cited as instances of divine sublimity.[110] The others are Iliadic: Longinus remarks on the sublimity of Homeric *theomachia* ("war of the gods"), which threatens the destruction of the world (Long. *Subl.* 9.6), before declaring that he prefers "those passages which represent divinity truthfully, as something immaculate and great and pure" (τὰ ὅσα ἄχραντόν τι καὶ μέγα τὸ δαιμόνιον ὡς ἀληθῶς καὶ ἄκρατον παρίστησιν, Long. *Subl.* 9.8), as exemplified in Homer's description of the passage of Poseidon from Samothrace to Aegae. This sequence of passages, all of which have origins in ancient Near Eastern writing,[111] points to a kind of sublimity that resides in theological notions and representations of the divine: as Longinus writes later in his treatise, "the sublime [*hupsos*] raises one up almost to the greatness of mind [*megalophrosunēs*] of divinity" (τὸ δ' ὕψος ἐγγὺς αἴρει μεγαλοφροσύνης θεοῦ, Long. *Subl.* 36.1). Moses, traditionally credited with authorship of the Pentateuch, serves as an exemplary figure for this kind of sublimity.

---

[108] Pearce 1733a: 301. Cf. the Greek text of Gen. 1:3 εἶπεν ὁ Θεός· γενηθήτω φῶς· καὶ ἐγένετο φῶς.
[109] On some of these various opinions see e.g. Rhys Roberts 1897.
[110] Usher 2007 shows that these passages "are bound together by programmatic words and phrases that serve the author as prompts or cues in composition" (293), proposing for example that Homer's treatment of Poseidon as one before whom "the sea parts with joy" (γηθοσύνη δὲ θάλασσα διίστατο, Long. *Subl.* 9.8) prompted the Genesis reference by reminding the author of Moses as one who parted the Red Sea in Exodus.
[111] West 1995 finds parallels for the Iliadic passages Longinus cites here in Sumerian, Akkadian, Ugaritic, and Hittite sources, concluding that "L's juxtaposition of Homer and Genesis in this section will now appear a little less strange" (342). See West 1997 for a broader study of Near Eastern influences on Greek poetry.

Philo of Alexandria, a Hellenized Jew who was a contemporary of Jesus and the Apostles, remarks on the "sublimity [*hupsēgoria*] in style" (κατὰ τὴν φράσιν ὑψηγορία, Philo *Det.* 79) of Genesis,[112] but also seems to have a conception of theological sublimity, as when he writes that Melchizedek "calls forth the notion of the Most High [*tou hupsistou*] from his conceiving of God not humbly and grovelingly but very grandly [*hupermegethōs*] and purely immaterially [*huperaulōs*] and sublimely [*hupsēlōs*]" (τὸ μὴ ταπεινῶς καὶ χαμαιζήλως ὑπερμεγέθως δὲ καὶ ὑπεραύλως καὶ ὑψηλῶς νοεῖν περὶ θεοῦ ἔμφασιν τοῦ ὑψίστου κινεῖ, Philo *Leg.* 3.82).[113] In fact the idea of the sublimity of God is not something that Philo has interjected into the biblical text. It is something already there. The passage of Genesis on which he comments here states that Melchizedek was the "priest of God the Most High [*tou hupsistou*]" (ἱερεὺς τοῦ θεοῦ τοῦ ὑψίστου, Gen. 14:18). The Greek *hupsistos* of the Septuagint translates the Hebrew *elyon*, derived from the verb *ala* ("to ascend"): *elyon* appears as a divine epithet not only in Hebrew but also in related West Semitic languages, applied to such deities as the Canaanite Baal, while the Greek translation *hupsistos* was used from the Hellenistic period onward not only for the Abrahamic God, both by Jews and by the authors of the books that would become the New Testament, but also, perhaps under the influence of the Septuagint, for Zeus or another supreme god by pagans in the Near East.[114] What this epithet signifies is the sublimity of the deity: it marks the deity as a divine being that is not sensible but transcendent.[115] That is obviously true in the case of the aniconic Yahweh, whom Jacob identifies by the awful and sublime name "the dread of Isaac" (*pachad yitschaq*, Gen. 31:42).[116]

In the final paragraphs of *European Literature and the Latin Middle Ages* Ernst Robert Curtius reflected on the fortunes of Longinus in the later centuries of the Roman Empire and in the Middle Ages, declaring that the apparent lack of interest in the *Peri hupsous* throughout this period constituted "one of the clearest symptoms of its debilitated intellectual energy."[117] Yet while late antique and medieval Latin Christendom may not have had any knowledge of Longinus, it clearly had a conception of what St. Bonaventure calls the "terrible sublimity" (*altitudo terribilis*) of God.[118] In the fourth century Zeno of Verona wonders: "What is more fortunate than when God in his paternal office condescends to

---

[112] See Kamesar 2016. [113] Translation adapted from Porter 2016: 538.
[114] See Toorn et al. 1999 s.v. elyon and s.v. hypsistos, as well as Parker 2017: 124–31.
[115] This appears to be the case even in pagan uses of ὕψιστος; Parker 2017 writes: "When in Amastris in Paphlagonia 'by the voice of the Unshorn One' an altar is dedicated 'of the Highest God who rules over all and is not seen,' a hierarchy is clearly being established between a lower god of sensible qualities, long-haired Apollo, and a supreme and invisible power who is unnamed; 'Highest' here is not mere rhetoric but embodies a theological vision" (128).
[116] See also Gen. 31:53. On the contested significance of this phrase see Toorn et al. 1999 s.v. fear of Isaac.
[117] Curtius 2013: 400; see 398–401.
[118] Quoted from Boitani 1989: 253. On medieval sublimity see ibid., passim as well as the papers collected in Jaeger 2010a.

attend to men and when that so great sublimity holds human insignificance dear or beloved?" (*Quid enim beatius, quam si homines deus paterno honore dignetur adtendere et tanta illa sublimitas humanam mediocritatem aut caram habeat aut dilectam?*, Zeno Tract. 1.61.6; cf. Tract. 2.9.8). His more famous contemporary, Augustine, interpreting that passage of Genesis which reads "and the Spirit of God was borne over the water" (*et spiritus dei superferebatur super aquam*), explains that the Spirit was not borne through physical "spans of space" (*spatia locorum*), but "by the power of its invisible sublimity" (*per potentiam invisibilis sublimitatis suae*, Aug. Gen. c. Manich. 1.5.8). The twelfth-century theologian Richard of St. Victor describes contemplative ecstasy in sublime terms, writing that the soul, "when irradiated by the divine light and suspended in wonder before the highest beauty, is so shaken with violent astonishment that it is forced completely out of place" (*quando divino lumine irradiata, et in summae pulchritudinis admiratione suspensa, tam vehementi stupore concutitur, ut a suo statu funditus excutiatur*), that it is "raptured above itself and elevated to sublime heights" (*super semetipsam rapta, in sublimia elevatur*), even comparing this experience to the Longinian image of a lightning bolt (*in modum fulguris coruscantis*).[119] Cathedrals and other church buildings like the Hagia Sophia in Constantinople, which Procopius says is a structure seemingly without mechanical explanation (*amēchania*, Procop. Aed. 1.1.49) in which "one's mind is lifted up to God and walks the air" (ὁ νοῦς δέ οἱ πρὸς τὸν θεὸν ἐπαιρόμενος ἀεροβατεῖ, Procop. Aed. 1.1.61),[120] or the Sainte-Chapelle in Paris, the experience of which Jean de Jandun says is "like being raptured to heaven" (*quasi raptus ad celum*), present architectural spaces whose sublime *magnificentia* ("magnificence") draws the worshipper toward the infinitely greater sublimity of God.[121] Jean also calls Notre-Dame "most terrible" (*terribilissima*), pointing to the association of consecrated spaces with *terror dei* ("the terror of God").[122] It is no accident that the words spoken by Jacob in the Vulgate upon waking from his dream of the ladder to heaven—"And shaking he said: How terrible is this place; this is none other than the dwelling-place of God and the gate of heaven" (*pavensque quam terribilis inquit est locus iste: non est hic aliud nisi domus Dei et porta caeli*, Gen. 28:17)—formed part of the entrance antiphon in the Latin liturgy for the consecration of churches, as used for the conversion of the pagan Pantheon in Rome in 609.[123]

---

[119] Quoted from Jaeger 2010b: 160.

[120] The word ἀμηχανία here signifies "that there did not seem to be any physical explanation for the effect it achieved" (Rousseau 1998: 122). Schibille 2014: 25–6 cites this with reference to the sublime.

[121] Quoted from Inglis 2003: 79. Jean here may be quoting 2 Cor. 12:2; my thanks to Karen Edwards for this suggestion. See Binski 2010.

[122] Quoted from Inglis 2003: 78. See Carruthers 2014 on medieval *terror*; although she concludes that "[t]here was no medieval Sublime because there was no need for such an idea. The two separate concepts of *terribilis* and *timor Dei* served its purposes" (31), I consider these instead as part of the medieval sublime.

[123] See Rankin 2010.

The theological species of the sublime is not primarily a matter of language but one of theological elevation, as Erasmus recognizes when he writes of Paul's Letter to the Ephesians that "his skill of speech does not match the sublimity of his thoughts" (*sensuum sublimitatem sermonis facultas non est assequuta*).[124] This line of thinking about divine sublimity continues into the period of the Reformation. John Calvin, in the *Institutio Christianae Religionis*, offers a prominent example. Calvin emphasizes the sublimity of God in relation to the total depravity of man, writing that human understanding "lies far beneath the sublimity of God's providence" (*longe infra providentiae Dei altitudinem subsidit*) and that "our infirmity does not reach up to his sublimity" (*ad eius altitudinem non pertingit nostra infirmitas*).[125] Elaborating on the commandment against taking the Lord's name in vain he declares that everything said and thought of God "should accord with the sacred sublimity of his name and be appropriate for exalting his magnificence" (*sacrae nominis eius sublimitati respondeat: denique ad extollendam eius magnificentiam aptum sit*).[126] He comments on a passage from Proverbs: "Solomon, in discussing the immeasurable sublimity of God, affirms that his son is as incomprehensible as himself: Speak his name, he says, and his son's name, if you can" (*Solomo de immensa Dei altitudine disserens, tam filium eius, quam ipsum incomprehensibilem affirmat: Dic nomen eius, si potes, inquit, aut filii eius*).[127] But Calvin was hardly alone in recognizing what the Dutch theologian Johannes Cocceius calls "the sublimity and majesty of God" (*Dei altitudo & majestas*).[128] Often this sense of sublimity was expressed, as in the Middle Ages, in terms of divine terror, with "the feare of Izhák" (Gen. 31:42) naming "the God whome Izhák did feare & reverence," as a marginal gloss in the 1560 Geneva Bible reads.[129] Edward Reynolds, later made Bishop of Norwich after the Restoration, describes the fear of the supreme deity in his sublime transcendence, writing that "to make him our *fear* (as he is called the *fear of Isaac*, Gen. 31.42.) is to acknowledge his infinite, peerless, surpassing, and unparallel'd excellencies and preheminence," while the Puritan preacher Jeremiah Burroughs makes the terrible sublimity of God more personal: "And dost thou walk in the fear of God? Hast thou not a bold spirit that goes in slight, presumptuous, bold base wayes? This is not like Jacob, he looked on Gods presence as terrible."[130]

Meanwhile Longinus' commendation of Genesis endeared him to early modern readers: as Isaac Casaubon wrote, "you might gather, perhaps not wrongly, that he was semi-Christian, based on that judgment which he made of the writings of Moses" (*semichristianum fuisse, non male fortasse colligas, propter illud quod facit de Mosis scriptis iudicium*).[131] Scholars, theologians, and preachers came to cite the *Peri hupsous* as a pagan testimony to the sublimity of Scripture, such as John

---

[124] Erasmus 1535: 591. [125] Calvin 1559: 64, 71. [126] Ibid. 131. [127] Ibid. 171.
[128] Cocceius 1662: 38. [129] [Anon.] 1560: 15. See e.g. Bussels 2016: 889ff.
[130] Reynolds 1657: 9; Burrough 1648: 57. [131] Casaubon 1603: 512 [510].

Stoughton, who writes that Longinus "saw so much majestie in the relation" of the *fiat lux* "that he confesses that narration had a seemely character and cognizance of the Divine power set upon it."[132] But Longinus was hardly the sole focus of early modern conceptions of the theological sublime: seventeenth-century texts are replete with references to the "divine *sublimitie*" of God, "the *glorious majesty and sublimity* of Gods divine nature," "the Majestie of God, and the divine sublimitie of his undefiled goodnesse," "his transcendent height and Sublimity over and above all other things or persons," "the sublimity and excellency of divine Majesty," "*the likeness of Divine sublimity.*"[133] As the author John Goodwin, a significant figure in the intellectual culture of the English Revolution who elsewhere quotes from Milton's *Tenure of Kings and Magistrates*, asserts, "the supertranscendent excellencie and sublimity of the divine nature, is such, that it is an object, proportioned only unto, and comprehensible only by, it self."[134]

In this chapter I hope to have illuminated at least the broad contours of the idea of the sublime as it would have been understood in the seventeenth century. I have traced the development of rhetorical notions of sublimity from Longinus and other ancient authors to the Renaissance, but also drawn attention to the physical and theological modes of the sublime. The following three chapters shall be concerned with the relevance of these three species of sublimity—rhetorical, physical, theological—to Milton.

---

[132] Stoughton 1640: 53. See Lazarus 2021 as well as Jansen 2019: 123ff.
[133] Wilkes 1608: 69; Pemberton 1613: 14; Wall 1627: 4; Fairclough 1650: 9; Dickson 1664: 54; Tombes 1667: 213.
[134] Goodwin 1648: 213; several references to Milton's *Tenure* can be found in Goodwin 1649 passim. On Goodwin see Coffey 2006.

2
Milton and the "Stile of Lofty"

In the twentieth century the problem of Milton's style became a major scholarly controversy, which culminated in Christopher Ricks's *Milton's Grand Style* (1963).[1] No one disputed that the style of *Paradise Lost*—the almost exclusive focus of the debate—is, in some sense, *grand*: rather, "the Milton controversy," as it came to be known, centered on the question of whether Milton's grand style succeeds in its ambitions, as the poet's defenders insisted, or whether it descends into tasteless orotundity and dull monotony, as his detractors claimed. In other words: is Milton's style truly *grand*, or really *grandiose*? In this chapter I am concerned with another question entirely, one that has never been properly addressed before. The Milton controversy was a matter of evaluative literary criticism, turning on varying estimations of the quality of the poet's verse. Here I am interested not so much in the appraisal of particular stylistic features and their local effects—though I shall of course touch upon these where appropriate—as I am in the literary-historical issue of Milton's own conception of the grand or sublime style, a conception which I think owes much to Longinus. This chapter therefore considers the evidence of Milton's prose and poetry in order to establish what Milton understood by the phrase "stile of lofty" (*CPW* 2: 401) and traces throughout his works the associations of sublime rhetoric with biblical style, inspired enthusiasm, and republican politics. I must begin, however, with Milton's acquaintance with the classical rhetorical tradition, which is a matter of education.

Milton's Education in the Sublime

In investigating the development of Milton's understanding of sublimity of style it is necessary to start by considering his early education "by sundry masters and teachers both at home and at the schools" (*CPW* 1: 809), as he recounts in *The Reason of Church-Government*.[2] Among these were the Scottish Puritan Thomas Young, who tutored Milton privately in his early years, and Alexander Gil, High Master of St. Paul's School, where Milton first enrolled sometime between 1615 and 1621. Isaac Vossius, writing in 1651, reports that Milton was, according to

---

[1] Ricks 1963. For a history of the controversy see esp. Leonard 2013: I 169–265.
[2] On Milton's education to 1625 see Barker 1937, Clark 1946 and 1964, and Fletcher 1956–61: I.

Milton, Longinus, and the Sublime in the Seventeenth Century. Thomas Matthew Vozar, Oxford University Press.
© Thomas Matthew Vozar 2023. DOI: 10.1093/oso/9780198875949.003.0003

Franciscus Junius, "a disciple of Patrick Young" (*discipulum Patricii Junii*), suggesting that the royal librarian, who from 1621 to 1624 also served as Prebendary and Treasurer of St Paul's Cathedral, might have been another.³ I would note that both Gil and Patrick Young were familiar, to varying degrees, with the *Peri hupsous*. Both Gil and his son of the same name, a friend of the young Milton, were associates of Thomas Farnaby, who cites Longinus several times in his *Index Rhetoricus*.⁴ Although the earliest known printed edition of this work did not appear until 1625, Gil the Elder must have read some version of the *Index* earlier in manuscript, since he quotes from it in his *Logonomia Anglica* (1619).⁵ Gil therefore would have at least come across the name of the Greek author. Patrick Young, to whom Milton sent a bound volume of his tracts in the late 1640s with the inscription "To the most learned man" (*Ad doctissim[um] virum, CW* 11: 373), was personally involved in King James's purchase of Isaac Casaubon's books in England in 1614, including Casaubon's annotated copy of Robortello's edition of Longinus, and later lent a copy of Robortello's edition, potentially Casaubon's, to Gerard Langbaine in the early 1630s.⁶ Hypothetically, either of these men might have introduced Milton to Longinus as early as his school years, though it is highly improbable that the difficult Greek of the *Peri hupsous*—a text not yet taught in the universities, much less in the grammar schools—would have been recommended to so young a pupil, even one as precocious as Milton must have been.

Among the papers of Thomas Gale is a manuscript entitled *The Constant Method of Teaching in St. Pauls Schoole London*, which represents the curriculum followed during Gale's period as High Master from 1672 to 1697.⁷ Its contents provide perhaps the best indication of what Milton's education at St Paul's might have been like several decades earlier: lessons in Latin, Greek, and Hebrew grammar; Latin theme writing and translation exercises; and readings of classical poetry (Homer, Aratus, Dionysius Periegetes, Vergil, Horace, Ovid, Persius,

---

³ Burmann 1727: III 618. Campbell 1997: 118 observes: "'Patrick' may be a slip for Thomas, JM's tutor, but Francis Junius is not likely to have confused his fellow scholar-librarian Patrick Young with the Smectymnuan Thomas Young," concluding that "it is at least possible, albeit improbable, that he had taught JM." As noted by Spencer 1957: Junius himself refers to Longinus throughout Junius 1637, which was translated into English (Junius 1638) and Dutch (Junius 1641).

⁴ Farnaby 1625: sig. A2r, 14, 30; noted in Spencer 1957: 137. Gil the Younger addressed a 1624 poem to Farnaby (Gil 1632: 18–19), as noted by Clark 1946: 142 and 1964: 89–91; Farnaby presented Gil the Younger with a copy of his edition of Juvenal and Persius, the detached inscription of which is now Harvard UL, Houghton Library MS Eng. 739, as noted by Poole 2018: 184 n.40. For more on Gil the Younger see Miller 1990 and Poole 2019.

⁵ E.g. Gil 1619: 102; see Clark 1964 passim and Dixon 1951: 79–80, 402–3.

⁶ The volume Milton sent to Patrick Young is Trinity College Dublin, Press B.4.16; Poole 2017a: 77 speculates that "the connection may have been Thomas Young, Milton's boyhood tutor, and possibly Patrick's kinsman." Casaubon's copy of Longinus is BL 1088.m.2; on the fate of Casaubon's library after his death see Birrell 1980, reprinted in Birrell 2013: 63–76, and Botley and Vince in Casaubon 2018: I 45–50, with reference to Young at 45–6. For the copy of Robortello's edition loaned to Langbaine see Langbaine 1636: *Notae* 115.

⁷ Trinity College Library (Cambridge), MS O.10.22. On Milton's education at St Paul's see Clark 1964, with a transcription of the Gale manuscript at 110–13.

Martial, Juvenal), oratory (Demosthenes, Cicero's speeches), and history (Sallust, Justin), as well as other texts like Aesop's fables, the *Distichs* of Dionysius Cato, Leonhard Culmann's *Sententiae Pueriles*, the mythographical *Bibliotheca* of Pseudo-Apollodorus, the Psalms, the Greek New Testament, and Erasmus' *Colloquia*. Not included in this list are any works of rhetorical theory, but other evidence suggests that Aphthonius' *Progymnasmata*, a handbook of rhetorical exercises recommended by the likes of Roger Ascham, formed part of the St Paul's curriculum in Milton's school years.[8] Providing an "easie entrance into Theames," or short prose compositions on assigned topics, the *Progymnasmata* was a standard rhetorical textbook in the grammar schools and a Renaissance bestseller, issued in 122 editions by 1620.[9] An extant Latin prose composition on the theme of early rising sometimes attributed to Milton suggests that at St Paul's he used the expanded edition of Reinhard Lorich, first published in 1542 and often reprinted.[10] But this rather pedestrian textbook on theme writing held no lessons in rhetorical sublimity: Aphthonius was probably one of the texts Milton had in mind when he complained in his essay *Of Education* of the "preposterous exaction" of "forcing the empty wits of children to compose Theams, verses, and Orations, which are the acts of ripest judgment and the finall work of a head fill'd by long reading, and observing" (*CPW* 2: 372).

Milton would have been more likely to have first encountered some sense of sublimity in rhetoric from Hermogenes, whose name was attached to a corpus of writings known to the Renaissance simply as the *Ars rhetorica*.[11] Upon his admission to Christ's College, Cambridge, in 1625, Milton's first year of study would have been devoted to rhetoric, in accordance with the Elizabethan statutes of the university, which specifically decreed that "the lecturer in rhetoric should teach Quintilian, Hermogenes, or one or another of Cicero's books of oratory" (*Praelector rhetorices Quintilianum Hermogenem aut aliquem alium librum oratoriarum Ciceronis [doceat]*).[12] Milton might have taken some sense of sublime

---

[8] Ascham 1570: 32r.   [9] Brinsley 1612: 121. See Johnson 1943 and Mack 2011: 27.
[10] Lorich 1542; see Clark 1964: 230–49. For the text of the Latin theme on early rising see *CW* 11: 382–5. University of Texas, HRC 127, the MS containing the theme and two verse exercises, was discovered in 1874 in the same box as Milton's commonplace book; see Kelley 1959 and Haan 2012: 25–36. Scholars since have generally considered the theme and poems to be Milton's, though Campbell 1997: 24 finds that "the handwriting does not resemble mature examples of JM's hand such as the supplicat of 1629" and Jones 2012b: 7 notes in passing that "the case for attribution remains less than secure." More recently, William Poole has classified the contents of the manuscript as *dubia*, arguing that these might just as easily be understood as the work of Milton's own pupils (*CW* 11: 378–82).
[11] On Hermogenes in the Renaissance see Patterson 1970 as well as Mack 2011 passim.
[12] CUL UA Luard 187, fol. 2r; Elizabeth 1852: I 457. On Milton's education at Cambridge (1625-2) see Fletcher 1956–61: II (201–18 on the teaching of rhetoric) and Skinner 2018: 118–38. The 1614-37 accounts of Joseph Mede, a tutor at Christ's, include records of books purchased by his students, collected in Fletcher 1956–61: II 553–622; judging from these, Mede's students were reading Cicero and Quintilian, together with modern authors like Omer Talon and Bartholomäus Keckermann, in their first year, rather than Hermogenes, no purchase of which is recorded. William Chappell, however, who was Milton's tutor in his first year, might well have assigned Hermogenes.

style from any of these authors, but especially from Hermogenes. The copious annotations on Hermogenes' *Peri staseōn* and *Peri ideōn* in Bartholomew Dodington's copy of the Portus anthology testify to the teaching of the author at Cambridge several decades earlier.[13] If Milton studied Hermogenes in the same edition that Dodington owned, he could have had Portus' text of Longinus before him as well.[14] Perhaps, then, his Cambridge years gave him his first taste of Longinus. In any case, the notions of rhetorical *megethos* ("grandeur") and *semnotēs* ("majesty") that Milton would have encountered in the *Peri ideōn* of Hermogenes would certainly have induced him to think in terms of rhetorical sublimity: he recalled the Hermogenic *ideai* later in the *Apology for Smectymnuus* in remarking on how few of the clergy "know to write, or speak in a pure stile, much lesse to distinguish the *idea's*, and various kinds of stile" (*CPW* 1: 934).[15] One way or another, Milton was clearly developing some sense of sublimity of speech by the time that he delivered the third of his academic orations or *Prolusiones* at Cambridge, perhaps in the Lent term of 1628 or 1629, in which he contrasts the arid scholastic philosophy then dominant in the university with the power of "divine poetry" (*Divina...Poesis*) to raise the soul on high (*in sublime*) and the ability of rhetoric not only to persuade but to seize (*capit*) and enslave (*in vincula pellectos*, *WJM* 12: 162).[16]

The question remains: when did Milton first become acquainted with Longinus? If not by the conclusion of his university years—Longinus was, after all, still rather obscure in England at this point—he may well have read him sometime during the course of his "studious retirement" (*CPW* 1: 319) in Hammersmith and Horton between 1632, when he received his Cambridge MA, and 1638, when he embarked on his tour of the Continent. It is plausible that in these years Milton might have had access to and occasionally visited major institutional collections like Sion College Library in London and the Bodleian Library in Oxford, in addition to the private libraries of acquaintances.[17] Sion College Library, newly established for the use of the London clergy, is suggested as

---

[13] CUL shelfmark Adv.d.4.4; see Leedham-Green 2004: 618–19.

[14] Franciscus Portus, I note, is named in Milton's life of Petrus Ramus, adapted from the *vita* by Johann Thomas Freigius, that is appended to the *Artis Logicae Plenior Instituto* (*WJM* 11: 512); see Miller 1972 on Milton's editing of Freigius. The edition of Euripides 1602 owned by Milton includes annotations by Aemilius Portus, son of Franciscus, to which the marginalia in Milton's copy (Bod. Don. d.27-28) refer several times (*WJM* 18: 310, 317, 320).

[15] On Milton and Hermogenes see Patterson 1970 passim.

[16] Third, that is, in the sequence in Milton 1674b: 88–95; on the date see Shawcross 1965: 265–6, Miller 1980: 80–1; Campbell 1997: 31; Campbell and Corns 2008: 36–7, 41–2. On the *Prolusiones* in general see e.g. Fletcher 1956–61: II passim, Hale 2005 passim, and Knight 2011. On this oration in particular see Fletcher 1956–61: II 469–71 and esp. Hale 2005: 86–90. Goode 1930 once proposed that some verbal parallels with Longinus could be detected in the *Prolusiones*, though Tillyard 1930 rightly argued that, while Milton had read and appreciated Longinus, these particular verbal similarities were tenuous.

[17] See Fletcher 1956–61: II 367–81 and esp. the more recent Poole 2012: 28–35 and *CW* 11: 11–33, who also suggests that Milton might have had access to the library of John Hales in Eton, on which see

such a candidate in a letter dated December 1634, in which Milton requests that his correspondent—Alexander Gil, son of Milton's former schoolmaster of the same name—act to advance his business (*negotium*) with "that Doctor, the yearly President of the College" (*illum Doctorem, annuum Collegii Praesidem, EF* 83).[18] The earliest printed catalogue of Sion College Library, published in 1650, lists the Portus edition of Longinus *in archivis*.[19] Anthony Wood reports that Milton incorporated his Cambridge MA at Oxford in the 1635-6 academic year, possibly because he was seeking access to the Bodleian Library, which was closer to Horton, where Milton was resident from May 1636, than Cambridge was.[20] A copy of the Portus edition is included in the 1635 catalogue of the Bodleian compiled by its librarian, John Rouse, to whom Milton a decade later addressed a Latin ode when sending the library a replacement copy of his 1645 *Poems*.[21] Possibly, given his potential connection to Patrick Young, Milton might even have had access to the Royal Library.[22] From this there emerges the possibility that Milton might have held in his hands that very copy of Robortello's Longinus which bears the annotations of Isaac Casaubon, the great English poet reading the Greek authority on the sublime with the notes of the renowned Huguenot scholar.[23]

Later, in Rome, Milton could have crossed paths with a translator of Longinus associated with the influential Barberini family, whose most prominent member at that time was Pope Urban VIII.[24] There, perhaps through a letter of introduction provided by Patrick Young, Milton made the acquaintance of the German humanist Lucas Holstenius, then the librarian of the pope's nephew, Cardinal Francesco Barberini.[25] It was Holstenius, as a letter addressed to him by Milton attests, who facilitated the English traveler's welcome into the Cardinal's circle.[26] Having attended a performance of the comic opera *Chi soffre, speri*—with a

---

Poole 2015. Hales is generally taken to be the "Mr. *H*." of Sir Henry Wotton's extant letter to Milton (*CW* 3: 61). Sir Henry Wotton calls Hales "our *Bibliotheca ambulans*" (Wotton 1672: 475), perhaps adapting Eunapius' praise of Cassius Longinus, as quoted in the dedication of the Portus volume, which Wotton owned (Stanford UL RBC KB1570.A6, on which see Vozar 2019). Jones 2002 considers Milton's possible use of the Kedermister Library at Langley, not far from Horton, but the 1638 catalogue, transcribed in Francis 1994: 72-5, does not include any editions of Longinus.

[18] See *CPW* 1: 322 n.5, Campbell and Corns 2008: 85, and Poole 2012: 30.

[19] Spencer 1650: 89, with the shelfmark G 64. *Arch*. The label *Arch*[*iva*] designates books in smaller formats, including octavos, held *in archivis* (on the closed-access shelves), which could be requested from the librarian—all of which were destroyed in the Great Fire of 1666; see McKitterick 2006: 613-14. On Sion College and its library in general see Pearce 1913.

[20] Wood 1691-2: I col. 880, though Parker 1958 and von Maltzahn 1994, among others, doubt Wood's report. See Campbell and Corns 2008: 86-88 and Poole 2012: 30.

[21] Rouse 1635: 114; *CW* 3: 276-83.   [22] Suggested by Poole 2012: 45 n.24.

[23] BL 1088.m.2.

[24] On the Barberini family and their patronage see Hammond 1994 and Rietbergen 2006. On Milton in Italy see di Cesare 1991 and Martin 2017. My thanks to Tomos Evans, who prompted this consideration.

[25] The possibility that Young provided a letter of introduction is suggested by Campbell and Corns 2008: 123. On Holstenius see Rietbergen 2006: 256-95; on Holstenius and England, including a discussion of his relationship with Young, see Blom 1984.

[26] On the extant holograph (BAV MS Barb. Lat. 2181, fols. 57r-58v) see Bottkol 1953.

libretto written by Giulio Rospigliosi, the future Pope Clement IX—at the Palazzo Barberini in February 1639, Milton professes to have been greeted at the door by Cardinal Barberini himself on account of Holstenius' report: "When for this sake I approached him the next day to pay my respects," Milton continues to Holstenius, "it was you yourself again who gave me access and the opportunity to speak with him" (*Qua ego gratia cum illum postridie salutatum accessissem, tute idem rursus is eras qui et aditum mihi fecisti et colloquendi copiam*, EF 147).[27] Holstenius, according to the same letter, gave Milton a tour of the Vatican Library, drawing attention to some Greek manuscripts on which he had been working; gifted him a copy of one of his books, probably either his volume of Pythagorean *sententiae* or his edition of Porphyry's life of Pythagoras; and tasked the Englishman with transcribing some passages from a Medicean codex at the Bibliotheca Laurenziana while he passed through Florence, though Milton was unable to fulfill this request.[28]

Given this connection with Holstenius, Milton could hardly have been unaware of the other great scholar-librarian of the Barberini circle, the Greek-born humanist Leone Allacci, alias Allatius. Holstenius and Allatius were rivals in scholarship as well as collaborators.[29] In 1638 the Typographia Vaticana printed Allatius' Greek-Latin edition of the Neoplatonic author Sallustius with notes by Holstenius, and both scholars contributed poems—Holstenius' Latin verses immediately follow Allatius' Greek—to the *Applausi poetici alle glorie della Signora Leonora Baroni* (1639), to which Milton's epigrams to Leonora may be indebted.[30] Holstenius would later praise Allatius as the foremost Hellenist in Europe: "In Greek letters, which he taught publicly for many years at the Greek College, he is without a doubt the best that Europe has, and he writes in prose and verse with facility and elegance like the ancients" (*Nelle lettere greche, che per molti anni publicamente insegnò nel Collegio greco, egli è senza dubio il primo che habbia l'Europa, e scrive in prosa e verso con facilità ed eleganza al pare degli antichi*).[31]

---

[27] On the identification of this opera as the one attended by Milton see Ademollo 1888: 25–34 and Smart 1913. While Milton may well have been greeted at the threshold by Francesco Barberini, as he claims, another attendee, Raimondo Montecuccoli, reports that it was Francesco's brother Antonio, also a cardinal, "who stood in person at the door for a huge crowd" (*che stava in persona alla porta, per una grandissima calca*, Ademollo 1888: 28).

[28] For details see EF 140–63. Miller 1991 identified the book gifted to Milton as Holstenius 1638, though Haan in EF 141 has recently proposed Holstenius 1630 as a likelier candidate.

[29] On the relationship between Holstenius and Allatius see Mirto 1999: 23–6 and Rietbergen 2006: 269–70.

[30] Allatius 1638, with Holstenius' notes at 113–19; Ronconi 1639, with Allatius' and Holstenius' contributions at 197–200 and 201–3, respectively. See Haan 1998: 99–117, who at 100 considers that Milton may have heard Leonora perform "at one of the many sumptuous musical entertainments overseen by Cardinal Francesco Barberini," who owned a copy of the *Applausi* (BAV shelfmark Stamp. Barb. JJJ.VI.67). Though the *Applausi* volume does not seem to have been published by the time of Milton's departure from Rome, Haan in EF 142 n.17 notes that poems from this collection "may have been circulating in manuscript in Rome or had received their trial performance in the city's academies."

[31] Biblioteca Nazionale Centrale di Firenze, MS Aut. Palat. IV.56, quoted in Mirto 1999: 24–5.

By the time of Milton's visit Allatius had completed a Latin translation of the *Peri hupsous* with textual commentary, manuscripts of which survive in the Fondo Allacci of the Biblioteca Vallicelliana and in the Fondo Barberini of the Vatican Library, and had referred to Longinus as an authority on rhetoric throughout his *De erroribus magnorum virorum in dicendo* (1635).[32] The Holstenius link opens the way to speculation that in Rome Milton could have been introduced to Allatius and could perhaps have even examined the Greek scholar's unpublished work on Longinus, though there is no positive evidence that this is the case.

The young Milton gives the impression of a bibliophile, someone who wanted not only to read books but to acquire them, meeting friends "among the booksellers" (*inter bibliopolas, EF* 83) and sending chests full of books back to England from his travels in Italy.[33] As the few extant books that can be identified as Milton's, nearly all of which are known to have been acquired in or around this period of his life, are mostly older Continental editions of classical authors purchased second-hand, one may well surmise that Milton might have procured a copy of some Swiss or Italian edition of Longinus, Portus' volume being the most likely, around this time, if not earlier.[34] My own survey of copies of Longinus in seventeenth-century English private libraries, however, indicates that Gerard Langbaine's edition, first published in 1636, was far more common than Portus' volume, the most popular of the Continental printings, let alone any other edition.[35] The numbers therefore suggest that Langbaine's may have been a more likely purchase. Upon its initial publication in 1636 Langbaine's edition would have attracted Milton's interest even if he had already encountered

---

[32] Biblioteca Vallicelliana, MS Allacci XXIX.1–8; BAV MS Barb. Gr. 190, fols. IIIr.–21r; Allatius 1635. See Costa 1985: 232–3; Fumaroli 1986; Refini 2016.

[33] In the *Defensio Secunda* Milton writes: "I saw to it that the books which I had acquired throughout Italy were placed on a ship" (*libros, quos per Italiam conquisiveram, in navem imponendos curassem, WJM* 8: 126); Edward Phillips recalls that his uncle "Shipp'd up a Parcel of curious and rare Books which he had pick'd up in his Travels; particularly a Chest or two of choice Musick-books of the best Masters flourishing about that time in *Italy*" (Darbishire 1965: 59). On Milton's book collecting see Poole 2012 passim and *CW* 11: 22–44.

[34] Books owned by Milton are thought to include, in chronological order of acquisition, a Sammelband containing Dante 1529, della Casa 1563, and Varchi 1555 purchased in 1629 (New York Public Library, shelfmark *KB 1529), on which see Kelley 1962; a copy of Aratus 1559 purchased in 1631 (BL shelfmark C.60.1.7), on which see Kelley and Atkins 1955; a copy of Lycophron 1601 acquired in 1634 (University of Illinois, shelfmark 881 L71601 copy 1), on which see Fletcher 1989; a copy of Euripides 1602 acquired in 1634 (Bod. shelfmark Don.d.27–28), on which see esp. Kelley and Atkins 1961 and Hale 1991; a copy of Chrysostom 1604 acquired in 1636 (CUL shelfmark Ely.a.272); a copy of Heraclides Ponticus 1544 purchased in 1637 (University of Illinois, shelfmark X881 H215 1544), on which see Fletcher 1948; and a copy of Boccaccio 1544 (Bod. shelfmark Arch. A f.145), on which see Poole 2014. I exclude from this list the Milton family Bible (BL Add. MS 32310). Other books have been previously identified as Milton's, though none of these attributions are now widely accepted. Perhaps most notably, a copy of Pindar 1620 (Harvard UL, shelfmark *OGC.P653.620 (B), edited in *WJM* 18: 276–304) was long thought to contain annotations by Milton, but Kelley and Atkins 1964 convincingly argued that the hand is not his. Most recently, the annotations in a copy of Shakespeare's First Folio (Free Library of Philadelphia, RBD EL SH15M 1623) have been identified as Milton's; see Bourne 2018 and esp. Bourne and Scott-Warren 2023.

[35] See the bibliographical appendix.

Longinus in Portus' volume, not least because Langbaine included in his edition both a Latin translation, taken from the 1612 Geneva edition of Gabriel de Petra, and 118 pages of his own scholarly notes. This was not an item the young bibliophile could easily disregard.

When in 1640, several months after his return to England, Milton took responsibility for the education of his nephews, Edward and John Phillips, the pedagogical potential of Langbaine's Longinus, a student edition addressed "to the youth of the academy" (*iuventuti academicae*), must have been on the new schoolmaster's mind:[36] Milton's one and only direct reference to Longinus appears in the program of his own ideal "*Academy*" (*CPW* 2: 379)—no doubt inspired at least in part by his own experience teaching—as laid out in the tract *Of Education*, first printed in June 1644 as a single eight-page quarto gathering.[37] In this brief work, dedicated to Samuel Hartlib, Milton sets out a *ratio studiorum* that, while fundamentally humanistic in its emphasis on the study of classical authors, is to a great degree oriented around practical and empirical disciplines such as those favored by the reformers of the Hartlib Circle.[38] In Milton's prescribed curriculum the student is expected to spend just one year learning classical languages, which constitute "but the instrument convaying to us things usefull to be known" (*CPW* 2: 369), before proceeding to a succession of subjects (agriculture, navigation, astronomy, engineering, medicine, moral philosophy, law) which culminates in the triad of logic, rhetoric, and poetics. In order to appreciate the context of Milton's one reference to Longinus it will be necessary to quote the whole passage:

> And now lastly will be the time to read with them those organic arts which inable men to discourse and write perspicuously, elegantly, and according to the fitted stile of lofty, mean, or lowly. Logic therefore so much as is usefull, is to be referr'd to this due place withall her well couch't heads and Topics, untill it be time to open her contracted palm[39] into a gracefull and ornate Rhetorick taught out of the rule of *Plato, Aristotle, Phalereus, Cicero, Hermogenes, Longinus*. To which Poetry would be made subsequent, or indeed rather precedent, as being lesse suttle and fine, but more simple, sensuous and passionate. I mean not here the prosody of a verse, which they could not but have hit on before among the rudiments of grammar; but that sublime art which in *Aristotles poetics*, in *Horace*,

---

[36] Langbaine 1636: sig. *2r. A. J. Hegarty, writing in *ODNB* s.v. Langbaine, Gerard (1608/9–1658), rightly characterizes it as a "student edition." On Milton and his nephews see Shawcross 2004: 73–134 and Coiro 2008.

[37] The date derives from George Thomason's copy, BL shelfmark E.50(12).

[38] On Milton's relationship with Hartlib see Raylor 1993; on the Hartlib Circle in general see Greengrass et al. 2002. There is some dispute concerning the question of how traditional or innovative the curriculum presented in *Of Education* really is, or whether it is best considered "a compromise between the new and old pedagogies" (Webster 2002: 113); see *CPW* 2: 184–216; *CPW* 2: 366 n.10; Lewalski 1994; Edwards 1995; Koslow 2008; Raylor 2009; Poole 2017a: 49–65.

[39] This is a commonplace, but it is perhaps worth noting that the title page of Langbaine 1636 features an open hand with the tag PUGNUS EXPANSUS ("fist opened up"); see Figure 4.

and the *Italian* Commentaries of *Castelvetro, Tasso, Mazzoni,* and others, teaches what the laws are of a true *Epic* Poem, what of a *Dramatic,* what of a *Lyric,* what decorum is, which is the grand master peece to observe. This would make them soon perceive what despicable creatures our common rimers and play-writes be, and shew them, what Religious, what glorious and magnificent use might be made of Poetry both in divine and humane things. From hence and not till now will be the right season of forming them to be able writers and composers in every excellent matter, when they shall be thus fraught with an universall insight into things. Or whether they be to speak in Parliament or counsell, honour and attention would be waiting on their lips. (*CPW* 2: 401–6)

It is easy to see why Milton's single reference to Longinus has been underestimated for so long: it seems to be nothing more than a name in a list, not only one name among many names but also in one list among many lists. There are, however, some very simple reasons to resist this intuition. That this is Milton's only known mention of Longinus does not necessarily mean that his interest in this author was passing or insignificant. In fact, Milton must have read *and appreciated* Longinus, or he would not have named him as a suitable author for students in his ideal academy. It should be remembered that in 1644, less than a decade after the appearance of Langbaine's Oxford edition and several years before the first published English translation, Longinus was not yet acknowledged as a standard classical authority among English readers. Milton's reference is one of the earliest known to Longinus in English. That Milton should not only go out of his way to mention Longinus at all, but endorse him alongside such recognized names as Aristotle and Cicero, is bold, and suggests a more than superficial knowledge. This, after all, appears to be the earliest instance of Longinus being prescribed for education in England.[40] The context of the reference, moreover, suggests that the *Peri hupsous* had by this point been assimilated into Milton's thinking. Of those classical rhetoricians whose names appear in Milton's list several, at least, were understood to be writing about the same thing, even if it went by various names, namely rhetorical sublimity: the antiquarian Edward Dering, for example, in a work published the same month as *Of Education,* writes that what Hermogenes called *megethos* and what Longinus called *hupsos* were both terms for "the sublime style of speaking" (*sublime dicendi genus*).[41] This is what Milton here calls the "stile of lofty."[42] Milton directly associates Longinus only with rhetoric, not with poetics, but that may just be a convenient place to pigeonhole the author for his present purposes: Milton would certainly have recognized that Longinus was writing about a quality found in "both poets and

---

[40] Later seventeenth-century examples include Blount 1654: 36 et passim and Cowley 1661: 49, as well as several Oxford tutors later in the century, on which see Feingold 1997: 258–9.
[41] Dering 1644: sig. A4r; on Dering and Milton see Rosenblatt 1982.   [42] See Clark 1953.

prose-writers" (ποιητῶν τε [...] καὶ συγγραφέων, Long. *Subl.* 1.3).[43] When he describes poetry as "lesse suttle and fine" than rhetoric, but "more simple, sensuous and passionate," it is the latter phrase that more closely resembles the Longinian sublime, which can take the form of starkly simple but powerful expressions like the *fiat lux* of Genesis and which has as one of its principal sources "vehement and enthusiastic passion" (τὸ σφοδρὸν καὶ ἐνθουσιαστικὸν πάθος, Long. *Subl.* 8.1). Sublimity is never "suttle." And surely Milton's description of poetry as "that sublime art" must owe something to Longinus.

The curriculum presented in *Of Education* is not organized as a series of authors but as a sequence of subjects, with specific authors to be read for their relevance to the teaching of some discipline: Cato, Varro, and Columella, for instance, are to be read as "Authors of *Agriculture*" (*CPW* 2: 387–388).[44] Rhetoric and poetics, as "organic" or instrumental arts, have the clear purpose of training students in the skills of written composition and public speaking, "forming them to be able writers and composers" and making them worthy "to speak in Parliament or counsell." This, then, is the intended end that Milton imagines for his students in their reading of Longinus: to put their oratorical and poetical abilities to "glorious and magnificent use," to write and speak sublimely, or as Langbaine puts it in the preface to his edition, which Milton may well have used for teaching, to cultivate "a genius capable of sublimity" (*capacem sublimitatis indolem*).[45] That this is how Milton did teach Longinus, and that he did bestow upon his pupils some sense of rhetorical sublimity, is indicated by one of the products of his pedagogy, Edward Phillips. Phillips' two later accounts of the educational regimen prescribed for him and his brother by their uncle, as related to biographer John Aubrey for his life of Milton and as printed in the preface to Milton's *Letters of State* in 1694, correspond closely to the curriculum elaborated in *Of Education*, suggesting that this plan of studies was not merely an abstract exercise but something that Milton actually put into practice.[46] Longinus is not mentioned in either of these accounts, but then neither are any other rhetoricians: there is no reason to think that these brief reports are, or are even intended to be, exhaustive, so the absence in them of any reference to Longinus does not argue against the likelihood that Phillips encountered the *Peri hupsous* under Milton's tutelage. Phillips' own literary-historical, educational, and lexicographical projects demonstrate a lifelong concern with rhetorical sublimity. In his dictionary *The*

---

[43] On the place of poetry in the curriculum set out in *Of Education* see Rajan 1945 and esp. Riggs 1992.

[44] On this point see Koslow 2008.   [45] Langbaine 1636: sig. *2r.

[46] Aubrey 2015: I 669–70, Phillips 1694: xvii–xix; Cyriack Skinner simply says that Milton "design'd in some measure to put [the program in *Of Education*] into practise" (Darbishire 1965: 24). See the helpful chart of Milton's Classroom Authors provided by Poole 2017a: 297–300, which shows how the authors featured in *Of Education* compare with those in Phillips' two accounts. Corns 2012b: 86 thinks it likely that Phillips "turned to the printed text in *Of Education* to refresh and inform his personal recollection," but I agree with Poole 2017a: 51, among others, that such skepticism is unwarranted.

New World of English Words he glosses "*Sublimity*" as the Latinate word for "heighth," and his entry for the latter is manifestly a definition of rhetorical sublimity: "*Heighth*, a vertue in writing or speaking, wherein the expressions are neither too inflate, nor too creeping, but observing a decent majesty between both."[47] In his later *Theatrum Poetarum*, in which he mentions Longinus and "his Book *de Sublimitate*" while also writing of "the heighth of Poetical rapture" and the "sublime vein in Poetry," Phillips characterizes the "*Decorum* to be observ'd in the style of the H[eroic] Poem" in the same terms in which he had described *heighth*, namely "that it be not inflate or gingling with an empty noise of Words, nor creepingly low and insipid, but of a Majesty suitable to the Grandeur of the subject."[48] For Phillips, then, the Longinian quality of *heighth* or sublimity is the appropriate style for epic poetry, so it is fitting that, in the *Compendiosa Enumeratio Poetarum* appended to his 1669 edition of Joannes Buchlerus' *Phrasium Poeticarum Thesaurus*, he should praise his uncle's recently released *Paradise Lost* as

> Poema quod sive sublimitatem Argumenti, sive Leporem simul & Majestatem Styli, sive sublimitatem Inventionis, sive similitudines & descriptiones quam maximè Naturales respiciamus, verè Heroicum, ni fallor, audiet, Plurium enim suffragiis qui non nesciunt judicare censetur perfectionem hujus generis poematis assecutum esse.[49]
>
> a poem which, whether we regard the sublimity of the argument, or the grace and at the same time the majesty of the style, or the sublimity of the invention, or the most natural similitudes and descriptions possible, will, if I am not mistaken, be known as truly heroic, for in the opinions of many who are not unable to judge it is thought to have achieved the perfection of this kind of poetry.

Here, in Milton's own lifetime, the poet's nephew becomes the first of many to describe *Paradise Lost* as sublime, as Nicholas McDowell notes.[50] The "*Decorum* to be observ'd in the style of the H[eroic] Poem" is *sublimitas* ("heighth"), and it is the rhetorical sublimity of Milton's epic—in theme (*sublimitatem Argumenti*), in style (*Majestatem Styli*), in invention (*sublimitatem Inventionis*)—that merits the

---

[47] Phillips 1658b s.v. sublimity, s.v. heighth; Phillips extensively appropriated material from Blount 1656, but these two entries are not among his borrowings. For a reevaluation of Phillips' dictionary see Miyoshi 2017: 73–85.

[48] Phillips 1675: 175 ("his Book *de sublimate*," a printing error corrected in the Errata), sig. *5r, 153, sig. **7r–**7v; he also writes of "sublime Poesy" (160) claims that "the more sublime the *Argument*, the nobler the Invention, and by consequence the greater the *Poet*" (sig. **5v); and judges that the pastoral poetry of William Browne, though "containing matter not unpleasant to the Reader," is "not of the sublimest strain" (189). On the *Theatrum Poetarum* see Terry 2001: Ch. 3 passim.

[49] Phillips 1669: 399, with *suffragiis* corrected from *saffragiis*. Cf. the remark in Phillips 1694: xxxix that *PR* was written "in a wonderful short space considering the sublimeness of it." On Phillips's *Enumeratio* see Howarth 1959.

[50] See McDowell 2019.

epithet "truly heroic" (*verè Heroicum*). Edward Phillips clearly shares his uncle's interest in questions of epic decorum, as expressed in *Of Education* ("what the laws are of a true Epic Poem, [...] what Decorum is"). It is not so far-fetched to think that his learned tutor had taught him that epic decorum requires sublimity, and that Milton had this in mind in composing his great epic of the Fall. For Milton, however, such sublimity of style was not merely—or not wholly—classical. It was also biblical.

Biblical Sublimity of Style and Milton's Soaring

In the eighteenth century Robert Lowth turned to Longinus to explain the sublimity of Hebrew poetry in his *De Sacra Poesi Hebraeorum*.[51] Already by Milton's time, however, divinely authored Scripture was increasingly recognized not only as a treasury of truth but as an exemplar of rhetoric, and it was widely understood that its style was sublime—"a sublime style for sublime things" (*hupsēlon hupsēlais*), as Isaac Casaubon put it: "Whatever Longinus and the other theorists of rhetoric say about how one attains sublimity [*hupsos*] in speech will all be found, brilliantly expressed, in the writings of the prophets" (*quicquid est apud Longinum et alios rhetoras quod τὸ ὕψος τῷ λόγῳ conciliet, id omne reperietur in prophetarum scriptis luculentissime expressum*).[52] For Casaubon, the "sublime style" (*sublimis stylus*) of the prophets was evident "especially in Isaiah" (*maxime in Isaia*).[53] Others agreed: in his *Pious Annotations* Giovanni Diodati, the uncle of Milton's friend Charles Diodati, affirmed that Isaiah was "endowed with a propheticke spirit in a most eminent degree for variety of visions, sublimenesse of sences, for power of demonstration, and for a most incomparable Majesty of stile," while Robert Boyle remarked that in the words of Isaiah many had "Admir'd that Lofty Strain which Artists have term'd the Sublime Character" ("Character" here having the sense of its Greek etymon *charaktēr* "style").[54] The rhetorical sublimity of Scripture was one of the very marks of its divine derivation: among the reasons that the preacher Robert Boughton gave in response to the question "What Arguments are there to assure us, that those bookes of the Old and New Testament are the Scriptures and undoubted Word of God?" was "the singular Maiestie and sublimitie of stile, which every where shineth in them."[55] For Theophilus Gale, "the *Majestie* of *Scripture stile* was the

---

[51] Lowth 1753; see Prickett 2016 on Lowth's biblical poetics and its contribution to English Romanticism.
[52] Bod. MS Casaubon 51, fol. 19r, quoted and translated in Grafton and Weinberg 2011: 107, 107 n.140. See Shuger 1988: Ch. 4 as well as Till 2012, Killeen 2013 (esp. 513–14), and Ossa-Richardson 2014.
[53] Bod. MS Casaubon 51, fol. 141, 19v, quoted in Grafton and Weinberg 2011: 107 n.141.
[54] Diodati 1643: sig. [A]1r; Boyle 1661: 173–4.   [55] Boughton 1623: 8.

original Idea and *exemplar* of that sublimitie of speech or *Rhetorick*, in use amongst the Heathens."[56]

One among the many comments on the sublimity of biblical style that Milton would have read comes from the famed Dutch scholar Hugo Grotius, whom Milton met in Paris in May 1638 at the beginning of his Continental tour.[57] Grotius is best known today for his contributions to the development of international law, but he also composed Neo-Latin poetry, edited Lucan, translated Stobaeus and Euripides, and authored a number of theological and exegetical works, including important commentaries on both the Old and New Testaments.[58] Commenting on the *fiat lux* passage of Genesis 1:3 in his *Annotata ad Vetus Testamentum* (1644) Grotius mentions Longinus but refers the reader to his earlier, more extensive commentary on the New Testament.[59] There, in his *Annotationes in Libros Evangeliorum* (1641) is found the following comment on Matthew 8:3, in which Christ heals the leper by uttering the passive imperative *katharisthēti* (KJV: "bee thou cleane"):

καθαρίσθητι] Actiones imperare etiam homines solent: at res solo imperio effectas dare vere divinum est. Ideo Christus ad miracula usus saepe est vocibus imperandi passivis: Nam & Moses creationem ita descripserat: *Et dixit Deus fiat lux & facta est lux*: quibus in verbis majestatem esse miram & σεμνότητα τοῦ λόγου recte animadvertit paganus homo Longinus rhetor.[60]

Be cleansed] Even humans are accustomed to command actions, yet to make things accomplished by command alone is truly divine. Therefore Christ often used the passive voice for commanding miracles, for also Moses had thus described the Creation: *And God said let there be light, and there was light*—in which words a pagan person, Longinus the rhetorician, rightly observes there to be an awesome majesty and solemnity of diction.

---

[56] Gale 1669: 382.   [57] See *WJM* 8: 122 and Campbell and Corns 2008: 106–7.

[58] It has long been speculated that his Latin verse drama *Adamus exul* (Grotius 1601) may have influenced Milton's choice of subject for his epic; see Evans 1968: 207–16 et passim as well as more recently Poole 2005: 106–7 and 2017a: 107. On Grotius' biblical commentaries see van Miert 2017 and Hardy 2017: Ch. 5 et passim.

[59] Grotius 1644: I 2 (*De his verbis vide Dionysij Longini locum, quem in dictis Annotatis protulimus*); Hardy 2017: 181 notes that "Grotius's biblical commentaries focused disproportionately on the New Testament." On earlier Genesis commentaries (1527–1633) in general see Williams 1948; most of these do not refer to Longinus, but some do, e.g. Vielmi 1575: 134. Grotius' interest in Longinus began relatively early: the name "Dion. Longinus" appears in the *excerpta theologica* (Amsterdam UL Remonstrant Collection, MS III C 4, fol. 336r col. b, transcribed in Posthumus Meyjes 1994: 12) that Grotius wrote in preparation for his earliest theological work, *Meletius* (written in 1611), in which he quotes Longinus' approval of Moses (Grotius 1988: 90). Grotius refers to the same passage in his popular apologetical work *Pro veritate religionis Christianae* (Grotius 1627: 28), which Milton cites in his Euripides marginalia (*WJM* 18: 318). On Grotius and Longinus see Jansen 2019 passim.

[60] Grotius 1641: 170.

Grotius shows how the inflection of a single word can demonstrate Christ's divine power to effect miracles "by command alone" (*solo imperio*). More pertinent to my purposes here, he also relates this to God's words at the moment of Creation, taking the *fiat lux* of Genesis and the *katharisthēti* of Matthew together as examples of "an awesome majesty and solemnity [*semnotēta*] of diction" (*majestatem... miram* & σεμνότητα τοῦ λόγου), or the Longinian sublime. Milton esteemed Grotius "of prime note among learned men" (*CPW* 2: 715), as he put it in *Tetrachordon*, and cited the *Annotationes in Libros Evangeliorum* a number of times throughout his divorce tracts.[61] He even refers to Grotius' commentary on Matthew in particular.[62] One can therefore be quite confident that Milton read Grotius' comment on the sublimity of Christ's command *katharisthēti*. This is just one probable example, however: Milton would undoubtedly have encountered elsewhere similar remarks on the rhetorical sublimity of the Bible, with or without reference to Longinus.

Milton, like Grotius and others, recognized that many varieties of biblical style could be just as sublime as biblical matter. In *De Doctrina Christiana*, for instance, he writes that "no one more sublimely and clearly declares the generation of divine nature" (*Divinae autem naturae generationem nemo neque sublimius neque disertius declarat*, CW 8.1: 134) than the author of the Epistle to the Hebrews: it is not just the subject that is sublime, but the way that the Apostle writes (*sublimius... declarat*).[63] But perhaps Milton's most important statement on biblical style comes in an exchange in *Paradise Regain'd*, when Satan tempts the Son with the entire intellectual and literary patrimony of "*Athens* the eye of *Greece*, Mother of Arts / And Eloquence" (*PR* 4.240–241), including the power of classical rhetoric:[64]

> Thence to the famous Orators repair,
> Those antient, whose resistless eloquence
> Wielded at will that fierce Democratie,
> Shook the Arsenal and fulmin'd over *Greece*
>
> (*PR* 4.267–270)

The verb *fulmin'd*, literally "thundered" (cf. Latin *fulmen*), evokes not only the figure of Pericles, who as previously noted was described as a "thundering" orator, but also Longinus, who made the Periclean *fulmen eloquentiae*, with its

---

[61] See *CPW* 2: 238, 329, 334–5, 344, 433–4. Milton also read the second volume of Grotius' New Testament commentary (*CPW* 7: 253), which features further references to Longinus (Grotius 1646: 108, 422). Conklin 1949: 19 seems to suggest that Milton was familiar with Grotius' Old Testament commentaries as well, as does Achinstein 2015: 273—a fair assumption.

[62] *CPW* 2: 433–4, 715; see Huguelet 1974: 205–6 and Rosenblatt 2007: 138–9.

[63] The editors note that "Milton now avoids declaring Paul as author of Hebrews" (*CW* 8.1: 230 n.viii).

[64] On this exchange see Lares 2001: Ch. 5, including a discussion of previous criticism. See also e.g. Lewalski 1966: 281ff.

unstoppable force ("resistless eloquence"), the emblematic image of rhetorical sublimity.[65] The Son rejects this, along with the rest of the classical inheritance, in favor of the Hebrew prophets:

> Thir Orators thou then extoll'st, as those
> The top of Eloquence, Statists indeed,
> And lovers of thir Country, as may seem;
> But herein to our Prophets far beneath,
> As men divinely taught, and better teaching
> The solid rules of Civil Government
> In thir majestic unaffected stile
> Then all the Oratory of *Greece* and *Rome*.
>
> (*PR* 4.353–360)

The Son affirms that the Greek and Roman orators were "Statists indeed"—that is, skilled in politics and affairs of state—but claims that the "divinely taught" Hebrew prophets are more fit for "teaching / The solid rules of Civil Government."[66] Yet the poet extols the superiority of Scripture not only in the matter that it teaches—namely, principles of law and political philosophy—but also in the style in which it is written: for Milton the "majestic unaffected stile" of Scripture matches, even excels, the "resistless eloquence" of the fulminating orators of Greece and Rome. Earlier, in his 1641 tract *Of Reformation*, Milton had referred to the "sober, plain, and unaffected stile of the Scriptures," but there "sober" and "plain" served to highlight the contrast between biblical style and "the knotty Africanisms, the pamper'd metafors; the intricat, and involv'd sentences of the Fathers" (*CPW* 1: 568). Here instead the "unaffected stile" of Scripture is called "majestic."[67] Why? Because Milton, like Grotius and his other contemporaries, understood biblical style to be sublime—for which "majestic" is another word.[68] The phrase "majestic unaffected stile" articulates the same notion found in the words of such disparate figures as Edward Chaloner, chaplain to Charles I, when he describes the *"forme of the stile"* of the Bible as "void of affectation, yet transcending in quicknesse, maiestie, and fulnesse, the Master-peeces of the most polite and elaborat Orators," and John Owen, one-time chaplain to Oliver Cromwell, when he writes of "that Majestick plainness, that unaffected Gravity" which would be obvious to "any Man, unto whose hands the Bible shall come."[69]

---

[65] Sublime rhetoric is here connected to "Democratie," as it is in Long. *Subl.* 44; on the politics of rhetorical sublimity see the section "Republicanism, liberty, and sublime rhetoric" below.
[66] See *OED* s.v. statist, *n.1* and *adj.* A.1.a.
[67] Milton also writes in *Tetrachordon* of "the Majesty of Scripture" (*CPW* 2: 613).
[68] See e.g. Phillips 1658b s.v. grandiloquence: "*Grandiloquence*, or *Grandiloquie*, (lat.) Majesty, or heigth of stile"—keeping in mind that Phillips glossed "*Sublimity*" as "heighth."
[69] Chaloner 1625: 38; Owen 1682: 19.

This notion of biblical style, Milton's notion, is Longinian: it is "majestic" and sublime, but at the same time simplex and "unaffected," decorously without that "over-elaboration" (*periergasia*) which Longinus regards as inimical to true sublimity (Long. *Subl.* 3.4). This is the quality exemplified in the words of the Mosaic *fiat lux*. The Son does not compare the sublime style of the pagan orators with the plain style of the Hebrew prophets, but rather one kind of sublimity with another, pagan rhetorical sublimity with biblical rhetorical sublimity.[70]

Milton's recognition of the rhetorical sublimity of the Bible was not just an idle notion, for throughout his writings, and in various ways, he attempts to imitate, emulate, reproduce, and reformulate biblical style.[71] This is, for obvious reasons, especially true of his three major poems on biblical subjects, *Paradise Lost*, *Paradise Regain'd*, and *Samson Agonistes*. In Raphael's narration of the Creation in *Paradise Lost*, Milton goes so far as to paraphrase that one passage of Genesis which Longinus had singled out for its sublimity: "Let ther be Light, said God, and forthwith Light / Ethereal, first of things, quintessence pure / Sprung from the Deep" (*PL* 7.243–245). It is striking just how closely the first line ("Let ther be Light, said God, and forthwith Light") approximates the biblical text ("And God said, Let there be light: and there was light," Gen. 1:3 KJV), channeling the original's exemplary sublimity, but Milton goes on to freely amplify his source ("Ethereal, first of things [...]"), as if to extend its majestic force: as Longinus notes, a crescendo of amplification (*auxēsis*) can intensify the sense of sublimity (Long. *Subl.* 11). In the same episode Milton also paraphrases God's other commands in the Genesis Creation narrative ("let ther be Firmament / Amid the Waters," *PL* 7.261–262; "Let there be Lights / High in th' expanse of Heaven to divide / The Day from Night," *PL* 7.339–341), reiterating not only the sense of the biblical passage but the form.[72] Indeed, Milton seems to have appreciated Grotius' affirmation of the rhetorical sublimity of divine orders that bring about their effects "by command alone" (*solo imperio*), for the poet's God begins the sequence of Creation by addressing the Son: "by thee / This I perform, speak thou, and be it don" (*PL* 7.163–164). The passive imperative here ("be it don") is a sublime expression comparable in form and function to the *fiat lux* of Genesis and to Christ's miraculous command to the leper in Matthew (*katharisthēti*).[73] The language of God in *Paradise Lost* has long been characterized as colorless and unpalatably plain, a perception that often coincides, predictably, with the

---

[70] McMurray 1998: 12 similarly observes that "[the Son's] response also describes a counter-sublime," a different "version of the sublime." See also Laskowsky 1981, who sees the Son's victorious response to Satan at the end of the poem ("Tempt not the Lord thy God," *PR* 4.561) as sublime.

[71] See Fisch 1967; Elliott 1974; Radzinowicz 1989 passim; McBride and Ulreich 2001.

[72] See Häublein 1975.

[73] McRae 2015 notes: "The verbs, which are in turn declarative, imperative, and jussive, further a sense of moment" (31).

valorization of the more seductive rhetoric of Satan.[74] Yet I would argue that here, at least, in the act of Creation, the simple and unadorned, yet potent and forceful speech of Milton's God achieves something of the sublime in its poetic imitation of the "majestic unaffected stile" (*PR* 4.359) of Scripture.

Sublime poetry is known in Eden, too: when Milton writes of Adam and Eve that before the Fall "neither various style / Nor holy rapture wanted they to praise / Thir Maker" (*PL* 5.146-148), he marks our primeval parents' prelapsarian song as one of sublime rapture. Peter Hume, Milton's earliest commentator, understood this when he glossed their hymns as "*Sublime Expressions of Praises to their Maker*," their rapture as "a sort of *Ectasie*, a suddain and pleasing Violence."[75] But Milton's conception of his own sublimity as a poet is perhaps most apparent in his invocation of the "Heav'nly Muse" (*PL* 1.6) at the beginning of *Paradise Lost*, where he marks his stylistic aspirations in explicitly sublime terms:

> I thence
> Invoke thy aid to my adventrous Song
> That with no middle flight intends to soar
> Above th' *Aonian* Mount, while it pursues
> Things unattempted yet in Prose or Rhime.
>
> (*PL* 1.12-16)

As he would later in *Paradise Regain'd*, Milton privileges the biblical over the classical, here transcending Hellenic Helicon ("th' *Aonian* Mount") through the power of the inspiring Spirit. Though this has sometimes been understood as professing the superiority of the poem's biblical subject matter over his pagan epic predecessors',[76] which would have been taken for granted, what Milton really presumes to surpass the ancients in is *style*: it is the "Song" that is the subject of "intends," the "Song" that aspires to "soar / Above th' Aonian Mount." The phrase "middle flight" signifies that the style is, to use Milton's own terms from *Of Education*, not "mean" but "lofty," that is, sublime.[77] It also announces Milton's departure from the Huguenot poet Du Bartas, who gave Milton his model for the Christian muse Urania. Du Bartas' "heedfull *Muse*," in the Jacobean translation of Josuah Sylvester, "keepes the middle Region: / Least, if she too-high a pitch

---

[74] See e.g. Stein 1953: 128; Samuel 1957: 603; Kranidas 1965: 135; Fish 1997: 59ff.; Hale 1997a; Forsyth 2003: 10. Bailey 1915: 158 notes that, "impossible as was the task of making the Infinite and Eternal an actor and speaker in a human poem, Milton's very failure in it is sublime."

[75] Hume 1695 ad loc. On the identity of the commentator (previously identified as *Patrick* Hume) see Harper 2019.

[76] See e.g. Fowler 2007 ad loc. ("Believing the matter he *pursues* higher than any in pagan antiquity").

[77] Cf. also "lofty rhyme" in *Lycidas* 11.

presume, / Heav'ns glowing flame should melt her waxen plume."[78] The poet of *Paradise Lost*, on the other hand, is one who takes "no middle flight" but "intends to soar," what Milton elsewhere, in *The Reason of Church-Government*, calls "a Poet soaring in the high region of his fancies" (*CPW* 1: 808). Unlike Du Bartas with his timid muse, Milton attempts the "unattempted," choosing to be bold and "adventrous," soaring upward and risking the plunge of Icarus with his "waxen plume," or the fall of Phaethon, both of whom according to Ovid failed to take the "middle" (*medium*) flight advised by their respective fathers, Daedalus and Apollo (Ov. Met. 8.203, 2.137).[79]

The poet's flight of Icarian and Phaethonic danger is manifestly sublime: Longinus, for whom sublimity is by nature literally "prone to fall" (*episphalē*, Long. Subl. 33.2), singles out Euripides' description of Phaethon's ascent, saying "Could you not say that the spirit of the writer mounts the chariot beside him and takes wing with [*sunepterōtai*] the horses, facing the danger with them?" (ἆρ οὐκ ἂν εἴποις, ὅτι ἡ ψυχὴ τοῦ γράφοντος συνεπιβαίνει τοῦ ἅρματος καὶ συγκινδυνεύουσα τοῖς ἵπποις συνεπτέρωται, Long. Subl. 15.4). Phaethon was clearly recognized in seventeenth-century England as an icon of Longinian sublimity and its perils. The title page of Langbaine's edition of Longinus, engraved by William Marshall, features the falling charioteer in the upper right of the composition (Figure 4), along with the Vergilian tag *Animos aequabit Olimpo* ("it will make souls equal to Olympus," Verg. Aen. 6.782).[80] Opposite Phaethon, Marshall includes an eagle soaring upward, accompanied by the phrase *In Sublime feror* ("I am borne on high"). Milton appropriates this sublime imagery too, becoming aquiline in his intention to "soar," a word he associates especially with eagles: Raphael flies "within soare / of Towring Eagles" (*PL* 5.270–271) and describes eagles and other high-flyers "soaring th' air sublime" (*PL* 7.421).[81] Hazarding the Icarian and Phaethonic danger of falling, soaring eagle-like with lofty flight, Milton in the proem clearly signals the sublimity of his poetic project.

Milton expressed his ambitions of sublime flight in a 1637 letter to Charles Diodati: "Let me speak to you of grand things.... What am I doing? I am growing wings [*pterophuō*] and intending to soar" (*te grandia loquar;* [...]. *Quid agam*

---

[78] Sylvester 1605: 6. See Lewalski 1985: 30; on Milton and Du Bartas generally see Taylor 1934 and, more recently, Poole 2017a passim.

[79] Quint 2004: 875. *PL* 1.16 adapts Ariosto's *cosa non detta in prosa mai, né in rima* (*Orl. Fur.* 1.2), but "unattempted" is Milton's (*cosa non detta* meaning "things not *said*"); Shore 2009: 197 calls it "the most substantial deviation."

[80] On the iconography of Marshall's title page see Hamlett 2012 and 2013 as well as Jansen 2019: 44–7. Marshall also engraved the infamous portrait of Milton in the 1645 *Poems* that provoked Milton to write the Greek epigram *In Effigiei Eius Sculptorem* criticizing the artist's "unskilled hand" (Ἀμαθεῖ...χειρί, 1); see Miller 1976: 15–18 and Skerpan-Wheeler 1999. This is, however, surely coincidental: Marshall was among the most prolific practitioners of his craft in Stuart England, and the portrait seems to have been commissioned by the publisher of the 1645 *Poems*, Humphrey Moseley, rather than Milton.

[81] On eagles in Milton see Edwards 2006: 134–9.

MILTON AND THE "STILE OF LOFTY" 61

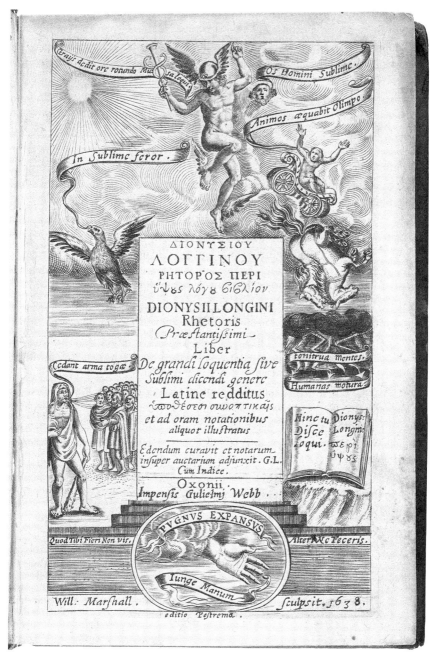

Figure 4 Title page of Gerard Langbaine's edition of Longinus (1638), STC 16789, used by permission of the Folger Shakespeare Library.

vero? Πτεροφυῶ, & volare meditor, EF 105). As one of the senses of the verb *meditor* is "to design, purpose, intend," it is possible to interpret the Latin phrase *volare meditor*, as I have here, as "intending to soar," perfectly prefiguring the expression in the proem of *Paradise Lost*.[82] The Greek verb *pterophuō* (*ptera* "wings" + *phuō* "I grow") carries a Platonic connotation, having been used to describe the flight of the soul in the *Phaedrus* (Pl. *Phdr.* 251c, 255d).[83] There is another instance with which Milton would have been familiar, in the Septuagint text of Isaiah 40:31: "they shall grow wings [*pterophuēsousin*] as eagles" (πτεροφυήσουσιν ὡς ἀετοί).[84] The biblical association of the verb points us to the notion that "soaring th' air sublime" is to assume the voice and station of a prophet, a connection Milton makes when he remarks of Revelation that "the whole Booke soares to a Prophetick pitch" (*CPW* 1: 714)—"pitch" here having the same sense as in Du Bartas' "too-high a pitch," namely a sublime height.[85] That the verb appears in Isaiah in particular gives *pterophuō* a special resonance, as in several places Milton defines his own prophetic role in Isaiahic terms. Twice he refers to the seraphim touching Isaiah's lips with a burning coal, a vivid biblical image of the prophetic vocation: in his early poetry he asks the sacred muse to "joyn thy voice unto the Angel Quire / From out his secret Altar toucht with hallow'd fire" (Nativity Ode 27–28), while in the same section of *The Reason of Church-Government* in which he speaks of the "Poet soaring" he writes of his intention to produce poetry inspired by the "eternall Spirit who can enrich with all utterance and knowledge, and sends out his Seraphim with the hallow'd fire of his Altar to touch and purify the lips of whom he pleases" (*CPW* 1: 821).[86]

The term prophecy (*prophetia*), as Milton observes in *De Doctrina*, can signify "the simple gift of teaching" (*simplex donum docendi*, *CW* 8.2: 788), but often implicit in the assumption of a prophetic role is a claim of divine inspiration. In the proem of *Paradise Lost* Book 9, Milton asks for an "answerable style" (*PL* 9.20)—that is, a style suited to the majesty of his subject, a sublime style for a sublime theme—from the muse who "inspires / Easie my unpremeditated Verse"

---

[82] L&S s.v. *meditor*. Translations of the phrase *volare meditor* include "learning to fly" (Tillyard 1932: 14), "meditating flight" (*WJM* 12: 27), and "practising flight" (*CPW* 1: 327, *EF* 104). Given the various possible senses of *meditor*, it is not obvious whether a more "meditative" sense of thinking about or intending, or on the other hand a more active sense of trying or practicing, should be preferred. Kerrigan et al. 2007: 775 print the Yale translation while commenting that the "verb translated as 'practicing' (*meditor*) is better rendered as 'contemplating'" (ibid. n.5); Dubrow 2008: 63, on the other hand, finds that the Yale version ("practising") is "supported by the subsequent phrase, which refers to a fledgling Pegasus raising himself on tender wings."

[83] See Quint 2004: 877 and Hale 2015: 72–3.

[84] On Milton's familiarity with the Septuagint see Campbell 1987; Milton cites Is. 40:31 in *De Doctrina Christiana*, but in Latin (*ascendunt pennis velut aquilae*, *CW* 8.2: 950). For *pterophuō* cf. also Philo *QE.* 2.65.

[85] *OED* s.v. pitch, *n*.2 sense V.a. On prophetic soaring in Milton see Reisner 2004 and 2009: 120ff.

[86] On Milton's prophetic role see Kerrigan 1974; Martz 1995; Lewalski 2013; see also Knott 1980: Ch. 5 passim. On Milton and Isaiah see Park 2000.

(*PL* 9.23-24) in her "nightly visitation" (*PL* 9.22).[87] It may seem here, and in other places where Milton speaks in terms of his own inspiration, that the poet is only gesturing toward the typical literary pretense of being inspired. After all, Milton in one place names his muse as Urania ("Descend from Heav'n *Urania*," *PL* 7.1), a poetic fiction with a classical name. Yet in the very first lines of the poem Milton specifies that the "Heav'nly Muse" whom he invokes is the same entity "that on the secret top / Of *Oreb*, or of *Sinai*, didst inspire" (*PL* 1.6-7) the prophet Moses. This would seem to imply a claim of real, literal inspiration, of words channeled through the poet by the Holy Spirit. Are Urania and the Spirit two different beings, two separate muses, or are they one and the same? This indeterminacy has occasioned some debate among scholars,[88] but for the poet's third wife, Elizabeth Minshull, the answer was manifest. In the biography of Milton prefixed to his 1749 edition of *Paradise Lost*, Thomas Newton relates the following anecdote about Minshull:

> being asked whether he did not often read Homer and Virgil, she understood it as an imputation upon him for stealing from those authors, and answered with eagerness that he stole from no body but the Muse who inspired him; and being asked by a lady present who the Muse was, replied it was God's grace, and the Holy Spirit that visited him nightly.[89]

The credibility of Newton's report is debatable, and I do not propose to ascertain whether Milton the man really did consider himself to be a latter-day prophet directly inspired by the Spirit: that is between Milton and God.[90] The point is that Milton's poetic invocation of the Spirit could easily be interpreted in this way: what is implied is that the poet's very utterances flow from the Spirit, that they are revealed to him, as to Moses before him—"That Shepherd, who first taught the chosen Seed, / In the Beginning how the Heav'ns and Earth / Rose out of *Chaos*"

---

[87] With regard to the sense of *unpremeditated* cf. *CPW* 3: 506 (God "left [...] our words to be put into us without our premeditation") and *PL* 5.148-149 ("in fit strains pronounc't or sung / Unmeditated"), the latter of which describes the "holy rapture" (*PL* 5.147) of Adam and Eve's prelapsarian speech.
[88] See e.g. Shaheen 1974; Ainsworth 2013; Lewalski 2013.
[89] Newton 1749: I lvi. Precisely which accounts Newton consulted are unknown. Newton writes that in addition to taking material from previous biographers (among whom no corroboration of this particular anecdote is to be found) he "also collected some other particulars from Milton's own works as well as from other authors, and from credible tradition as well as from written testimonies" (Newton 1749: I sig. B1v). It is quite possible that the anecdote is merely a fanciful elaboration of those moments where Milton writes of his muse's "nightly visitation" (*PL* 9.22). At the same time, however, Minshull lived on until 1727, so some thitherto unrecorded oral tradition of an encounter later in her life is not on its face implausible. But of course even if she did say what Newton reports, that does not necessarily mean that the poet himself spoke in such terms.
[90] David Masson in 1874 could write confidently: "That Milton believed himself to be, in some real sense, an inspired man, admits of little doubt" (Masson 1874: III 114). Kerrigan 1974 argues this point strongly, but scholars have not always found Masson's proposition so obvious; see e.g. the skeptical Radzinowicz 1976 and 1978: 350ff.

(*PL* 1.8–10)—by God. As William Poole puts it: "When Milton sat down (or slept, as he claimed) to compose *Paradise Lost*, was he not continuing, rather than simply commenting on, the creative powers of the first author, of God himself?"[91]

Sublime Style and the Problem of Enthusiasm

Milton must have understood that his pretensions of divine inspiration could make him vulnerable to the charge of what was known as *enthusiasm*.[92] While the word carries no special technical sense today, in early modern English *enthusiasm* was a term of polemical abuse applied to any number of unorthodox individuals or groups, from Anabaptists to experimental philosophers.[93] In particular, it was applied to those who made claims of divine revelation by way of prophetic visions, dreams, and other means of inspiration, consistent with the word's Greek etymon, *enthousiasmos*, which signifies that inspired state in which the god (*theos*) comes to dwell within (*en*) a mortal being.[94] Henry More, in his 1656 tract *Enthusiasmus Triumphatus*, defined it succinctly as "nothing else but a misconceit of being inspired."[95] Given that claims of direct inspiration by God could—and often did—challenge established authorities, in seventeenth-century England enthusiasm was seen to pose an acute threat to Church and State alike. Thomas Hobbes warns in *Leviathan* that those who "take their owne Dreames, for the Prophecy they mean to bee governed by, and the tumour of their own hearts for the Spirit of God" end up "destroying all laws, both divine, and humane" and "reduce all Order, Government, and Society, to the first Chaos of Violence, and Civill warre."[96] Similarly the scholar and theologian John Spencer in his *Discourse Concerning Vulgar Prophecies* warns that these "*are of very evil consequence in the State. The monuments of our own and forrein Nations assure us that there is not a more fruitful womb of seditions and confusions in States.*"[97]

The word *enthusiast* seems to first appear in English in Richard Taverner's 1536 translation of Philip Melanchthon's *Apologia Confessionis Augustanae*, which refers to "enthusiastes whiche fayned them selves to be inflate and inspired by the divine influence and power."[98] But by the Jacobean period *enthusiasm* was being used beyond the religious sense, namely in relation to poetry, signifying the *furor poeticus* or inspired frenzy of the poet: Josuah Sylvester, in the

---

[91] Poole 2007.
[92] Newton, commenting on Milton's invocation of the Spirit in the proem of *PL* 1, writes that "some may think that he incurs a worse charge of enthusiasm," concluding that "his works are not without a spirit of enthusiasm" (Newton 1749: 9).
[93] See Tucker 1972 on the shifting semantics of the word, including the gradual loss of its negative connotation beginning in the eighteenth century.
[94] For general overviews of early modern enthusiasm see Knox 1950 and Heyd 1995.
[95] More 1656: 2. [96] Hobbes 1651: 232. [97] Spencer 1665: 8.
[98] Taverner 1536: sig. N6v.

"Index of the Hardest Words" appended to his translation of Du Bartas, glosses "*Enthousiasmos*" as "poeticall furie," while John Marston, in his 1606 play *Parasitaster*, writes of "*Estro* or *Enthusiasme*, / (For these are phrases both poeticall)."[99] Following the political and religious upheavals of the middle of the seventeenth century, it became critically important to distinguish between the two senses of the term *enthusiasm*, between the relatively unthreatening enthusiasm of the poets and the real, potentially dangerous enthusiasm of those supposedly inspired by the Spirit. Henry More neatly epitomizes the issue when he writes that "a *Poet* is an *Enthusiast in jest*, and an *Enthusiast* is a *Poet in good earnest*."[100]

Enthusiasm—or to be precise, "vehement and enthusiastic [*enthousiastikon*] passion" (τὸ σφοδρὸν καὶ ἐνθουσιαστικὸν πάθος, Long. *Subl.* 8.1)—constitutes one of the main sources of sublimity of style in Longinian rhetoric.[101] Already in the *editio princeps* of the *Peri hupsous* Francesco Robortello identified the origin of sublimity as inspired *furor*.[102] John Spencer, like More and other contemporary anti-enthusiastic writers, treats enthusiasm primarily as a physiological disorder, but he also ties it to a Longinian notion of divine inspiration:

> Now our admired Prophets having this natural fervor and pregnancy of Spirit to wing their Fancies, and this heat intended by the new forces of an ἀτμός ἔνθεος (as *Longinus* stiles the Earthy vapor which inspired the *Pythia*) an enthusiastick vapor of heated Melancholy arising from the *hypochondria*, it cannot fail of displaying it self in such rapturous and lofty strains of divine rhetorick; as shall be verily thought to flow *e vena Israelis*, from the same Divine Spirit which inspired the Prophets.[103]

Spencer seems to implicate Longinus and the sublime style in the enthusiasm of false prophets, making the "enthusiastick vapor" (ἀτμὸν ἔνθεον, Long. *Subl.* 13.2) of Delphi, with which Longinus compares the inspiration of sublime writers, the root cause of enthusiasm, and describing the sublime speech of enthusiasts as "rapturous and lofty strains of divine rhetorick" such as could be mistaken for the rhetorical sublimity of the Hebrew prophets. Yet Spencer may well have recognized that while Longinus often speaks of the sublime in terms of inspiration, he mocks the "enthusiasm" (*enthousia*) of writers who believe themselves to be truly inspired by the gods, those who, as the Lansdowne manuscript translation reads, "under a fond supposall of their being actuated by some Enthusiastick Spiritt think they speak by inspiration when indeed it is all but a childish Prate and Babble."[104] The Lansdowne translator appears to make some effort to appropriate

---

[99] Sylvester 1605: sig. XX4v; Marston 1606: D3r. [100] More 1656: 20.
[101] For previous work on the rhetoric of enthusiasm (without reference to Longinus) see Hawes 1996 and McDowell 2003 passim.
[102] Robertello 1554: 26 (marginal note at Long. *Subl.* 13.2).   [103] Spencer 1665: 75.
[104] BL MS Lansdowne 1045, fol. 167v (Long. *Subl.* 3.2).

Longinus as an anti-enthusiastic writer. Here the manuscript's phrase "Enthusiastick Spiritt" translates the Greek *enthousia*, but the translator must have been aware of the connotation of this particular choice of words.[105] Even more telling is the passage in which Longinus condemns the quality of certain episodes in the *Odyssey*: "Can we call these anything other in truth than the dreams of Zeus [*tou Dios enupnia*]?" (τί γὰρ ἂν ἄλλο φήσαιμεν ταῦτα ἢ τῷ ὄντι τοῦ Διὸς ἐνύπνια, Long. *Subl.* 9.14). The Lansdowne MS concludes the list of episodes: "All which odd conceits are but a better sort of Enthusiastick dreams."[106] Thus Longinus' *tou Dios enupnia* ("dreams of Zeus") is reinterpreted for seventeenth-century readers as "Enthusiastick dreams," or the dreams through which enthusiasts claim to receive divine revelations.

Meric Casaubon, son of Isaac Casaubon and an important scholar in his own right, also understood that Longinian enthusiasm was rhetorical rather than dangerously radical. Casaubon, in his *Treatise Concerning Enthusiasme*, makes a point of discriminating carefully between rhetorical enthusiasm and the enthusiasm that is the object of his polemic, writing: "I will not take advantage of the words, ἐνθουσιασμός, ἐνθουσιάζειν, or any other equivalent unto them: because often by *Greek* Authors used figuratively, where no real *Enthusiasme* or super-naturall agitation, so farre at least as can be collected from the words, is intended."[107] Casaubon turns to the *Peri hupsous* to illustrate this, citing among others those passages in which Longinus writes that sublime passion "inspires and possesses one's words as if [*hōsper*] by some madness and enthusiastic [*enthousiastikōs*] spirit" (ὥσπερ ὑπὸ μανίας τινὸς καὶ πνεύματος ἐνθουσιαστικῶς ἐκπνέον, Long. *Subl.* 8.4) and that the orator Demosthenes spoke "as if [*hoionei*] he had been possessed by Apollo" (οἱονεὶ φοιβόληπτος γενόμενος, Long. *Subl.* 16.2). From these examples Casaubon deduces that Longinus is not speaking of literal divine inspiration, but only a rhetorical mode of enthusiasm:

> It appears by those qualifications, ὥσπερ and οἱονεὶ, that he intended it only after a sort, as things may be compared, not really. Indeed *Longinus*, though a heathen by profession, yet was not very superstitious; as may appear by this, that he durst challenge *Homer*, (upon whom especially all heathenish *Theology* was grounded,) though but a Poet, of Atheisme and grosse absurdity, for making his Gods to fight with men; and not only to fight, but receive wounds also.[108]

Casaubon considers Longinus to be "not very superstitious," on the evidence of his criticism of Homer's profane portrayal of the gods as excessively human (Long.

---

[105] Hall 1652 pointedly avoids the use of the term enthusiasm in his translation: "Such are *Amphicrates*, *Hegesias*, and *Matris*, who many times when they conceive themselves in a *fury*, vent not *raptures* but childish *petulancies*" (5).
[106] BL MS Lansdowne 1045, fol. 170v.   [107] Casaubon 1655: 141; see Stark 2009: Ch. 5.
[108] Casaubon 1655: 142.

Subl. 9.7), and accordingly not one to believe that the enthusiasm of the poet or orator is a form of actual divine inspiration. Longinus, as Casaubon notes, deliberately qualifies his frequent talk of sublime inspiration with adverbs like *hōsper* ("just as, as it were") and *hoionei* ("as if"), which signify that he speaks of the inspiration of the sublime speaker and the real enthusiasm of false prophets "as things may be compared, not really." While a superficial reading of the *Peri hupsous*, with its many references to divine inspiration and possession, might suggest that Longinian sublimity is really divinely inspired, Casaubon strives to separate Longinus from genuine "superstitious" enthusiasts.

When *Paradise Lost* was first published in 1667, Milton's inspired poetry, with its invocations of the Holy Spirit as its motivating muse, would have posed for Restoration readers the question of whether Milton's enthusiasm was real or whether it was merely rhetorical. The question was not trivial, especially considering Milton's infamy as a defender of regicide. Was his inspiration simply a literary conceit, or was it a dangerous claim of divine revelation? Scholars such as Sharon Achinstein and John West have previously shown how Marvell and Dryden were forced to confront this problem with regard to Milton, as the poet's inspired style came to be interpreted as a form of religious enthusiasm.[109] Here I would like to propose the possibility that Milton himself was aware of this predicament, and that *Paradise Lost* contains something like a preemptive response to it.

Milton's own direct comments on enthusiasm are polemical—understandably so, since *enthusiast*, like *fanatic*, was a derogatory term, not a label with which one identified. Milton only ever uses the term *enthusiast*, or rather its Latin cognate *enthusiasta*, in his *Defensiones* of the revolutionary government. In the *Defensio pro Populo Anglicano* he criticizes his opponent, the French classical scholar and monarchist Claudius Salmasius, for judging the principle of popular sovereignty "to be utterly new and merely dreamt up *by the deliriums of Enthusiasts*" (*novam esse prorsus et* Enthusiastarum *tantummodo deliriis somniatam*, WJM 7: 186). Here Milton clearly wants to rebut the accusation that his political ideas are tainted with enthusiasm: he does not wish for his countrymen to be libeled as "fanatics" (*Fanaticos, WJM* 7: 552), or as his contemporary John Lilburne translates it, "*Fantastic Enthusiasts*."[110] Later in the same work, however, Milton for a moment assumes the role of enthusiast, if only rhetorically: "seeing that we English are so often to you enthusiasts and inspired men and prophets, let me be the prophet, to say that God and men threaten you as avengers for so great a crime" (*quandoquidem Angli* Enthusiastae, *et* Enthei, *et* Vates *toties tibi sumus, me vate scito, Deum tibi atque homines tanti piaculi ultores imminere, WJM* 7: 360, 362). Rather than turn the charge of enthusiasm against his opponent, as he does

---

[109] See Achinstein 1996 and 2003: Ch. 6; see also West 2018: 44–53 et passim.
[110] Lilburne 1652: 16.

once in the *Defensio Secunda*—castigating a poet who defended Salmasius as one who "does not in fact make verses, but is simply insane, he himself being the most mad of all those enthusiasts whom he so rabidly attacks" (*vero non versos facit, sed plane insanit enthusiatarum omnium quos tam rabide insectatur, ipse amentissimus*, WJM 8: 80, adapting Hor. *Serm.* 2.7.117)—Milton agrees to play the prophet (*me vate scito*) so that he can summon God's wrath polemically against Salmasius. Here it is merely a polemical ploy, but it reminds one of Milton's assumption of a prophetic voice in his early poetry, as in *Lycidas*, and of his desire, as expressed in *Il Penseroso*, to "attain / To somthing like Prophetic strain" (*Il Penseroso* 173-174).[111]

At times Milton seems somewhat sympathetic toward groups that were often described as enthusiasts, as when he notes in *The Reason of Church-Government* that "Primitive Christians in their times were accounted such as are now call'd Familists and Adamites, or worse" (*CPW* 1: 788). He writes derisively in *The Doctrine and Discipline of Divorce* of "the sort of men who follow *Anabaptism, Famelism, Antinomianism,* and other *fanatick* dreams" (*CPW* 2: 278),[112] but the second edition, issued the following year, adds the parenthetical remark "(if we understand them not amisse)" (*CPW* 2: 278). The parenthesis softens the sense and suggests some reservation of judgment, though Milton still insists that, if his proposals were implemented, "many they shall reclaime from obscure and giddy sects" (*CPW* 2: 355), the word "giddy" here referring to the divine madness of the enthusiasts.[113] By 1660 Milton was using the term *fanatic* to describe not the sectaries but royalists and supporters of the established church, as for instance when he rebukes Matthew Griffith, former chaplain to Charles I, in his *Brief Notes upon a Late Sermon*: "you and your Prelatical partie are more truly schismatics and sectarians, nay more properly *fanatics* in your *fanes* and guilded temples, then those whom you revile by those names" (*CW* 6: 548).[114] Beyond the polemical prose, in the Samson of *Samson Agonistes* who is incited by the "rouzing motions" (*SA* 1382) of the Spirit to the commission of an act of religious violence that has sometimes been described in modern terms as terrorism, Milton may offer a portrait of a violent enthusiast who would have put Restoration readers in mind of the failed uprising against the newly restored Charles II by Thomas Venner and

---

[111] On the prophetic voice in *Lycidas* see Wittreich 1979; Ulreich 1983; Dietz 1997. Given the poem's guiding theme of melancholy, Milton's closing reference in *Il Penseroso* to "somthing like Prophetic strain" (v. 174) seems to put him in the company of anti-enthusiastic writers like More who associated melancholy with enthusiasm.

[112] Shoulson 2008 finds the passage from which this excerpted to be "strikingly continuous with Casaubon's or More's explanation of the fancies of enthusiasts" (228).

[113] See *CPW* 2: 278 n.2; Loewenstein 2001: 242 n.2; *OED* s.v. giddy, *adj.* ("The primary sense thus appears to be 'possessed by a god, ἔνθεος'").

[114] See also *CW* 6: 511, 542. On Milton's play on words (*fanatics/fanes*) see the note at *CW* 6: 777 n.96.

the Fifth Monarchy Men in 1661.[115] Whether Milton endorses Samson's enthusiastic violence, of course, is a matter of considerable debate.[116]

What is perhaps Milton's boldest statement on enthusiasm is found in *Areopagitica*, in which Milton deplores the notion that a book might be prohibited publication due to "one sentence of a ventrous edge, utter'd in the height of zeal, and who knows whether it might not be the dictat of a divine Spirit" (*CPW* 2: 534). Milton displays a remarkably radical openness to the possibility that a contemporary book could be divinely inspired.[117] The fact that he describes the language of the envisaged book in sublime terms ("ventrous," "height") invites one to consider, finally, how the poet's rhetorical sublimity relates to the potential charge of enthusiasm in *Paradise Lost*.[118] Just as the Hebrew prophets who achieved the "majestic unaffected style" (*PR* 4.359) of the Bible were "divinely taught" (*PR* 4.357), so Milton's sublime style demands to be understood as the rapturous strain of one inspired by God: as Edward Phillips writes, "the height of Poetical rapture hath ever been accounted little less then *Divine Inspiration*."[119] Milton's enthusiasm and sublimity come together in the proem of Book 3, with its invocation of "holy Light" (*PL* 3.1). Like the "divinely taught" (*PR* 4.357) prophets, Milton here claims to have been "Taught by the heav'nly Muse to venture down / The dark descent, and up to reascend" (*PL* 3.19–20), divinely instructed how to plunge to a sublime depth and soar to a sublime height, before concluding with the request that the divine light invest him with prophetic vision: "Shine inward, and the mind through all her powers / Irradiate," (*PL* 3.52–53), he asks, "that I may see and tell / Of things invisible to mortal sight" (*PL* 3.54–55). But at the same time that he marks his sublime flight "with bolder wing" (*PL* 3.13), Milton expresses his anxiety about such a venture, opening the invocation with the question: "May I express thee unblam'd?" (*PL* 3.3).[120] While the potential blame pondered here

---

[115] On *SA* and terrorism see Mohamed 2005 and 2011: Ch. 4. On Samson's enthusiasm see Hill 1977: 428–48; Loewenstein 1996 and 2001: Ch. 9; Edwards 2003; Prawdzik 2017: Ch. 5; Milton wrote prior to Venner's uprising that if the state would cease interfering in church matters "I verily suppose ther would be then no more pretending to a fifth monarchie of the saints" (*CW* 6: 512). On Milton's attitude to enthusiasm in the other of his 1671 poems, see Shoulson 2008 (and 2013: Ch. 5), who finds Milton in *Paradise Regain'd* "shifting his poetics from a literary enthusiasm to one far more ambivalent about the ideological and religious implications of such a mode" (244).

[116] Serjeantson 2009, besides treating some of the extensive scholarship on this subject, provides a powerful intervention based on the Reformed commentary tradition, favoring a regenerationist reading.

[117] Knott 1980 cites this as evidence that Milton "believed in the possibility of prophetic utterance" (119); Wilding 1986 comments that Milton "covertly insinuates the subversive alternative of divine inspiration" using language that is "part of the rhetoric of the radical sects" (18). Cf. later in *Areopagitica* where Milton writes that "now the time seems come" in which "all the Lords people are become Prophets" (*CPW* 2: 555–6).

[118] The connection between sublimity and enthusiasm is observed in passing, though only in relation to Milton's Restoration reception, by Achinstein 1996: 16 and West 2018: 52.

[119] Phillips 1675: sig. *5.

[120] On Milton's anxiety in the proems see Fallon 2007: 210–32, which informs much of my analysis here.

might refer to the specific terms in which the divine light is described ("offspring of Heav'n first-born, / Or of th' Eternal Coeternal beam," *PL* 3.1-2), it could refer more broadly to the poet's assumption of a prophetic role and aspiration to a sublime height.[121]

The danger of Milton's sublime enthusiasm is given vivid expression in the proem of Book 7. The poet opens with the invocation of Urania "whose Voice divine / Following, above th' *Olympian* Hill I soare, / Above the flight of *Pegasean* wing" (*PL* 7.2-4). These are familiar terms, looking back to the proem of Book 1, where Milton announces that in his sublime flight he "intends to soar / Above th' *Aonian* Mount" (*PL* 1.13-14). The allusion to the winged horse Pegasus ("*Pegasean* wing"), however, prepares the reader for an extended simile in which the poet compares himself to Bellerophon, the Greek hero who mounted Pegasus in an attempt to ascend to Olympus, only to be struck down to the earth, where he was left to wander blind for the rest of his days.[122] Addressing the muse, Milton writes:

> Up led by thee
> Into the Heav'n of Heav'ns I have presum'd,
> An Earthlie Guest, and drawn Empyreal Aire,
> Thy tempring; with like safetie guided down
> Return me to my Native Element:
> Least from this flying Steed unrein'd, (as once
> *Bellerophon*, though from a lower Clime)
> Dismounted, on th' *Aleian* Field I fall
> Erroneous there to wander and forlorne.
>
> (*PL* 7.12-20)

The poet registers the anxiety that he has been presumptuous in undertaking his visionary ascent to "the Heav'n of Heav'ns" where he has "drawn Empyreal Aire." There, he recognizes, he is a "Guest," a word which may signify that he is one who is welcome, but which may also be understood in the sense of one who is foreign to a place, a stranger, one who does not belong (cf. Greek *xenos*).[123] Milton fears that such presumption could bring him to a calamitous fall, indeed one worse than that of Bellerophon, for the Greek hero dropped from "a lower Clime"—he seeking only to reach Olympus, the poet to soar far beyond. Through the figure of Bellerophon, of a kind with Phaethon and Icarus, Milton imagines the danger of

---

[121] Fallon 2007 writes that the poet "realizes the gravity of his prophetic claim and the implications if he is in error" and notes the sense of "the danger of the vertical movement" (219). Kerrigan 1974 comments: "The poet seems to fear that he has violated a mystery, broken a taboo" (129).

[122] Important early sources for the myth, conflated in the mythological tradition, include Hom. *Il.* 6.155-210, Hes. *Theog.* 319-25, and Pind. *Isthm.* 44-7.

[123] *Pace* Fallon 2007: 226; see *OED* s.v. guest, *n*. 2.a. as well as the etymological note.

falling that necessarily attends the flight of sublime style, which is, as Longinus says, literally "prone to fall" (*episphalē*, Long. *Subl.* 33.2).[124] The poet wishes to be "with like safetie guided down" from the sublime height, brought down to his "Native Element" where he no longer risks falling: "Standing on Earth, not rapt above the Pole, / More safe I Sing with mortal voice" (*PL* 7.23–24). Here Milton climbs down not only from his sublime flight but also from his claims of divine inspiration. The verb *rapt* appears in two other places in the poem, in both cases describing the divine transport of prophets to heaven: Elijah "Rapt in a Chariot drawn by fiery Steeds" (*PL* 3.522), Enoch "Rapt in a balmie Cloud with winged Steeds" (*PL* 11.706).[125] Ceasing to be "rapt above the Pole," sublimely raptured or transported beyond the visible universe, Milton seems to downplay, if not renounce, his own prophetic role. Inhabiting this role, as Milton understood, laid him open to the charge of enthusiasm, and his hesitation is connected with a palpable fear of retribution. Continuing, he urges the muse:

> But drive farr off the barbarous dissonance
> Of *Bacchus* and his revellers, the Race
> Of that wilde Rout that tore the *Thracian* Bard
> In *Rhodope*, where Woods and Rocks had Eares
> To rapture, till the savage clamor dround
> Both Harp and Voice; nor could the Muse defend
> Her Son. So fail not thou, who thee implores:
> For thou art Heav'nlie, shee an empty dreame.
>
> (*PL* 7.32–39)

For Milton, the threat of *sparagmos*, of being rent into pieces like Orpheus, was not just figurative: in the months immediately following the restoration of Charles II there was a real possibility that Milton, the renowned apologist for regicide, would be hanged, drawn, and quartered—his body mutilated—for treason against the Crown.[126] The riotous Bacchantes that threaten to tear apart the Orphic poet here have long been interpreted as a reference to the carousing Cavaliers of the Restoration court, an identification supported by a parallel in *The Readie and Easie Way to Establish a Free Commonwealth* where Milton describes proponents of the restoration of Charles II as "these tigers of Bacchus, these new fanatics of not the preaching but the sweating-tub, inspir'd with nothing holier then the Venereal pox" (*CW* 6: 509–511).[127] The parallel is, I think, more telling than has been recognized, for in representing the Restoration court as the frenzied sectaries of Bacchus, Milton makes those who mutilate Orpheus into "fanatics," that is,

---

[124] See Burrow 1999: 496, who notes in passing the Longinian tenor, as well as Quint 2004: 875–6.
[125] Noted by Fallon 2007: 209–10. Cf. the use of *rapture* in *CPW* 1: 752. [126] See Lieb 1994.
[127] Noted by Corns 1994: 25.

enthusiasts—adopting the same tactic that he used in his polemical prose, turning the charge of enthusiasm back against his opponents.[128] That it reappears here, in *Paradise Lost*, suggests Milton's awareness that, as an inspired poet who, like Orpheus, has the power to "rapture" his audience with sublime rhetoric, he invites the dangerous charge of enthusiasm, and thereby the doom of dismemberment. In response, he frames his enemies themselves as the real enthusiasts: "more properly *fanatics* in your *fanes* and guilded temples, then those whom you revile by those names" (*CW* 6: 548).

In the Restoration the enthusiasm of the sublime poet, as described by Longinus, could be interpreted as real enthusiasm, as a dangerous claim of inspiration by the Spirit, and could thereby potentially provoke retribution, as evoked in the image of murderous Bacchantes in *Paradise Lost*. But careful readers like Meric Casaubon understood that Longinus himself, while drawing on the Platonic notion of the poet's divine inspiration, "intended it only after a sort, as things may be compared, not really," and indeed that he mocked those who, as the Lansdowne translation reads, "under a fond supposall of their being actuated by some Enthusiastick Spiritt think they speak by inspiration when indeed it is all but a childish Prate and Babble."[129] Milton, whose sublime flights of rhetoric, together with his poetic professions of divine inspiration and his radical reputation, made him vulnerable to the charge of enthusiasm, seems to have understood the same: he freely calls upon the Spirit to inspire his poetry, but never in a way that is unequivocally enthusiastic, and he composes his epic in a sublime style, but one that is qualified—let us recall Longinus' use of *hōsper* and *hoionei*—as only "*somthing like* Prophetic strain" (*Il Penseroso* 173–174).[130]

Republicanism, Liberty, and Sublime Rhetoric

Rhetoric, as the Greeks and Romans well understood, is a public and political art. The association between enthusiasm and the sublime opens up the broader question of the politics of sublime rhetoric, a question broached by Longinus himself at the very end of the *Peri hupsous*. There he reports a conversation with a philosopher who, taking up the well-worn trope that "democracy is a fit nurse of the great" (ἡ δημοκρατία τῶν μεγάλων ἀγαθὴ τιθηνός, Long. *Subl.* 44.2), attributes the decline of letters to the despotism of the Roman emperors. The authorial voice counters that it is inner liberty, freedom from the passions, which is the true requisite of greatness, and that the literary decadence of the Empire is due not to

---

[128] Examples of Bacchantes described in terms of enthusiasm include Anyan 1615: 31 ("*enthusiasme* of *Bacchus*"), Hammond 1659: sig. B1v ("*Bacchus*'s Enthusiasts"); and Gale 1669: 289 ("the *Dithyrambus*, or Song dedicated to *Bacchus*, was a kind of Enthusiastick *Rapture* [...sung by] persons *Ecstatick*, or rather *phrenetick*, and mad").

[129] Casaubon 1655: 142; BL MS Lansdowne 1045, fol. 167v.   [130] Emphasis mine.

political bondage but to passions that "enslave" (*doulagōgousi*, Long. *Subl.* 44.6) the soul.

This was a passage of which Isaac Casaubon took notice. He opens a set of notes on the *Historia Augusta*—a late antique collection of sometimes wildly inaccurate biographies of the Roman emperors from Hadrian to Numerian, Casaubon's edition of which was published in 1603—with an approving reference to "that which Longinus admirably contends in the *Peri hupsous* regarding corrupted eloquence under the Emperors" (*Quod praeclare disputat Longinus in περὶ ὕψους, de corrupta sub Imperatoribus eloquentia*).[131] Casaubon and his contemporaries identified the author of the *Peri hupsous* with Cassius Longinus, the Greek philosopher of the third century AD who joined the court of the renegade queen Zenobia in Palmyra. This only heightened the political charge of the final section of the *Peri hupsous*: according to the *Historia Augusta*, Cassius Longinus was put to death by Aurelian for his alleged authorship of a defiant letter that was sent by Zenobia to the emperor shortly before the Romans reconquered Palmyra (*Hist. Aug.* Aurel. 30.3). The fate therefore of Cassius Longinus, and by extension the author of the *Peri hupsous*, could be understood as an illustration of the dangers of speaking freely against imperial power.[132] Given this background, it is perhaps not surprising that in the synoptic preface to his 1612 edition of the text Gabriel de Petra interprets the political conclusion of the *Peri hupsous* esoterically: as the matter under consideration, the question of why letters are in a state of decline, is "slippery and dangerous" (*lubricam & periculosam*), Longinus added the moral explanation "in order to avoid the opprobrium of the previous solution, since he deservedly suspected that the Emperor could be immoderately offended by it" (*ut prioris solutionis invidiam declinet, quippe qua non mediocriter Imperatorem offendi posse suspicabatur merito*).[133] Reading between the lines, de Petra determines that Longinus is in fact a secret republican who blames imperial despotism for the decadence of rhetoric but "cautiously evades" (*caute eludit*) retribution through the device of ascribing his real opinion to the anonymous philosopher.[134]

Many English readers of Longinus would have read de Petra's esoteric interpretation, as his preface was reprinted in the popular Oxford edition of Gerard Langbaine.[135] Scholars including Annabel Patterson, Nigel Smith, and David Norbrook have previously drawn attention to the resonance of the republican Longinus for Milton and his contemporaries.[136] Among these were the Greek

---

[131] Bod. MS Casaubon 1, fol. 51r, quoted in Hardy 2017: 40 n.76; Casaubon's edition of the *Hist. Aug.* was published as Casaubon 1603.
[132] On the valuation of freedom of speech in the early seventeenth century see Colclough 2005; see also Dzelzainis 2012 on Milton and *parrhēsia*.
[133] De Petra 1612: 30. On esoteric writing see Strauss 1988; Patterson 1993; Melzer 2014.
[134] De Petra 1612: 31.   [135] Langbaine 1636: sigg. B2v–B6v.
[136] Patterson 1993: 258–70; Smith 1994 passim; Norbrook 1999 passim.

author's English translator, the young John Hall, who was by this time employed by Parliament as a political pamphleteer.[137] Hall's biographer, John Davies, reports that his *Dionysius Longinus of the Height of Eloquence* (1652), was "much esteemed in both Universities," and a number of copies can be traced to Oxford and Cambridge graduates.[138] The book was issued, as Samuel Hartlib noted, "with a large preface dedicated to Lord Whitlock"—that is, Bulstrode Whitelocke, a member of the revolutionary Council of State.[139] In this preface Hall makes explicit what the mere fact of dedication implies, enlisting Longinus in "the *Best* and *Justest* cause that ever mankind can engage in" and offering his work as a rhetorical guide for "*civil* persons" in the new political order.[140] Hall recognizes that "the *Crisis* of eloquence," or the event of political persuasion, "is not a little altered" from the circumstances of "*Senates* and *Harangues* to the people" in antiquity and laments that "the corruption of time hath diseas'd most Governments into *Monarchies*."[141] Nevertheless, he insists that Longinus is not "obsolete" and asserts that "these old precepts may very well conduct the greatest wits, and the sharpest observatours."[142] The effect, as David Norbrook has observed, is to give the sublime "a distinctively republican accent."[143] Republican authors like Hall ascribed the thunderous power of the sublime to the New Model Army and to major personalities of the revolutionary cause: in the newsbook *Mercurius Britanicus Alive Again* Hall writes that the force of Sir Thomas Fairfax, then commander of the army, "like an impetuous *torrent*, carries down all before it" just as Longinian sublimity "bears down all before it like a whirlwind," while Andrew Marvell in *An Horatian Ode upon Cromwel's Return from Ireland* sublimely describes Oliver Cromwell, then soon to be Lord Protector, as "like the three-fork'd Lightning, first / Breaking the Clouds where it was nurst" and as a conflagration forging a "fiery way" and "burning through the Air."[144] Abraham Cowley only reinforces the association when he subverts Marvell's depiction of Cromwell in the *Horatian Ode* with his own royalist vision of the return of Charles II as St. George riding a flame from heaven ("From a fair clowd, which rather ope'd, than broke, / A flash of Light, rather than Lightning came"), distinguishing the restrained majesty of the King from the violent sublimity of the usurper.[145]

Milton was well aware of the possible political connotations of certain forms of writing, having famously described his use of blank verse in *Paradise Lost* as "an example set, the first in *English*, of ancient liberty recover'd to Heroic Poem from

---

[137] *CSP Dom.* (1649) 139.
[138] Hall 1656: sig. b5r. For book owners see the bibliographical appendix.
[139] HP 28/2/42A.   [140] Hall 1652: sig. A3v, A4v.
[141] Hall 1652: sig. A7v, A8r; on the sense of Hall's phrase "the *Crisis* of eloquence" see Smith 1994: 188 and Raymond 2005: 273–5.
[142] Hall 1652: sig. A6r, A7r.   [143] Norbrook 1999: 137.
[144] Hall 1648 (June 8, 1648): 28, quoted in Norbrook 1999: 176; Hall 1652: 3; Marvell 1971: I 91–2, on which see Norbrook 1990: 155–8 and 1999: 267–71.
[145] Cowley 1660: 80; see McDowell 2008: 257–8.

the troublesom and modern bondage of Rimeing."[146] As conjectured above, Milton probably read Langbaine's edition of the *Peri hupsous*, including Gabriel de Petra's comments on Longinus' republicanism, and it would be strange if he had not come across Hall's translation as well: Hall seems to have had some contact with Milton as early as December 1646, when he reports to Samuel Hartlib his receipt of "a loving & Modest express from Worthy Mr Milton," and the two were almost certainly acquainted by the 1650s, when both were serving the Council of State.[147] From Langbaine and Hall Milton would have acquired a clear sense of the republican character of Longinian sublimity. Like Hall and Marvell, Milton in his political prose of the late 1640s and 1650s writes of the revolution and its icons in sublime terms. Milton signals the sublimity of the revolutionary project in the *Defensio Secunda*, claiming that his cause is so noble (*nobilissimam*, *WJM* 8: 10) that he can "barely restrain myself from soaring more high and more bold than is fitting for the purpose of an exordium, and from searching for something more grand that I could utter" (*mihi vix temperare, quin altius atque audentius quam pro exordii ratione insurgam; & grandius quiddam, quod eloqui possim, quaeram*, *WJM* 8: 12).[148] There too he describes Cromwell's deeds as "loftier than the popular aura of titles, as the tops of pyramids bury themselves in the sky" (*velut pyramidum apices coelo se condunt, populari titulorum aura excelsiores*, *WJM* 8: 222) and praises the Lord Protector for allowing himself "to descend from the heights" (*ex sublimi descendere*), "having scorned the name of kings for a majesty far more majestic" (*regium nomen majestate longe majore aspernatus*, *WJM* 8: 224). Marvell explicitly recognized the republican sublimity of the *Defensio Secunda* when writing to its author that it represented "the Height of the Roman eloquence"—using the same word (*Height*) that Hall had chosen as his translation of Longinus' *hupsos*.[149]

Some sense of sublimity can even be detected in Milton's treatment of the execution of Charles I in 1649. In *The Tenure of Kings and Magistrates*, his apology for that action, he castigates those

---

[146] Lewalski 2007: 10.
[147] HP 60/14/3B. On the Hall–Hartlib correspondence see Turnbull 1953, with reference to Milton at 227–8. The nature of Milton's "express" to Hall is unclear, but over the next few months Hall repeatedly asked Hartlib to help facilitate their correspondence, writing: "I am much Ambitious of the Accquaintance of Mr Milton (who is here said to be the Author of that excellent discourse of Education yow were pleasd to impart) I beseech yow be a means to bring us to a Correspondency, if yow can" (HP 60/14/5A; it is possible, though this is only speculation, that Milton's reference to Longinus in *Of Education* inspired his young admirer to translate the work). In the final letter to mention Milton Hall writes: "I am sorry Mr Milton dos abundare suo sensu" (HP 60/14/39B), borrowing a phrase from the Vulgate text of Romans 14:5 translated in the KJV as "bee fully perswaded in his owne minde." McDowell 2008: 61 interprets this as signifying that Milton "did not wish to become involved in the efforts of the Hartlib circle to found an Office of Address." On Milton and Hall see also Patterson 1993: 259–60. Campbell 1997: 100 suggests that Hall was employed by Parliament "possibly to share JM's growing workload."
[148] See Norbrook 1999: 331–8.   [149] Marvell 1971: II 306.

> who comming in the cours of these affaires, to have thir share in great actions, above the form of Law or Custom, at least to give thir voice and approbation, begin to swerve, and almost shiver at the Majesty and grandeur of som noble deed, as if they were newly enter'd into a great sin   (CW 6: 153)

Milton is writing of nothing less than the sublimity of regicide, the "Majesty and grandeur" of that most revolutionary act of political violence before which the more timid among the parliamentarians "almost shiver." Shuddering before this act of sublime terror was indeed the reaction among many royalists: John Evelyn wrote in his diary that the event "struck me with such horror that I kept the day of his *Martyrdom* a fast," while the clergyman Philip Henry, in his well-known testimony, recalled that at the moment of the fatal blow "there was such a Grone by the Thousands then present, as I never heard before & desire I may never hear again."[150] Within a few months of the publication of Milton's *Tenure* Hall would affirm the sublimity of the founding of the new order in *An Humble Motion to the Parliament of England Concerning the Advancement of Learning*, where he addresses the members of the Rump Parliament as "men of sublime mindes, that have carried you beyond all the doubts and objections of flesh and blood, above the extent of your owne designs, or almost the latitude of your owne wishes, beyond the dictates of common Law and reason."[151] Milton chastises those who shuddered and shrank before the sublimity of the regicide, while Hall accordingly praises the "sublime mindes" who had carried it out.

Milton's sonnets, to turn to the poetry, are often marked by what the Italians called *asprezza*, literally roughness or difficulty, a quality that Tasso, whom Milton associates with the "sublime art" (*CPW* 2: 404) of poetry in *Of Education*, links to the sublime.[152] A specifically republican sublimity is apparent in Milton's heroic sonnets addressed to Fairfax and Cromwell.[153] In the sonnet to Fairfax, written in July 1648, the general is said to fill Europe's "jealous monarchs with amaze" (3), to strike them dumb with sublime terror and stupefaction, while the sonnet to Cromwell, dated May 1652, seems to draw from the sublime imagery of Marvell's *Horatian Ode*, praising its subject as figure who breaks "through a cloud" (1) to make his "glorious way" (4).[154] John Aubrey, in a letter written to Anthony Wood on May 24, 1684, pointed to the "sublimitie of Witt" of these two sonnets:

---

[150] Evelyn 1955: II 547; Henry 1882: 12.
[151] Hall 1649: 15. See Norbrook 1999: 214 and McDowell 2008: 206.
[152] See Prince 1962 passim; Leonard 2009; Lehtonen 2019: 218–19.
[153] On these sonnets, together with the sonnet to Henry Vane, as "heroic" see Smart 1921: 40–1, Prince 1962: Ch. 2 and Ch. 6, and Schlueter 1995.
[154] I quote the corrected Trinity College Library (Cambridge), MS R.3.4 texts of the sonnets in *CW* 3: 285–6. See *OED* s.v. amaze, *n*. The possible influence of Marvell's *Ode* on Milton's sonnet to Cromwell has been suggested (apparently independently?) by Herz 1978: 240–1 and Crane 1986. The sonnet is dated May 1652, while the *Ode* was probably written in 1650.

Mr. J. Milton made two admirable Panegyricks (as to sublimitie of Witt) one on Ol: Cromwel, & the other on Th. Ld Fairfax, both which his nephew Mr. Philips hath; but he hath hung back these 2 yeares, as to imparting copies to me for the Collection of mine with you. Wherefore I desire you in your next, to intimate your desire, of having these 2 copies of verses aforesaid. Were they made in the commendacion of the Devill, 'twere all one to me. 'tis the ὕψος that I looke after.[155]

Aubrey, I would note in passing, reminds one that while sublimity may be associated especially with the more weighty genres of epic and tragedy, a form as small as the sonnet can be sublime, too: Longinus preserved for posterity Sappho's short lyric beginning φαίνεταί μοι because he found this poem to be as worthy of the epithet *sublime* as the *Iliad* (Long. *Subl.* 10.2) and his judgment of the Greek lyricist may possibly have influenced such women poets of the Renaissance as Gaspara Stampa and Louise Labé.[156] Milton's sonnets to Cromwell and Fairfax, to return to the matter at hand, did not appear in print until after the poet's death, when they were published by Edward Phillips in the 1694 edition of his uncle's *Letters of State*, as such bold encomia to republican heroes were anathema after the Restoration and before the Revolution of 1688.[157] When Marvell's *Horatian Ode* and other Cromwellian poems were printed in 1681, for instance, the sheets containing them were systematically removed from all but two known copies of the volume.[158] Aubrey struggled to obtain copies of Milton's sonnets, complaining that the author's nephew "hath hung back these 2 yeares, as to imparting copies to me," but the poems were, apparently, circulating in manuscript around this time. A rare contemporary example is provided by the so-called Danvers anthology of mostly political poetry, including anti-Stuart satire, the table of contents of which records poems "On Lord Fairfax Crom & Vane"—which are very likely Milton's heroic sonnets on the figures named,

---

[155] Bod. MS Wood F. 39, fol. 372r. Aubrey continues: "I have been told 'tis beyond Waller's or anything in that kind"—presumably thinking of Waller's *Panegyric to my Lord Protector*. Hale 1995: 144 wisely notes: "Though this was said after Milton's death, I see no reason to suppose it was not what Aubrey—and the impartial learned or the intellectually curious—thought during Milton's life."

[156] I say "short lyric" because the text as preserved in Longinus consists of four complete Sapphic stanzas as well as part of another. D'Angour 2006 provides a plausible reconstruction of the fragmentary stanza but D'Angour 2013 suggests that the poem may have continued for several more stanzas. The poems of Labé and Stampa were published around the same time (1554/5) as the Robortello and Manutius editions of Longinus, so they would not have had access to these previously, but they may well have read (or at least become acquainted with) Longinus in MSS then circulating; see Rigolot 1997: 43–6, 57–67 and Martin 2012: 79 on Labé and Longinus, Tylus 2015 and Falkeid 2015 on Stampa and Longinus.

[157] See Fulton 2010. Von Maltzahn 2016: 305 notes that Milton's diminishing estimation of both Cromwell and Fairfax may also have played a role; see Patterson 1997: Ch. 2 passim.

[158] Marvell 1681; the exceptional copies are BL shelfmark C.59.i.8 and Huntington Library, shelfmark 79660. *CSP Dom.* (1681) 382 records that the printer, Robert Boulter, was arrested in July 1681, but it is not clear that this was related to the publication of Marvell's volume.

though the relevant pages have long since been removed.[159] Yet while the apparent inclusion of Milton's sonnets in the Danvers manuscript seems due at least in part to their political charge, for Aubrey the politics of the sonnets are irrelevant: "Were they made in the commendacion of the Devill, 'twere all one to me. 'tis the ὕψος that I looke after." Longinian sublimity was often represented as implicitly republican, but for Aubrey, a tolerant royalist and friend to republicans like James Harrington, *hupsos* is a quality above politics.[160]

That Aubrey conceived of *hupsos* in this way offers an admonition not to overstate the partisan character of sublimity in early modern rhetoric. Boileau, after all, opened the book of *Oeuvres Diverses* in which his famed translation of Longinus first appeared with his *Discours au roi*, a poem in praise of that most monarchical of monarchs, Louis XIV, and assumed the position of historiographer to the Sun King in 1677.[161] In the late seventeenth and early eighteenth centuries Whigs and Tories alike turned to Longinian sublimity, and even its Miltonic exemplum, for their own purposes.[162] Yet one need not look past Milton's lifetime to find sufficient indications of this. In the 1630s Gerard Langbaine, later an ardent royalist who as provost of Queen's College would oppose the parliamentary visitation of Oxford, had no qualms about preparing and publishing his extensive *Notae* on the text of the *Peri hupsous*, despite having undoubtedly read de Petra's interpretation of the final chapter. His edition featured what is apparently the first printed imprimatur of an Oxford Vice-Chancellor, namely Richard Baylie, a close associate of Archbishop Laud who would be ejected from the presidency of St John's College by Parliament in 1648.[163] Abraham Cowley, who served as secretary to Henrietta Maria in France in the 1640s, did not hesitate to recommend Longinus as an authority on rhetoric in his proposed educational program.[164] Framed as suitable instruction "for the Improvement of Oratory," the Lansdowne manuscript translation of the *Peri hupsous*, though its expansive interpretation of *theomachia* ("war of the gods," Long. *Subl.* 9.6) in one place as "Civill Warrs of the Gods" may have been motivated by the conflicts of the 1640s, betrays no real sense of a political understanding of the work.[165] Instead, given its attempts to tame the sublime, as when Longinus' "vehement and enthusiastic passion" (τὸ σφοδρὸν καὶ ἐνθουσιαστικὸν πάθος, Long. *Subl.* 8.1) is changed to "A due and discreet Ordring

---

[159] BL Add. MS 34362; see von Maltzahn 2008: 43 n.71 and 2016: 306. The MS is inscribed "Sam^II Danvers. 1664" (fol. 1r) and "F Danvers" (f. 164v), and may possibly have belonged to the Danvers family of Northamptonshire, though Love 1998: 242 n.24 regards this as "a red herring," offering the alternative explanation that "the scribe was utilizing a blank book that had been so signed by Danvers."

[160] See *ODNB* s.v. Aubrey, John (1626–97). Von Maltzahn 2016: 306 suggests that Aubrey struggled to obtain copies of the sonnets because "the poems might not be yielded to those viewed as politically unsympathetic," but as Phillips was happy to supply Aubrey with information for his life of Milton this does not seem to me to be the most probable explanation.

[161] Boileau 1674: 1–6.   [162] See von Maltzahn 2001; Noggle 2001; Williams 2005: Ch. 5.

[163] Johnson and Gibson 1946: 9; Gadd 2013: 564. See *ODNB* s.v. Baylie, Richard (1585/6?–1667).

[164] Cowley 1661: 49.   [165] BL MS Lansdowne 1045, fols. 166v, 169v.

of our Passions," the Lansdowne Longinus can potentially be seen as a kind of conservative counterpart to the radical translation of John Hall.[166] Even Hall's direct republican claim to Longinus could not repel readers who were otherwise inclined politically: copies of his translation were owned by such figures as the clergyman David Stokes, a resolute supporter of Charles I who was restored as canon of Windsor in 1660, and Sir William Godolphin, diplomat for Charles II.[167]

Most curiously, Edward Phillips, who unlike his uncle was apparently something of a royalist, borrows extensively from Hall's preface to Longinus in the introduction to his *Mysteries of Love & Eloquence*, a kind of Cavalier rhetorical handbook concerned with the very sort of "Court Amours" (*PL* 4.767) and other frivolities of the Caroline court derided by Milton.[168] As Nicholas McDowell has found, Phillips closely paraphrases Hall's words, as when he writes that "the Learned compare Eloquence to the Chymists Elixar; it contains all qualities in it, yet it should not have one perceivable" (Hall: "the *Chymist's Elixar* conteining all Qualities in it, yet not one perceivable") or describes eloquence as "*a way of Speech prevailing over those we have designed to prevail over*" (Hall: "*A way of speech prevailing over those whom we designe it prevail*").[169] These appropriations betray nothing of the political charge of Hall's preface, which Phillips could not but have noticed. To this I would add the example of Thomas Blount's *The Academie of Eloquence*, another one of those courtly rhetorical manuals not uncommonly entitled "Academies"—Phillips', in fact, was later reprinted as *The Beau's Academy*.[170] Blount was a Catholic royalist who upon the Restoration published *Boscobel*, an account of the providential preservation of Charles II after the Battle of Worcester in 1651: "Expect here," he writes in the introduction to that work, "to read the highest Tyranny and Rebellion that was ever acted by Subjects, and the greatest hardships and persecutions that ever were suffer'd by a *King*."[171] Yet Blount, remarking that Longinus had been "lately well translated into English," felt free to incorporate material from the preface and translation of "Mr. *Hall*" in several places throughout the *Academie*.[172] Like Phillips, Blount was apparently happy to make use of Hall's Longinus as a classical edition while nevertheless discounting the translator's manifest political intentions.

Now this is not to say that Longinian sublimity had no political overtones. Gabriel de Petra and John Hall both recognized republican tendencies in the text of the *Peri hupsous*. Authors like Hall, Marvell, and Milton made use of

---

[166] Ibid. fol. 169r.   [167] See the bibliographical appendix.
[168] On Edward Phillips's politics see Shawcross 2004: 73–94.
[169] Phillips 1658a: sig. a2r, sig. a2v; Hall 1652: sig. B2r, sig. B1v. See McDowell 2019.
[170] Phillips 1699. On such rhetorical "Academies" see Barnes 2016: 140.
[171] Blount 1660: sig. A5r. Hirst 1990: 143–4 notes that already in the *Academie* "among the sample letters he prints are several which emphatically manifest his commitment not only to a gentle but also to a Stuart order."
[172] Blount 1654: 36, 66, 87, 91, 144, 145.

sublime rhetoric in describing parliamentary icons. Meanwhile, enemies of the Cromwellian regime pictured the revolutionaries as Phaethonic figures sublimely soaring to dangerous heights: John Taylor, the Thames waterman turned poet and defender of the monarch, warned Parliament that if it did not relent, "you fall (like *Phaeton*) for presuming to guide that Chariot whose lustre dazled your eyes, and whose sublimity astonisheth, yea confounds your understandings," while a verse in the royalist newsbook *Mercurius Melancholicus* judged similarly: "Your lofty Flight doth predicate a Fall."[173] Another author, perhaps Marchamont Nedham, in a *"Trage Commedie"* of *"Crafty Crumwell"* likewise asks: "Why *Oliver*, shouldst thou so high aspire, *Phaeton* like."[174] In some satirical verses printed not long after the Restoration the poet and playwright Thomas Jordan, a dedicated supporter of the monarchy, even mocked Parliament for their "Sublime Rhetorick" in particular, a rhetoric whose force could make "prisons" seem like "libertie":

> Heroic Sirs, you glorious nine or ten,
> That can depose the King, and the Kings men,
> Who by your Sublime Rhetorick agree,
> That prisons are the Subjects libertie[175]

In the seventeenth century rhetoric and poetics did not always neatly align with political allegiance, and the sublime is no exception.[176] Nevertheless, there was one side in the Civil Wars that appears to have been especially associated with "Sublime Rhetorick," the side that in its violent acts of revolution and regicide, in its overturning of established forms of government and culture, in its sometimes millenarian hopes of ushering in a new era of human history, seemed to fly too close to the sun.

As the examples from his political writings and heroic sonnets adduced earlier indicate, Milton seems to have had a strong sense of the republican character of sublimity, as he would have drawn from de Petra's esoteric interpretation, printed in Langbaine's edition, of the closing chapter of the *Peri hupsous*. At the same time, however, Milton could not have easily dismissed Longinus' supposedly insincere reply to the philosopher, that the cultural decadence of imperial Rome was due not to the end of republican government but rather to the slavery of the passions. Milton subscribed to what Quentin Skinner has called a Neo-Roman conception of civil liberty as self-mastery: to be a free person, to be a non-slave, one must be one's own master, which requires not only freedom from the

---

[173] Taylor 1644: 35–6; Hackluyt 1648: 4.
[174] [Nedham] 1648: sig. B4v; see McDowell 2008: 251–2.
[175] Davidson 1998: 309. Festa 2006: 66 notes that "Jordan's comparison of stern MPs to 'Schoolmasters' bears a close resemblance to the aspersions cast on Milton by Peter du Moulin."
[176] See McDowell 2008 passim.

domination and enslavement of another but also control of one's passions.[177] Personal liberty is therefore a prerequisite for any form of political liberty, as slavery of the mind leads to literal enslavement: Milton opens the *Tenure* with the plea that his fellow Englishmen not yield to the "double tyrannie, of Custom from without, and blind affections within" (*CW* 6: 151), while an entry in his commonplace book under the heading *Respublica* notes "the error of the noble Brutus and Cassius who felt themselves of spirit to free an nation but consider'd not that the nation was not fit to be free," leading the Romans to become "slaves to thire owne ambition and luxurie" (*CW* 11: 187).[178] In *Paradise Lost* Michael explains to Adam that

> inordinate desires
> And upstart Passions catch the Government
> From Reason, and to servitude reduce
> Man till then free. Therefore see hee permits
> Within himself unworthie Powers to reign
> Over free Reason, God in Judgement just
> Subjects him from without to violent Lords
>
> (*PL* 12.87–93)

Milton also connects the state of letters to personal virtue, as when he writes in the *History of Britain* that "Eloquence, as it were consorted in the same destiny, with the decrease and fall of vertue corrupts also and fades" (*CPW* 5: 40).[179] Therefore even while Milton may have found the esoteric republican interpretation of the final chapter of the *Peri hupsous* compelling and gleaned from it a sense of the republican character of the sublime, he would also have acknowledged the wisdom of Longinus' reply to the philosopher, that self-mastery is required for the attainment of true sublimity.

It is with this in mind that I turn to Milton's exemplar of *false* sublimity. I mean of course Satan in *Paradise Lost*. While there is surely something sublime in Satan's sheer verticality of movement and his audacious ambitions,[180] here I would like to put the emphasis more squarely on his vaunting rhetoric. For it has not been noticed that Satan's speech is actually characterized in the poem as sublime. In Book 1, as the legions of fallen angels are summoned, Satan lifts their spirits ("rais'd / Thir fanting courage, and dispel'd thir fears," *PL* 1.529–530) with

---

[177] Skinner 2008; on Neo-Roman liberty in general see Skinner 1998, with references to Milton passim. On Milton's politics see also inter alia Armitage et al. 1995; Parry and Raymond 2002; Rahe 2004; Tournu and Forsyth 2007.
[178] See Martindale 2012a: 58.
[179] On eloquence in the *History of Britain* see von Maltzahn 1991: 65–9 et passim.
[180] For previous studies touching on Satan's sublimity in this respect see Feinstein 1998; Stark 2003; Sedley 2005: Ch. 4; Cheney 2009b; Lehtonen 2019.

"high words" (*PL* 1.528), sublime diction.[181] Yet these high words have "Semblance of worth, not substance" (*PL* 1.529): Satan's overreaching rhetoric fails to attain true sublimity, amounting to nothing more than vain bombast, or what Longinus called *psuchrotēs*.[182] Later in the poem, just as Satan prepares to convince Eve to taste the forbidden fruit, Milton makes the *hupsos*, the height of his eloquence, into the subject of a simile:

> As when of old som Orator renound
> In *Athens* or free *Rome*, where Eloquence
> Flourishd, since mute, to som great cause addrest,
> Stood in himself collected, while each part,
> Motion, each act won audience ere the tongue,
> Sometimes in highth began, as no delay
> Of Preface brooking through his Zeal of Right.
> So standing, moving, or to highth upgrown
> The Tempter all impassiond thus began.
>
> (*PL* 9.670–678)

The comparison of Satan to "som Orator renound / In *Athens* or free *Rome*" might put one in mind of Demosthenes or Cicero, but Milton pointedly declines to name any particular individual.[183] Instead he specifies societies to which the classical orator of the simile might belong, the democratic Athenian city-state or the Roman Republic ("In *Athens* or free *Rome*").[184] These are places "where Eloquence Flourishd, since mute," a phrase that echoes the ancient commonplace, voiced by such authors as Seneca the Elder, Tacitus, and of course Longinus, of the decline of oratory under the monarchical rule of the emperors.[185] The orator of the simile achieves, moreover, a "highth" of eloquence, a literal translation of *hupsos* which Milton emphasizes by repetition.[186] The simile therefore does not compare Satan with Demosthenes and Cicero, nor with ancient orators more generally, but with a sublime republican orator.

It has long been recognized that Satan, in his refusal "To bow and sue for grace / With suppliant knee" (*PL* 1.111–112) and to join in what Milton in *The Readie*

---

[181] The high words that Satan delivers to the demonic host here are not given; Milton only speaks to their effect.

[182] Similarly, Satan's "grandeur and majestic show" (*PR* 4.110), as the Son calls the temptation of world rule in *PR*, "though call'd magnificence" (*PR* 4.111), is not actually such. Stark 2003 usefully applies the Longinian notion *psuchrotēs* to Milton's Satan, but takes the sense of "frigidity" too literally.

[183] Shore 2012: 108–9; Hale 2016b: 35. On the figure of the orator in Milton's prose see Wittreich 1974; on Milton and Ciceronian rhetoric see Dzelzainis 1997.

[184] On the Miltonic *or*, which I return to in Chapter 3, see Herman 2003; Leonard 2020.

[185] Sen. *Contr.* 1 *praef.* 6–7, Tac. *Dial.* 36.2, Long. *Subl.* 44. See Russell 1964 at Long. *Subl.* 44 and Russell 1990: 309–10.

[186] Pallister 2008: 204 identifies this as "the grand style" but does not make the connection to *hupsos* and Longinus.

and Easie Way called "the perpetual bowings and cringings of an abject people" (*CW* 6: 488), presents himself as a republican, a revolutionary who confers with the other fallen angels in a parliament called Pandemonium and who seeks to overthrow "the Throne and Monarchy of God" (*PL* 1.42).[187] Satan also in places resembles the tyrannical Caesar of Lucan's sublime republican epic *Pharsalia*.[188] It is the combination of these affinities that suggests something of Cromwell in Milton's Satan. Having by the end of the 1650s come to regard the Protectorate as "a short but scandalous night of interruption" (*CPW* 7: 274), as he put it in the *Likeliest Means to Remove Hirelings*,[189] Milton implicitly likens Satan, who "with necessitie, / The Tyrants plea, excus'd his devilish deeds" (*PL* 4.393–394), to Cromwell, who famously told Parliament that he was "ready to excuse most of our actions—aye and to justify them as well as to excuse them—upon the grounds of necessity."[190] Milton had previously exalted Cromwell, in the 1652 sonnet addressed to him, with sublime imagery borrowed from Marvell's *Horatian Ode*, but in *Paradise Lost*, after the poet's disillusionment, it is the demonic sublimity of Satan in his "aerie flight / Upborn with indefatigable wings" (*PL* 2.407–408) that seems to recall the soaring Cromwell of the *Ode*, whom Marvell had addressed with the same sesquipedalian Latinism: "But thou the Wars and Fortunes Son / March indefatigably on."[191]

Milton ends the simile comparing Satan to a sublime republican orator by associating his rhetorical "highth" with passion: "to highth upgrown / The Tempter all impassiond thus began" (*PL* 9.677–678). Satan's "impassiond" state is consonant with the "vehement and enthusiastic passion" (τὸ σφοδρὸν καὶ ἐνθουσιαστικὸν πάθος, Long. *Subl*. 8.1) which Longinus considers among the principal sources of *hupsos*. At the same time, however, Longinus warns of the danger of being too "impassiond," of becoming enslaved to one's passions. Satan's ambitions of usurpation inexorably arise from the hold that his passions have upon him, principally "Monarchal pride" (*PL* 2.428) such as could also be attributed to the Lord Protector. Milton may well have been thinking of Cromwell when in 1657 or 1658 he added an entry to his commonplace book under the heading *Rex* containing a paraphrase of Augustine: "If there is some slavery in political rule, he who is in charge is really more of a slave than he who lies under him" (*Si in principatu politico aliqua est servitus, magis proprie servus est*

---

[187] Chernaik 2017: 124ff. provides a useful recent overview of the question of Satan's politics. My own thinking here is influenced especially by Hill 1977: 365–75, Worden 1991 and 2009: 344–7, and Norbrook 1999: 438–67.

[188] See Blissett 1957; Norbrook 1999: 438–67. On the English reception of Lucan in the decades leading up to the Civil Wars see Paleit 2013.

[189] See esp. Woolrych 1974, followed by among others Worden 2009: 41–4, though for doubts about the anti-Cromwellian meaning of the phrase, and about Milton's disillusionment with Cromwell generally, see most recently Gregory 2015.

[190] Cromwell 1937–47: IV 261; see Worden 2009: 347 and Ch. 13.

[191] See Patterson 2009: 5–8.

qui praeest, quam qui subest, CW 11: 255).[192] "Presumptuous aspiration," notes Christopher Hill, "pride and arrogance: they are the vices against which Milton and other radicals had warned Oliver Cromwell and his generals."[193] The seraph Abdiel, who alone stood "unmov'd, / Unshak'n, unseduc'd, unterrifi'd" (*PL* 5.898–899) by Satan's forceful argument for rebellion, refutes Satan's pretension that obedience to God constitutes "Servilitie" (*PL* 6.169) thusly:

> This is servitude,
> To serve th' unwise, or him who hath rebelld
> Against his worthier, as thine now serve thee,
> Thy self not free, but to thy self enthrall'd
>
> (*PL* 6.178–181)

Service to an unworthy ruler, like that of the legions of Satan, is true servitude, but so too is the thralldom of the self, the enslavement of the mind by the passions, the internal subjection that Satan himself suffers ("to thy self enthrall'd"). Satan revolts against what he perceives to be the illegitimate absolute power of the divine monarch, but "with passions foul obscur'd" (*PL* 4.571), as Uriel once describes him, Satan is "not free." He lacks that self-mastery that Milton regarded as necessary for political liberty. And in this, as Hill indicates, there is a potential imputation against those who had served the Good Old Cause. Satan, bound by pride, fails in his ambitions of revolution; he also fails, for the same reason, in his aspirations to sublimity. In Satan Milton portrays a sublimity that is republican in spirit yet which nevertheless fails due to the slavery of the passions, which as Longinus says—sincerely or not—prevents the achievement of the sublime. Here the hubris of the revolutionary cause meets and aligns with the overreaching *huperbolē* of the sublime. Greek and Hebrew wisdom agree on the result. Longinus writes that sublimity is "prone to fall" (*episphalē*, Long. *Subl.* 33.2). Solomon says: "Pride goeth before destruction: and an hautie spirit before a fall" (Prov. 16:18 KJV).

---

[192] Hammond 2019: 674 ponders the association with Cromwell, noting that "Milton's summary is more robust, and implicitly more condemnatory, than the original passage in Augustine." See August. *De civ. D.* 19.14.
[193] Hill 1977: 368.

3
Sublime Physics in *Paradise Lost*

Seventeenth-century philosophical and scientific debates, as Stephen Fallon and others have shown, prompted Milton to develop a peculiar understanding of substance that can be characterized as at once monist, in that substance is understood as singular; materialist, in that substance is understood as matter; and vitalist or animist, in that substance is understood as living.[1] What I am concerned with in this chapter, to speak in terms of the Aristotelian categories that paraded about on the occasion of the performance of *At a Vacation Exercise*, is not so much substance but rather quality and especially quantity.[2] For in writing *Paradise Lost* Milton was confronted with the problem of how to represent the alien magnitudes of his cosmic subject matter. His response, as I shall attempt to demonstrate here, was to contrive a sublime physics in which the extremes of material size and scale evoke the sublime Lucretian *horror ac divina voluptas* recognized by Andrew Marvell in his verses On Mr. Milton's Paradise Lost: "At once delight and horrour on us seize."[3] In this Milton was indebted both to ancient authors such as Longinus and Lucretius, who were participants in a classical tradition of natural-philosophical sublimity, and to modern scientists such as Galileo and Robert Hooke, whose experiments with technologies of magnification allowed new vistas to be pictured, and others imagined, for the very first time.[4] I shall begin with a focus on Etna, a Longinian exemplar of physical sublimity, before turning to Milton's similes of material magnitude more generally, and will then conclude by considering the sublime spaces of the poem.

---

[1] See esp. Fallon 1991 and Rogers 1996. Sugimura 2009 and 2014b has usefully called attention to the relevance of Renaissance Aristotelianism to Milton's understanding of matter, though without, in my view, successfully overturning the general consensus on Milton's monism.

[2] On this occasion Milton played the role of *Ens* (Being), while his fellow undergraduates were Aristotelian categories (Substance, Quantity, Quality, etc.): "*The next* Quantity *and* Quality, *spake in Prose, then Relation was call'd by his Name*" (*At a Vacation Exercise* between ll. 90–91). For some comments on Aristotelian quantity and quality in Milton see Sugimura 2009 passim.

[3] Marvell 1971: I 138.

[4] On Hooke and contemporary natural history in relation to Milton see Edwards 2005 passim. Milton's attitudes toward and knowledge of the new science is a matter of some debate: Svendsen 1956 and Lovejoy 1962 found Milton to be quite conservative in this regard, but recent scholarship (Fallon 1991; Marjara 1992; Rogers 1996; Martin 2001; Edwards 2005; Duran 2007; Sarkar 2012; Leonard 2013: Ch. 11; Danielson 2014; Martin 2019), has tended to emphasize Milton's interest in the new science. For a recent caveat see Poole 2004. On this matter see also Vozar 2021b.

Milton, Longinus, and the Sublime in the Seventeenth Century. Thomas Matthew Vozar, Oxford University Press.
© Thomas Matthew Vozar 2023. DOI: 10.1093/oso/9780198875949.003.0004

Etna, Typhon, and Satan

The publication of *Mundus Subterraneus* (1664-5), a compendium of geological knowledge written by the Jesuit polymath Athanasius Kircher, was a highly anticipated event. Around September 1665 Henry Oldenburg, editor of the newly founded Royal Society's *Philosophical Transactions*, lamented in a letter to Spinoza that Kircher's book "has not yet appeared in our English world, on account of the plague, which prohibits almost all commerce" (*nondum in mundo nostro Anglico comparuit, ob pestem, omnia fere commercia prohibentem*).[5] By November of the same year a nine-page review of the "long expected *Subterraneous World*" appeared in the sixth issue of the *Transactions*, aiming to "give the *Curious* a taste of the *Contents* of this Volume, and thereby to excite them to a farther search into the recesses of Nature."[6] Other articles in the *Transactions* from the late 1660s refer to Kircher's volume, while Robert Hooke, in a series of lectures on earthquakes delivered before the Society over the years 1667-70, returned to Kircher's book repeatedly.[7] Kircher's interest in subterranean phenomena had been provoked by his encounters with earthquakes and volcanic eruptions during a journey to southern Italy in the late 1630s. He personally witnessed an eruption of the Sicilian volcano Etna, and the *Aetnae Descriptio* provided in the *Mundus* is correspondingly vivid. The two-page illustration of the eruption "as observed by the Author in the year 1637" (*ab Authore Observati A°. 1637*), with the smoldering volcano towering over the city of Catania (Figure 5), reinforces the sense of sublime terror produced by the text, in which Kircher remarks on the "terrifying appearance" (*horrenda facies*) of Etna, its "precipice horrible to see" (*visu horribile praecipitium*), and its "horrendous roar" (*horrendo mugitu*).[8] Kircher did not need to have read Longinus, who had singled out Etna as being singularly "wonder-worthy" (*axiothaumastoteron*, Long. *Subl.* 35.4), in order to feel a sense of terrifying awe before the sight of exploding Etna. Like Longinus, he was writing in a tradition of describing the sublime Lucretian *horror* in natural phenomena. Kircher's personal experience thus coincides with the testimonies of classical authorities and the new science alike: "you could scarcely find an author either among the ancients or among the moderns whom the power of this rampaging nature does not draw into awe and amazement" (*vix Authorem sive ex Antiquis, sive Neotericis reperias, quem non in admirationem & stuporem hujus ferocientis naturae vis traxerit*).[9]

The pyroclastic destructive power of volcanoes like Etna was part of this discourse of physical sublimity, as were massive mountains more generally by

---

[5] Spinoza 1925: IV 164 (Latin) and 1985-2016: II 10 (English).   [6] Oldenburg 1665a: 109.
[7] Oldenburg 1665b and 1669: 968, noted by Nicolson 1938: 506 n.7; Hooke 1705: 210-450 (references to the *Mundus Subterraneus* at 295 et passim), on which see Rappaport 1986. Hooke owned copies of this and other works by Kircher; see URL=<hookesbooks.com>.
[8] Kircher 1664-5: I 186.   [9] Kircher 1664-5: I 186.

Figure 5 Illustration from Athanasius Kircher's *Mundus Subterraneus* (1678), vol. 1, between p. 200 and p. 201, BSB-ID 2166670, courtesy of the Bayerische Staatsbibliothek and the Munich Digitization Center.

virtue of their sheer size.[10] Longinus takes the Homeric image of mountains stacked on top of one another, Pelion upon Ossa upon Olympus, as an illustration of dispassionate sublimity, a representation of huge physical stature that requires no emotional charge to provoke awe. Just as *pathos* is not always sublime, he writes, "so on the other hand sublimity is often without passion, as in, among many other places, those lines ventured by the Poet upon the Aloadae" (ἔμπαλιν πολλὰ ὕψη δίχα πάθους, ὡς πρὸς μυρίοις ἄλλοις καὶ τὰ περὶ τοὺς Ἀλωάδας τῷ ποιητῇ παρατετολμημένα, Long. *Subl.* 8.2), quoting Homer: "They strove to set Ossa on Olympus, and on Ossa to set quivering-leafed Pelion, that heaven might be scaled there" (Ὄσσαν ἐπ᾽ Οὐλύμπῳ μέμασαν θέμεν, αὐτὰρ ἐπ᾽ Ὄσσῃ/Πήλιον εἰνοσίφυλλον, ἵν᾽ οὐρανὸς ἀμβατὸς εἴη, *Od.* 11.315–316).

[10] On the early modern "aesthetics" of mountains see esp. Nicolson 1963 and Barton 2017, with occasional references to the sublime passim.

This certainly puts one in mind of the mountain-hurling of the angels in the war in heaven, to be treated in the next chapter.[11] But Milton recycles the sublime Homeric idiom directly in his 1626 poem *In Quintum Novembris*, one of several Anglo-Latin epics written about the Gunpowder Plot in the early seventeenth century, when he describes the tower of *Fama* (Rumor) as "nearer the golden stars / than Athos or Pelion superimposed upon Ossa" (*rutilis vicinior astris/Quàm superimpositum vel Athos vel Pelion Ossæ*, 173–174).[12] With its connotations of impious rebellion—the Aloadae, from the original Homeric context, were Giants who revolted against the Olympian gods—the sublime image of Pelion piled on Ossa here portrays the tower of "Titanean *Fama*" (*Titanidos...Famae*, 172) as a kind of Babel insolently building toward heaven, despite the fact that Milton soon goes on to valorize *Fama* for her role in the uncovering of the Plot.[13] Less ambiguous is the Satan of *In Quintum Novembris*, who is rendered, as in other Anglo-Latin gunpowder epics, the ultimate mastermind of the 1605 conspiracy. Just before hatching his violent plans, Satan reacts with furious envy at the sight of England's green and pleasant land:

> suspiria rupit
> Tartareos ignes & luridum olentia sulphur.
> Qualia Trinacriâ trux ab Jove clausus in Ætna
> Efflat tabifico monstrosus ab ore Tiphœus.
>
> (In Quintum Novembris 34–37)

He broke forth sighs reeking of Tartarean fires and lurid sulphur, like those that monstrous fierce Typhoeus, imprisoned by Jupiter in Trinacrian Etna, blows from his wasting mouth.

Milton's use of Etna, that exemplar of physical sublimity, to characterize Satan is not without precedent. Tasso, similarly, had likened the "black breaths" (*negri fiati*) of Satan to the "sulfurous and burning fumes" (*fumi sulfurei, ed infiammati*) of Etna (Tasso *Ger. Lib.* 4.8).[14] Yet Tasso compares Satan directly to Etna, while Milton compares him instead to Typhoeus or Typhon, the dragon trapped within the huge volcano. Milton's is the more apt comparison: just as Satan, the allegorical dragon of Revelation (Rev. 12:3ff.; see *PL* 4.1–5), was condemned to Hell for his rebellion against God, so Typhon was hurled down to the earth and "imprisoned by Jupiter in Etna" (*ab Jove clausus in Ætna*) for his attempt to overthrow the

---

[11] Cf. also in this respect *PL* 5.756–758, noted by Quint 2004: 864.
[12] On *In Quintum Novembris* and other Anglo-Latin Gunpowder Plot poems see Haan 1992. On the figure of Fama see Hardie 2012, with *In Quintum Novembris* treated at 429–38.
[13] Hardie 2012: 435 sees the Pelion-Ossa image, along with Milton's choice of the epithet "Titanean" (*Titanidos*, 172), as "suggesting a gigantomachic insubordination against the divinity."
[14] Hume 1695: 15 notes this passage of Tasso in his comment on *PL* 5.233, on which see below; cf. Spenser *FQ* 1.11.44.

Olympian. Typhon had "dared to hope for ethereal thrones" (*aetherias ausum sperare...sedes*, Ov. *Met.* 5.348), as Ovid wrote. Accordingly, the popular Italian mythographer Natale Conti took Typhon to represent "the fury of ambition" (*ambitionis furor*), while George Sandys, in his 1632 commentary on Ovid's *Metamorphoses*, declared: "Typhon is the type of Ambition; ascending, as all other vices, from hell."[15]

In his gunpowder epic Milton was drawing upon a tradition of Christian allegoresis which interpreted the Titans and Giants of Greek mythology as the fallen angels, with Typhon himself as Satan, and the same is true in *Paradise Lost*.[16] Early in the first book of the poem Milton writes that Satan and his comrades, cast out of heaven, fell for "Nine times the Space that measures Day and Night" (*PL* 1.50), alluding to the *Theogony*, in which Hesiod explains that it would take nine days and nights for a bronze anvil to fall the distance that the rebellious Titans fell (Hes. *Theog.* 722–725). Later in the same book Milton directly compares Satan to Typhon, as he did in *In Quintum Novembris*, but also to Briareos, the monstrous ally of the Titans. The poet describes Satan as

> in bulk as huge
> As whom the Fables name of monstrous size,
> *Titanian*, or *Earth-born*, that warr'd on *Jove*,
> *Briareos* or *Typhon*
>
> (*PL* 1.196–199)

Milton had referred to the "monstrous size" (*portentosa magnitudo*) of the same pair in one of his university exercises:

> an Terra novam in superos Deos enixa est portentosae magnitudinis prolem? An vero *Typhoeus* injectam *Aetnae* Montis eluctatus est molem! an denique, decepto Cerbero, catenis adamantinis subduxit se *Briareus*? (*WJM* 12: 122, 124)

> Has the earth given birth to a new offspring of monstrous size against the gods above? Has Typhoeus really struggled out of the mass of Mount Etna thrown upon him? Has Briareus, Cerberus having been deceived, removed himself at last from his adamantine chains?

Milton's likening of Satan's "bulk" to the massive physicality ("monstrous size") of these gigantomachic figures "that warr'd on Jove" attempts to intimate the truly colossal scales involved here. Just as Conti had described Typhon as being "of

---

[15] Conti 1602: 651; Sandys 1632: 190.
[16] See Harding 1946: 85–8; Hughes 1965: 196–219; Labriola 1978; Revard 1980: 192–4; Butler 1998; Forsyth 2003: 28–35.

astonishing magnitude of body" (*admirabili corporis magnitudine*), so Milton's Satan appears incomprehensibly large, sublimely "huge"—a word which Peter Hume glosses as "vastly great, from *Oga*, Sax. terror, fright."[17]

Some thirty lines later in *Paradise Lost*, continuing the Satan–Typhon parallel, Milton compares the domain of the one with the domain of the other, Hell to Etna. The passage begins with Satan setting out from the lake of fire:

> Then with expanded wings he stears his flight
> Aloft, incumbent on the dusky Air
> That felt unusual weight, till on dry Land
> He lights, if it were Land that ever burn'd
> With solid, as the Lake with liquid fire;
> And such appear'd in hue, as when the force
> Of subterranean wind transports a Hill
> Torn from *Pelorus*, or the shatter'd side
> Of thundring *Aetna*, whose combustible
> And fewel'd entrals thence conceiving Fire,
> Sublim'd with Mineral fury, aid the Winds,
> And leave a singed bottom all involv'd
> With stench and smoak: Such resting found the sole
> Of unblest feet.
>
> (*PL* 1.225–238)

The "hue"—not merely the color, but more generally the form or appearance—of the infernal ground upon which Satan alights is compared to that of the ruined terrain produced by the related phenomena of earthquakes ("a Hill / Torn from *Pelorus*") and volcanic eruptions ("the shatter'd side / Of thundring *Aetna*"), both supposedly caused by the action of "subterranean wind."[18] Milton's diction draws on Vergil's in Book 3 of the *Aeneid*, where Etna is similarly described as "thundring" (*tonat*, Verg. *Aen*. 3.571) and spewing out its "entrals" (*viscera*, Verg. *Aen*. 3.575), though Milton does not go so far as to imitate his Roman predecessor's statement that Etna "licks the stars" (*sidera lambit*, Verg. *Aen*. 3.574),

---

[17] Conti 1602: 643; Hume 1695: 12, the etymology probably taken from Skinner 1671 s.v. huge.

[18] See *OED* s.v. hue, *n*.1 1a. Lewalski 2007, from which I cite *PL*, reproduces the punctuation of the early printed editions (Milton 1667 and 1674a), with a semicolon after "liquid fire" and a comma after "hue"—differing from the punctuation of the surviving MS of Book 1, which served as printer's copy for the first edition: "as the Lake with liquid fire, / And such appear'd in hew"; (Morgan Library and Museum, MA 307, fol. 6v). Darbishire 1931: xxxix argued that the punctuation in the printed editions limited the simile "to the one aspect of colour," but Wright 1947: 147 correctly points to the broader early modern meaning of *hue*, concluding: "It would follow that the words 'and such appear's in hue' were intended to introduce the simile and that the punctuation of the first edition is therefore justified as a correction of the manuscript."

which, one ancient critic complained, Vergil "uselessly and vainly exaggerated" (*vacanter... accumulavit et inaniter*, Gell. *NA* 17.10.17).[19] Joseph Addison, in his Miltonic translation of *Aeneid* Book 3, also pointedly omits the phrase: there Etna simply "casts out dark Fumes and pitchy Clouds, / Vast Show'rs of Ashes hov'ring in the Smoak" (ll. 4–5).[20] In this Milton, like Addison, avoids the fault of bombastic absurdity which Longinus associates with expressions like "the vomiting up to heaven" (τὸ πρὸς οὐρανὸν ἐξεμεῖν, Long. *Subl.* 3.1) of flames.[21]

It is possible to interpret "the force / Of subterranean wind" erupting from beneath the earth as Typhon, whose name was associated with the etymologically unrelated *typhoon*: Milton later writes of fallen angels who "with vast *Typhoean* rage more fell / Rend up both Rocks and Hills, and ride the Air / In whirlwind" (*PL* 2.539–541).[22] Coming so soon after the comparison of Satan to "*Briareos* or *Typhon*" (*PL* 1.199), the Typhonic typhoon could then be identified as Satan.[23] Yet surely it is just as significant that Milton does *not* mention Typhon: instead of ascribing subterranean phenomena to the movements of a buried giant, as Vergil does in his description of Etna, (Verg. *Aen.* 3.578), Milton offers what then remained a standard geological explanation, reaching for the natural-philosophical vehicle rather than the mythical one.[24] Drawing on a tradition that extends from Lucretius and Seneca to moderns like Kircher, Milton turns to sublime natural phenomena, the uncreating forces of earthquakes and eruptions, in his attempt to express the *horror* of the alien inferno, with the awesome Etna at the center of the simile. When Milton writes of the "entrals" of Etna being "Sublim'd with Mineral fury," he uses the verb *sublime* in the alchemical sense, meaning to vaporize by heat, but the word nevertheless maintains its sense of vertical movement—Peter Hume glosses it here as "Raised, height'ned," adding the etymology "*Sublim'd*, of *Sublimis*, Lat. high, lofty"—and its appearance in this context may well signal a sense of Longinus' nomination of Etna as an exemplar of physical sublimity.[25] For Hume even Vergil's verses "seem short" of Milton's: "our Author has given us the Philosophy of this Fiery Mountain."[26]

Yet at the same time that Milton presents a sublime natural-philosophical portrayal of Etna, his vocabulary verges on the scatological, the "subterranean wind" which results in "a singed bottom all involv'd / With stench and smoak"

---

[19] See Sullivan 1972: 186. Besides Verg. *Aen.* 3.570–582 Milton would have been familiar with classical literary depictions of Etna in e.g. Ov. *Met.* 15.340–355 and probably the pseudo-Vergilian *Aetna* as well; Carlo Dati cites this poem in a letter to Milton dated November 1, 1647: "Vergil, or better to say with Scaliger 'Cornelius Severus,' in the *Aetna*...." (*Virgilio o per dir meglio con lo Scaligero Corn. Sev. in Aetna*, *WJM* 12: 303).
[20] Cited from the text in Davis 2015: 244–7, who notes the omission at 248, 266.
[21] On the passage with which Longinus is concerned see Wright 2016–18: II 64–5.
[22] See *OED* s.v. typhoon, *n*. as well as s.v. typhon, *n.2*.
[23] Fish 1997: 18 observes: "The 'force' that 'transports a Hill / Torn from *Pelorus*' is not identified, but since the 'Archfiend' is the nearest available agent, it is attached to him, as is the entire image."
[24] Kerrigan et al. 2007 ad loc.   [25] Hume 1695: 15.   [26] Ibid.

suggesting flatulence.[27] In effect, the simile builds up Satan as a sublime Etna-like force of nature only to deflate him, as it were, with Rabelaisian humor. I would note a further correspondence in the simile which brings more mockery. This follows from the legend that Empedocles dove into the fires of Etna in the hopes of apotheosis, recalled later in the poem when the philosopher appears in the Paradise of Fools: "he who to be deemd / A God, leap'd fondly into *Aetna* flames, / *Empedocles*" (*PL* 3.469-471). Looking forward to Empedocles, who similarly coveted godhood only to meet infernal flames, the very mention of Etna ridicules Satan for his suicidal "fondness" or foolishness.[28]

To close this section, it is perhaps worth noting the probable biographical detail that Milton may have had some first-hand experience of volcanic phenomena. In one of his university exercises, written in the late 1620s, Milton had envisioned "approaching flaming Etna unharmed" (*ad Aetnam flammigantem impune accedere*, *WJM* 12: 170) in pursuit of knowledge, but he never had the opportunity to see the volcano himself: as part of his Continental tour Milton had supposedly intended to travel south to Sicily, and thence to Greece, from Naples, where he stayed for some time in late 1638, but these plans never came to fruition.[29] In the environs of Naples, however, Milton could have encountered the volcanic topography of the Campi Flegrei or Phlegraean Fields, from the Greek verb *phlegō* ("burn"). There he was introduced to the then septuagenarian Giovanni Battista Manso, Marquis of Villa, who presided over the Accademia degli Oziosi, among the most notable of the Italian academies, and who was formerly the patron of such illustrious Italian poets as Torquato Tasso and Giambattista Marino.[30] In the short prose preface to the Latin hexameters that he addressed to the Neapolitan, Milton wrote of Manso: "He honored the author, while he was staying in Naples, with the highest favor, and conferred upon him many courtesies of humanity" (*Is authorem Neapoli commorantem summa benevolentia prosecutus est, multaque ei detulit humanitatis officia*, *Mansus* pref. 8-9).[31] Manso's villa, where Milton could have attended meetings of the Oziosi, was located very near to the volcanic crater Solfatara, the sulfuric stench of which pervades the neighboring city of Pozzuoli still today, as I can personally attest: its Roman name, Puteoli, is said to derive

---

[27] See Lieb 1970: 28-34, esp. 29-32 n.15. On Miltonic scatology see also Lieb 1978, McCluskey 1997, and Lehnhof 2007. On the Restoration reception of Milton's "subterranean wind" see Blackwell 2004.

[28] See *OED* s.v. fond, *adj.* and *n.*1 sense A2.

[29] Milton refers to Etna elsewhere in the *Prolusiones* (*WJM* 12: 122, 228) as well as in *In obitum Procancellarii medici* 46 and *Ad Patrem* 49. In the *Defensio Secunda* Milton claimed: "I was intending to cross over to Sicily as well and to Greece when the sad news from England of civil war called me back" (*In Siciliam quoque et Graeciam traiicere volentem me, tristis ex Anglia belli civilis nuntius recvocavit*, *WJM* 8: 124). While Sicily is a plausible destination, Greece is less so, and the reason Milton gives for curtailing his travel plans, news of civil war from England, must be either an erroneous recollection or a polemical fabrication; see Campbell and Corns 2008: 121-2.

[30] See Campbell and Corns 2008: 120-1. On the Oziosi see de Miranda 2000.

[31] On this poem see Low 1984 and Haan 2012: 124-32. Manso's epigram addressed to Milton was included among the testimonia introducing the Latin half of Milton's 1645 *Poems*.

from the Latin verb *putere* ("to stink").[32] Manso himself mentions "the fires of Pozzuoli" (*gli fuochi di Pozzuoli*) as one of the more notable features of the area in his life of Tasso, while Giulio Cesare Capaccio, secretary of the city of Naples and a fellow member of the Oziosi, found Solfatara a source of awe: "Does what has been said of Solfatara not arouse great astonishment in one who reads of it? Now what will it do to one who sees it?" (*Quel che si è detto della Solfatara, non reca stupor grande à chi lege? Hor che farà à chi la vede?*).[33] It is not implausible that Milton would have included the site in his itinerary: another Englishman, the previously mentioned translator of Ovid George Sandys, had visited Solfatara in 1610 and had written about it in a travelogue which became a popular guidebook among his countrymen, recommended to university students by the likes of the Cambridge don Richard Holdsworth.[34] If Milton did visit Solfatara, recollection of its fumaroles and pools of boiling mud may well have inspired his depiction of Hell in *Paradise Lost*.[35] Kircher in the *Mundus Subterraneus* wrote of the Phlegraean Fields, which he passed through in the same year that Milton was there, that amidst the smoke and flame "you might say that you had been placed in Hell" (*in inferno te constitutum diceres*).[36]

Milton's Hyperbolic Similes

The Typhon and Etna similes feature multiple correspondences between tenor and vehicle: Typhon, for instance, recalls Satan's ambition and defeat, while Etna marks the vanity of his Empedoclean designs on godhood. Such is the homologation, to use the term first introduced by James Whaler, which is so characteristic of Milton's complex similes.[37] But the Typhon and Etna similes also feature

---

[32] On the location of Manso's villa see Appendix V in Walker 1799: xxvi–xxxi. Milton's account in the *Defensio Secunda* makes no mention of the villa: Manso, he says, "himself took me around the areas of the city and to the court of the Viceroy, and he came more than once himself to my lodging for the purpose of visiting me" (*ipse me per urbis loca et Proregis aulam circumduxit, & visendi gratia haud semel ipse ad hospitium venit, WJM* 8: 124). Campbell and Corns 2008: 120 state that "it is not clear that he received Milton in the villa" since "Milton says that he stayed at an inn," but even if Milton stayed somewhere else, that would not necessarily have prevented him from visiting the villa. On Milton and the Oziosi see Haan 1998: 118–29, who at 122 remarks that "it is probable that it was at the Puteoli villa, with its beautiful coastal setting, that [Manso] played host to Milton."

[33] Manso 1634: 191; Capaccio 1607: 163–4. On Capaccio see Cocco 2007 passim and 2013 passim.

[34] Sandys 1615: 267–9. On Sandys see Ellison 2002. Holdsworth's *Directions for a Student in the Universitie*, on the authorship of which see Trentman 1978, is edited in Fletcher 1956–61: II 623–64, with reference to Sandys at 647. On Milton's possible knowledge of Sandys' travelogue see Nicolson 1938 and Cawley 1951: 102–8 et passim.

[35] Proposed by Nicolson 1938, though I have found the suggestion entertained as early as James 1820: 104.

[36] Kircher 1664–5: I 178.

[37] See Whaler 1931a, 1931b, 1931c, and 1932. Some other notable studies of Milton's similes include Hartman 1958 and Fish 1997: 22–37, 162–80. On critical debates over the similes, with an emphasis on interpretations of digression vs. homologation, see Leonard 2013: I 327–90.

multiple related vehicles, linked by the conjunction *or*: "*Titanian*, or *Earth-born*" (*PL* 1.198), "*Briareos* or *Typhon*" (*PL* 1.199), "or" indeed "that Sea-beast / *Leviathan*" (*PL* 1.200–201); "a Hill / Torn from *Pelorus*, or the shatter'd side / Of thundring *Aetna*" (*PL* 1.231–233).[38] What unites all of these is a comparison of quantity. While other elements of the similes have rightly been brought to the fore by greater attention to Miltonic homologation over the previous century—the illusory island in the extended Leviathan simile (*PL* 1.203–208), in a now standard example, is recognized as a traditional image of Satanic deception—at the same time one should not lose sight of the simple fact that so many of Milton's similes are concerned with hyperbolically demonstrating physical magnitude, sublime extremes of quantity.[39]

Here it may be worthwhile to consider briefly the place of quantity (*quantitas*) in the theory of comparison outlined in Milton's *Artis Logicae Plenior Institutio*. This Ramist textbook, a close adaptation of the *Dialectica* of Petrus Ramus and George Downame's commentary upon it, was first published in 1672 but was probably written well before then, perhaps in the 1640s while Milton was still teaching his nephews.[40] Though most of the words are not his own, this treatise can nevertheless offer important insights into Milton's thinking about logic, with potential relevance to the poetry.[41] Milton follows Ramus in dividing his subject into *inventio*, the discovery of arguments, and *iudicium* or *dispositio*, the arrangement of arguments. Among the forms of argument featured in the former category is comparison (*comparatio*), including comparisons of quantity, defined as that property "by which things are declared great or small, many or few" (*qua res magnae vel parvae, multae vel paucae dicuntur, WJM* 11: 92). Quantitative comparison deals with both the more measurable notion of mathematical quantity, as in size and number, as well as a more abstract notion of logical quantity (*WJM* 11: 154). It follows therefore that things are compared not only with respect to strictly calculable quantities but perceived ones: "it is not only in the nature of the thing itself, but even in the opinion of the one discoursing" (*idque non solum rei ipsius natura, sed vel opinione disserentis, WJM* 11: 168).

In this light many of the similes in *Paradise Lost* can be understood as arguments of quantitative comparison generated by a process of Ramist *inventio*. In treating the colossal figures of his fable, Satan especially, Milton is forced to invent

---

[38] On the Miltonic *or* see esp. Herman 2003, though I side with Leonard 2020 in not taking these generally as points of aporia or incertitude.

[39] The traditional resonance of the illusory island was first noted by Pitman 1925. On hyperbole in baroque literature see Johnson 2010.

[40] See esp. the extensive introduction in *CPW* 8: 144–205; on the date see also Dahlø 1979, who argues that the work instead belongs to Milton's Cambridge years. On Ramism generally see Ong 1958; Feingold et al. 2001; Hotson 2007; Reid and Wilson 2011.

[41] See Grose 1971; Adams 1983; Connor 2006; Wilson 2010; Skerpan-Wheeler 2013. On Milton's complicated relationship with Ramism see also Duhamel 1952; Sugimura 2009: Ch. 1 passim; Ettenhuber 2021.

arguments of comparison which, by virtue of human fallibility, cannot adequately express the true quantity of the things themselves yet which, in their sublime *huperbolē*, point upward, like an exponential function, toward a perfect perception of the things compared. Often Milton will discover a classical argument of quantitative comparison, only to magnify it to hyperbolic proportions. Consider the much discussed double simile describing the arms of Satan:

> his ponderous shield
> Ethereal temper, massy, large and round,
> Behind him cast; the broad circumference
> Hung on his shoulders like the Moon, whose Orb
> Through Optic Glass the *Tuscan* Artist views
> At Ev'ning from the top of *Fesole*,
> Or in *Valdarno*, to descry new Lands,
> Rivers or Mountains in her spotty Globe.
> His Spear, to equal which the tallest Pine
> Hewn on *Norwegian* hills, to be the Mast
> Of some great Ammiral, were but a wand
>
> (*PL* 1.284–294)

The basic images are Homeric in origin: in the *Iliad* Achilles' shield is said to shine like the moon (*Il.* 19.373–374), while in the *Odyssey* Polyphemus' club is compared to a mast (*Od.* 9.322).[42] What Milton does with this material, however, is quite different. Satan's spear is not directly compared to a mast, but is instead represented by a proportional relationship. James Whaler modeled the simile with the ratio: Spear > Pine = Pine > Wand.[43] As Stanley Fish keenly recognized, Milton plays with the expectation of a Homeric comparison of weapon-as-mast, which is the impression given in the first two and a half lines: "His Spear, to equal which the tallest Pine / Hewn on *Norwegian* hills, to be the Mast / Of some great Ammiral."[44] It is only after the caesura that the syntax resolves, and the sense with it, as Milton declares that to such a mast Satan's spear "were but a wand." For Fish the sequence of reading associates pine with wand "by an abstract term of relationship (equal)," resulting in a diminution of the Adversary: "a miniature Satan supports himself on a wand-like spear."[45] Yet the verb *equal* here need not denote an abstract relationship of equality but may instead mean something like "liken, compare" or "rival."[46] In any case the logic of the simile clearly dictates a proportional relationship of quantity which does not diminish but, on the contrary, inflates the size of the spear and, by association, its bearer. This is not to say

---

[42] On these and other precedents see Fowler 2007 ad loc.
[43] Whaler 1931c: 1064.   [44] Fish 1997: 22–7.   [45] Ibid. 23, 25.
[46] As noted by Fowler 2007 ad loc. and Leonard 2013: I 382; see *OED* s.v. equal, *v.* 2 and 3.

that Milton is making a claim of literal proportionality. To repeat what he writes of quantitative comparison in the *Ars Logicae*: "it is not only in the nature of the thing itself, but even in the opinion of the one discoursing" (*idque non solum rei ipsius natura, sed vel opinione disserentis, WJM* 11: 168). What Milton offers instead, what he has discovered through his process of *inventio*, is an argument of quantity via his own limited *opinio* ("conjecture") of how hyperbolically huge such a spear must be.

Milton does something similar with Satan's shield in the lines preceding. The Homeric antecedent compares Achilles' shield to the moon in its brightness, while Milton's simile foregrounds not the brightness of Satan's shield but its immensity, its "broad circumference."[47] But then the Homeric and Miltonic vehicles are not really the same. Milton's is not the orb visible in the night sky by unaided sight but the new world, an America of the heavens, whose features can only be perceived through the novel technology of the telescope.[48] Milton claimed to have met the "*Tuscan* Artist" in person when staying in Florence, recalling in *Areopagitica* that he had "found and visited the famous *Galileo* grown old, a prisner to the Inquisition, for thinking in Astronomy otherwise then the Franciscan and Dominican licencers thought" (*CPW* 2: 538).[49] Yet the significance of Galileo in this simile has been disputed. Some have seen him as a noble contrast to the Archfiend; others have found that his optical artifice associates him with the Deceiver.[50] Yet while there is, to be sure, a link between optics and demonic deceit—as with the "Optic Skill" (*PR* 4.40) of which Satan avails himself in *Paradise Regain'd*—here in the simile there is no suggestion of visual illusion. Instead I would posit that in the schema of the simile Galileo functions as the "artist," the *artifex*, of the technology that can intimate, if necessarily imperfectly, the true proportions of Satan.[51] Sharon Achinstein argues that "since we see the telescope magnifying Satan's shield to its epic proportions, Satan's heroism is diminished," but exactly the opposite is the case: Galileo's glass is the borrowed instrument by which Milton can approach in metaphor the unimaginably "broad circumference" of the shield.[52]

---

[47] Milton's adjectives (*ponderous, massy, large*) read like an elaboration of the Homeric phrase μέγα τε στιβαρόν τε (*Il.* 19.373), signifying the object's size (*mega*) and density (*stibaron*).

[48] On the telescope in Milton's poetry generally see Nicolson 1935 and Konečný 1974.

[49] Beginning with Liljegren 1918: 12–36, skepticism has occasionally been expressed that this meeting ever occurred, as Milton's testimony is the only evidence for it, though my sense is that this is a minority opinion. See also Wright 1933; Nicolson 1935; Rebora 1953; *CPW* 2: 538 n.180; Wood 2001; Butler 2005; Campbell and Corns 2008: 112–13.

[50] For the former opinion see Broadbent 1967: 72; for the latter see Webber 1979: 142–3, and also Harris 1985, Flannagan 1986, and Friedman 1991.

[51] Cf. Brady 2005: 139, who argues that Galileo should be understood "himself as prosthetic to his 'glass,' a supplement whose rhetorical and pedagogical activities are crucial to the instrument's production of knowledge."

[52] Achinstein 1994: 171, who also notes that the simile has "been read as an instance of the Miltonic sublime" (170), with reference to Samuel Johnson (259 n.63).

This is not to say that Satan is valorized: Satan's spear is a walking stick ("He walkt with to support uneasie steps," *PL* 1.295), and the lunar spots made visible by the telescope suggest Satan's blemishes. Yet the overall function of the double simile is to stretch the reader's imagination toward sublime physical proportions far beyond the normal scales of human perception. Like those Homeric lines on Ossa and Olympus singled out by Longinus, Milton's similes are perfect examples of sublimity without pathos. They provoke no intense emotion, nor are they intended to: dispassionately, rather, by overwhelming quantitative comparisons, they mark Satan, his arms, and his dominion as utterly alien, beyond human comprehension, in their massive monumentality. So too later when Satan, confronted by Gabriel, prepares himself for battle:

> On th' other side *Satan* allarm'd
> Collecting all his might dilated stood,
> Like *Teneriff* or *Atlas* unremov'd:
> His stature reacht the Skie, and on his Crest
> Sat horror Plum'd
>
> (*PL* 4.985–989)

Milton's model here is Vergil, who wrote that Aeneas, preparing for single combat with Turnus, stood "as huge as Athos, or as huge as Eryx" (*quantus Athos aut quantus Eryx*, Verg. Aen. 12.701).[53] Milton follows a similar pattern, but in place of Grecian Athos and Sicilian Eryx he substitutes Tenerife, in the Canary Islands, and Atlas, in the Maghreb. These names are found together as examples of sublime mountain heights in the 1657 poetry handbook of Josua Poole, appearing in close proximity under the headword *High* in the phrases "Tall as Atlas pillars which did tack" and "A cliffe / As high as the Canarian Tenariffe."[54] But Milton would have known of both from various sources. In the travel writings assembled by Samuel Purchas, which Milton read extensively, the poet could have read an account of Tenerife by Sir Edmund Scory, who registered his sense of awe before the magnitude of the mountain: "The great mountaine of Teyda, commonly called the Pike of Tenariffe, is a Mountaine which begets I know not whether a greater attention, when you come to it, or when you behold from a farre off: but in both very great."[55] Robert Burton wonders: "The pike of *Teneriffe* how high

---

[53] In fact, as Ferguson 1920 shows, much of the end of *PL* 4 looks to the last 300 lines of the *Aeneid*.
[54] Poole 1657: 343. On Poole's appropriations from Milton's 1645 *Poems* see Farrell 1943. Marvell uses the same rhyme in *Upon the Hill and Grove at Bill-borow* ("Discerning further then the Cliff / Of Heaven-daring Teneriff," 27–8).
[55] Purchas 1626: 784. On Milton and Purchas generally see Cawley 1951: 96–101, Pennington 1997: 9–10, and *CW* 11: 405–6. Milton cites Purchas in his extant commonplace book (*CW* 11: 120, 138–9); there is also an annotation referring to Purchas in Milton's copy of the Shakespeare First Folio (Free Library of Philadelphia, RBD EL SH15M 1623); see Bourne 2018 and Bourne and Scott-Warren 2023. In 1648 Samuel Hartlib recorded the report of Theodore Haak that "Milton is not only writing a

it is?"[56] Atlas of course would have been familiar from classical sources like the *Aeneid*, in which Mercury alights upon the mountain "which props up heaven on its top" (*caelum qui vertice fulcit*, Verg. *Aen.* 4.247). That Atlas was also a rebellious Titan makes the reference especially apt. Partly the simile stresses Satan's resolution: "unremov'd," like the island Tenerife and the load-bearing Atlas, he will stand his ground.[57] But like Vergil's it is principally concerned with demonstrating *quantitas*, greatness of size or extent.

Once again a Miltonic *or* ("Like *Teneriff* or *Atlas*") reveals that the exact metaphorical referents of the simile are almost beside the point: the key is that these two summits of towering mass prepare the way for the sublime claim that when "dilated"—that is, amplified and enlarged—Satan's "stature reacht the Skie." Longinus marveled at "the interval between heaven and earth" (τὸ ἐπ' οὐρανὸν ἀπὸ γῆς διάστημα, Long. *Subl.* 9.5) that defines the size of Eris in the *Iliad*: "her head strikes heaven and she walks upon the ground" (οὐρανῷ ἐστήριξε κάρη καὶ ἐπὶ χθονὶ βαίνει, *Il.* 4.443).[58] Here Milton may well have been thinking of Homer, indeed reading Homer through Longinus: presented as a colossus whose height stretches from the ground all the way to the firmament, Satan here projects a similarly sublime image of physical size.[59] That Satan should do so in imitation of Eris—literally "strife"—is all the more fitting.[60] And with a final flourish, as if to heighten the already sublime appearance of Satan, Milton adds that "on his Crest / Sat horror Plum'd," a terrifying abstraction which evokes Vergil's description of the crest of Turnus along with its reference to the sublime Etna: "his high helmet, haired with triple plume, holds up a Chimera breathing from its jaws the fires of Etna" (*cui triplici crinita iuba galea alta Chimaeram/sustinet, Aetnaeos efflantem faucibus ignis*, Verg. *Aen.* 7.785-786).[61]

Such similes serve to instill a sense of terrible awe before the immense magnitude of Satan. Yet quantitative comparisons can thoroughly belittle, too, as at the

---

Universal History of England but also an Epitome of all Purchas volumes" (HP 31/22/21A). One likely product of this attempted epitome is *A Brief History of Moscovia*, for which Purchas was one of Milton's principal sources; see *CPW* 8: 454-538 passim.

[56] Burton 1989-94: II 36.

[57] The word *unremov'd* has sometimes troubled readers: Bentley 1732 ad loc. felt compelled to emend it to *undismay'd*; some decades later William Hayley, taking issue with Bentley's emendation ("Who ever suppos'd that Atlas or Teneriff were sometimes dismay'd?"), preferred the line to read "Like Teneriff or Atlas Mount, unmov'd" (Murray and Rushdy 1994: 230). But *OED* s.v. unremoved, *adj.* 1.c. ("Chiefly *poetic*. Fixed in place; firmly grounded or stationed.") offers, just before Milton's line, a very close parallel from 1648: "But his resolves remaine / As unremov'd as Rocks."

[58] As Longinus' observation follows a major lacuna, the Homeric passage is not quoted, but the reference to Eris makes clear that this was what Longinus had in mind, as the commentators (e.g. Russell 1964 ad loc.) agree.

[59] As proposed by Machacek 2011: 131.

[60] On interpretations of Homeric Eris in the Renaissance see Wolfe 2015, including Ch. 5 on Milton (though without reference to this passage).

[61] Harding 1962: 50.

end of Book 1, when the fallen angels are made to shrink to the size of dwarfs, pygmies, and elves as they pack Pandemonium:

> Behold a wonder! they but now who seemd
> In bigness to surpass Earths Giant Sons
> Now less then smallest Dwarfs, in narrow room
> Throng numberless, like that Pigmean Race
> Beyond the *Indian* Mount, or Faerie Elves,
> Whose midnight Revels, by a Forrest side
> Or Fountain some belated Peasant sees,
> Or dreams he sees
>
> (*PL* 1.777–784)

"Behold a wonder!" offers a bathetic *mirabile visu* for a transformation that is anything but sublime. Lest there be any doubt that some insult is intended, Milton adds: "Thus incorporeal Spirits to smallest forms / Reduc'd thir shapes immense, and were at large" (*PL* 1.789–790). Dwarfs *at large*: Christopher Ricks calls it a "superbly contemptuous pun."[62] The general comparison is one of quantity, but as often there is much greater relevance to Milton's selection of metaphorical vehicles. The "Faerie Elves" in particular have attracted attention in this regard, whether as the knavish devils of English folklore familiar from Shakespearean comedy or even, according to a medieval tradition discussed by C. S. Lewis, as former angels exiled for refusing to take sides in the war in heaven.[63] Milton's pygmies, on the other hand, have been rather overlooked.

While the word *pygmy* was applied at the very end of the seventeenth century by the anatomist Edward Tyson to the chimpanzee, and later in the nineteenth century to the hunter-gatherer tribes of the Congo, for Milton and his contemporaries pygmies were figures of classical mythology, diminutive humanoids often represented as fighting with cranes.[64] In *Pseudodoxia Epidemica*, first published in 1646, Thomas Browne considers accounts of pygmies ranging from Homer to the sixteenth-century Italian naturalist Ulisse Aldrovandi and finds the evidence for their existence wanting: "that there is, or ever was such a race or Nation, upon exact and confirmed testimonies, our strictest enquiry receaves no satisfaction."[65] As Karen Edwards has argued, Browne avoids engaging with the potential political import of the pygmies as a defeated people in the 1640s, whereas Milton, earlier in Book 1 of *Paradise Lost*, exposes "that

---

[62] Ricks 1963: 15.
[63] See Callander 1750: 164–5, Wright 1962: 104–6, and Lewis 1964: 122–38. See also Leonard 2013: Ch. 5 passim.
[64] See Tyson 1699. [65] Browne 1981: I 330.

small infantry / Warr'd on by Cranes" (*PL* 1.575–576) as an example of evanescent military valor.[66] If that is the case, the comparison of the shrunken devils to the "Pigmean Race" may speak to their own martial failure. But there is a further possible point of correspondence which has not been noted before. "Enslaving practices are easy to begin to list," Cedric Brown has written of the council in Pandemonium, among them "the diminishing of the size of the people."[67] The aptness of this comment, linking the fallen angels' physical diminishment with enslavement, will soon become clear.

In the final chapter of the *Peri hupsous*, as discussed in Chapter 2, Longinus presents as his interlocutor an anonymous philosopher who argues that eloquence has declined with the establishment of monarchical empire. Imperial rule, he says, makes citizens slaves, and slaves, who cannot speak freely, are so molded that they can never be great orators. It is at this point in his discourse that the philosopher speaks of pygmies (*pugmaioi*):

'ὥσπερ οὖν, εἴ γε' φησὶ 'τοῦτο πιστὸν ἀκούω, τὰ γλωττόκομα, ἐν οἷς οἱ Πυγμαῖοι καλούμενοι δὲ νᾶνοι τρέφονται, οὐ μόνον κωλύει τῶν ἐγκεκλεισμένων τὰς αὐξήσεις, ἀλλὰ καὶ συναραιοῖ διὰ τὸν περικείμενον τοῖς σώμασι δεσμόν· οὕτως ἅπασαν δουλείαν, κἂν ᾖ δικαιοτάτη, ψυχῆς γλωττόκομον καὶ κοινὸν δή τις ἀπεφήνατο δεσμωτήριον.' (Long. *Subl*. 44.5)

"And so," he says, "if what I hear is credible, that the cages in which pygmies or so-called dwarfs are kept not only hinder the growth of those confined within, but also compress them through the bondage that surrounds their bodies, so one could say that all slavery, even if most just, is a cage of the soul and a common prison."

What is described here is a brutal practice in which young slaves are forced into cages in order to stunt their growth and even shrink them.[68] "Cage" does not do justice to the Greek: the word *glōttokomon* literally means "tongue-bag," referring to a pouch containing the reed of the *aulos*, an ancient wind instrument. The same term is used in the New Testament to refer to Judas' coin purse (John 12:6, 13:29). Whatever its exact dimensions, the pygmy's *glōttokomon* must be imagined as excruciatingly restrictive. Though Longinus' philosopher expresses some doubts, it is certainly conceivable that such attempts at "pygmification" were sometimes made: the Romans were disgusted but also greatly amused by physical abnormalities, and Plutarch even mentions a "monster market" (τῶν τεράτων ἀγοράν, Plut. *Mor*. 520c) that specialized in deformed slaves.[69] In any case the existence of

---

[66] Edwards 2008. The pun on *infant* was first noted by Addison 1970: 87; see Leonard 2013: I 20, 33. On Milton's pygmies see also Teague 1986 and Welch 2016 passim.
[67] Brown 1995.   [68] On this passage see Russell 1964 ad loc. and Connor 2011.
[69] Dasen 1988; Garland 2010: 46–8; Trentin 2011.

such a practice was considered credible by early modern readers. Isaac Casaubon, commenting on a reference to *pumili* ("dwarfs") in Suetonius' life of Augustus, cites this passage of Longinus as evidence that "slave traders would rear boys locked up in cages and bound with ligatures in order to make them dwarfs" (*Mangones, ut efficerent nanos, conclusos alebant in arca pueros et fasciis revinctos*).[70] The credibility of Longinus' report was probably increased by the fact that dwarfs were highly prized by Renaissance royalty, to the extent that there were occasionally even schemes to breed them: Isabella d'Este, Marchioness of Mantua, found her dwarf Nanino a female mate, Nanina, in the hope that they would produce a *razza* ("race, line") of their kind.[71] In England Henrietta Maria cherished the court dwarf Sir Jeffrey Hudson, or "Lord Minimus," who was presented to her as a gift—he leapt out of a pie at a banquet—from the Duchess of Buckingham in 1628.[72]

It is with this passage of Longinus in mind that Milton's pygmies may begin to bear a new significance. The anonymous philosopher writes of slaves crammed into Procrustean cages so that they will shrink into pygmies. The fallen angels are compressed "in narrow room" such that they come to resemble "that Pigmean Race." The comparison of Satan's followers to pygmies can thus be seen to work on several levels of correspondence. It points, of course, to their smallness, their actual quantitative diminution. It marks them as a humiliated army, like the pygmies vanquished by the cranes. And finally, via Longinus, it shows them to be slaves: their pygmification is a sign of enslavement. The devils think Pandemonium is their Parliament. It is their prison.

Astronomy and the Sublimities of Space

Thus far in this chapter I have mostly been concerned with Milton's engagement with the physical sublimity of extreme size. I turn now to the sublimity of space. Longinus gives some sense of this when he comments on a passage of the *Iliad* which represents the strides of the horses of the gods as spanning impossibly long distances (*Il.* 5.770-772): Homer "measures their motion with a cosmic interval. Because of the excess of extent anyone might declare, with reason, that if the horses of the gods moved two times in succession they would find no space left in the cosmos" (τὴν ὁρμὴν αὐτῶν κοσμικῷ διαστήματι καταμετρεῖ. τίς οὖν οὐκ ἂν εἰκότως διὰ τὴν ὑπερβολὴν τοῦ μεγέθους ἐπιφθέγξαιτο, ὅτι ἂν δὶς ἐξῆς ἐφορμήσωσιν οἱ τῶν θεῶν ἵπποι, οὐκέθ' εὑρήσουσιν ἐν κόσμῳ τόπον, Long. Subl. 9.5). Longinus finds this passage of Homer so sublime precisely because it involves the vastness of cosmic distances.

---

[70] Casaubon 1605: 166, on Suet. *Aug.* 83.   [71] Shaw 2019: 166.
[72] See *ODNB* s.v. Hudson, Jeffery (1619-82). On royal women and dwarfs see Brown 2015.

That some affinity was recognized in seventeenth-century England between the soaring sublimity of Longinus and the celestial spaces of the new observational astronomy is suggested by the iconography of the engraved title page of *A Discourse Concerning a New World and Another Planet* (1640). The author of this book was the polymathic John Wilkins, later a founding member of the Royal Society.[73] The first part of the volume, previously printed as *The Discovery of a World in the Moone*, explores the implications of the lunar discoveries of Galileo and Kepler, while the second part offers a new defense of the Copernican theory against the criticisms of the Scottish clergyman Alexander Ross.[74] Its title page, engraved by William Marshall, features a model of the heliocentric universe, beneath which stand the three figures of Copernicus on the one side and Galileo and Kepler on the other (Figure 6). Situated between Copernicus and the pair is an unraveled scroll containing the title of the book superimposed upon what is presumably a map of the lunar surface, representing those "new Lands,/Rivers or Mountains in her spotty Globe" (*PL* 1.290–291) observed by Galileo's telescope, also pictured.[75] The iconography derives chiefly from the title page of the *Dialogus de Systemate Mundi* (1635), Matthias Bernegger's Latin translation of Galileo's *Dialogo sopra i due massimi sistemi del mondo* (1632), engraved by Strasbourg printmaker Jacob van der Heyden (Figure 7)—itself a reworking of Stefano Della Bella's *antiporta* to the original Italian edition of the *Dialogo* (Figure 8)—but, as Natalie Kaoukji and Nicholas Jardine have pointed out, it also borrows one element from Marshall's earlier engraved title page to Langbaine's edition of Longinus (Figure 4).[76] The element is a soaring eagle (Figure 9), which in the Longinus engraving ascends toward the sun with the words *In Sublime feror* ("I am borne on high"). On the title page of Wilkins' *Discourse*, the same eagle ascends toward the sun, though in this case it is not the sun as seen in the sky but the sun as the center around which the planets revolve (Figure 10). The eagle on Wilkins' title page does not speak, but just next to it there are two banderoles with words. One has Galileo, who is pointing upward toward the bird with his left hand, saying *Hic eius oculi* ("Here, his eyes"), expressing the power of the telescope, which Galileo holds in his right hand, to give humans the keen sight that is proverbially the possession of eagles.[77] The other banderole gives Kepler the words *Utinam et alae* ("If only [we had] wings too"), expressing the desire to soar into the sublime heights of the heavens, a possibility entertained by Wilkins in the *Discourse* when he ponders "what meanes there may bee conjectured, for our

---

[73] On Wilkins see Poole 2017b.   [74] See McColley 1936 and Henderson 2017.
[75] Nonnoi 2003: "The context and the subsequent content of the treatises hint at the fact that it is a map of the lunar surface, with mountains, valleys, watercourses and vegetation" (241).
[76] Kaoukji and Jardine 2010: 435 ("The only other instance of actual copying we have found"). See also Nonnoi 2003: 238–44.
[77] Nonnoi 2003: 242.

SUBLIME PHYSICS IN *PARADISE LOST* 103

Figure 6 Title page of John Wilkins' *A Discourse Concerning a New World & Another Planet* (1640), STC 25641, used by permission of the Folger Shakespeare Library.

Figure 7 Title page of Galileo's *Dialogus de Systemate Mundi* (1635), BSB-ID 14444526, courtesy of the Bayerische Staatsbibliothek and the Munich Digitization Center.

SUBLIME PHYSICS IN *PARADISE LOST* 105

Figure 8 Title page of Galileo's *Dialogo sopra i due massimi sistemi del mondo* (1632), BSB-ID 11799516, courtesy of the Bayerische Staatsbibliothek and the Munich Digitization Center.

Figure 9 Detail of William Marshall's title page for Langbaine's Longinus (1638), STC 16789, used by permission of the Folger Shakespeare Library.

ascending beyond the sphere of the earths magneticall vigor," whether "the application of wings" or "a flying Chariot."[78]

Why Marshall should imitate the astronomical art of Galileo's book is obvious. Marshall's reuse of his Longinian eagle, too, must be more than accidental. Wilkins may well have instructed the engraver to include it: he was familiar

---

[78] Wilkins 1640: I 237–8; Kaoukji and Jardine 2010: 441–2.

SUBLIME PHYSICS IN *PARADISE LOST* 107

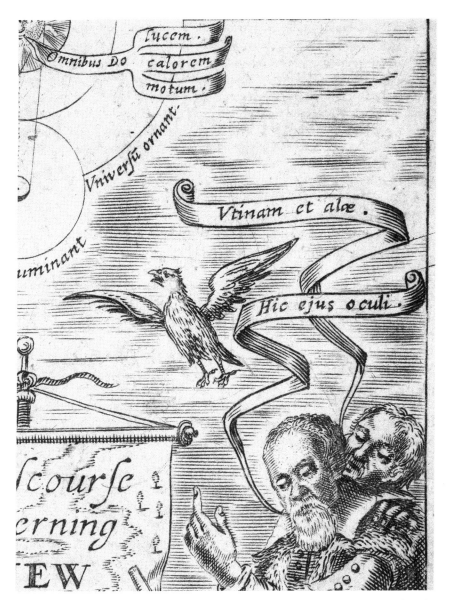

Figure 10 Detail of William Marshall's title page for John Wilkins' *Discourse* (1640), STC 25641, used by permission of the Folger Shakespeare Library.

with Longinus, probably from Langbaine's edition.[79] The iconographic link speaks to the notion that to study the heavens one must look sublimely upward. As Plato wrote in the *Timaeus*: "God invented and gave us vision so that, beholding the

---

[79] Wilkins 1675: 401. On the popularity of Langbaine's edition see the bibliographical appendix.

orbits in the heavens, we might use them for the revolutions of thought within us" (θεὸν ἡμῖν ἀνευρεῖν δωρήσασθαί τε ὄψιν, ἵνα τὰς ἐν οὐρανῷ τοῦ νοῦ κατιδόντες περιόδους χρησαίμεθα ἐπὶ τὰς περιφορὰς τὰς τῆς παρ' ἡμῖν διανοήσεως, Plat. Tim. 47b). Ovid wrote that a god "gave man a face sublime" (os homini sublime dedit, Ov. Met. 1.85) and made him stand erect so that he could observe the stars. The Ovidian tag os homini sublime is featured on the title page of the Langbaine Longinus, and Wilkins in his Discourse quotes Ovid's verses as evidence of the excellence of his science: "God gave to man an upright face, that he Might view the stars, & learn astronomy."[80] Thomas Browne is more skeptical of this anatomical etiology:

> To opinion that man is erect to looke up and behold the heavens, is a conceit onely fit for those that never saw the fish Uranoscopus, that is, the Beholder of heaven; which hath its eyes so placed, that it lookes up directly to heaven [...]; and therefore men of this opinion understood not Plato when he said that man doth *Sursum aspicere*, for thereby was not meant to gape or looke upward with the eye, but to have his thoughts sublime, and not onely to behold, but speculate their nature with the eye of the understanding.[81]

For Browne such an interpretation of Plato's comment is too literal: it does not signify that the human eye was uniquely endowed for stargazing, but rather that the species should aspire to "thoughts sublime."[82] But perhaps Christopher Wren, Dean of Windsor and father of the architect of the same name, is right when he comments in his copy of the first edition of the *Pseudodoxia Epidemica*: "This is too Paedantical; And captious; For Plato sayd plainlye Astronomiae causâ datos esse Homini oculos. But not to other Creatures, thoughe they haue their Heads more erect then Hee, and far better sight."[83] In any case what pertains to Langbaine's Longinus and Wilkins' *Discourse* is the continuing association of sublime vision and astronomy as a commonplace.

Milton, who granted his Adam an "Eye sublime" (*PL* 4.300), had a demonstrable interest in this science, though much of his reading in the subject was rather traditional. That was certainly the case for the curriculum at Cambridge in the late 1620s and early 1630s. The Elizabethan statutes enjoined: "The professor of mathematics, if teaching astronomy, should expound Ptolemy" (*Mathematicus professor* [...] *si astronomiam* [*docet*], *Ptolomaeum enarret*).[84] Students were encouraged to read other classical sources such as Aristotle and Pliny, though in practice, if Joseph Mede's students at Christ's College are any indication, much

---

[80] Wilkins 1640: 237.　　[81] Browne 1981: I 293.　　[82] On this passage see Edwards 2005: 55.
[83] Quoted in Browne 1981: II 902. Wren's copy is Bod. shelfmark O 2.26 Art.Seld. On Wren's marginalia see Colie 1960.
[84] CUL UA Luard 187, fol. 2r; Elizabeth 1852: I 457.

was taught from derivative modern compendia.[85] Studying at Cambridge a generation after Milton, the future naturalist and Fellow of the Royal Society Francis Willughby would include an extensive entry in his commonplace book under the heading "On the new philosophy and the motion of the earth" (*De novâ Philosophia & terrae motu*), but even by the middle of the century the new science was far from general acceptance at Cambridge, and John Hall, while an undergraduate at St John's College, could jest about "the circle *Galileo's* found, / Though not drunk, thinking that the earth ran round."[86] Devising his own curriculum in *Of Education*, Milton prescribes the cosmic Lucretius together with the astronomical poets Aratus and Manilius, besides including astronomy more generally among those disciplines whose "principles" are worthy of study (*CPW* 2: 391–6).[87] Edward Phillips later records that under his uncle's tutelage he was taught these authors as well as the Hellenistic astronomer Geminus and the medieval cosmologist Johannes de Sacrobosco.[88] Milton's annotated copy of Aratus' *Phaenomena* survives, demonstrating his careful attention to that text, but even when reading a literary work like *Iphigenia in Aulis* Milton was highly attuned to astronomical questions: where Euripides places the "scorching star" (ἀστήρ... /σείριος, Eur. *IA* 6–7), or Sirius, near the Pleiades, Milton notes in his extant copy that "Scaliger in his preface to Manilius rightly wonders how this could accord with astronomy" (*haec astronomia qui possit constare merito dubitat Scaliger in proaemio ad Manilium*, *WJM* 18: 310).[89] This particular annotation is written in Milton's post-1638 hand, as indicated by his use of the Italic *e* rather than the Greek ε, suggesting perhaps that Milton thought this was important information for the pupils whom he began to instruct after his return from the Continent.[90]

The examples presented thus far might give the impression that Milton's knowledge of astronomy was limited to long-established authorities, but Milton was hardly unaware of more recent developments. When, for instance, he refers to

---

[85] See Skinner 2018: 129–30, 133. Mede's records are collected in Fletcher 1956–61: II 553–622.
[86] Nottingham UL, Mi LM 15/1, 325–30; Hall 1646: 5. See Serjeantson 2016: 74ff.
[87] On Milton and Manilius see DuRocher 2001: Ch. 4.
[88] Phillips 1694: xvii–xviii. Poole 2017a: 52–3 finds it likely that Milton used the *editio princeps* of Geminus 1590, "a premonition of how searching Milton's own study of classical astronomy would prove to be" (52). Martin 2001: 236 points out that "Geminus [...] did not actually exclude the heliocentric hypothesis," but the evidence for this comes from an excerpt of Geminus' commentary on Posidonius' *Meteorology* quoted in Simplicius (text in Diels 1882–1909 IX: 291–2; translation Geminus 2006: 252–5); "*Geminus's* Astronomy" (the astronomical textbook Εἰσαγωγὴ εἰς τὰ Φαινόμενα, or in Latin *Elementa Astronomiae*), which is what Phillips 1694: xvii reports that he read with his uncle, does not itself take up the question. On Milton and Sacrobosco see Gilbert 1923.
[89] Milton's copy of Aratus is BL shelfmark C.60.1.7, on which see Kelley and Atkins 1955. Milton's copy of Euripides 1602 is Bod. Don.d.27–28; on the annotations see Kelley and Atkins 1961, Hale 1991, Festa 2004, and McDowell 2016 passim. Milton here must be referring to Scaliger 1600: sig. βv. For another example of astronomically-minded annotation see *WJM* 18: 312 on Eur. *Rhes*. 530.
[90] On the dating of Milton's adoption of the Italic *e* see Darbishire 1933. On the pedagogical purpose behind Milton's post-1638 annotations see Festa 2004, with the date noted at 59 n.17.

"*Prutenick* tables" (*CPW* 2: 243) in *Areopagitica* he aligns himself with the new science of astronomers such as Erasmus Reinhold, whose *Prutenicae Tabulae* offered astronomical tables based on the calculations of Copernicus.[91] Milton may have represented Galileo in *Areopagitica* primarily as a victim of Catholic censorship, "a prisner to the Inquisition," but he also acknowledged that this was the result of the Italian's novel "thinking in Astronomy" (*CPW* 2: 538), and a reference in the same work to a book with "5 *Imprimaturs*" (*CPW* 2: 504) makes it highly likely that Milton returned to England with a copy of Galileo's *Dialogo*.[92] In *Paradise Lost* Milton points to the discoveries reported by Galileo in *Sidereus Nuncius* (1610) when he describes the "spotty Globe" (*PL* 1.291) of Satan's shield, or indeed when he compares Raphael's sight of the earth to the astronomer's view of the moon: "As when by night the Glass / Of *Galileo*, less assur'd, observes / Imagind Lands and Regions in the Moon" (*PL* 5.261–263).[93]

But Milton's most direct engagement with the new science is the dialogue on astronomy at the beginning of *Paradise Lost* Book 8, when "*Adam* inquires concerning celestial Motions," as the argument states, thus taking on the role of the curious Sagredo in Galileo's *Dialogo*.[94] Adam asks Raphael why it is that the inconceivably huge apparatus of the *primum mobile* should revolve around a minuscule and stationary earth:

> When I behold this goodly Frame, this World
> Of Heav'n and Earth consisting, and compute
> Thir magnitudes, this Earth a spot, a graine,
> An Atom, with the Firmament compar'd
> And all her numberd Starrs, that seem to rowle
> Spaces incomprehensible (for such
> Thir distance argues and thir swift return
> Diurnal) meerly to officiate light
> Round this opacous Earth, this punctual spot,
> One day and night; in all thir vast survey
> Useless besides, reasoning I oft admire,
> How Nature wise and frugal could commit
> Such disproportions
>
> (*PL* 8.15–27)

Besides a hint of Hamlet ("this goodly frame the Earth, seemes to me a sterill Promontory"), one may detect here, as in other places in the dialogue, the

---

[91] Reinhold 1551; see Martin 2001: 243 and Leonard 2013: II 710–11.   [92] See Miller 1971: 355.
[93] Galileo 1610; Sarkar 2012: 157. See also *PL* 3.588–590. Hume 1695 ad loc. explicitly relates *PL* 1.287–291 to *Siderius Nuncius*; Poole 2017a: 342 n.43 notes that Hume mentions Galileo eight times.
[94] Lewalski 2007: 196. See Gilbert 1922; Lewalski 1985: 46–50; Herz 1991 (esp. 155).

influence of Wilkins' *Discourse*: "And alas, what is this unto the vaste frame of the whole *Universe*? but *punctulum*, such an insensible point, which do's not beare so great a proportion to the whole, as a small sand do's unto the Earth."[95] If he had in fact read Wilkins—not, given his interest in the new science, an implausibility—Milton might have recognized the iconographic link with Langbaine's Longinus in the title page. In any case, it is clear that in this passage of what one might call poetic *meteoroscopy*, or what Edward Phillips defined in his English dictionary as "that part of Astrology, which handleth the difference of Sublimities, and distance of Stars," Milton's attention to cosmological details foregrounds the vastness of space, its "sublimities."[96] Adam intuits what was well known to seventeenth-century astronomers: that a geocentric system, whether the old Ptolemaic model or the geoheliocentric variation proposed by Tycho Brahe some twenty years before Milton's birth, presupposed stars moving over incredible distances— "a sumless journey" (*PL* 8.36)—at incredible velocities—"Speed, to describe whose swiftness Number fails" (*PL* 8.38).[97] *Number fails*: arithmetic itself cannot reckon it. These are sublimities beyond estimation.

When he tries to "compute / Thir magnitudes," the "disproportions" between the mere *punctulum* of Earth and the "numberd Starrs, that seem to rowle / Spaces incomprehensible" can only leave Adam to "admire," meaning both to wonder how that is the case and to experience a sense of sublime awe before the extreme magnitudes contemplated. Raphael disambiguates the signification of *admire* in his response, firmly situating the word in the second sense:

> This to attain, whether Heav'n move or Earth,
> Imports not, if thou reck'n right, the rest
> From Man or Angel the great Architect
> Did wisely to conceal, and not divulge
> His secrets to be scann'd by them who ought
> Rather admire
>
> (*PL* 8.73–75)

Here "admire" stands in opposition to "scann'd," making clear that humans are meant not so much to measure as to marvel.[98] Astronomical observers, whether Adam himself or those of the postlapsarian future, should not analyze the heavens but yield to sublime *admiratio*. If Adam's question ("When I behold this goodly

---

[95] Shakespeare 1623: 262, on the potential implications of which see Herz 1988; Wilkins 1640: 111. Parallels with Wilkins (and with Ross) are noted in McColley 1937. Leonard 2013: II 775, while rightly questioning McColley's claim that Milton sides with Ross, judges of the parallels: "Individually, these might be dismissed as coincidence, but the cumulative evidence is plausible."
[96] Phillips 1658b s.v. Meteoroscopie; cf. *OED* s.v. meteoroscopy, *n.* 1: "Observation of celestial objects."
[97] See Fowler 2007 ad loc. and Danielson 2014: 171–2.
[98] On both instances of *admire* see Brady 2007: 177–8.

Frame," *PL* 8.15) reprises the psalm attributed to David ("When I consider thy heavens, the worke of thy fingers, the moone and the starres which thou hast ordained," Ps. 8:3 KJV), it does so imperfectly, for it approaches celestial phenomena with calculation rather than awe.[99] Understood properly ("if thou reck'n right"), the scientific dispute over geocentrism versus heliocentrism is irrelevant ("Imports not").[100] What is crucial is that Adam admire the sublimities of the universe designed by God.

Raphael goes on to defend, provisionally at least, the integrity of the geocentric model, not, however, in the mathematical terms favored by Adam (e.g. "compute," *PL* 8.16) but on theological and anthropological grounds:

> And for the Heav'ns wide Circuit, let it speak
> The Makers high magnificence, who built
> So spacious, and his Line stretcht out so farr;
> That Man may know he dwells not in his own;
> An Edifice too large for him to fill,
> Lodg'd in a small partition, and the rest
> Ordain'd for uses to his Lord best known.
> The swiftness of those Circles attribute,
> Though numberless, to his Omnipotence,
> That to corporeal substances could adde
> Speed almost Spiritual; mee thou thinkst not slow,
> Who since the Morning hour set out from Heav'n
> Where God resides, and ere mid-day arriv'd
> In Eden, distance inexpressible
> By Numbers that have name.
>
> (*PL* 8.100–114)

If the sublime scale of "Heav'ns wide Circuit," the revolution of the vast *primum mobile* around the earth, overwhelms humble human intellection, it does not give reason for doubt ("something yet of doubt remains," *PL* 8.13) but rather testifies to the "high magnificence" of the deity "who built / So spacious, and his Line stretcht out so farr," referring to the question put to Job: "Who hath layd the measures thereof, if thou knowest? or who hath stretched the line upon it?" (Job 38:5 KJV).[101] The sublimities of the universe speak to the sublimity of God. If Adam doubts such astounding velocities as are entailed by the geocentric model,

---

[99] Edwards 2014: 113.
[100] On geocentrism/heliocentrism in *PL* see esp. the revisionary views of Martin 2001, Danielson 2010 and 2014, and Leonard 2013: Ch. 11.
[101] Van Eck 2012 comments: "In a complete reversal of the classical aesthetic favoring clarity, transparence and regularity, the architecture of the cosmos is now sublime because it is incomprehensible" (235).

he need only look to Raphael himself as an example: the archangel has traveled from Heaven to Eden in a matter of mere hours, across a "distance inexpressible / By Numbers that have name." Again human notions of number fail utterly at comprehending the distance involved: by the mid-seventeenth century the English language had begun to assimilate names for large numbers like *billion, trillion,* and *quadrillion* from French, but no such name in creature-arithmetic can even attempt to express just how far Raphael has flown, whichever unit of measurement one might use.[102]

Yet immediately following this tentative apology for geocentrism Raphael veers suddenly into considering the possibility that the Copernican model is correct: "What if the Sun / Be Center to the World" (*PL* 8.122-123), he asks, pronouncing the same *Quid si sic*? ("What if so?") that Copernicus speaks on the title page of Wilkins' *Discourse*.[103] This is one of a series of what-ifs explored by Raphael, among which is a speculation that often attended the Copernican hypothesis, the potential plurality of worlds: "other Suns perhaps / With thir attendant Moons thou wilt descrie" (*PL* 8.148-149), he tells Adam.[104] Indeed, this is a possibility voiced at various points throughout the poem: when Satan plunges into the world wherein he seeks God's prophesied new creature, he flies "Amongst innumerable Starrs, that shon / Stars distant, but nigh hand seemed other Worlds" (*PL* 3.565-566); when Raphael descends from Heaven to instruct that same creature, he "Sailes between worlds and worlds" (*PL* 5.268); angels describe the firmament as being "Of amplitude almost immense, with Starr's / Numerous, and every Starr perhaps a World" (*PL* 7.620-621). Raphael may exhort Adam to "Dream not of other Worlds" (*PL* 8.175), but Milton clearly wants his readers to do so, if only to imagine the infinitude of God's power.

Lucretius had imagined worlds "more than innumerable in number" (*numero magis innumerali*, Lucr. 2.1086), but in Renaissance Europe this notion could be considered gravely heretical: it was chiefly for his belief in the plurality of worlds that Giordano Bruno, the most prominent early modern proponent of the idea, was tried by the Roman Inquisition and burned alive at the Campo de' Fiori in 1600.[105] Yet that did not deter such speculation in seventeenth-century England, where the *libertas philosophandi* prevailed to a much greater

---

[102] See e.g. Morland 1666: 8, not noted in *OED* s.v. billion, *n.*; s.v. trillion, *n.*; s.v. quadrillion, *n.* and *adj.* To be clear, Raphael has traveled from Heaven, that is, from *outside of* the created world whose arrangement, geocentric or heliocentric, is the subject of Adam's inquiry, but the "distance inexpressible" traveled by Raphael speaks to the possible velocities of the stars *within* the created world and, in part, to its size.
[103] In attributing to Copernicus the phrase *Quid si sic?* Wilkins/Marshall appropriate a phrase previously associated with Tycho Brahe; see Remmert 2005: 58-60* as well as Kaoukji and Jardine 2010: 435-6 and (in relation to Raphael's what-ifs in *PL*) Danielson 2014: 124-8.
[104] On the plurality of worlds in *PL* see McColley 1932; Dodds 2008; Danielson 2014: Ch. 8.
[105] See recently Martinez 2016.

extent than it did on the Continent: Wilkins in his *Discourse* defended the proposition "*That a plurality of worlds doth not contradict any principle of reason or faith*," while Robert Burton in "*a Digression of the Ayre*" in *The Anatomy of Melancholy* writes favorably of the view, which he credits to Bruno among others, that "there be *infinite Worlds*, and infinite Earths or systemes, *in infinito æthere*."[106] Milton, one suspects, would have thought of Bruno in much the same way that he thought of Galileo, as an intellectual martyr condemned by the tyrannical Roman Church. But what I wish to stress here is the way that Milton makes use of this controversial cosmological hypothesis to magnify the scale of the created world in *Paradise Lost*.[107] If the scope of the world system discussed by Adam and Raphael is already too big to measure, its manifold multiplication, prompted suddenly by the "stupendous plural," in John Leonard's words, of "other Suns" (*PL* 8.148), inflates the universe even further, to such magnitudes of vastness, such cosmic sublimities, that can only provoke a sense of awesome Lucretian *horror*.[108] Juan d'Olivar's frontispiece to the *Entretiens sur la pluralité des mondes* (1686) of Bernard le Bovier de Fontenelle, though printed a little over a decade after Milton's death, supplies a striking example of how a near contemporary envisioned such an overwhelming spectacle (Figure 11).[109]

Peering through an aperture in its outer shell, Satan "Looks down with wonder at the sudden view / Of all this World at once" (*PL* 3.542–543): "Such wonder seis'd" (*PL* 3.552) him, Milton repeats.[110] But the fact that Satan can view the entirety of this physical apparatus *ab extra* indicates that it comprises only a small part of a much greater whole. Thus far I have only considered the world or universe created by God, but for Milton the world, be it Ptolemaic or Copernican—or indeed the plurality of worlds, if plural they be—does not signify the sum of all that is. Dennis Danielson has usefully suggested that we speak of Milton's *multiverse*, which consists of not only the created universe, containing the earth and various celestial phenomena (sun, moon, planets, stars), but also the other created realms of Heaven and Hell and, what is more, infinite Chaos.[111] Perhaps no passage gives a better sense of the place of Adam's world within this multiverse than Satan's arrival at the edge of Chaos, from which standpoint he is able

---

[106] Wilkins 1640: 20; Burton 1989–94: II 52, on which see Barlow 1973.

[107] Sarkar 2012 notes: "He is using an idea that the astronomy of the early modern period had provided him with [...] in order to create a sense of tremendous space" (90).

[108] Leonard 2013: II 742. Norbrook 2013 asserts that *PL* "offered a plurality, though not an infinity, of worlds (3.566–7), and appealed to [a] mid-century Protestant celebration of reformed greatmindedness against the anti-sublime spirit of the old religion." See Janowitz 2010 on Lucretius and the sublimity of plural worlds in the eighteenth century.

[109] On early modern visual representations of the plurality of worlds, including d'Olivar's, see Ayala 2014.

[110] Leonard 2016a remarks on the movement from the Paradise of Fools (*PL* 3.440–97) to this passage as "a shift from satire to sublimity" (68).

[111] See Danielson 2014: 50 et passim.

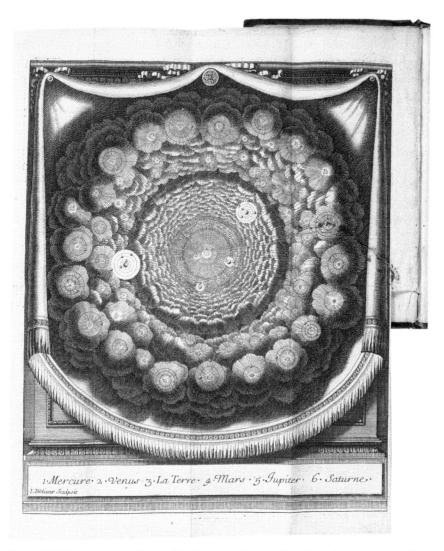

Figure 11 Frontispiece to Bernard le Bovier de Fontenelle's *Entretiens sur la pluralité des mondes* (1686), 228–339q, used by permission of the Folger Shakespeare Library.

> to behold
> Farr off th' Empyreal Heav'n, extended wide
> In circuit, undetermind square or round,
> With Opal Towrs and Battlements adorn'd
> Of living Saphire, once his native Seat;
> And fast by hanging in a golden Chain
> This pendant world, in bigness as a Starr
> Of smallest Magnitude close by the Moon.
>
> (*PL* 2.1047–1053)

"This pendant world" does not, as commentators before Zachary Pearce misinterpreted it, denote the earth alone, but rather the entire created universe, as Leonard has recently noted.[112] Like the pendant that dangles from a necklace, this pendant world *hangs*—the etymological sense of *pendant*, from Latin *pendere*— "in a golden Chain" from a Heaven which is so vast ("extended wide / In circuit") that one cannot even discern whether its shape is rectilinear or curved ("undetermind square or round").[113] The crucial image of scale is to be found in the description of this world as "in bigness as a Starr / Of smallest Magnitude close by the Moon"— that is, the pendant world compared to Heaven is like the faintest star beside the full lunar orb. If the size of the created world already astounds, it is dizzying to zoom out and find that this immense universe—containing the earth, the planets, the sun, and all the stars, but also potentially teeming with other systems, even exoplanets with undiscovered extraterrestrial creatures—is itself minuscule when set beside Heaven. Adam calls the earth but a "punctual spot" (*PL* 8.23) within the universal frame, but here the universal frame itself is revealed to be a mere point. If critics have sometimes erred in mistaking Milton's "pendant world" for the earth alone, rather than the entire sidereal universe, their failure highlights the difficulty of imagining the true sublimities, the incredible expanses, of Milton's cosmos.

No sublimities can compare with the endless expanse of space in which this pendant world floats, "the vast immeasurable Abyss" (*PL* 7.211) that is "fitliest call'd *Chaos*."[114] Milton reasons in *De Doctrina Christiana* that the orthodox doctrine of creation from nothing (*ex nihilo*) is impossible and the alternative of creation from pre-existing matter (*ex materia*) incoherent, concluding therefore that "all things were from God" (*fuisse omnia ex Deo*, CW 8.290). In *Paradise Lost*, accordingly, Chaos emerges as God withdraws—Milton's verb is "retire" (*PL* 7.170)—from his own substance. Like God, Chaos is limitless, unbounded, infinite: "Boundless the Deep, because I am who fill / Infinitude" (*PL* 7.168-169), says the Father. This is the stuff of which worlds are born, not only the created universe inhabited by humankind but, potentially, other universes entirely: Milton writes that God might "ordain / His dark materials to create more Worlds" (*PL* 2.915-916), a prospect voiced earlier by Satan when he claims that "Space may produce new Worlds" (*PL* 1.650). Milton's use of *space* in this cosmological sense was somewhat novel in 1667, but it corresponds to the usage of John Evelyn and Lucy Hutchinson in their 1650s Lucretius translations, where English *space* renders Latin *spatium*.[115] Like "the void profound / Of unessential Night" (*PL* 2.438), which translates Lucretius' *inane profundum* (Lucr. 1.1108), the

---

[112] Pearce 1733b: 81-2; see Leonard 2013: II Ch. 11 passim, esp. 726.   [113] Fowler 2007 ad loc.
[114] Lewalski 2007: 11. Norbrook 2013 takes the infinite space of Milton's Chaos as evidence of "a deep imaginative engagement with creative potential that accords with the republican sublime." Some recent scholarship on the nature of Milton's Chaos includes e.g. Sugimura 2009: Ch. 7 and Danielson 2014: Ch. 2.
[115] See Evelyn 1656: 69 and Hutchinson 2011: 73. See also *OED* s.v. space, *n*.1 8.

cosmological sense of *space*, as John Leonard has shown, points to a distinctive Lucretian influence on Milton's Chaos.[116] When Milton calls Chaos "The Womb of nature and perhaps her Grave" (*PL* 2.911), reworking Lucretius' "the same all-mother of nature its common grave" (*omniparens eadem rerum commune sepulcrum*, Lucr. 5.259), Milton suggests, with a wavering "perhaps," the sublime Lucretian *horror* of this hostile expanse which, in its infinitude, "with utter loss of being / Threatens" (*PL* 2.440-441).[117] At the moment of the Creation violent Chaos menaces the whole Miltonic multiverse with ruin, with its "surging waves, as Mountains to assault/Heav'ns highth, and with the Center mix the Pole" (*PL* 7.214-215).[118]

C. S. Lewis detected an abhorrence of infinite space, a kind of cosmic "agoraphobia," in Milton.[119] Chaos, with its limitless, immeasurable extension, is the locus of this *horror*. Its vacuum can swallow and devour for eternity: Satan "drops / Ten thousand fadom deep, and to this hour / Down had been falling" (*PL* 2.933-935) were it not for a force acting upon him ("The strong rebuff of som tumultuous cloud / Instinct with Fire and Nitre," *PL* 2.936-937) to change his trajectory, illustrating the first law of motion defined in Isaac Newton's *Principia* two decades later.[120] Milton first describes the space into which Satan slips, in what might otherwise have been a perpetual free fall,[121] as an

> Illimitable Ocean without bound,
> Without dimension, where length, breadth, & highth,
> And time and place are lost
>
> (*PL* 2.891-894)

If the span of the finite universe is sublime, as it was for Longinus, then the "Illimitable Ocean" of Chaos—the domain, that is, rather than its personified

---

[116] Leonard 2000: 203 (and see passim). For Lucretian influences on *PL* generally see also Hardie 2009: 264-79; Quint 2004; Calloway 2009; Norbrook 2013.

[117] Rumrich 1996: 119 asserts "no one disputes that in *Paradise Lost* chaos is 'the Womb of Nature,'" but Leonard 2000: 207 does, holding that this line refers to Night; Rumrich 2000: 219 acknowledges that Night is often associated with womb imagery but maintains that this line does refer to Chaos. While we should take care to differentiate between Chaos and Night, unformed matter and lightless void, it is perhaps no accident that it is not always clear to which of these Milton is referring: as the portrayal of personified Night as Chaos' "Consort" (*PL* 2.963) suggests, the two are allegorically "wedded," which is to say *coextensive in space*. In my discussion of Chaos as sublime space therefore I do not sharply distinguish between Chaos and Night. But I hide my diminished head as I acknowledge the justice behind the parenthetical remark of Leonard 2013: "it is remarkable how often Chaos forces critics to seek refuge in footnotes" (II 786). Here I incline toward those who emphasize the hostility of Chaos (Schwartz 1988: 8-39; Leonard 2000) as opposed to those who consider it essentially good (Danielson 1982: 24-57; Rumrich 1996: 118-46 and 2000). On Chaos and Lucretian *horror* see previously Norbrook 2013.

[118] Leonard 2000: 203 and 2013: 804 sees here an echo of Lucr. 1.1108. See also *PL* 2.924-27.

[119] Lewis 1964: 99-100; see also Martin 1996 and Leonard 2013: 816-18.

[120] Newton 1687: 12; see Trubowitz 2017: 49.

[121] Leonard 2000 notes: "Critics have shrunk from the implications of that phrase [i.e. "to this hour"], but Milton really does open the possibility of a fall lasting thousands of years" (208).

ruler—is infinitely more so. Whatever the allegorical status of Chaos, in Milton's multiverse it represents an extradimensional sublimity that exceeds even the very qualities ("length, breadth, & highth") that notionally define space and surpasses human understandings of quantity and proportion. At a time when English mathematicians such as John Wallis were exploring the possibilities of the infinite, preparing the way for Newton's infinitesimal calculus, Milton, who professed in the *Defensio Secunda* an interest in "anything new in mathematics" (*novum quidpiam in Mathematicis, WJM* 8: 120), was attempting to imagine, in his Chaos, infinity *in extenso*, infinite space.[122]

Milton's Chaos represents a degree of physical sublimity that far surpasses not only the other spaces of his multiverse but also the sublime similes that characterize Satan. Consider the group of similes describing the passage of Satan through Chaos near the end of Book 2, when he

> Springs upward like a Pyramid of fire
> Into the wilde expanse, and through the shock
> Of fighting Elements, on all sides round
> Environ'd wins his way; harder beset
> And more endanger'd, then when *Argo* pass'd
> Through *Bosporus* betwixt the justling Rocks:
> Or when *Ulysses* on the Larbord shunnd
> *Charybdis*, and by th' other whirlpool steard.
>
> (*PL* 2.1013–1020)

The simile of the "Pyramid of fire" is simple and brief but symbolically rich. Playing, like Milton, on the *figura etymologica* that derives Greek *puramis* ("pyramid") from *pur* ("fire"), Plato in the *Timaeus* assigns the element of fire to the tetrahedron because its angles make it "most piercing and most sharp" (τμητικώτατόν τε καὶ ὀξύτατον, Pl. *Tim.* 56b). This gave the pyramid associations of destruction and transgression, as can be seen when Milton writes in the *The Reason of Church-Government* of "Prelaty thus ascending in a continuall pyramid" as "her pyramid aspires and sharpens to ambition" (*CPW* 1: 790).[123] But Milton's simile also suggests a comparison with the physical magnitude of the ancient pyramids at Giza, a survey of which the mathematician John Greaves had published in his *Pyramidographia* (1646), as Peter Hume's comment implies: "The famous Egyptian Pyramids, the expensive and astonishing Tombs of their Kings, are of this Figure."[124] It is tempting, if problematic, to take the use of a capital letter for "Pyramid" in both the 1667 and the 1674 editions to support this

---

[122] On Milton and the new mathematics see Duran 2007: 179–207, expanded from Duran 2003, Webster 2015, and Trubowitz 2017.
[123] See Gorecki 1976: 103–5.   [124] Hume 1695 ad loc.

interpretation.[125] In any other context a "Pyramid of fire" would be astonishing, an image of superlative size much like those we have seen previously in Milton's hyperbolic similes. Shooting into the unbounded infinitude of Chaos, however, Satan's pyramid is dominated by "the wilde expanse," his fire just one among innumerable "fighting Elements." The simile becomes lost, like Satan himself, amidst the vast emptiness of Chaos. Satan finds himself "harder beset / And more endanger'd" than Jason and Ulysses. Comparison to these Greek heroes might otherwise magnify, but here it diminishes Satan, whom infinite Chaos makes its plaything, whom it imperils with oblivion, as the rocks do the Argonauts, as the whirlpools do the Ithacan. Satan may succeed in escaping the danger of Chaos, as the Greek heroes do theirs, but his struggle ("So he with difficulty and labour hard / Mov'd on, with difficulty and labour hee," *PL* 2.1021–1022) does not leave one in doubt of which is the superior force. For all of Satan's sublimity, the space through which he pilots is far sublimer. Like his minions disfigured into pygmies, he is utterly dwarfed by the amplitude of infinite Chaos.

---

[125] Milton 1667 and 1674a. The position, as expressed by Darbishire 1952–5: I ix–xxxxv, that Milton was highly attentive to punctuation and spelling, for instance "us[ing] the capital letter to mark out a distinct use of a word" (xiv), has over the decades come under attack by e.g. Adams 1955: 60–111, expanded from Adams 1954, as well as Creaser 1983 and 1984; see also Dobranski 1999 passim. But Darbishire's view has recently been taken up, at least in part, by Poole 2017a: 154–5.

4
Milton and the Theological Sublime

Longinus commended Moses as a sublime author not only for the manner in which he communicated the nature of the divine but also for his theological comprehension. Having examined in the two preceding chapters Milton's notions of rhetorical and physical sublimity, respectively, I turn now to his engagement with the theological sublime. Milton believed that the office of the poet was a religious vocation in and of itself, one that entailed the elucidation of sublime theological truth: as he put it in *The Reason of Church-Government*, the poet, whose "abilities, wheresoever they be found, are the inspired guift of God, rarely bestow'd, but yet to some (though most abuse) in every Nation" (*CPW* 1: 816), has a duty to teach "whatsoever in religion is holy and sublime" (*CPW* 1: 817). The many who "abuse" this heavenly endowment are those afflicted by moral or theological misunderstanding: "'Most' heathens," Ralph Haug comments in the Yale edition, "and some Christians as well, abuse the gift; their *matter* is faulty."[1] In treating Milton's sublime theological matter I shall begin with *A Maske Presented at Ludlow Castle, 1634* before turning to the later poetry and *De Doctrina Christiana*.

The "Sublime Notion" of Virginity

Milton's *Maske* was written to celebrate the inauguration of John Egerton, 1st Earl of Bridgewater, as Lord President of Wales and was performed at Ludlow Castle in the Welsh Marches on Michaelmas 1634.[2] Milton family friend Henry Lawes, who presumably secured the young poet this commission, composed the music, some of which survives.[3] The Egerton children acted most of the main roles: Alice, the eldest, played the part of the Lady accosted by the god of revels Comus, while John, Lord Brackley and Thomas played the Brothers. Lawes, their tutor in music, took on the role of the protective "Daemon" or "attendant Spirit." The actor who played Comus himself remains unknown.[4]

---

[1] *CPW* 1: 816 n.108.
[2] Trinity College Library (Cambridge), MS R.3.4, Milton's working draft, is headed simply "A maske" (13). The popular title *Comus* follows the usage of Toland 1699: 46; see Fletcher 1971: 153ff. and Greteman 2016.
[3] See *CW* 3: 587–98.
[4] It has sometimes been suggested (e.g. Parker 1968: I 142; Orgel 2003: 38) that Milton himself may have acted the part of Comus, but there is no evidence that Milton was even in attendance at the Ludlow performance, much less that he assumed any role.

The text of the masque was therefore written as a script for the Ludlow performance, of which the Bridgewater manuscript presented to Lord Egerton, with its cuts and other alterations, seems to provide the best record.[5] For my purposes here, however, I am not so much interested in the event of performance as I am in the Miltonic opus itself, the literary qualities of which were lauded by Sir Henry Wotton in a letter which was prefixed to the masque in the 1645 *Poems*: "I should much commend the Tragical part, if the Lyrical did not ravish me with a certain Dorique delicacy in your Songs and Odes, wherunto I must plainly confess to have seen yet nothing parallel in our Language: *Ipsa mollities*" (*CW* 3: 61). With the words *Ipsa mollities* ("suppleness itself"), Wotton was, no doubt quite consciously, making use of a programmatically charged term in Augustan poetics, in which context Latin *mollis* ("soft") denotes that which is light and refined—characteristically, the slighter, more Callimachean genres, amatory elegy particularly—in opposition to that which is *durus* ("hard"), like the heavy stuff of epic and tragedy.[6] *Ipsa mollities* therefore is appropriate praise for the light entertainment of a masque, but Wotton's language of rapture ("ravish") hints at a sense of the work's sublimeness, too, a passionate lyrical sublimity like that of the Sappho poem Longinus so admired.

Yet the true sublimity of the work is not so much literary as intellectual. Milton's masque is "a kind of philosophical ballet," in the words of Charles Williams, one which sets the ethereal virtue of chastity, as embodied by the virginal young Lady, against the worldly vices of the seductive Comus.[7] The figure of Comus, ekphrastically described in the third-century *Imagines* of Philostratus (Philostr. *Imag.* 1.2), had briefly appeared on stage in Ben Jonson's 1618 masque *Pleasure Reconciled to Virtue*, but Milton's character would seem to owe more to *Comus sive Phagesiposia Cimmeria*, a Neo-Latin moral satire by the Dutch humanist Erycius Puteanus, first published in 1608 but reprinted in Oxford in the very year that the Ludlow masque was composed and performed.[8] Like Puteanus' Comus, who espouses the hedonistic credo "What is the life of mortals without pleasure? It is punishment" (*Quae mortalium sine voluptate vita? poena est*), Milton's voluptuary advocates a sort of Cyrenaic doctrine of sensual indulgence, ridiculing "those budge doctors of the *Stoick* Furr" (*Maske* 708) who urge "lean and sallow Abstinence" (*Maske* 710).[9] But on hearing the "Divine inchanting

---

[5] BL Loan MS 76; see *CW* 3: cxlviii–cl.

[6] For a recent treatment of *versus molles* see Weber 2019, with some previous scholarship indicated in n.2.

[7] Williams 1950: 255. On the influence of Williams' Milton criticism see Leonard 2013 passim.

[8] Singleton 1943 was the first to establish Puteanus' work as a highly plausible source, with other correspondences explored by Mish 1967 and Leasure 2002: 65–71. Brown 1985: 191 n.15 notes that "[t]he reprinting of this text in Oxford in the same year as Milton's masque makes an additional reason for taking the possibility of influence seriously, but it may simply be that those responsible for the new edition were commenting on current aristocratic luxury, that is, were responding to the present historical context in a way similar to Milton's."

[9] Puteanus 1608: 22.

ravishment" (*Maske* 245) of the Lady's song Comus recognizes a numinous power: "Sure somthing holy lodges in that brest, / And with these raptures moves the vocal air / To testifie his hidd'n residence" (*Maske* 246-248). The sense of sublime ravishment and rapture that Comus experiences threatens to overwhelm him.[10] For as the Elder Brother assures the Younger, their sister is protected by "the arms of Chastity" (*Maske* 440): the petrifying aegis of the virgin Minerva was in fact "But rigid looks of Chast austerity, / And noble grace that dash't brute violence / With sudden adoration, and blank aw" (*Maske* 450-452). Such is the "sudden adoration, and blank aw"—a line Milton labored over, as his working draft in the Trinity manuscript indicates—provoked in Comus when he first encounters the Lady.[11]

Chastity, the Elder Brother continues, *sublimes* the mind, "turns it by degrees to the souls essence, / Till all be made immortal" (*Maske* 462-463): Milton will use just that verb later in *Paradise Lost* to describe the ascent from "body up to spirit" (*PL* 5.478) as earthly fruits are "by gradual scale sublim'd" (*PL* 5.483).[12] The sublimation of the Lady's virginity entails an elevation from sexual body to spiritual perfection.[13] Among Milton's models for such sublimation is the Christian poetry of Dante and Petrarch: in his 1642 antiprelatical tract *An Apology Against a Pamphlet* Milton claims that, despite his early enjoyment of pagan love poets like Ovid, in his maturity he "preferr'd the two famous renowners of *Beatrice* and *Laura* who never write but honour of them to whom they devote their verse, displaying sublime and pure thoughts, without transgression" (*CPW* 1: 890).[14] Milton's conception of erotic sublimation is exhibited in a passage following soon after which commentators have long linked back to the Ludlow masque, as he discourses on "how the first and chiefest office of love, begins and ends in the soule, producing those happy twins of her divine generation knowledge and vertue," which he calls "abstracted sublimities" (*CPW* 1: 892): the sense is of rarified essences, spiritual purities extracted or drawn out from (the literal sense of the Latin root *abstractus*) the erotic impulse.[15]

Comus assails the Lady with various arguments for his philosophy of carnal delights, but the virtuous virgin refuses to yield. Her final speech, in the early manuscript versions, asserts the superiority of the "holy dictate of spare

---

[10] Perhaps with a sense of the cognate *rape* (from Latin *raptus*); see Thomas 2006: 448.

[11] See Trinity College Library (Cambridge), MS R.3.4, p. 20.

[12] On alchemical and spiritual sublimation, respectively, in Milton see recently Nicholls 2016 and 2019 and Earle 2020.

[13] Shullenberger 2008: 197 writes of the Lady's chastity as a form of "sublimation," but conceives of this primarily in terms of Freudian psychoanalysis rather than in the contemporary alchemical *cum* hermetical sense ("its Renaissance spiritual and alchemical resonances").

[14] For some possible echoes of Dante in *Maske* see Samuel 1966: 285 and Leasure 2002: 71; several commentators have suggested that Milton's "Sun-clad power of Chastity" (*Maske* 783) may allude to Petrarch's *Vergine bella, che di sol vestita* (*Canzoniere* 366.1); see e.g. Brown 1985: 138.

[15] See e.g. *CPW* 1: 892 n.128.

Temperance" (*Maske* 768). But in the 1637 text of the masque, which Milton revised for its first print publication,[16] the Lady's speech is expanded with a testimony to the sublimity of chastity:

> Thou hast nor Eare, nor Soul to apprehend
> The sublime notion, and high mystery
> That must be utter'd to unfold the sage
> And serious doctrine of Virginity,
> And thou art worthy that thou shouldst not know
> More happines then this thy present lot.
> Enjoy your deer Wit, and gay Rhetorick
> That hath so well been taught her dazling fence,
> Thou art not fit to hear thy self convinc't;
> Yet should I try, the uncontrouled worth
> Of this pure cause would kindle my rap't spirits
> To such a flame of sacred vehemence,
> That dumb things would be mov'd to sympathize,
> And the brute Earth would lend her nerves, and shake,
> Till all thy magick structures rear'd so high,
> Were shatter'd into heaps o're thy false head.
>
> (*Maske* 785–800)

Virginity is a "sublime notion, and high mystery," the very utterance of which would rouse the Lady to a divine fury, inciting her "rap't spirits" to "a flame of sacred vehemence." Her sublime rapture is contrasted with the "gay Rhetorick" of Comus and its "dazling fence," over which the Lady's "pure cause" triumphs.[17] Milton may have appreciated the rhetorical style of the sublime, but he could also acknowledge the superiority of a "sublime notion" of theological truth like the virtue of chastity over any display of rhetoric. As Calvin writes in the *Institutes*, the style of the Evangelists may be simple, but their matter is sublime, such that John, "thundering from on high" (*e sublimi tonans*), strikes down the infidel "more powerfully than any thunderbolt" (*quolibet fulmine validius*).[18] The *fulmen divinitatis* transcends the *fulmen eloquentiae*. Particularly apposite is a comment offered by the Huguenot theologian Daniel Chamier in his four-volume *Panstratia Catholica*, a work which Milton cites in *Tetrachordon*.[19] In a chapter on the question of "Whether the Church should exhibit the Scripture in the vulgar tongue" (*An Scripturam Ecclesia proposuerit lingua vulgari*), Chamier makes the following argument for the affirmative:

---

[16] This passage, as well as Comus' response, is absent from the MSS; see esp. Brown 1985: 137–41.
[17] See Gay 1995 on the possible resonances of 2 Corinthians 12.2–5 here.
[18] Calvin 1559: 20.   [19] See *CPW* 2: 697.

> Maiestas non pendet a vocabulis, sed a rebus ipsis. Nihil enim sanctum est, quod non habeat suam maiestatem, non adventitiam, & accidentariam, sed sibi insitam. Itaque, quancunque in linguam transferantur, ab ea destitui non possunt. Sic Longinus περὶ ὕψους, quanquam Mosen Hebraice non legisset, tamen observavit in Greco idiomate, eius styli maiestatem.[20]
>
> Majesty does not depend on words, but on the things themselves. For nothing is sacred that does not have its own majesty, which is not extrinsic and accidental but inherent in itself. And so whatever language they are translated into, they cannot lack of this. Thus Longinus *On the Sublime*, although he had not read Moses in Hebrew, nevertheless perceived in the Greek idiom his majesty of style.

The passage continues with a quotation of Longinus on the *fiat lux* in the original Greek and, fittingly, in a Latin translation. Chamier is making a theological point about Scripture: if even a pagan Greek like Longinus, who presumably knew no Hebrew, could appreciate the sublimity of Genesis in translation, then surely the Bible could be communicated in the vernacular. But what interests me here is Chamier's understanding of biblical *maiestas* as something that lies not in anything literary or rhetorical, but in ideas, in sacred ideas: "Majesty does not depend on words, but on the things themselves." In the Ludlow masque that majesty is manifest in the "sublime notion" of virginity, as it is also in the divine wrath it portends: "the brute Earth would lend her nerves, and shake, / Till all thy magick structures rear'd so high, / Were shatter'd into heaps o're thy false head." As commentators going back to Thomas Warton have recognized, Milton's "brute Earth" reproduces Horace's *bruta tellus* (Hor. *Carm.* 1.34.9).[21] In the poem from which this phrase derives, Horace relates how the destructive power of Jupiter's thunder has instilled in him a newfound fear of the gods: "By this ode," the late antique commentator Porphyrion writes, "he signifies that he is making repentance, because having followed the Epicurean sect he was irreligious" (*Hac ode significat, se paenitentiam agere, quod Epicuream sectam secutus inreligiosus extiterit*, Porph. *Comm. Hor. Carm.* 1.34.1). But the verbal parallels, as Cedric Brown has shown, go beyond *bruta tellus*: "shake" seems to look to Horace's *concutitur* ("is shaken," *Carm.* 1.34.12), while the infernal subjects of Horace's verb (*Styx et invisi horrida Taenari/sedes*, *Carm.* 1.34.10–11) are reflected in the immediate reply of Comus, another 1637 addition:

> a cold shuddring dew
> Dips me all o're, as when the wrath of Jove
> Speaks thunder, and the chains of *Erebus*
> To som of *Saturns* crew.
>
> (*Maske* 803–806)

---

[20] Chamier 1626-30: I 389.   [21] Warton 1785 ad loc.

More than a passing allusion, Horace's poem seems to have given structure to the revised dialogue: "the Lady claims the power of heaven in her arguments against epicureanism; Comus, a creature known to hell, acknowledges the fear of God induced by thunder."[22] More particularly, the Lady's power is the "sublime notion" of virginity, divine endorsement of which animates the Jovian threat of thunder: for if sublime ideas are sacred matter, they carry with them always, whether implicitly or explicitly, the intimation of sacred wrath. If, as the Elder Brother claims, she who is chaste "may pass on with unblench't majesty" (*Maske* 430), it is the prospect of God's wrath that renders her secure from ill-doers. Sublime virginity also effects the Lady's liberation at the end of the masque by the nymph Sabrina, who is "swift / To aid a Virgin, such as was her self / In hard besetting need" (*Maske* 855–857)—a deus ex machina of the sort favored by Euripides, a two-volume edition of whose tragedies Milton acquired in 1634, the same year as the composition and performance of the masque.[23] But it is the final exchange between the Lady and Comus that suggests the deep connection, to be further explored throughout this chapter, between the sublimity of theological ideas—a *maiestas rerum*, in Chamier's terms—and divine violence.

The War in Heaven as Sublime Theomachy

In *Paradise Lost* there is no greater spectacle of divine violence than the war between the heavenly host of angels and their rebellious counterparts in Book 6.[24] As for the poem as a whole, Milton's most authoritative source for the episode is Scripture, in this case Revelation.[25] At the same time this part is, again like much of the epic whole, replete with echoes of classical and Renaissance epic poetry. To take just a couple of examples, Milton's portrayal of the conflict as an "Intestine War" (*PL* 6.259) bears comparison with Lucan's epic of civil war, while some of the particulars of angelic battle seem to allude to the Neo-Latin *Christiad* of Marco Girolamo Vida.[26] More generally, perhaps Milton's most salient extra-biblical model is the theomachy, or combat of the gods, in classical epic.[27] In his narration of the war in heaven Raphael struggles to communicate divine things to the earthbound Adam, "lik'ning spiritual to corporal forms" (*PL* 5.573), but it is the fighting gods of the *Iliad* to which he turns for the closest analogue, as when Satan and Michael contend:

---

[22] Brown 1985: 140.   [23] Bod. Don.d.27–28.
[24] On the war in heaven in *PL* see esp. Revard 1980; on Milton and war more generally see Freeman 1980 and Fallon 1984.
[25] See Dobbins 1975: 26–52.
[26] For comparisons with Lucan see Martindale 1986: 218–20 and Norbrook 1999: 447–50; on parallels with Vida see Haan 2003.
[27] See Hughes 1965: 196–219 and Martindale 1986: 93–102.

> They ended parle, addresst for fight
> Unspeakable; for who, though with the tongue
> Of Angels, can relate, or to what things
> Liken on Earth conspicuous, that may lift
> Human imagination to such highth
> Of Godlike Power: for likest Gods they seemd,
> Stood they or mov'd, in stature, motion, arms
> Fit to decide the Empire of great Heav'n.
>
> (*PL* 6.296–303)

Their fight is literally "unspeakable," in that its true nature cannot be apprehended by human intelligence, even Adam's prelapsarian one. That which so challenges Raphael's communicative abilities is the sublimity of the divine phenomenon, the "highth / Of Godlike Power." The best that he can do to relate this to Adam is to compare the combatants to classical divinities: "likest Gods they seemd." Milton would have known that Homeric theomachy is among the key examples of theological sublimity supplied in the *Peri hupsous*. Writing that "the images of theomachy are also sublime" (ὑπερφυᾶ καὶ τὰ ἐπὶ τῆς θεομαχίας φαντάσματα, Long. *Subl.* 9.6), Longinus cites a conflated passage of the *Iliad* speaking of the fear that "earthshaking Poseidon might tear open the earth" (γαῖαν ἀναρρήξειε Ποσειδάων ἐνοσίχθων, *Il.* 20.63) and addresses his reader: "Look, friend, how the earth is torn apart from its depths, and Tartarus itself is laid bare, and the whole universe is seized by ruin and disintegration" (ἐπιβλέπεις, ἑταῖρε, ὡς ἀναρρηγνυμένης μὲν ἐκ βάθρων γῆς, αὐτοῦ δὲ γυμνουμένου ταρτάρου, ἀνατροπὴν δὲ ὅλου καὶ διάστασιν τοῦ κόσμου λαμβάνοντος, Long. *Subl.* 9.6).[28] For Longinus, theomachy, as a conflict of almighty powers threatening universal destruction, constitutes a singularly sublime epic subject.[29]

Making Christian figures play the part of the pagan gods in epic poetry could be regarded as a ludicrous travesty in itself: so in *L'Art poétique* (1674) Boileau criticizes those who "propose to make God, the saints, and the prophets act like the gods hatched from the brains of poets" (*Pensent faire agir Dieu, ses Saints, & ses Prophetes,/Comme ces Dieux éclos du cerveau des Poëtes*, 3.195–196) or have Satan "contend for victory with God" (*avec Dieu balance la victoire*, 3.208).[30] Nevertheless, the profusion of angelic combat scenes in Renaissance epic, as in Vida's *Christiad*, suggests that Boileau's was a minority view.[31] As for Milton's version, criticism has long been split between those who find it sublime, like

---

[28] On Longinus' quotation of the *Iliad* see Usher 2007: 294–6.
[29] On theomachy and the Longinian sublime see Chaudhuri 2014 passim and Bolt 2019: 311–12.
[30] Boileau 1674: 125–6. The phrase *avec Dieu balance la victoire* means literally "balance the victory with God," the verb *balancer* here having the sense "put in suspense, render uncertain."
[31] Gregory 2006: 43 writes that "the readers of less sophisticated hexaemeral narratives than Milton's evidently did not find it absurd for Michael and Lucifer to slug it out for several contested rounds."

Joseph Addison, and those like Voltaire who think it farcical.[32] Arnold Stein, in a noteworthy reading of the episode, characterized it as intentionally comic, a sort of mock-heroic burlesque.[33] As the reader will expect, I take the view that Milton's war in heaven is much more sublime than it is ridiculous. Here Addison, writing in one of his 1712 *Spectator* essays on the poem, is a perceptive guide: "Let the judicious reader compare what Longinus has observed on several passages in Homer, and he will find parallels for most of them in the *Paradise Lost*."[34] For if one heeds Addison's exhortation, a number of passages in Book 6 will indeed suggest the influence of the sublime Longinian reading of Homeric theomachy on Milton's construction of the episode.[35]

Longinus foregrounds the laying bare of Tartarus in Homer's theomachy; Milton, similarly, uncovers the horrible depths of Hell to which Satan's forces are doomed, "the Gulf / of *Tartarus*, which ready opens wide / His fiery *Chaos* to receave thir fall" (*PL* 6.53–55). Milton, moreover, emphasizes the sublime terror of this vision, calling the "spacious Gap" which the wall of heaven "disclos'd / Into the wastful Deep" a "monstrous sight" provoking "horror" (*PL* 6.861–863). The war in heaven also features another theomachic image praised by Longinus for its sublimity, the throwing of mountains (Long. *Subl.* 8.2): "Hills amid the Air encounterd Hills / Hurl'd to and fro with jaculation dire" (*PL* 6.664–665). As noted earlier, Homer describes the Aloadae piling Pelion on Ossa (*Od.* 11.315–316). Hesiod, similarly, writes that the Giants "hurled three hundred rocks from their sturdy hands, one after another" (οἵ ῥα τριηκοσίας πέτρας στιβαρῶν ἀπὸ χειρῶν/πέμπον ἐπασσυτέρας, Hes. *Theog.* 715–716), thus burying the rebellious Titans with whom Satan and his "horrid crew" (*PL* 1.51) were identified.[36] Mountains, by virtue of their scale, are exemplary instances of physical sublimity, as discussed in the preceding chapter. But of course these mountains are not really mountains at all: they are rather the corporeal forms to which spiritual phenomena are likened. The mountains tossed about in the war in heaven are therefore equally, if not more so, instances of theological sublimity, representations of the power of divine beings ("Gods") in terms understandable at the limits of human imagination. As God's obedient angels lift "the seated Hills with all thir load" (*PL* 6.644), the devils themselves are stunned in sublime horror by the prospect "so dread" (PL 6.648) of mountains ripped from their foundations and hurled through the air: "Amaze, / Be sure, and terrour seis'd the rebel Host" (*PL* 6.646–647).

Most sublime, perhaps, are the terrifying portents of cosmic ruin, another Longinian theme. The single combat of Michael and Satan is compared to the

---

[32] On the critical tradition see Leonard 2013: 272–4, 301–3 et passim.
[33] Stein 1953: 17–37.   [34] Addison 1970: 72.
[35] Some similar parallels had been previously noted in passing by Machacek 2011: 131–2, though without attention to the context of Milton's theomachy.
[36] Revard 1980: 192–4.

clashing of planets in the heavens "if Natures concord broke" (*PL* 6.311), in imitation of Lucan (Lucan *Phars.* 1.72–81).[37] The din of angelic battle, "clamour such as heard in Heav'n till now / Was never" (*PL* 6.208–209), is such that it could rattle the whole of earth, had it then existed:

> all Heav'n
> Resounded, and had Earth bin then, all Earth
> Had to her Center shook. What wonder? when
> Millions of fierce encountring Angels fought
> On either side
>
> (*PL* 6.217–221)

The poet's interrogative "What wonder?" (i.e. "Why should it surprise?") equally represents an exclamation—"What wonder!"—at the sublime spectacle of the war in heaven, an effect heightened by the sharp enjambment of the conjunction ("when") breaking into a sprawling dactyl ("Millions of"). It can be no accident that the destructive potential of Chaos is elsewhere described similarly, for Chaos, ruinous disorder, is exactly what is threatened by this sublime theomachy.[38] More than a mere war as that phenomenon is known to mortals, this is a conflict of beings so powerful that their actions could tear apart the heavens:

> Warr seem'd a civil Game
> To this uproar; horrid confusion heapt
> Upon confusion rose: and now all Heav'n
> Had gone to wrack, with ruin overspred,
> Had not th' Almightie Father where he sits
> Shrin'd in his Sanctuarie of Heav'n secure,
> Consulting on the sum of things, foreseen
> This tumult, and permitted all, advis'd
>
> (*PL* 6.667–674)

The terms could not be exaggerated: "horrid confusion heapt / Upon confusion" (*confusion* bearing the now obsolete sense of "ruin, destruction, perdition"); "all Heav'n / Had gone to wrack."[39] The devastation is almost impious, implying that the war might actually uncreate God's kingdom, and seems only partly mitigated by crediting the Father as the one who allows and, ultimately, curtails the fight. Other Christian poets had written scenes of angelic combat, but Milton, as Stella Revard notes, "adheres rather more closely than most of his predecessors to the classical model that portrayed the devastation of a war of the gods."[40] What this

---

[37] Noted in Norbrook 1999: 447.
[38] *PL* 2.924–927, 7.213–215; see Schwartz 1988: 26.
[39] *OED* s.v. confusion sense 1a.
[40] Revard 1980: 192.

does is demonstrate the sublime power of the angels at war, a recurring threat to the fabric of the universe: when Satan stands opposite Gabriel "Like Teneriff or Atlas unremov'd" (*PL* 4.987) at the end of Book 4, Milton writes that, had God not intervened, "the Starrie Cope / Of Heav'n perhaps, or all the Elements / At least had gon to wrack" (*PL* 4.992–994). Such visions of universal ruin may skirt the edge of blasphemy, invoking the thought of a cosmos beyond God's control, but their association with the combat of the angels firmly establishes the episode as a Christian iteration of the classical epic theomachy as it was understood by Longinus.

Arnold Stein found all of these passages—the gap of Tartarus, the throwing of mountains, the prospect of a heaven "gone to wrack" (*PL* 6.670)—to have been "made comic by controlled excess," memorably comparing the angels' mountain-hurling to the slapstick tossing of custard pies.[41] But Stein mistook that excess as silly when really it is the *huperbolē* of the sublime. Partly this is due to a misreading of Milton's language. Stein singles out the Latinate *jaculation* ("Hills amid the Air encounterd Hills / Hurl'd to and fro with jaculation dire," *PL* 6.664–665) as "the kind of exaggerated word that is calculated to embarrass the exaggeration, after the manner more familiar in mock-epic," but in this he infers a humorous connotation not obviously present (and one which the adjective *dire* in fact argues against).[42] When, for instance, John King, then Vice-Chancellor of the University of Oxford and later Bishop of London, in a sermon delivered at Whitehall on the third anniversary of the Gunpowder Plot preached that the infamous undercroft beneath the House of Lords had been like a bow "*strongly strung* with 36. barrels of gun-powder great and small, for the more violent iaculation, vibration, and speed of the arrowes," his tone could hardly be anything but serious.[43] Rather than a humorously pedantic Latinism, *jaculation dire* should be understood as a sublime expression well suited to the Gigantomachic terror of the scene, a phrase of Vergilian gravity.[44]

But Stein also erred in neglecting Milton's earliest readers. Like Boileau, a few objected on the grounds that any such scenes of angelic combat, Miltonic or otherwise, were theologically problematic: so in 1695 Samuel Morland refuses to, "in imitation of a late learned Author, try to squeeze a plausible

---

[41] Stein 1953: 23, 24 (straining the meaning of "amaze" and "terrour" in *PL* 6.646–647).

[42] Ibid. 24. One wonders whether the prevalent sense of *ejaculation* as seminal emission in late modern English (attested but not predominant in the seventeenth century; see *OED* s.v. ejaculation, *n*. senses 1 and 2) has made Milton's *jaculation* sound funny to twentieth- and twenty-first-century readers, even if that was not the case for Milton and his contemporaries.

[43] King 1608: 20, cited in *OED* s.v. jaculation, *n*.

[44] Broadbent 1972: 137 asks: "If 'jaculation dire' is meant to impress, doesn't it rather oppress us with fatiguing lexicography?" But to an educated early modern reader, for whom Latinity was almost as natural as it was for the Romans, *jaculation* (from the common verb *iacere*, "to throw") would have been regarded as a rare but wholly natural Anglicization, indeed one suitable to epic decorum, not a demand for dictionary-diving. On Milton's Latinisms see Hale 1997b: 105–20, who observes that generally "Latinisms conduce to a continual varying *gravitas*" (119).

Description of LOST PARADISE, out of St. *John*'s Vision in the Isle of *Patmos*, and fancy to my self a formal and pitch Battle," while in 1698 Charles Leslie complains of the "Adventurous Flight of *Poets*, who have Dress'd *Angels* in *Armor*, and put *Swords* and *Guns* into their Hands, to Form *Romantick Battles* in the *Plains* of *Heaven*, a *Scene* of Licentious *Fancy*."[45] In general, however, "early readers agreed that Books 1, 2, and 6 were the most noble of *Paradise Lost*," as Leslie Moore writes, and "they were equally certain that Book 6 surpassed all others in sublimity."[46] Samuel Barrow, the "S.B. M.D." whose Latin verse tribute to *Paradise Lost* was included in the 1674 edition, praised "the sublime poetry of the great Milton" (*grandia magni/Carmina Miltoni*) particularly for its depiction of "heaven in conflict" (*in certamine Coelum*), including the hurling of "mountains like missiles" (*Montes ceu Tela*) and the threat that heaven might "not survive its battles" (*pugnae non superesse suae*).[47] Commenting on the line "Hurl'd to and fro with jaculation dire" (*PL* 6.665), Peter Hume in his 1695 *Annotations* acclaimed the scene as "a Nobler *Idea* of the Warring Angels, than any of the Poets have given us, of the *Gigantic* Invasion of Heaven by the *Titans*, they endeavour'd to make their *Scalado*, by heaping the Mountains one upon another."[48] John Dennis, writing in 1696, affirms that "the most delightfull and most admirable Part of the sublimest of all our Poets, is that which relates the Rebellion and Fall of these Evil Angels."[49] And Joseph Addison, who declared that Milton's "distinguishing excellence, lies in the sublimity of his thoughts," devotes his March 22, 1712 *Spectator* essay to explicating the sublimity of Book 6, highlighting especially the scene of Homeric mountain-throwing.[50] Though not determinative, the cumulative testimony of these close readers of *Paradise Lost*, contemporary or near-contemporary, should give pause to anyone who thinks that Milton was simply making a mockery of the epic tradition. But the best argument that Milton was aiming at sublimity in Book 6 of the poem is simply that all of the aspects of the war in heaven considered thus far do have clear parallels in Longinus, just as Addison says. In writing the war in heaven, the evidence suggests, Milton adapted the traditional epic scenario of theomachy, and he did so in a specifically Longinian manner emphasizing the episode's sublimity. In this, moreover, Milton, with what Marvell calls his "Theme sublime," even surpassed the sublimity of the ancients: as Barrow concludes his dedicatory verses to *Paradise Lost*, "Whoever

---

[45] Morland 1695: 13; Leslie 1698: sig. A2r. Le Comte 1982: 180 notes that these were "two theological writers, who had a battle-axe to grind."

[46] Moore 1990: 109 (see also passim); see also von Maltzahn 2001.

[47] Lewalski 2007: 5. Lieb 1985: 75 notes that the emphasis on the war in heaven (which in fact takes up around half of Barrow's poem) "demonstrates the extent to which Milton's earliest readers were inclined to single out the War in Heaven as an event of paramount importance."

[48] Hume 1695: 206.   [49] Dennis 1696: 129; see also Dennis 1721: 1–20.

[50] Addison 1970: 72, 122–9.

reads this will think Homer sang only of frogs, Vergil of gnats" (*Haec quicunque leget tantum cecinesse putabit/Maeonidem ranas, Virgilium culices*).[51]

Now this is not to say that the war in heaven is devoid of comedy entirely. While the combat of the angels on the whole is a scene of sublime violence, illustrating by grandeur the divine power of the combatants, its sublimity is not diminished for being interspersed with points of humor, though manifestly not the humor of slapstick or farce. Gloating over their success with artillery, Satan and Belial pun on their enemies' predicament in "gamesom mood" (*PL* 6.620), though their ridicule is as serious as it is fun: their words are, as Satan admits, spoken "in derision" (*PL* 6.608), a mockery born of disdain.[52] But the chief object of mockery is of course Satan, as the Son indicates near the end of the preceding book: in words recalling the Psalmist's verse "Hee that sitteth in the heauens shal laugh: the Lord shall haue them in derision" (Ps. 2:4 KJV), the Son responds "Mightie Father, thou thy foes / Justly hast in derision, and secure / Laugh'st at thir vain desinges and tumults vain" (*PL* 5.735–737).[53] Such mockery is apparent in the wounding of Satan by Michael's sword:

> then *Satan* first knew pain,
> And writh'd him to and fro convolv'd; so sore
> The griding sword with discontinuous wound
> Pass'd through him, but th' Ethereal substance clos'd
> Not long divisible, and from the gash
> A stream of Nectarous humor issuing flow'd
> Sanguin, such as Celestial Spirits may bleed
>
> (*PL* 6.330–331)

The immediate healing of the wound was fodder for Alexander Pope in *The Rape of the Lock*, in which a sylph guarding Belinda is snipped "in twain" (3.151), only for the cut to seal spontaneously: "(But Airy Substance soon unites again)" (3.152).[54] But as Addison noted, Milton's passage "is in imitation of Homer," whose gods also heal and bleed ichor.[55] John Leonard, questioning the degree to which Pope's humor is "at Milton's expense," has recently drawn attention to Pope's comment on the line "Such Stream as issues from a wounded God" in his popular translation of the *Iliad*.[56] Leonard is interested in the fact that Pope seems to write approvingly of Milton's imitation of Homer with regard to

---

[51] Lewalski 2007: 6. Barrow alludes here to the *Batrachomyomachia* and the *Culex*, poems spuriously attributed to Homer and Vergil, respectively.

[52] For the puns see *PL* 6.558–567, 6.609–627 passim. On classical and Renaissance notions of laughter as derisive see Skinner 2002: III 142–76.

[53] On the Psalms parallel see Gilbert 1942: 20.

[54] Pope 1938–68: II 130. On the adaptation of Milton's sublime epic to mock-heroic ends see Welch 2016.

[55] Addison 1970: 127; see Leonard 2013: 273.   [56] Leonard 2016b: 459.

"Angels in the Christian System, when *Satan* is wounded by *Michael*," but more pertinent to my concerns is the very beginning of Pope's note: "This is one of those Passages in *Homer* which have given occasion to that famous Censure of *Tully* and *Longinus, That he makes Gods of his Heroes, and Mortals of his Gods.*"[57] Pope is referring to Longinus' treatment of Homeric theomachy: just after the passage quoted at the beginning of this section, in which he praises the laying bare of Tartarus and the vision of universal ruin, Longinus objects to the gods' "wounds" (τραύματα, Long. *Subl.* 9.7) as detracting from their divine sublimity. Satan's wound may mend on its own—a tenet Milton might have derived from, among other places, the Byzantine demonology of Michael Psellos—but the fact that he can be physically injured at all is a painful humiliation, an experience unknown to God's partisans, impervious to any blow, who can, at most, simply be moved ("unobnoxious to be pain'd / By wound, though from thir place by violence mov'd," *PL* 6.404-405).[58] Longinus, then, may well provide the model not only for the sublime battle itself but also for the bathetic injury that punctures Satan's pretension to godhood.

"High in the midst exalted as a God," Satan affects divine sublimity, riding "his Sun-bright Chariot" as an "Idol of Majesty Divine" (*PL* 6.99-101). But on the third day he and his horde are routed by true majesty divine: the Messiah, in the fiery chariot of Ezekiel, "on the wings of Cherub rode sublime" (*PL* 6.771), and "under his burning Wheeles / The stedfast Empyrean shook throughout, / All but the Throne it self of God" (*PL* 6.832-834), leaving Satan's forces "astonisht" (*PL* 6.838), thunderstruck.[59] The sublime theomachy of the war in heaven stresses the power of the godlike angels, but the Son's sublime theophany at its conclusion reminds us that their power is nothing compared to the omnipotence of God. Which brings us, finally, to Milton's sublime conception of the deity.

Milton's Sublime God

For John Colet, the humanist who founded Milton's alma mater, St Paul's School, the hexameral narrative of Creation in Genesis, accommodated to the understanding of the masses, constituted a degraded explanation of "the most sublime knowledge of Moses about God and about divine things and the creation of the world" (*Moysis altissima sapiencia de deo deque divinis rebus creationeque mundi*).[60] The story told in Genesis was a vulgarization of sublime theological truth. As Colet wrote: "all things of God, when they are handed down to humans,

---

[57] Pope 1938-68: VII 287.
[58] On Psellos as a source West 1955: 146-7 as well as Fowler 2007 ad loc. Stein 1953: 22 rightly noted that the wound "renders him physically ridiculous."
[59] On the Son in Book 6 see esp. Revard 1980: 235-63.
[60] Cambridge, Parker Library, MS 355, p. 226. An English translation is available, together with a Latin text, in Colet 1876: 3-28, 165-82.

degenerate from their sublimity" (*omnia dei quum hominibus tradantur a sua sublimitate degenerent*).[61]

Milton, too, acknowledges that Genesis does not provide a literal depiction of the act of Creation but instead a narrative accommodated to its audience. In reality the Creation did not take place over the course of six days, but instantaneously: "Immediate are the Acts of God, more swift / Then time or motion, but to human ears / Cannot without process of speech be told" (*PL* 7.176–178). Yet for Milton, as these verses suggest, biblical accommodation is not so much social—speaking to the masses, as Colet understands it—as it is epistemological, speaking to the limited comprehension of the human mind.[62] Milton therefore takes a higher view of the Genesis narrative *qua* narrative, in line with his general position, articulated in *De Doctrina Christiana*, that the manner in which God represents himself in the Bible is the manner in which he wishes to be understood by humanity.[63] That is why Raphael's hexameral account in Book 7 follows the text of Genesis so closely, reassembling and amplifying the Hebrew original in English verse.[64] Even in translation the Mosaic notion of the divine is conspicuous, such that the pagan Longinus could recognize the sublimity of Genesis even as he read it in the Greek Septuagint, for as Daniel Chamier observed: "Majesty does not depend on words, but on the things themselves" (*Maiestas non pendet a vocabulis, sed a rebus ipsis*).[65] Just after his judgment of the wounds suffered by the gods in the *Iliad*, Longinus affirms that the sublimity of Homeric theomachy is far surpassed by that of the account of the Creation in Genesis because the latter is among "those passages that represent divinity as it really is, something immaculate [*achranton*] and great [*mega*] and absolute [*akraton*]" (τὰ ὅσα ἄχραντόν τι καὶ μέγα τὸ δαιμόνιον ὡς ἀληθῶς καὶ ἄκρατον παρίστησιν, Long. *Subl*. 9.8). What Longinus found so sublime about the *fiat lux* of Genesis 1:3 in particular was that it properly showed "the power of God" (τὴν τοῦ θείου δύναμιν, Long. *Subl*. 9.9). When Milton reconstructs the biblical verse in the lines "Let ther be Light, said God, and forthwith Light / Ethereal, first of things, quintessence pure / Sprung from the Deep" (*PL* 7.243–245), he implicitly endorses the Genesis narrative not only as an exemplum of sublime rhetoric, as discussed earlier, but also as a faithful depiction of the nature of God's power. Such is the sublime telling of the Creation which Adam, with a suggestion of the Lucretian *horror ac voluptas*, declares he has "heard / With wonder, but delight" (*PL* 8.10–11).

Colet attends directly to the problem of representing divine sublimity in a treatise on the theology of Pseudo-Dionysius the Areopagite in which he states that writers of sacred literature like John were possessed of a sublime knowledge

---

[61] Cambridge, Parker Library, MS 355, p. 226.
[62] This distinction with regard to Milton was first offered by MacCallum 1962 (with reference to Colet at 402).
[63] See *CW* 8.1: 28–33 and below.   [64] See Häublein 1975 and Chapter 2 above.
[65] Chamier 1626–30: I 389.

of God that can only be shadowed (*adumbravit*) in Scripture: "The sublimity of John's mind has so shadowed by its figures that which he perceived in that kind, that almost no one besides himself understands unless he is roused by the same prophetic spirit" (*Sublimitas mentis Iohannis quod in illo genere cernebat ita adumbravit suis figuris, ut nemo fere intelligat nisi ipse nisi eodem prophetali spiritu agitetur*).[66] The apophatic theology of Dionysius encouraged negation as a means of figuring the "unknown god" (*agnōstos theos*) of whom Paul preached on the Athenian Areopagus in Acts 17, when he converted the Dionysius from whom the theologian takes his pseudonym. So alluding to the "inaccessible light" (*phōs aprositon*) of 1 Timothy 6:16, Dionysius writes: "The divine darkness is the 'inaccessible [*aprositon*] light' in which God is said to dwell, which is invisible [*aoratō*] due to the excessive brightness [*tēn huperechousan phanotēta*] and inaccessible [*aprositō*] due to the excess [*huperbolēn*] of the supersubstantial [*huperousiou*] flood of light" (Ὁ θεῖος γνόφος ἐστὶ τὸ «ἀπρόσιτον φῶς», ἐν ᾧ κατοικεῖν ὁ θεὸς λέγεται, καὶ ἀοράτῳ γε ὄντι διὰ τὴν ὑπερέχουσαν φανότητα καὶ ἀπροσίτῳ τῷ αὐτῷ δι' ὑπερβολὴν ὑπερουσίου φωτοχυσίας, *Ep.* 5 1073A). The alpha privatives of *aoratos* and *aprositos* define God by negation as that which is not visible (*a-* + *oratos*) nor approachable (*a-* + *prositos*), but the *huper-*terms *huperechō* ("exceed"), *huperbolē* ("overthrowing"), and *huperousios* ("over-being") simultaneously emphasize the hyperbolic excess that is the mark of divine sublimity (*hupsos*).[67]

Scholars such as N. K. Sugimura and Paul Cefalu have highlighted Milton's affinities with the specifically negative or apophatic approach to accommodation promoted by Dionysius,[68] which are perhaps nowhere more evident than in the very similar Dionysian figuration of the deity in the angelic hymn of Book 3:

> Fountain of Light, thy self invisible
> Amidst the glorious brightness where thou sit'st
> Thron'd inaccessible, but when thou shad'st
> The full blaze of thy beams, and through a cloud
> Drawn round about thee like a radiant Shrine,
> Dark with excessive bright thy skirts appear,
> Yet dazle Heav'n, that brightest Seraphim
> Approach not, but with both wings veil thir eyes.
>
> (*PL* 3.375–382)

Others have gestured to Dionysius as a source for this passage, but it has not been stressed just how close Milton's word choice is to the Greek: "invisible" (*aoratos*),

---

[66] Colet 2013: 130. Though unspecified, the mention of John, then generally considered the author of both the eponymous Gospel and Revelation, almost certainly refers to the latter, given the emphasis on obscure "figures" (*figuris*).

[67] Stang 2012: 122 observes that "Dionysius instructs the reader how best to understand these privatives: not as signifying lack but rather superabundance."

[68] Sugimura 2009: 196–230 and Cefalu 2016 (with reference to Colet at 215–16).

"inaccessible" (*aprositos*), "excessive bright" (*huperechousa phanotēs*).[69] I would note in passing that this is as good an example as any of the Hellenism of Milton's language, which was well known to early generations of readers but is too often forgotten today: Benjamin Stillingfleet, for instance, commenting on *Paradise Lost* in the 1740s, wrote that "Milton's Diction is formed on the Gr. Language."[70] Here the unseen God is decorously adumbrated ("shad'st") by the blinding light and clouds that surround him in a sort of chiaroscuro effect, offering a representation of the deity as, in Longinian terms, "immaculate" (*achrantos*), "great" (*megas*), and "absolute" (*akratos*, Long. *Subl.* 9.8). Milton's God is presented as a *Deus absconditus* whose sublime Dionysian excess ("Dark with excessive bright") and incomprehensibility ("Thron'd inaccessible") puts him beyond all human reach, indeed beyond even seraphic vision.[71] C. S. Lewis, though wishing that Milton had exercised "more poetical prudence" and made his God "sufficiently awful, mysterious, and vague," nevertheless had to admit that this particular passage silences any such "theological scruples."[72]

Milton's God, as the mention of Lewis may prompt one to recall, has long been a subject of critical controversy.[73] On the level of language, God's speech has sometimes been impugned as colorless, but this might perhaps be better understood instead, as I have suggested earlier, as a mode of biblical sublimity, or what Milton elsewhere calls a "majestic unaffected stile" (*PR* 4.359). The more serious issue, however, is of course theological. Lewis famously declared, with some justice: "Many of those who say they dislike Milton's God only mean that they dislike God: infinite sovereignty *de jure*, combined with infinite power *de facto*, and love which, by its very nature, includes wrath also—it is not only in poetry that these things offend."[74] As Blair Worden has put it more recently, with reference to a *locus classicus* of the debate: "Ever since William Empson went to school at Winchester and decided that the God that he met in the classroom there was 'very wicked', the failure of the Old Testament deity to accommodate himself to the moral requirements of twentieth-century liberal agnosticism has been a problem to Milton's readers."[75] Lewis's emphasis on wrath in particular is penetrating, for it is perhaps above all else the hatred and anger of the deity, his *odium* and *ira*, that has provoked so much revulsion among God's detractors.

Universal *agapē*-love, the sublimity of the Creation—these are easy enough to adore. On the other side is that which Belial calls God's "red right hand"

---

[69] Hunter et al. 1971: 93–4; see also Lieb 1981: 204–6, though he does not cite the particular passage of Dionysius quoted above. Milton surely also had in mind 1 Tim. 6:16 itself, which he cites in *De Doctrina* (*CW* 8.1: 26).
[70] BL shelfmark C.134.h.1, interleaved page facing sig. B4r, on which see Adlington 2015. The notes in this volume seem to represent only a partial transcription of Stillingfleet's notes, as discussed by Sugimura 2021. On Milton's Greek see also Hale 2016a.
[71] On Milton's God as *Deus absconditus* see Lieb 2006 passim.   [72] Lewis 1943: 126.
[73] For an overview of the critical tradition see Leonard 2013: II 477–525.   [74] Lewis 1943: 126.
[75] Worden 1991: 240, though of course distaste for Milton's God goes back a good deal further than Empson. The reference is to Empson 1965: 10 ("I think the traditional God of Christianity very wicked, and have done since I was at school, where nearly all my little playmates thought the same").

(*PL* 2.174), a phrase which, like the "brute Earth" made to "shake" (*Maske* 798) in Milton's Ludlow masque, recapitulates a Horatian image of Jovian violence: "striking the sacred citadels with his red right hand he terrified the city" (*rubente/dextera sacras iaculatus arcis/terruit urbem*, Hor. *Carm.* 1.2.2–4).[76] God refers to himself as "Th' incensed Deitie" (*PL* 3.187) whom the sinful must appease, an expression that mimics George Chapman's paraphrase of the Homeric "wrath of the gods" (θεῶν μήνιμα, *Od.* 11.73) in his *Odysses*.[77] If, as Milton proposes in the proem of Book 9, the subject of his epic is "Not less but more Heroic than the wrauth / Of stern *Achilles*" (*PL* 9.14), "or rage / Of Turnus" (*PL* 9.16–17), "Or *Neptun*'s ire or *Juno*'s" (*PL* 9.18), then it is God's "Anger and just rebuke" (*PL* 9.10), as an inevitable reaction to creaturely disobedience, that constitutes Milton's greater argument.[78] At the outset of the war in heaven Milton's God of wrath assumes the sublime appearance of the aniconic deity encountered by Moses at Sinai in Exodus 19:16–19,[79] whose theophany on the mountain is accompanied by volcanic smoke and fire:

> So spake the Sovran voice, and Clouds began
> To darken all the Hill, and smoak to rowl
> In duskie wreathes, reluctant flames, the signe
> Of wrauth awak't: nor with less dread the loud
> Ethereal Trumpet from on high gan blow
>
> (*PL* 6.56–60)

This is the wrath made manifest through God's agent, the Son, who, telling the Father "whom thou hat'st, I hate, and can put on / Thy terrors" (*PL* 6.734–735), drives the rebellious angels into the Tartarean abyss: mounting his sublime chariot, the Son "into terrour chang'd / His count'nance too severe to be beheld / And full of wrauth bent on his Enemies" (*PL* 6.824–826); in his pursuit, "Eternal wrauth / Burnt after them to the bottomless pit" (*PL* 6.865–866).[80]

With this scene in mind Neil Forsyth suggests that "the problem for many readers is that, in spite of the claims in the invocation to Book 9, their wrath [i.e. the Son's and God's] is not different from that of their predecessors," concluding that wrath as a theme of classical epic "genuinely contaminates" Milton's poem.[81] On this point Forsyth quotes approvingly the sentiment of Sin, who disdainfully speaks of "his wrath, which he calls Justice" (*PL* 2.733). But one must be careful not to give too much credit to that which comes from the mouth of Sin. *Pace* Forsyth, the comparison of Milton's matter to that of classical epic in the proem of

---

[76] First noted, I believe, by Bentley 1732 ad loc., who with his customary textual-critical abandon inferred that, "being spoken of *Vengeance*, it must be HER *right hand*."
[77] Chapman 1614: 162.   [78] See Flannagan 1998: 584 n.13.   [79] See Murrin 1980: 156–7.
[80] On *odium Dei* in *PL* see Lieb 2006: 163–83.   [81] Forsyth 2003: 214.

Book 9 does not contaminate so much as it elevates: set beside the selfish and capricious furies of the pagan gods and heroes, the wrath of Milton's God can only appear transcendently superior, a truly "just rebuke" (*PL* 9.10) for ill doings. When Milton actually portrays his God of wrath, it is as the "Sovran voice" (*PL* 6.56) wreathed with smoke and flame at Sinai: the model is not classical epic but the description in Exodus. The author of the Pentateuch, as Longinus recognized, knew well how to represent "the power of God" ($\tau\grave{\eta}\nu$ $\tau o\hat{v}$ $\theta\epsilon\acute{\iota}ov$ $\delta\acute{v}\nu\alpha\mu\iota\nu$, Long. *Subl.* 9.9), and Milton's Mosaic depiction of the God of wrath represents in a biblically sanctioned mode the sublime power of the deity.

Forsyth seems to imply that God's hatred is proof enough of wickedness: one may detect a certain animus in the tone of his conclusion that, while hatred may be Satan's, "it is also both Milton's God's and the Christian's."[82] But to conflate pagan and Christian wrath, demonic and divine hatred, as Forsyth does, obscures real differences. Who could really confuse the *mēnis* of Achilles with the wrath of Milton's God?[83] Hatred, in itself, is not evil. Not for Milton, at least. Milton the man, by the evidence of his polemical prose, does not come across as one wholeheartedly averse to the hatred of an enemy.[84] More importantly, Milton did not think it indecorous to imagine God experiencing such a passion. While most theologians, going back to the early church, taught that God does not have emotions, others asserted the contrary: Lactantius, for one, argued this point in *De ira Dei*, a work that Milton cites in his commonplace book.[85] In *De Doctrina Christiana* Milton rejects *anthropopatheia*, or the ascription of specifically human emotions to divinity, as such, but nevertheless maintains that we should conceive of the deity as Scripture dictates: "It is safest for us to understand God with our mind just as he exhibits himself and describes himself in sacred letters" (*Nobis tutissimum est, talem nostro animo comprehendere Deum, qualem in sacris literis ipse se exhibet, seque describit*, *CW* 8.1: 28).[86] Milton's God may at times be hateful, wrathful, violent, distant, terrible, but then so too is the deity who appears in the Old Testament, in which text "the majesty of God" (*Dei maiestatem*, *CW* 8.1: 30) is justly represented. The wrath of Milton's God, then, should not be seen as a moral-theological blemish but rather as a manifestation of his all-powerful and ultimately incomprehensible sublimity.

As Milton's most explicit and extensive opinions on the nature of God are to be found in his systematic theology, my examination of divine sublimity can

---

[82] Ibid. 216.
[83] This is of course not to deny the force of classical models of wrath in the poem, on which see, in addition to ibid. 188–216, Kilgour 2008.
[84] See Loewenstein 1990: 20–5, who remarks: "The wrath of God in history finds its counterpart in the wrath of the militant polemicist" (21).
[85] *CW* 11: 113–14. On Lactantius and Milton see Hartwell 1929.
[86] On Milton's conception of God's passibility see esp. Lieb 2006: 127–62.

hardly neglect *De Doctrina Christiana*.[87] I turn to this work not as an interpretive key to the poetry but rather as an index of Milton's enduring conception of the deity, which is my primary concern here.[88] Something like half of the entire text of *De Doctrina* consists of strings of biblical proof texts, and Milton's choices in this respect can reveal certain emphases in his theological thought.[89] That he twice cites Ephesians 3:18 on the "profundity and sublimity" (*profunditas et sublimitas*, CW 8.2: 610, 650) of divine love, quoting Theodore Beza's Latin translation of the Greek *bathos kai hupsos*, marks sublimity as a quality to be associated with God.[90] Indeed, in approaching controversial issues of theology, it is the very sublimity of the subject that so concentrates Milton's mind on Scripture. The most heterodox position expressed in *De Doctrina* is surely antitrinitarianism, or the rejection of the doctrine of the Trinity, for which heresy the Spanish polymath Michael Servetus was infamously burnt at the stake in 1553.[91] When Milton argues against the Trinity he recognizes that he is dealing with a "sublime" (*sublimis*) matter before which human reason fails, writing of the relationship of the Father and the Son that "in a matter so

---

[87] The manuscript of *De Doctrina*, National Archives, SP 9/61, was discovered in 1823 at the Old State Paper Office in Whitehall together with transcriptions of Milton's State Papers. Charles Sumner, then the royal librarian, at the behest of George IV prepared an edition and translation into English (Sumner 1825); on the editorial tradition see Hale 2010. With the noteworthy early exception of Burgess 1829 (on which see Hunter 1993; Hill 1994; and Moshenska 2013), the authorship of the treatise was taken for granted until 1991, when William Hunter challenged this consensus largely upon the basis of supposed theological inconsistencies between De Doctrina and Milton's other works. See Hunter 1992, with responses by Barbara Lewalski and John Shawcross and a short reply from Hunter in Lewalski et al. 1992. Hunter turned to Bishop Burgess for support in Hunter 1993 and further developed his argument in Hunter 1998. Other forays into the controversy published around this time include Kelley 1994 and Hill 1994, with the response of Hunter 1994 in the same issue. In response to this challenge and the debate it engendered Thomas Corns instigated a collaborative research effort with Gordon Campbell, John Hale, David Holmes, and Fiona Tweedie to study the manuscript itself as well as its provenance, style, and theology, the results of which supported the traditional assumption of Milton's authorship; see Campbell et al. 1997 and esp. Campbell et al. 2007. It should be noted that skepticism about Milton's authorship, though (now as ever) a minority view, continues, as demonstrated by a roundtable led by Hugh Wilson and James Clawson at the Twelfth International Milton Symposium at the University of Strasbourg in June 2019. For a different perspective on the debate, which nevertheless affirms Milton's authorial role, see Kerr 2015.

[88] Kelley 1941, notably, offered an important and useful study of *De Doctrina* as a "gloss" upon *PL*, but on the limits of this approach, as well as the problems of reading *De Doctrina* in relation to the poetry more generally, see Lieb 2009. On *De Doctrina* in its own right see also Lieb 2006 passim as well as more recently Hale 2019.

[89] On biblical citations in *De Doctrina* see Hale 2019: 27–37 as well as Milton's own statement at CW 8.1: 8.

[90] On the biblical translations of which Milton made use in *De Doctrina* see CW 8.1: xlvii–li. Beza here follows Erasmus 1535: 602, who features a short comment on the Vulgate translation *Sublimitas & profundum*, based on the alternative Greek word order *hupsos kai bathos*; see Erasmus 2004: 519.

[91] On Milton's antitrinitarianism generally see esp. Bauman 1987; Rumrich 1998; Lieb 2006: 213–78; Dzelzainis 2007; on the relevant chapter of *De Doctrina* see also Hale 2019: 103–13. For the view that Milton subscribed to "subordinationism," rather than antitrinitarianism proper, see Hunter et al. 1971. From Burgess 1829 to Hunter 1992, controversy over Milton's understanding of the Son has intersected with the authorship debate concerning *De Doctrina*.

sublime and set beyond reason, in the very elements of faith and as it were in its primary postulates, faith can rely on the word of God alone, and that most clear and distinct, not on reason alone" (*in re tam sublimi supraque rationem posita, in ipsis fidei elementis et quasi primis postulatis, solo Dei verbo, eoque clarissimo ac disertissimo, non sola ratione, fides niti potest*, *CW* 8.1: 148). The Reformation principle of *sola scriptura* stands for Milton as the only available resort to approach a sublime God who lies beyond human comprehension.

Milton elaborates on his conception of the sublimity of God in the second chapter of *De Doctrina*, entitled *De Deo*. Here Milton adduces the Pauline passage that inspired his verses on God dwelling in inaccessible light ("Amidst the glorious brightness where thou sit'st / Thron'd inaccessible," *PL* 3.376–377) as testimony to the sublime remoteness of the deity: "God, as he is in himself, far exceeds human thought, much less perception: 1 Tim. 6:16 *dwelling in inaccessible light*" (*Deus, prout in se est humanam cogitationem, nedum sensus longè superat: 1. Tim. 6. 16. lucem habitans inaccessam*, *CW* 8.1: 26). At another point in *De Deo* God's Hebrew epithets suggest his sublime power: *Elion* signifies "most high," or what the Septuagint renders with the Greek *hupsistos*, while *Shaddai*, which Milton glosses as "literally sufficing" (*ad verbum sufficiens*, *CW* 8.1: 38), relates, according to a possible etymology which would not have been missed by the Hebraist Milton, to the root verb *shadad* ("to violently destroy"), implying a sense of *El Shaddai* as "God the Destroyer."[92] The final theme to which Milton turns in the chapter concerns, again, the distance and unreachability of the sublime deity. Calling attention to the Mosaic passage that lies behind his verses on the "Sovran voice" (*PL* 6.56) wreathed with smoke and flame, Milton offers the theophany at Sinai as the image that best intimates the nature of God in its obscurity: "Of this divine glory, as much as mortals can grasp it, there exists some description: Exodus 19:18 etc. *Mount Sinai was smoking*" (*Huius divinae gloriae quantum capere mortales possunt, extat aliqua descriptio, Exod. 19. 18. &c.* mons Sinai fumabat, *CW* 8.1: 46). Milton concludes his chapter with an emphasis on the sublime grandeur, wonder, and incomprehensibility of the deity: "Therefore finally he should be called by us wonderful and incomprehensible: Judg. 13:18 *Why do you ask about my name, since it is wondrous?* Ps. 145:3 *His grandeur cannot be fully examined.* Isa. 40:28 *There is no full accounting of his knowledge*" (*Unde nobis denique mirabilis & incomprehensibilis dicendus est: Iud. 13. 18.* quid rogitas de nomine meo, cum sit mirificum? *Psal. 145. 3.* magnitudinis eius non est pervestigatio. *Esa. 40. 28.* nulla est pervestigatio prudentiae eius, *CW* 8.1: 46).

---

[92] See Toorn et al. 1999 s.v. elyon, s.v. hypsistos, and s.v. shadday. The gloss on *Shaddai* seems to come from Tremellius, as noted in *CW* 8.1: 39 n.xiii. On Milton's Hebrew see Miller 1984 as well as Hale 1997b passim.

Timor Dei and Timor Idololatricus

In all his power and unknowability, Milton's God inspires fear of his wrath, a sublime dread that one might even be erased from existence: so Abdiel warns Satan that, when God's "wrauth / Impendent" (*PL* 5.890–891) ensues, then "who can uncreate thee thou shalt know" (*PL* 5.895), while the Son, accepting the mission of executing the Father's wrath, professes to "put on / Thy terrors" (*PL* 6.734–735).[93] The terror of divine wrath might even be said to lie at the foundation of Abrahamic religion, given that the earliest Hebrew expression for religion means simply *fear of God*.[94] In *De Doctrina*, as Michael Lieb has stressed, Milton establishes *timor Dei* as an integral part of the worship (*cultus*) of the deity: "Fear of God is that by which we revere God as supreme father of all and judge and supremely fear offending him" (*Timor Dei est quo Deum sicut summum patrem omnium et iudicem reveremur, eiusque offensionem summe timemus*, CW 8.2: 952).[95] Even the semantics of the verb *reveremur* suggest the close association between worship of God and divine terror: the word means at once revere and reverence, stand in awe of, fear.[96] This is among those many places in the text where Milton has appropriated the words of Johannes Wollebius.[97] Wollebius, a Swiss Calvinist theologian whom Milton accounted, according to Edward Phillips, among "the ablest of Divines," provided what one might even go so far as to call a base text for *De Doctrina* with his *Compendium Theologiae Christianae* (1626).[98] Notwithstanding major theological divergences, not least its antitrinitarianism, *De Doctrina* not only assumes much of the structure of Wollebius' *Compendium* but sometimes even adapts its wording, as here with Wollebius' definition of *timor Dei*: "Fear of God is that by which we so revere the Word and Majesty of God that we avoid offense of the so beneficent Father in any way, not so much out of dread of punishment as love of God." (*Timor Dei est quo Dei Verbum & Majestatem sic reveremur, ut offensam tam benigni Patris omnibus modis praecaveamus non tam poenae formidine, quam Dei amore*).[99] Milton's alterations, though slight, are telling. Instead of Wollebius' "beneficent Father"

---

[93] See also *PR* 3.219–220, 4.625–626. An expanded version of this section, with more on the background of *timor Dei* and *timor idololatricus*, has appeared as Vozar 2021a.

[94] See Pfeiffer 1955.

[95] Lieb 2006: 184–209, to which my discussion of this topic is deeply indebted.

[96] L&S s.v. *revereor*: "to stand in awe or fear of; to regard, respect, honor; to fear, be afraid of; to reverence, revere."

[97] Kelley 1967: 39 notes the "close verbal agreement" without further comment.

[98] Darbishire 1965: 61. On Wollebius' influence on *De Doctrina* see Sewell 1939: 35–45; Scott-Craig 1940; Kelley 1935, 1941 passim, and 1967; and most recently Hale 2014.

[99] Wollebius 1655: 251 (I cite the 1655 Oxford edition). Apropos my mentioning *fear of God* as an expression for religion generally, I would note that Wollebius ibid. clarifies: "*Fear of God* is sometimes taken for the whole worship of God, but in this place that virtue is understood which is called *filial fear*" (Timor Dei *quandoque pro toto Dei cultu sumitur: hoc vero loco ea virtus intelligitur, quae* timor filialis appellatur).

(*benigni Patris*), *De Doctrina* has the more stern "supreme father of all and judge" (*summum patrem omnium et iudicem*). Wollebius writes that "we avoid offense" (*offensam... praecaveamus*) not out of "dread of punishment" (*poenae formidine*) but out of "love of God" (*Dei amore*), while Milton states more starkly: "we supremely fear offending him" (*eiusque offensionem summe timemus*). Finally, unlike Wollebius, Milton deploys a succession of biblical verses as textual support, including those that enjoin believers to "exult with trembling" (*exultate cum tremore*, Ps. 2:11) and "prepare your own salvation with fear and trembling" (*cum timore ac tremore vestrum ipsorum salutem conficite*, Phil. 2:12). The differences are clear. Wollebius takes care to associate *timor Dei* with a benign deity and the love that he evokes; Milton prefers a theology of fear and trembling before his sublime God. His God does not only provoke but *is* dread, as Milton recognizes in the Hebrew divine name *pachad yitschaq* ("the fear of Isaac") when, citing Gen. 31: 53 "Jacob swore by the dread of his father" (*iuravit Iacob per pavorem patris sui*), he adds the gloss "that is, God" (*i.e. Deum*, CW 8.2: 1000).[100]

Milton, again following Wollebius, contrasts *timor Dei* as a proper part of Christian *cultus* with "idolatrous" (*idololatricus*, CW 8.2: 954) fear, though he does not directly define what this is. *Timor idololatricus* seems to have been a recurring theme in Reformed systematic theologies, apparently originating in the monumental *Syntagma Theologiae Christianae* (1609/1610) of the German theologian Amandus Polanus, under whom Wollebius studied, and to whose chair of Old Testament studies he eventually succeeded, at the University of Basel.[101] Polanus defines *timor idololatricus* as the kind of fear exemplified in the pagan dread of idols, as well as the Catholic veneration of the saints:

Timor idololatricus, est quum timetur ab idolis: qualis erat timor Gentilium, qui a signis caeli, a diis suis metuebat: Atqui dii Gentilium metuendi non sunt, quia non sunt. Gentiles imitantur Papani, timentes *a sanctis*, quos iratos sibi fore arbitrantur, nisi honore eo illos afficiant, quo Papa jubet: qui metuunt indignationem Petri & Pauli, quam incursuros Papa minatur eos, qui edictis ejus contraveniunt.[102]

Idolatrous fear is when there is fear on account of idols: such was the fear of the Gentiles, who feared the signs of heaven as of their gods: and the gods of the Gentiles should not be feared, because they do not exist. Papists imitate

---

[100] Lieb 2006: 195. On the divine name see Toorn et al. 1999 s.v. fear of Isaac.
[101] Polanus 1609–10: II sigg. NNNNnn4v–OOOoo1r. On Polanus see Letham 1990; on Polanus and *De Doctrina* see Hale 2019: 60–1. A dedicatory poem at the beginning of Wollebius' *Compendium* draws a line from Calvin through Polanus to Wollebius (Wollebius 1655: sig. A3r). On Polanus and Wollebius in the context of Reformation Basel see Burnett 2006 passim. *Timor idololatricus* appears also in the systematic theology of the Dutch Reformed theologian Andreas Essenius (Essenius 1665: 123, 126), whose inclusion of Catholic veneration of the saints in this category indicates that his source is Polanus, rather than Wollebius.
[102] Polanus 1609–10: II sig. OOOoo1r.

the Gentiles, being afraid *of the saints*, whom they think are angry at them unless they treat them with the honor that the Pope commands, they who fear the indignation of Peter and Paul, which the Pope threatens that those who contravene his edicts will incur.

For Wollebius, *timor idololatricus* signifies a fear of both idols and things of this world: "Idolatrous fear is that by which man fears for himself not only on account of idols, but on account of humans and the World, more than God" (*Timor idololatricus non solum is est, quo ab idolis, sed quo ab hominibus, & a Mundo magis sibi metuit homo, quam a Deo*).[103] But Milton sets the latter in a separate category, fear "of any things whatsoever except God" (*rerum quarumcunque praeter Deum*, CW 8.2: 954). In this respect Milton seems closer to Polanus, who also has a separate category for "fear of humans more than God" (*Timor hominum potius quam Dei*).[104] This would seem to suggest that Milton understands *timor idololatricus* specifically as that fear which relates to idols, an inference that finds support in his choice of 2 Kings 17:33 as a biblical example of this category: "They revered Jehovah, and they worshipped their own gods according to the custom of the nations that they had brought over there" (*Iehovam reverebantur, et deos suos colebant ex ritu gentium quas deportaverant inde*, CW 8.2: 954).

Milton's fervent opposition to various forms of idolatry—references in his extant commonplace book (*vide de Idolatria* [sic], CW 11: 218; *vide Idolatria*, CW 11: 291) indicate that his lost *Index Theologicus* included a section devoted to the topic—has attracted a good deal of scholarly attention.[105] Yet despite passing mentions by Lana Cable and Tobias Gregory it has not been widely recognized that *timor idololatricus* constitutes a distinct category in Milton's thought.[106] Chief among contemporary purveyors of idolatry, in Milton's view, were the Church of Rome and its Laudian emulators in England, and the secondary sense of *timor idololatricus* as Catholic dread of idols in Polanus echoes in the antiprelatical tracts of 1641–2, as when Milton writes of the Lord's Supper in *Of Reformation*: "that Feast of love and heavenly-admitted fellowship, the Seale of filiall grace became the Subject of horror, and glouting adoration, pageanted about, like a dreadfull Idol" (*CPW* 1: 523). But the primary sense of *timor idololatricus* as dread of pagan gods comes to the fore in *Paradise Lost*. Among the figures that appear in the epic catalogue of Book 1, which lists the "various Idols through the Heathen

---

[103] Wollebius 1655: 252. [104] Polanus 1609–10: II sig. OOOoo1r.

[105] On Milton and idolatry generally see Loewenstein 1990 passim; Cable 1995; Lewalski 2003; Shore 2012: 85–104. Campbell 1977 recognized that the organization of the *Index Theologicus* corresponds with that of Bellarmine's *Disputationes* and on this basis argued that Milton had once intended to write an anti-Bellarmine polemic. More recent scholarship, however, has cast doubt upon this assumption, noting that this type of polemical organization was a common practice in contemporary theological commonplace books; see Poole 2009: 368, Miller 2011, and Poole's appendix in *CW* 11: 83–92.

[106] Cable 1995: 202 n.21; Gregory 2010: 256 n.19.

World" (*PL* 1.375) that the fallen angels eventually came to be known as, are "*Moloch*, horrid King besmear'd with blood / Of human sacrifice" (*PL* 1.392–393), "*Chemos*, th' obscene dread of *Moabs* Sons / From *Aroar* to *Nebo*, and the wild / Of Southmost *Abarim*" (*PL* 1.406–408) and the half-fish god Dagon "dreaded through the Coast / Of *Palestine*, in *Gath* and *Ascalon* / And *Accaron* and *Gaza's* frontier bounds" (*PL* 1.464–466).[107] Here Moloch, Chemos, and Dagon are all associated with a kind of theological horror or dread that conforms with the sense of *timor idololatricus* in *De Doctrina*.[108] Dread names their worship and veneration: to be "dreaded," in the sense that Dagon is, is to be revered with fear and awe.

It has long been known that Milton's depictions of Semitic deities in the catalogue are deeply informed by his reading of John Selden's *De Diis Syris*, and the case of Chemos, also called Peor ("*Peor* his other Name," *PL* 1.412), is no exception.[109] The word *obscene*, which refers to the "lustful Orgies" (*PL* 1.415) that the Moabite god is supposed to have encouraged, comes directly from Selden's description of the "obscene practices" (*obscoenos mores*) of his cult—though Selden himself does not credit such reports, as Peter Hume notes in his comment on Milton's Chemos: "our Learned *Selden* disagrees, and not without sufficient Reason on his side, for Idolatry throughout the Old Testament is every where exprest, by going a Whoring after strange Gods."[110] Hume offers an astute observation on the phrase *th' obscene dread* with the gloss "*Dread*, for Deity; *Primus in orbe deos fecit timor* [Fear first made gods in the world]."[111] For dread is grammatically in apposition to the god: "*Chemos*, th' obscene dread of *Moabs* Sons." Chemos *is* the obscene dread, just as God is the dread of Isaac (*i.e. Deum*, CW 8.2: 1000). Milton's phrase, it will noticed, formally mimics the divine name of dread with its subjective genitive: Chemos is *the dread of Moab's sons*, as God is *the dread of Isaac*. Biblically, Chemos-Peor is most prominent in the episode of Numbers 25 in which the Moabite women seduce the men of Israel into performing idolatrous sacrifices: as Milton recounts in the catalogue, the god "entic'd / *Israel* in *Sittim* on thir march from *Nile* /To do him wanton rites, which cost them woe" (*PL* 1.412–414). Milton earlier summoned up this episode in *Of Reformation* in condemning the "horror" of revelries on the Sabbath as approved by the Laudian establishment: "Thus did the Reprobate hireling Preist *Balaam* seeke to

---

[107] On the demonic catalogue see Rosenblatt 1975; Lyle 2000; Quint 2007.

[108] On the ancient deity see Toorn et al. 1999 s.v. Chemosh. The name Chemos does not appear elsewhere in Milton's works, but for other references to Peor see *Nativity Ode* 197, *CPW* 1: 589, *WJM* 18: 233.

[109] See Selden 1617: 65–74. On Selden as Hebrew scholar see esp. Rosenblatt 2006 and 2021, with references to his influence on Milton throughout, as well as Toomer 2009 passim.

[110] Selden 1617: 70 (see also 68, 69); Hume 1695 ad loc. On this point see Rosenblatt 2006: 86–7. Achinstein 2015 has called into question just how closely Milton read his Selden, which this discrepancy could be taken to support, though there are obvious dramatic reasons for Milton to contradict his source here. On the obscenity of Milton's Chemos see also Flinker 1980 passim.

[111] Hume 1695 ad loc. The Latin expression is proverbial, but appears in this form in e.g. Stat. *Theb.* 3.661.

subdue the Israelites to *Moab*, if not by force, then by this divellish *Pollicy*, to draw them from the Sanctuary of God to the luxurious, and ribald feast of *Baal-peor*" (*CPW* 1: 589). Chemos-Peor competes with God as an alternative object of religious fear, though a patently false one. The perverse imitation of God's divine name thus marks both pagan and Judeo-Christian veneration as outwardly similar forms of theological dread, while nevertheless not confusing *timor idololatricus* with proper fear of God.

Another pagan deity of dread appears in Book 2 of *Paradise Lost*, among the retinue of personified Chaos and his consort Night: "and by them stood / *Orcus* and *Ades*, and the dreaded name / Of *Demogorgon*" (*PL* 2.963–965). In an earlier mention of Demogorgon, in the first of his Cambridge prolusions, Milton purports to have gained his knowledge about this god from "among the most ancient mythographers" (*Apud vetustissimos... Mythologiae scriptores*, *WJM* 12: 126), but in fact Demogorgon was a name unknown to the ancients.[112] It appears to have emerged from a late-antique commentary on the *Thebaid* of Statius, in which a mysterious deity summoned by Tiresias, "the supreme one of the triple world, whom it is taboo to know about" (*triplicis mundi summum quem scire nefastum*, Stat. *Theb.* 4.516), is identified by the scholiast as the demiurge or creator god of the Platonic tradition: "he means the demiurge, whose name it is not permitted to know" (*dicit deum δημιουργόν, cuius scire non licet nomen*).[113] The Greek δημιουργόν was likely transliterated into Latin script as *demiourgon*, which, corrupted, ultimately yielded the god that would be canonized in medieval and early modern mythography as Demogorgon.[114] As C. S. Lewis remarked: "This is perhaps the only time a scribal blunder underwent an apotheosis."[115]

Milton would have been familiar with references to Demogorgon in two of his favorite modern poets, Tasso and Spenser, but Harris Fletcher has argued that his principal mythographical source was Boccaccio's *Genealogia Deorum Gentilium*, which sets Demogorgon at the head of the genealogical tree of the gods.[116] It is therefore significant that Boccaccio locates the origin of Demogorgon's worship in pagan "dread" (*horrore*), which ostensibly motivated a taboo on uttering the name of this deity among the archaic Arcadians, "whether they thought it indecent for so sublime a name to come into the mouths of mortals, or perhaps feared that if

---

[112] Milton makes another reference to Demogorgon at *WJM* 12: 134.   [113] Sweeney 1997: 293.
[114] See the app. crit. in ibid. On Demogorgon in medieval and early modern mythography see Landi 1930; Quint 1975; Pade 1997.
[115] Lewis 1964: 40.
[116] Fletcher 1958. For other traces of the influence of the *Genealogia* on Milton see the comments in Hughes 1957 passim as well as Butler 2003. See also Poole 2014, who has identified Bod. shelfmark Arch. A f.145 as Milton's copy of Boccaccio's *Vita di Dante*, which is cited in his commonplace book (*CW* 11: 211–12). On Milton and mythography generally see Mulryan 1996 passim. For Demogorgon in the poets see Tasso, *Ger. Lib.* 13.10 and Spenser, *FQ* 1.5.22, 4.2.47, noted by Hume 1695 ad loc.; cf. also *FQ* 1.1.43.

named he would bring his wrath upon them" (*seu existimantes indecens esse tam sublime nomen in buccas venire mortalium, vel forte timentes ne nominatus irritaretur in eos*).[117] The sublime name (*sublime nomen*) of the ineffable and aniconic Demogorgon can only be compared to that of the one true God, the *Deus absconditus* of fuming Sinai, the *agnōstos theos* of the Areopagus.[118] Discussing the etymology of *Demogorgon*, Boccaccio first offers the derivation "god of the earth" (*daemon + gorgon*) before considering the alternative "'terrible god,' since it is said about the true God who dwells in heaven: 'Holy and terrible is his name'" (*'deus terribilis,' quod de vero Deo qui in celis habitat legitur: 'Sanctum et terribile nomen eius'*).[119] With his quotation of Psalms 110:9, Boccaccio calls attention to the superficial resemblance between these two deities whose names are "terrible" (*terribilis*), though of course he does not fail to distinguish between them: "But God is terrible for another reason, for he is terrible in judgment on account of the integrity of his justice against those who do evil, while that one is terrible for those that ignorantly believe in him" (*Verum iste aliam ob causam terribilis est, nam ille ob integritatem iustitie male agentibus in iudicio est terribilis, iste vero stolide existimantibus*).[120] That Milton represents Demogorgon as a "dreaded name" clearly looks back to the *sublime et terribilis nomen* that he found in Boccaccio, with its evocation of pagan theological dread and its suggestion of a resemblance between Demogorgon and the Christian deity—a point that Peter Hume picks up on, without mentioning Boccaccio, in his comment that the name of Demogorgon "was concealed in imitation of that ineffable appellation of God, seldom pronounced by the Jews."[121] Milton's reference to Demogorgon may be brief, but encapsulated in it is an anthropology of pagan religion as a phenomenon based in ignorant fear.[122]

Daniel Shore has likened the catalogue of pagan gods in *Paradise Lost* to a *Götzenkammer* (literally "chamber of idols"), which preserved pre-Reformation images of the saints in some German Protestant churches, contemplation of which makes the Reformed observer—or reader, in Milton's case—joyful for having overcome sinful idolatries.[123] With regard to Chemos, dread of the Moabites, or outside the catalogue to Demogorgon's dreaded name, the specific transgression exhibited is *timor idololatricus*, understood as a perversion and diabolical imitation of the right practice of *timor Dei*. In *Samson Agonistes* the blind and captive protagonist rebukes Dalila for not being able to distinguish between the two:

---

[117] Boccaccio 2011: 34.   [118] See Solomon 2012.   [119] Boccaccio 2011: 38.
[120] Ibid.   [121] Hume 1695 ad loc.
[122] On Boccaccio's historical and anthropological perspective on pagan myth see Lummus 2012, with reference to Demogorgon passim.
[123] Shore 2012: 95, 103–4, who also dubs this an experience of the "idolatrous sublime" (86, 102–3), though the sublime here is mostly understood in a Kantian mode rather than in some sense that Milton might recognize.

> To please thy gods thou didst it; gods unable
> To acquit themselves and prosecute their foes
> But by ungodly deeds, the contradiction
> Of their own deity, Gods cannot be:
> Less therefore to be pleas'd, obey'd, or fear'd
>
> (*SA* 896–900)

Samson dismisses any pious motivation on Dalila's part because Dagon and the other pagan gods are not gods at all and therefore deserve no religious fear ("Less therefore to be [...] fear'd"). As the first Semichorus proclaims, the Philistines dread what is only an idol, rather than the true God whose name is Dread itself: "Chaunting thir Idol, and preferring / Before our living Dread who dwells / In *Silo* his bright Sanctuary" (*SA* 1662–4). The Philistines may be "jocund and sublime" (*SA* 1659), but theirs is a false sense of sublimity, the sensual elevation that comes from intoxication and the orgiastic exaltation of idols ("Drunk with Idolatry, drunk with Wine," *SA* 1660). The sublime God of the Hebrews, on the other hand, manifests his divine power through the action of his agent Samson, which he promises "with amaze shall strike all who behold" (*SA* 1635).[124] The real "horrour" (*SA* 1540), the "horrid spectacle" (*SA* 1532) that ensues, immanentizes the transcendent sublimity of the one true God whose name is Dread.

In Milton's theological thought *timor idololatricus* is exposed as the historical and psychological basis of pagan religion and to an extent of idolatry more generally, including Catholic and Laudian ritual. The Reformed should be able to perceive that this sense of religious awe and dread is misplaced which should belong to God alone, and in this they might feel superior. But there is also a sympathetic recognition that some form of theological dread lies at the heart of all religious worship, Catholic and Reformed, pagan and Christian alike. In this, if in little else, Milton could agree with a Laudian royalist like Alexander Ross, who in his work of comparative religion *Pansebeia* (1653) answers the question "*How doth it appear that Religion is the foundation of Common-wealthes, or humane societies?*" with the reply "Because Religion teacheth the fear of God," and "it was this fear that begot Religion in the world, *Primus in orbe Deos fecit timor*"— quoting the same Latin proverb that Peter Hume does in his comment on Milton's Chemos.[125] For Milton this understanding of theological dread may be not only negative, indicating the ignorant inferiority of the pagan idolator, but also positive: for while *timor idololatricus* may be a demonic reflection of *timor Dei*, in its very similarity it serves a protreptic function, reminding the Christian of the fear that is due to the sublime deity whose name is Dread.

---

[124] As Loewenstein 1990: 188 n.61 notes: "What distinguishes the God of Israel from other gods, of course, is precisely the fact that He 'only doeth wondrous things' (Psalms 72:18; cf. Psalms 86:8, 10)."

[125] Ross 1653: 519, 520. On this work see Mills 2016 and Hartmann 2018: 225–38.

Conclusion

For Milton and his contemporaries, as I hope to have demonstrated, notions of the sublime could be found in natural-philosophical and theological contexts as much as in rhetorical ones. Longinus, whom Milton may have taught to his nephews, among other rhetoricians supplied him with an ideal of *hupsos* as a model of biblical style, which nevertheless invited the charge of religious enthusiasm. Milton also seems to have meditated on the republican-inflected but ultimately ambiguous politics of the *Peri hupsous*, even going so far as to configure Satan as a sublime republican orator—a sign of potential disillusionment with the Good Old Cause that should be taken into account in future readings of *Paradise Lost*. Material sublimity, on the other hand, helped Milton to describe the indescribable otherness of his otherworldly theme through comparisons of massive scale and magnitude, inspiring what I have called his hyperbolic similes. Significantly, Milton engaged with a Longinian idea of the physically sublime through the new science, as the vistas of astronomical discovery allowed the poet to imagine the sublimities of the created universe in its immensity, and even more so Chaos in its infinitude. Finally, but no less crucially, Milton inherited from Longinus and others a sense of the sublimity of the divine, which manifests in writings ranging from the 1634 *Maske* to his late theological treatise *De Doctrina Christiana*. This bears on the interpretation of his poetry, as in the episode of the war in heaven in *Paradise Lost*, which I see as a sublime theomachy following Longinus' exegesis of Homer. But it is also relevant more generally for Milton's conception of the deity in his transcendent obscurity, in his awesome wrath, and in the terrible fear that is his due as "our living Dread" (*SA* 1663).

In the process of making this argument I have also aimed to add to an expanding body of scholarship on the diffusion and reception of the *Peri hupsous* in early modern Europe. Further evidence of the attention that Longinus attracted in England in this period is featured in the appendices that follow. The bibliographical appendix supplies a study of copies of Longinus that I have been able to trace to seventeenth-century English private libraries, documenting the dissemination of several editions, particularly Gerard Langbaine's, among various English book owners from the Elizabethan period to the Restoration. The textual appendix provides an edition of the Lansdowne Longinus, the previously unknown seventeenth-century English translation of the *Peri hupsous* that I discovered in a manuscript at the British Library. Together these additional studies offer ample testimony that texts of Longinus circulated widely and drew a diverse readership in England in the decades before the appearance of Boileau's translation.

In the introduction to this study I quoted the judgment of Leslie Moore that Milton's sublimity is "a fiction of eighteenth-century criticism."[1] The preceding chapters have attempted to contest this claim, of which Moore's statement is only the most succinct iteration. As I have argued, various notions of the sublime, Longinian and otherwise, were very much current in seventeenth-century England, and this work has suggested some of the ways that Longinian *hupsos* and other modes of sublimity left their imprint on Milton's writings and thought. If my interpretation is correct, it may resolve a certain tension that can be detected when Moore's phrase is set in its original context: "The 'sublime Milton' may well be a fiction of eighteenth-century criticism, but it functions as a near truth in literary history."[2] If Milton's sublimity really was an invention of his eighteenth-century critics, how can it still seem so *true* in a literary-historical sense? I submit that it is not an eighteenth-century invention, and that early readers such as Edward Phillips, Samuel Barrow, Andrew Marvell, and John Aubrey, as much as later ones such as John Dennis, Joseph Addison, and Jonathan Richardson, perceived in Milton's verse and prose alike a *sublimitas* that the author himself consciously fashioned. If Milton's sublimity helped guarantee his place in a nascent canon of English literature, this may be due as much to his own intentions as to the work of his critics.[3] That is to say: the "sublime Milton" is an epithet not so much bestowed as earned.

---

[1] Moore 1990: 2. [2] Ibid.
[3] On the early modern sublime and the English literary canon see esp. Cheney 2018b: 252–64. On the formation of the English canon in general see inter alia Guillory 1993, Ross 1998, and Kramnick 1999.

BIBLIOGRAPHICAL APPENDIX

Longinus in English Private Libraries to 1674

In 1657 the bookseller William London listed an octavo of Longinus among "the most vendible books in England."[1] While a merchant would have obvious commercial motives for promoting items in his stock as bestsellers, the advertisement nevertheless prompts a couple of questions. Which editions? And "vendible" to whom? For despite increasing attention to the reception of Longinus in England before Boileau's 1674 translation, the evidence of book ownership has not yet been considered.[2] This bibliographical study is intended to supply preliminary answers to these questions, drawing on the documented provenance of books now in British and American collections, on contemporary references to book ownership, and on book auction catalogues published in the 1670s and 1680s.[3] The focus here is on private libraries rather than institutional ones, though it is certainly the case that collections such as the Bodleian Library and the Sion College Library also held copies of Longinus in this period.[4] Given the limits of available sources, this study, far from being exhaustive, can only uncover a small part of the wider ownership of the various editions of Longinus which must have been circulating in the thousands in England before Boileau's translation arrived from across the Channel. That, however, should prove sufficient to show the diverse backgrounds and persuasions of those who owned copies of Longinus in this period.

At least seven different editions of Longinus, according to my research, were held in English private libraries before 1674, representing the majority of those then printed: the *editio princeps* of Francesco Robortello, printed by Johannes Oporinus in 1554; the edition of Franciscus Portus (1511–81), included after the texts of Aphthonius and Hermogenes in his 1569/70 volume of Greek rhetoricians printed by Jean Crespin, which served as the *textus receptus* until the early eighteenth century; the 1612 edition of Gabriel de Petra, which paired the Greek text with a Latin translation in parallel columns; Gerard Langbaine's edition, which featured de Petra's Greek and Latin on facing pages with Langbaine's notes at the end, first published in 1636 and reprinted in 1638 and 1650; the 1644 edition produced by the Bolognese printer Carlo Manolessi, which included de Petra's Greek and Latin texts as well as two other Latin translations; the first printed English translation, by John Hall, published in 1652; and the 1663 edition of Tanneguy Le Fèvre (1615–72), which provided a Greek text, de Petra's Latin translation, and Le Fèvre's notes.

With regard to Robortello's *editio princeps*, the only copy I have been able to place in England before 1674 is that of the famous Huguenot scholar Isaac Casaubon (1559–1614), who moved to England in October 1610 and whose library was purchased at his death by

---

[1] London 1657: sig. Gg2v, noted by Lazarus 2021.
[2] For a tabulation of references to Longinus in Dutch book sales catalogues between 1600 and 1650 see Jansen 2019: 285–6.
[3] On book trade catalogues see Munby and Coral 1977 and Myers et al. 2001.
[4] Rouse 1635: 114; Spencer 1650: 89; see Chapter 2. On private libraries in seventeenth-century England see Pearson 2012 and 2021.

James I, whence it ultimately came to the British Library.[5] The earliest edition widely circulating in England was probably that of Portus—which should not be surprising, since Robortello's edition, like that of Paulus Manutius published the following year, presents only the text of Longinus, while Portus' volume also includes Hermogenes' *Ars Rhetorica* and Aphthonius' *Progymnasmata*, both of which were popular school texts in the Elizabethan period.[6] As a matter of fact, Longinus seems to have completely escaped the attention of the first known English owner of Portus' volume, Bartholomew Dodington (1535/6–95), Regius Professor of Greek at Cambridge.[7] Dodington, who acquired his copy of Portus in 1573, removed the texts of both Aphthonius and Longinus from the book and had the text of Hermogenes interleaved for his copious annotations: clearly he was only interested in Hermogenes, then a required teaching text in the Cambridge syllabus.[8] Dodington's counterpart at Oxford, the classical scholar Sir Henry Cuffe (1562/3–1601), who was executed for his role in Essex's Rebellion, also seems to have owned a copy of Portus' edition, probably for the same reason.[9] Elizabethan readers' priorities are perhaps also suggested by the record of two copies of Portus possessed by the Cambridge-based French bookseller John Denys (d. 1578), which refers to the volume as *hermogenes Apthonius et alij Rethorici greci genevae vetus <8o>*: Hermogenes, it seems, was the principal draw for those who acquired Portus' volume, followed by Aphthonius, while Longinus does not even merit a mention.[10] Nevertheless, it was probably through Portus' edition that Longinus first attracted the attention of English readers: some, at least, of those who acquired the volume for its texts of Hermogenes and Aphthonius must have been curious about a little known Greek rhetorician whose subject was "sublimity" (*hupsos*). That much is suggested by an annotated copy of Portus with the autograph of Sir Henry Wotton (1568–1639), which features not only interlinear glossing and marginalia in the Hermogenes text but also section numbering in Greek numerals and some underlining added to the text of Longinus.[11] Another copy of Portus was owned by the Huguenot émigré Peter Cardonnel (1614–67), whose library was sold at auction in 1681.[12] For some, at least, Portus came to be valued more for containing the text of Longinus than anything else: a near mirror image of Dodington's, the copy owned by John Hacket (1592–1670),

---

[5] BL shelfmark 1088.m.2. On Casaubon see *ODNB* s.v. Casaubon, Isaac (1559–1614).
[6] See Patterson 1970 and Mack 2011 passim.
[7] On Dodington see *ODNB* s.v. Dodington, Bartholomew (1535/6–95).
[8] CUL shelfmark Adv.d.4.4, signed and dated "B. Dodingtonus 1573" on the title page; see Leedham-Green 2004: 618.
[9] BL shelfmark 1089.e.7, if I am correct in identifying the Henry Cuffe of the inscription on the title page (*Henrici Cuffi liber*); see *ODNB* s.v. Cuffe [Cuff], Henry (1562/3–1601). The manuscript annotations on Longinus in this copy cannot be Cuffe's, as they cite de Petra's 1612 edition.
[10] Leedham-Green 1986: II 29. Similarly, even a century later the auction catalogue for the library of Thomas Jessop lists the volume as *Apthonius Hermogenis &c. Graec. Porti* (Millington 1681a: 3). I have been able to definitively place no other copies of Portus in England before the end of the 16th c. besides Dodington's and the two sold by Denys. Allen 2013: 52 n.169 supposes "it would seem likely" that a volume recorded in a 1585 list of books donated to the Westminster School and Westminster Abbey libraries by William Cecil, 1st Baron Burghley as *Comentarii in Aphthonii progymnasmata cum commentariis in Hermoginis Rethorica Graece* (Burghley House, Muniments Drawer 49/5/2; see Bowden 2005) was a copy of Portus' edition. Portus' edition, however, does not contain any commentaries: the Burghley list probably refers instead to a copy of the Aldine *Rhetores Graeci* (Manutius 1508). Nevertheless, it is not improbable that some number of the books recorded simply as *Aphthonius et Hermogenes* vel sim. in Elizabethan library lists were copies of Portus' volume.
[11] Stanford UL, call number KB1570.A6; for more on this copy see Vozar 2019. On Wotton see *ODNB* s.v. Wotton, Sir Henry (1568–1639) and Thrush and Ferris 2010 s.v. Wotton, Sir Henry (1568–1639).
[12] Cooper 1681: 15. On Cardonnel see Malcolm 2002: 259–316.

Bishop of Lichfield, possibly acquired as a gift in the 1610s, has had Hermogenes and Aphthonius removed, leaving only the pages of the *Peri hypsous*.[13]

De Petra's bilingual Greek and Latin text of 1612, which was reprinted in both Langbaine (1636) and Manolessi (1644), as well as the English translation of Hall which appeared in 1652, would have made Longinus much more accessible to seventeenth-century readers. Samuel Cholmley (fl. 1647-54) of Peterhouse, Cambridge autographed his copy of Langbaine's edition in 1647.[14] So did ejected minister Richard Byfield (1598-1664) in 1649.[15] The Durdans library of Sir Robert Coke (1587-1653) contained a copy of de Petra's edition.[16] Robert Sidney, 2nd Earl of Leicester (1595-1677) had accumulated no fewer than four copies of Longinus in his Penshurst library by 1665, including copies of Langbaine's 1636 edition, its 1638 reprint, Manolessi's edition, and Hall's translation.[17] While he once lamented that he had "always wanted Language, Especially Greek," with these various translations, Latin and English, in his library Sidney's lack of confidence in his Greek need not have precluded his study and enjoyment of Longinus.[18] Besides these, five others can be named. The architect Sir Roger Pratt (1620-84) had a book by "Dionysius Cassius" bound in January 1664—probably Longinus in Langbaine's edition.[19] Sir William Godolphin (1635-96), diplomat for Charles II, probably acquired his copy of Hall's translation before leaving for Spain in 1666.[20] The Anglican clergyman and royalist David Stokes (c. 1590-1669), according to the auction of his library in 1685, owned both a Langbaine edition and a Hall translation.[21] Abiel Borfet (c. 1633-1710) inscribed his Langbaine edition in 1671, the same year he was appointed vicar of Lyminge, Kent, and added copious notes throughout.[22] And there was a copy of Langbaine in the library of John Cosin (1594-1672), Bishop of Durham.[23] Booksellers in the middle of the century ensured that Longinus kept circulating among buyers: George Thomason (c. 1602-66), two years after selling Sidney his copy of Manolessi's edition, acquired a copy of Hall's translation

---

[13] CUL shelfmark P*.14.30(F). Liam Sims (personal communication, 2018) notes that the name "Sherley" is written upside down on the front endpaper and suggests that Hacket might have received the book as a gift, perhaps from a Walshingham Sherley who was at Trinity College during Hacket's period of study there; see Venn and Venn 1922-7 s.v. Walshingham Sherley. If that is the case, Hacket's possession of this copy can be dated to the 1610s. Hacket quotes Longinus in a posthumously published work (Hacket 1692: 39), citing the page number of the Portus edition. On Hacket see Matthews 1948: 49 and *ODNB*. s.v. Hacket, John (1592-1670).

[14] Durham UL, shelfmark Bamburgh L.6.52, which according to Danielle Westerhof (personal communication, 2018) features underlining at sigg. A4v, A5r, A5v, and A6r. See Venn and Venn 1922-7 s.v. Samuel Cholmley.

[15] Yale UL, call number GfL29 b636ba. On Byfield see Matthews 1934 s.v. Byfield, Richard and *ODNB*. s.v. Byfield, Richard (bap. 1598, d. 1664).

[16] Lambeth Palace Library, shelfmark C11/AP4 02. On Coke see Thrush and Ferris 2010 s.v. Coke, Sir Robert (1587-1653).

[17] Warkentin et al. 2013: 142-3. On Sidney see *ODNB* s.v. Sidney, Robert, second earl of Leicester (1595-1677) and Thrush and Ferris 2010 s.v. Sidney, Sir Robert (1595-1677).

[18] BL Add. MS 4464, f. 1r., cited in Warkentin et al. 2013: 24.

[19] Skelton 2009: 43. On Pratt see *ODNB*. s.v. Pratt, Sir Roger (bap. 1620, d. 1685).

[20] Wadham College Library (Oxford), shelfmark unlisted. Godolphin spent most of his time abroad after 1666; see *ODNB* s.v. Godolphin, Sir William (bap. 1635, d. 1696). Sandra Bailey (personal communication, 2018) observes that the binding appears original, English rather than Spanish, and that there are no indications of earlier ownership.

[21] Cooper 1685: 20, 61. See Matthews 1948: 380 and *ODNB* s.v. Stokes, David (1590x92-1669).

[22] Bod. shelfmark 8° W 30 Med.Seld. On Borfet see Venn and Venn 1922-7 s.v. Borfett, Abiell.

[23] Durham UL, shelfmark Cosin W.5.15. On Cosin see Matthews 1948: 140 and *ODNB* s.v. Cosin, John (1595-1672).

on November 22, 1652, the month after it was published,[24] while in 1667 Thomas Rookes listed Hall's translation among the wares still available at his shop in Gresham College after the Great Fire of London.[25]

In addition to these more securely dated examples, it is reasonable to consider cases in which the evidence of book ownership or death of the owner postdates Boileau's translation by a couple of decades or so, working on the assumption that most, if not all, of the pre-1674 Longinus editions in this category were acquired before the publication of Boileau's volume. Anthony Wood (1632–95), in a catalogue of his personal library prepared in March 1680 or 1681, has an entry for "Dr Langbaynes notes on Longinus."[26] The Bodleian has copies of the 1636 and 1638 Langbaine editions featuring the inscription of the orientalist Edward Pococke (1604–91).[27] The collection of Anglican theologian Edward Stillingfleet (1635–99), which was purchased on his death by Narcissus Marsh and remains part of Marsh's Library in Dublin today, contains copies of both Hall's translation and the Le Fèvre edition.[28] Stillingfleet was aware of Longinus by 1662, for in his *Origines Sacrae*, first published that year, he writes: "The testimony of *Longinus* is sufficiently known, that Moses was no man of any vulgar wit (οὐχ ὁ τυχὼν ἀνήρ)."[29]

The last quarter of the seventeenth century also supplies the invaluable evidence of printed book auction catalogues. The first known English book auction catalogue, printed in 1676, was that of the nonconformist Lazarus Seaman (d. 1675), and Andrew Cambers has remarked on the prevalence of dissenters among those whose libraries were sold at auction in the 1670s and 1680s, noting that the English book auction probably developed in part as a means of dispersing dissenters' libraries in the absence of appropriate institutions to which they might be donated.[30] Copies of Longinus are listed in the catalogues for a number of these dissenters' libraries: among the books of Seaman, Portus; Thomas Manton (1620–77), Langbaine and Le Fèvre; Samuel Brooke (fl. 1627–76), Langbaine; Stephen Charnock (1628–80), Hall; Ralph Button (1611/12–80) and Thankful Owen (1620–81), two Langbaines and Hall; John Owen (1616–83), Langbaine; Thomas Jacomb (1622–87), Langbaine.[31] But copies of Longinus were owned by many others besides. Copies of Portus were owned by the polymath Benjamin Worsley (1618–77), and by an Edward Palmer,

---

[24] BL shelfmark E.1294.(2.), with the annotation "Nou. 22;" see Fortescue 1908: I 891. On Thomason see *ODNB* s.v. Thomason, George (c. 1602–66). Leicester's purchase of Manolessi from Thomason was recorded August 2, 1650; see Warkentin et al. 2013: 142.

[25] Rookes 1667: sig. K2v ("Dionysius Longinus of Eloquence Eng."), sig. tt2r ("Dionysius Longinus of eloquence").

[26] Bod. MS Wood E. 2(70), fol. 39, cited in Kiessling 2002: 397. Wood 1691-2: II 140 mentions the Longinus edition in his biography of Langbaine. On Wood see *ODNB* s.v. Wood, Anthony [Anthony à Wood] (1632–95).

[27] Bod. shelfmarks 8° St.Amand 152, 8° St.Amand 438; on Pococke see *ODNB* s.v. Edward Pococke (1604–91).

[28] Marsh's Library, shelfmarks unlisted.   [29] Stillingfleet 1662: 117.

[30] Cambers 2011: 131–4.

[31] Cooper 1676: 67; Cooper 1678a: 18; Cooper 1680: 20; Millington 1680a: 26 (but says "Engl. by Evelin"); Millington 1681b: 12, 15, and 12 in the separately numbered English section; Millington 1684: 30; and Millington 1687a: 42. Charnock's library is one of five considered in Pearson 2010. On these individuals see the relevant entries in Matthews 1934 and the *ODNB*. For the Brooke catalogue ESTC refers to Samuel Brooke (d. 1631), Master of Trinity College, Cambridge, but the catalogue's reference to Brooke as a former fellow of Katharine Hall, as well as its inclusion of books postdating 1631, indicate that the owner must have been the Samuel Brooke who was Bursar of Katharine Hall 1639–40, 1647–8, and 1649–50, as pointed out by Poole 2013: 179 n.49. I have taken the additional step of tentatively identifying him with both the Samuel Brooke listed in Matthews 1948: 39, one of the fellows of Katharine Hall removed for refusing the engagement in 1650, and the former fellow of Katharine Hall Samuel Brooks listed as an ejected minister in Matthews 1934 s.v. Brooks, Samuel.

Esq. (d. 1680).[32] Thomas Jessop (fl. 1659–78), vicar of Coggeshall, Essex, owned a Portus and a Langbaine.[33] James Chamberlaine (c. 1635–84), fellow of St. John's College, Cambridge and Arthur Annesley, 1st Earl of Anglesey (1614–86) each owned a Langbaine.[34] Thomas Watson (d. 1679/80), head of Charterhouse School from 1662 to 1679, owned the edition of Le Fèvre, while the library of an anonymous owner auctioned in 1686 included a copy of Hall's translation.[35] Copies of Langbaine's edition are listed in the book catalogues for a number of joint auctions, including those of ejected minister Stephen Watkins (fl. 1632–64) and physician and natural philosopher Thomas Sherley (1638–78); Robert Greville, 4th Baron Brooke (c. 1638–77), one of the six peers sent to invite the return of Charles II in 1660, and ejected minister Gabriel Sangar (1608–78); civil lawyer and parliamentarian John Godolphin (1617–78) and Owen Phillips (c. 1625–78), Under Master of Winchester College; and William Sill, prebendary of Westminster Abbey from 1681 to 1687, and a Cornelius Callow of London.[36] The "very choice Library," in Anthony Wood's words, of Edward Bysshe (c. 1610–79) apparently contained a total of four editions of Longinus: Langbaine, Manolessi, Hall, and, Le Fèvre.[37]

These can represent only a fraction of those who owned copies of Longinus before 1674. Nevertheless, some simple observations can be made. The book owners enumerated above include scholars, schoolteachers, lawyers, diplomats, members of Parliament, peers, physicians, scientists, an architect, a member of the Hartlib Circle, and Fellows of the Royal Society. Predominant, however, and perhaps not unsurprisingly, are clergymen. These include several orthodox Anglicans, including two bishops, but many dissenters. This may well be an effect of an overrepresentation of dissenters' libraries in the book auction catalogues of the 1670s and 1680s, as noted above, but it could also indicate a genuine preference: Longinus' emphasis on simple, direct, powerful language that proceeds as if divinely inspired might have been taken to accord especially well with Puritan principles of speech.

By my count, the books owned by these men include twenty-five copies of Langbaine's edition; eleven of Portus' rhetorical anthology; ten of Hall's translation; and fewer than five

---

[32] Dunmore and Chiswell, 1678: 25; Millington 1680b: 3. On Worsley see *ODNB* s.v. Worsley, Benjamin (1617/18–77) and Leng 2008. For the Palmer catalogue ESTC refers to an Oxford alumnus of this name who matriculated at Queen's College July 14, 1665 (Foster 1888–91 s.v. Edward Palmer), but it may well be another person of the same name, such as e.g. the Cambridge alumnus admitted pensioner at Peterhouse July 29, 1655 (Venn and Venn 1922–7 s.v. Edward Palmer).

[33] Millington 1681a: 3, 5; the latter lists *D. Longini Rhetorica, Gr. & Lat. (sine titulo) cum notis*, the *notae* probably identifying it as Langbaine's edition. Matthews 1934 s.v. Jessop, Thomas notes: "Calamy calls him an after-conformist, but no evidence of his nonconformity."

[34] Millington 1686: 9; Philipps 1686: 45. On Chamberlaine see Venn and Venn 1922–7 s.v. James Chamberlaine; on Annesley see *ODNB* s.v. Annesley, Arthur, first earl of Anglesey (1614–86).

[35] Millington 1680c: 12; Cooper 1686: 32. Cambers 2011: 132 includes the Watson catalogue among dissenters' libraries, presumably taking this to be the ejected minister Thomas Watson who died in 1686, on whom see Matthews 1934 s.v. Watson, Thomas and *ODNB* s.v. Watson, Thomas (d. 1686). The 1680 catalogue, however, clearly refers to the books' owner as "late Master of the *Charter-house School*," so it clearly cannot be the same Thomas Watson.

[36] Cooper 1679: 29; Ranew 1678: 34; Cooper, 1678b: 47; Millington 1687b: 9. On Watkins see Matthews 1934 s.v. Watkins, Stephen; on Sherley see *ODNB* s.v. Sherley, Thomas (bap. 1638, d. 1678); on Greville see Cokayne 1887–98: II 33; on Sangar see Matthews 1934 s.v. Sangar and *ODNB* s.v. Sangar, Gabriel (1608–78); on Godolphin see *ODNB* s.v. Godolphin, John (1617–78); on Phillips see Cook 1917: 71.

[37] Wood 1691–2: II 484; Dunmore 1680: 26, 29, 70. The copy at 26 is listed with the publication date of Langbaine's edition (1636), but the city of Manolessi's (*Bon.[oniae]*, i.e. Bologna), and it includes Cassius as part of Longinus' name, as does Manolessi's edition; I therefore understand it as Manolessi's. On Bysshe see *ODNB* s.v. Bysshe, Sir Edward (c. 1610–79).

copies, respectively, of the editions of Robortello, de Petra, Manolessi, and Le Fèvre.[38] While such a small sample severely limits the accuracy of any extrapolation, this tabulation points to a plausible relationship between the bibliography of the *Peri hypsous* and knowledge of Longinus in the period before Boileau's 1674 translation appeared. Portus' volume was probably acquired, at least at first, for the texts of Aphthonius and Hermogenes, but this was likely the first edition of Longinus circulating in England and the first place English readers encountered him. Langbaine's 1636 edition, which made the Greek text available alongside de Petra's Latin translation and his own copious notes, made Longinus appreciable by a much larger audience and probably remained the edition of choice in England throughout the half a century before Boileau, as suggested by its 1638 and 1650 reprints, but Hall's English translation attracted a fair number of readers as well. The *Peri hypsous* may not have been such a staple of the seventeenth-century English private library as, say, the Church Fathers, but as this study has shown, it was far from uncommon.

---

[38] I exclude booksellers from this count but include Dodington's Portus, despite the missing text of Longinus.

TEXTUAL APPENDIX

The Lansdowne Longinus

British Library MS Lansdowne 1045, fols. 166–172 contains an English translation of Longinus that I have tentatively dated to the middle of the seventeenth century (Figure 12, Figure 13). Below is an edited text of this work. The original spelling has been maintained, but deletions have been removed, punctuation added or changed, capitalization normalized, and section numbers standardized. For a semi-diplomatic transcription of the text, and for further information, see my article in *The Seventeenth Century*.[1]

Of Sublimity of Stile, or the Raptures of Eloquence, from Dionysius Longinus Περὶ Ὕψους, Done from the Greek in to English for the Improvement of Oratory.

1

[167r] When we jointly perused, most dear Terentian, that tract of Cecilius which he composed on this argument of sublime, you well know that we both agreed on this censure of it, that the stile was too creeping for so lofty a subject, that some of the most materiall points were passd by unobservd, and that therefore it would prove of no great advantage to the reader, which yet ought to be the cheifest aim of every one that presses toward the repute of an author. Beside for the handling of any art or science, there are two things that deserve our more especiall regard. The first is to propound and explain that subject which is to be discoursd upon. The second in order, though for dignity it meritts the praecedence, is to shew by what means and methods the art so propos'd is most readily to be acquir'd. In the latter of these Cecilius his guilty of a gross defect, for he has indeed with more of copiousness than was requisite demonstrated that there is such a thing as sublimity of speech, as if that were so much to be questioned. But then as to the instructing by what measures we might artificially come to an attainment hereof, this as if it were less pertinent he has unhappily omitted. And yet we may have so much charity as to allow that this author is not so much to be blam'd for his being in some things deficient, as to be commended for his industry and first adventure upon this subject. And now since your commands oblige me to attempt somewhat upon this same topique of sublime, let us consider what can be there upon said which may prove of advantage to such as find frequent occasion to speak in publique. But here at my entrance on this tasque I must beg leave, dear sir, to engage you that you judge and censure the performance with all the freedom and sincerity that a cordiall friendship obliges to, without being brib'd or biass'd from the naked truth. For that philosopher made an honest reply who when askt wherein we might approve our selves most like unto the gods wisely answred: in doing good and in speaking truth. And in writing to you who are so great a master of all learning I have this advantage, that I am freed from the trouble of making any taedious introduction, & shall therefore only in short advise you that by sublime I understand the highest advance and most exalted pitch of eloquence, that from whence poets and other writers have all borrowed their respective reputations, and

[1] Vozar 2020.

Figure 12 Title page of the Lansdowne Longinus, MS Lansdowne 1045, fol. 166v, © The British Library Board.

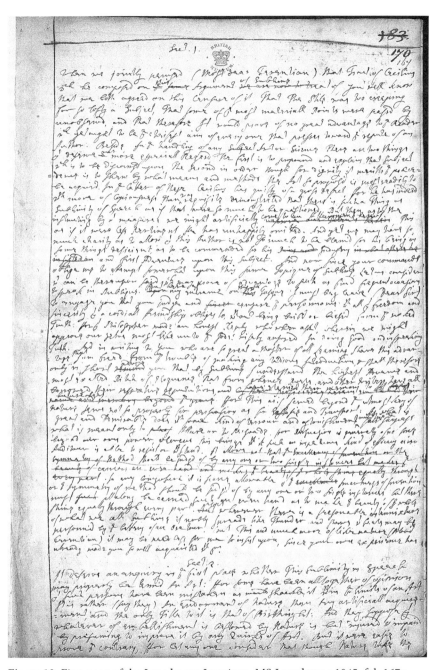

Figure 13 First page of the Lansdowne Longinus, MS Lansdowne 1045, fol. 167r, © The British Library Board.

have eterniz'd their memory to all future ages. For this as if seemed beyond the utmost key of nature seems not so properly for persuasion as for exstasie and transport: as what is great and admirable does with some kind of terrour and astonishment outstrip & farr surpass what is meant only to allure or to persuade. For persuasion is generally of no force beyond our own power, whereas this brings with it such an impetuous kind of efficacy as no auditour is able to resist or withstand. In any composure it is scarce allowable that the smartness of invention or the symmetry of method should be judg'd of by any one or two single instances, but there must all along be carried such an even hand as to make the beauty of the whole shine equally through every part. Yet wherever there is a seasonable intermixture of what we call sublime it nobly spreads like thunder and shews what feats may be perform'd by the battery of an oratour. But this and much more of like nature, alov'd Terentian, it may be need less for me to insist upon, since your own experience has already made you so well acquainted with them.

2

It deserve an enquiry in the first place whither this sublimity in speech may properly be term'd an art: for some have been alltogether of opinion that such persons have been mistaken as would shackle it within the limits of an art. It is rather, say they, an endowment of nature than any artificiall acquirement, and the only title to it is that of birthright. And they suppose that whatever of embellishment is bestowed by nature is but injured & impaird by praesuming to improve it by any quirks of art. But it were easie to prove the contrary, for let any one consider that though nature take [167v] a very licentious range in these sublime and lofty strains of speech, yet is this not altogether so unbounded as to scorn a confinement within rule & order. It is true the foundation and platform of this and all other habits is laid by nature, but then the superstructure and improvement, the due regulating and the becoming practise of it is all the laborious attainment of art. For as vessells are soon liable to overset except when pois'd by their just ballance, so would this sublimity run the frequent risque of miscarryige if it were left to the torrent of nature without being restrain'd and managed by art and method. It would be sometime so headstrong as to need a curb and at other times so jadish as to provoke the spurr. Demosthenes has observd that the cheifest good attainable in this life is to be happy, but there is another property of a no whit inferiour nature without which the other would be but of a short continuance, and that is to be cautious and discreet, which vertue ought to extend as well to our words as to our actions and behaviour. And this prudence or discretion is that which must give a due meen and decorum to our attempts upon a sublimity or loftiness of discourse, for otherwise we may be too apt to stumble upon those faults that require a more than ordinary care to avoid, the first whereof is that of excess when ones stile is too big, too swelling, and too much strain'd, which is a peice of affectation that that tragaedian was guilty of who us'd these flanting expressions: the curling waves of flame, to vomit in the face of heaven, to make the huffing god of wind a piper, and such like heights which are all as it were a note beyond ela. They obscure the stile and purle the understanding rather than sound truly great, and if we calmly make a more narrow search in to any of them they will their first appearance of terrible sink by degrees into scorn and contempt. And if a too immoderate height be indecent in tragaedie, which yet naturally requires some magnificence and admitts of more than usuall flights and raptures, it must needs be much more unbecoming in our familiar discourse. Among others Gorgias his liable to be caught at for this fault when he calls Zerxes the Persian Iove and terms vultures, living sepulcres. There are some things in Callisthenes likewise which are not so truly high and lofty as soaring beyond all bounds of modesty. Clitarchus is yet much more to be condemnd being a very vain & conceited writer, one that according to Sophocles

> whistles altogether out of tune.

The same censure must be pased on Amphicrates, Hegesias & Matris who under a fond supposall of their being actuated by some enthusiastick spiritt think they speak by inspiration when indeed it is all but a childish prate and babble. And really there is no fault we are more prone to than this of being over-lofty. For all men by nature aiming at what's great & high and industriously shunning what's mean despicable, they generally dash upon this rock, as judging it

> No scandall to miscarrie in great attempts.

Though tumours and excrescencies in discourse are like those in the body that betray a corrupt and distempred constitution, and make us oft feel an effect contrary to their appearance, for thus though moisture be the cause of a dropsie yet is there none more drie than him that is afflicted with it. The speaking therefore too big and swelling is that which would exceed and vainly goe beyond sublime. There is another fault which we may term a being boyish or paedantick which is very opposite to a true grandeur and sublimity, for it is really sordid, & narrow soul'd and in truth a most degenerating vice. If it be askd wherein this boyishness consists I answer it is a kind of school infirmitie that by overstraining falls into what's meerly flat and dull. Those who are most subject to incurr this fault are such as run upon incredible stories and fictions, and such as affect the use [168r] and imitation of rhetoricall figures. Next to this is a third sort of vice which arises from the ill management of our affections which Theodorus calls a sort of madness. It is a being needlessly and unseasonably pathetick where no passion is required, or the being immoderate where we should keep within bounds: for thus some as if they were scarce sober betray unseemly passions not such as are proper to the occasions they apply them to but such as they were unluckily born with or at best such as they childishly learnt at school, whereby they become tiresom & nauseous to their unconvicted auditors, pretending themselvs to be mightily movd when yet they can make no impression on others. But as to what relates to the passions we may find some other occasion to discourse of.

3

In one of those vices that we have mentioned (I mean that of cold or boyish) Timaeus is too abounding, who is indeed a person otherwise completely qualified, not barren of some noble expressions, very learnd and rationall, but being too forward in the censure of others faults and too winking in the espiall of his own, being likewise very fond of broaching new notions, he fell sometime in to what was extremely flat and childish. As I shall give one or two instances of those many more that Caecilius has already observ'd. Speaking in commendation of Alexander the Great: He conqured all Asia, sais he, in fewer years than Isocrates spent in the composure of his panegyrique wherein he advizes King Philip to an expedition against the Persians. A wonderfull comparison indeed between a monarch of Macedon and a petty sophister: at this rate of drawing paralells, good Timaeus, it may as well be prov'd that the Lacaedemonians fall short of the meritts of Isocrates since they foold away 30 years in the taking of Messene, whereas this latter dispatchd his panegyrique in barely ten. And what an exclamation does he make upon occasion of the Athenians being took captive in Sicily. It was, sais he, a deserved peice of vengeance inflicted for their impiety toward Hermes or Mercury in pulling down his Statues, and this punishment received under the conduct of one who from his ancestors had took the name of Hermes, the injur'd deity being calld Hermocrates from his father Hermon. Upon my creditt, dear Terentian, I can't but wonder that he did not make a like reflexion on Dionysius the tyrant and pretend that because he had highly injured Iupiter and Hercules he was upon this account expelld his kingdom by Dion and Heraclides, the first whereof in Greek comes neer to Iupiter as the other does to Hercules. But why should I insist longer on Timaeus? Since those more eminent heroes (I mean Zenophon and Plato) though bred in the School of Socrates, have yet sometime so shamefully forgot themselvs as to utter what was extremely flat and dull. As for instance the former in that treatise which he wrot upon the Lacaedemonian republick has these expressions: you shall no sooner hear their voice than if they were dumb stones, no more procure them to cast a look than if they were brasen statues, and in fine you would think them as modest as the very babies in our eyes. It had become Amphicrates better than Zenophon to have made the babies in our eyes the test of modesty, as if he suppos'd that all mens eyes were truly bashfull whereas some persons impudence is no way more notorious than in their looks or eyes. Thus Homer calls an impudent fellow a drunken flaring doge-eyed sot. But Timaeus was so much a plagiarie as to borrow this fancie however ridiculous from Xenophon, for thus in his life of Agathocles he plaies upon the Greek word κοράι which signifies virgins as well as one part of our eyes. There was one, sais he, that by force carried away his Neece who had been married to another person, the very next day after the wedding: which peice of impudence, proceeds he, who could have been guilty of except the babies in his eyes were harlots rather than chast virgins. And what shall we think of the divine Plato who speaking of the Tables made of cypress wherein were recorded their historicall memoirs: the writers of them, sais he, that hang up in the temples their monuments of cypress. And in another place he delivers himself thus: As to the walls, O Megillus, I am clearly of the Spartans opinion who thought them not proper for a city, and therefore since they are falln down I would have them take their rest upon the ground and not be disturbd [168v] or raisd again. And that of Herodotus is not much better where fair women are calld the torments of our eyes. Though this indeed is the more excusable because the persons who so phras'd it were rude, ignorant and drunk. But we should not so farr copie after these mens example as to blunder upon the same vice and so purchase for ourselves an infamy to succeeding generations.

4

These faults which are so unseemly doe all spring from this peice of affectation, that persons are too fond of newfangled notions, which is a madness that our modern writers are more especially guilty of. For good and evill, profitt and mischeif doe frequently ow their birth to the same originall. Thus those graces which does most deck and imbellish a discourse, the beautie, the vigour, the loftiness, and the aptness of it, and such like ornaments doe many times by an indiscreet usage degenerate in to what's quite contrary to their intention. For so it fares oft with high strain'd hyperboles & rhetoricall exaggerations. The danger of this we shall take occasion to shew hereafter. It is requisite at present that we make enquiry how we may best avoid those vices that sublimity is apt to be attended with. And this, my freind, will be the more easie if we can form to our selve a cleer notion and give a solid judgment of what is truly sublime, which is indeed a very difficult performance. For a good judgment is the happy result of a very long experience, for the better gaining whereof I shall lay down such directions as may prove most effectuall for the attainment of it.

5

It must be confessd, most dear Terentian, that in relation to our ordinary course of life, nothing, whereof the contempt does argue somewhat of greatness, can it self be said to be truly great. And thus fares it with riches, honour, glory, empire and such like enjoyments, whose outsides glisten with a darling pomp and splendour, but to a wise man that can see in to them they seem neither so great nor excellent but that he thinks it a vertue to scorn and despise them: so as their respective owners are not so much to be admir'd as those more noble souls whose greatness of spiritt has plac'd them above the acceptance of them. This may be applied to composures in poesy & oratory wherein we must be cautious that we be not imposd upon what bears a fair resemblance of great by having much of fiction and romance, which if more narrowly searchd in to will be found so crase and spungy that they may exercise our wonder much less than our scorn and derision. For our souls at the apprehension of what's truly sublime are by nature raisd and elevated, they suffer some kind of transport, they grow big with joy and complacency as if they themselvs had invented what they barely hear recited. So as whatever is delivered by never so wise and learn'd a person, if it doe not move the soul and leave some durable impression behind it, if upon result of second thoughts it flag and sink from that esteem that we first entertaind of it, it is no not truly sublime because the sense flies away as it were with the sound of the words and we retain it no longer than while we hear it spoke. That rather is truly great & sublime which will bear the touch of recollection and remain, which will stand the shock of a thorough search, and after all continue steady fixd and immoveable, so rivetted into the memory as no way possible ever to be forgot. Again, you may judge that to be really sublime which pleases equally all persons and at all times. For when persons of different professions, passions, ages and opinions doe all jump and agree in the same approbation, this harmony and consent of so many severall persuasions must needs give a firm and indisputable testimony of what's truly great and wonderful. [169r]

6

There be five most copious springs or fountains of sublimity, to all which must be praesupposd as a common basis or foundation, a faculty of speaking well, without which all the rest are insignificant. The first and most considerable is a dextrous management of our thoughts and invention, as I have already observd in what I wrot upon Zenophon. The second is a due and discreet ordring of our passions. These two requisites of sublime are in great part the endowments of nature whereas those that follow are the attainments of art. The third therefore is an exact forming of figures, which figures are of two sorts, those of thought, and those of words. The next to this is a nobleness of expression, which is made up of two parts, a fitt choice of words and smooth elaborate periods. The fifth ingredient of grandeur or sublimity, which crowns and consummates all the rest, is the right marshalling of all to the best advantage of order & connexion. Upon each of these five heads we shall take occasion hereafter to enlarge, but we shall first observe that some of these have been omitted by Caecilius, as to instance he has made no mention of patheticallness or the ordring of our passions. If he thought that sublime and patheticall did not differ from each other, but were every way the same, he was grandly mistaken. For there are many passions which are so farr distant from sublime that they are low and beggerly, as pity, greif and fear. And on the other side there are many instances of sublime which have nothing of passion, as among thousand others, is apparent from those bold stroaks of Homer upon the Aloides:

> Promoted Ossa crown'd Olympus head
> And over Ossa Pelion lay spread
> Thus mountains serv'd for stairs to th' blest abodes
> To chink the {...} of heaven and reach the gods.

And that which follows is yet more lofty:

> Nor would the project have come short &c.

And thus among orators, panegyriques and such like stately subjects are altogether lofty and sublime when yet they are destitute of all passion: nay those orators who are most patheticall are least fitt for encomiums or panegyrick and those again who are most excellent at panegyrique are worst qualified for raising of the passions. Or on the other hand if Caecilius suppos'd that a being patheticall added no grace nor ornament to sublimity and therefore thought it not worth the allowing he was again deceived. For I dare be so bold as to assert that nothing does more contribute to the true spiritt of sublime than a vehement, if seasonable, passion that argues somewhat of a divine phrensie and transport as if we uttered oracles and spake all by inspiration.

7

Of those five forementioned heads that which is of most moment & ought to lead the van is the elevation of our thoughts, which though it is an enjoyment that we possess by donation rather than by our own getting, yet ought we as much as possible to cherish and improve our souls in this facultie and make them alway goe big of some noble conceptions. If it be enquir'd by what means this may be perform'd: I answer that I have in another place observ'd that this elevation of thought is as it were the reflex image of a great soul. And thus many times where nothing at all is spoke yet even in silence we admire some inexpressible greatness of thought. Thus in one of Homers Odysses Ajax by holding his peace betraied more of a great spiritt than by any thing he could have spoke, since under those circumstances his greatest eloquence was to be dumb. We must first therefore have regard to that requisite of sublimity which is to be the foundation of all the rest, namely that an oratour must entertain no low nor vulgar thoughts: for those persons that debase their minds to a mean, ordinary, servile way of thinking, it is impossible they should ever bring forth any thing that is admirable or worthy of posterity. Their expressions only can be great and lofty whose thoughts likewise are of the same strain. And hence what's truly great & sublime falls cheifly from persons of a high and generous spiritt, as [169v] appears in that becoming reply of Alexander when Darius offred him his only daughter & the one half of his empire for a dowrie with her. Were I Alexander, sais Parmenio, I would accept of the proffer. Yes, sais Alexander, and so would I, were I Parmenio. Than which nothing could have been said more princely and heroick. To this that of Homer bears a neer resemblance where speaking of the goddess of discord he sais of her that

> Her head reachd heaven while her feet trod earth.

No less a distance than twixt this low orb and heaven above, which vast extent may be said to be the measure of Homers witt rather than of the goddess he describes. How much beneath this is that expression of Hesiod concerning the goddess of darkness, or (as some interpret it) of greif (if at least the poem which bears the title of Aspsis may be justly fathred on him), of whome he tell us:

> She from her shent nose run streams of snot

Now this is not to dress her up for terrible but makes her rather hatefull & nauseous. Whereas on the other side see what majestick grandeur Homer attributes to his gods:

> The kenning sailour of the sharpest eye,
> Observe how farr much of distance he can spie
> Before the seas seem compiled to the skie:
> So farr the hard mouth'd racers of the gods
> Launch every stride they make—

He gives them no shorter a reach than the dimension of a clear horizon: so as any one surprisd at the vastness of this hyperbole may well imagine that if these divine coursers should take but one more step forward the world it self could offoard no farther room to tread on. These fancies likewise in his description of the civill warrs in heaven are beyond wonder admirable, where he sais:

> The fright made heaven shiver, & stout Olympus quake.

And again:

> The sooty king of shades hears the alarm
> Doubts hell, no shelter from the threatned harm,
> Leaps from his furnace throne and owns a fear
> Least Neptune so employ his dung fork spear;
> As missing of his well intended blow
> It fall with vengeance on the earth below,
> And make so wide a breach i' th' roof of hell
> That day should rush where night and darkness dwell
> And seeping light new paint the smoak dried cell
> While men and gods with easie glance decrie
> What depth before had {...} from every eye.

You see, sir, how the caverns of the earth gape, how the recesses of hell are discovered, and the whole world seems summon'd to its change or dissolution, while the severall parts of it, heaven, hell, mortall & immortall beings doe all bear a part in the hazardous effects of this dreadfull combat. These kind of fancies are indeed great and soaring, yet if they be not taken in an allegoricall sense they argue too much of impiety and make too bold with the sacredness of that subject they are applied to. And indeed I must confess that Homer in my opinion while he attributes to the gods wounds, jarrs, revenge, teers, imprisonment, and such like sufferings, he seems designedly to advance his heroes engag'd at the seige of Troy into the reputation of gods, and to degrade the gods into the more dishonourable state of men. Nay their condition at that rate would be much worse than ours, for amidst the sharpest storms of humane misfortune it is some comfort that death at least will be a safe & certain harbour, whereas the gods must have their misery as well their nature durable to eternity. I shall now cite such passages as are much better than those we have already mentioned in the combat of the gods, that repraesent a deity in true [170r] and more proper colours, with no allay of what's indecent or misbecoming. As among others is observable that place (which many others have oft taken notice of) concerning Neptune:

> While Neptune round the earthy campagne roves
> His feet strike palsie to the hills & groves

And again:

> He treads the bearing waves while th' fishes play
> And thuss by instinct their allegiance pay,
> Nor subject waves their well known lord adore
> And glad huzza's in foaming billows roar;
> Nay they divide in banks to make more room
> While the alarm'd whales in legions come
> And then ambitious to approach more nigh
> As conscious of their sloth attempt to fly.

And thus that Iewish legislatour who was a more than ordinary person from a right conception of the excellence of a divine being, has attributed to him the height of all power & majesty, while at the introduction to his laws he thus writes[2]

Nor I hope, sir, will you think it taedious while for our better information I cite you one more passage from our poet that relates to the character of men to let you see in what an heroique strain Homer describes his men. Amidst the depth of night and darkness the Graecian army could not see to engage their enemy. Att this Ajax impatient of delay thus addresses him self to Iupiter:

> Dispell, great Iove, the cowardising night
> And let our eyes direct our hands to fight,
> Let's see but where we strike and then we dare
> Even thou thy self against us to appear.
> Wee'd brisqly be content to march by day
> To th' night of death but hate to grope the way.

See here the courage of a true bred champion: he does not pray for life, that were a trifle beneath a heroe to ask for, but since by night he lost the opportunity of shewing his valour, in some anger at his being detaind from action, he begs for a speedy break of day, resolving then to push on & purchase an honourable grave though Iove himself should take the enemies side. And in the following citation our poet does as it were gently fan and enflame the heat of that fury he describes and seems himself in that transport he relates of Hector when he sais of him:

---

[2] An empty space remains on the page where the quotation of Genesis is expected.

> He rav'd like Mars wading through streams of bloud,
> Or like the blazing tapers of a wood
> Fir'd at midnight to outvie the moon
> And bid defiance to the cooler sun.
> A foam oreflow'd his lips &c.—

But the same author in his Odysses falls short of these enlivening heights, and directs us thereby to observe (what upon severall accounts seems not unworthy the remarque) that the fancie of poets droops in their declining years when tales & trifles become their only divertisement. For that Homer scen'd his Odysees after his more talking Iliads may be clear'd beyond deniall. The Odysses, containing no more than a rehearsall (with additions) of severall misadventures first recited in the Iliads and is indeed no better than a 2d pt or continuation of the Trojan warr: many disasters which hapned in the story of the Iliads being by the heroes in Odyses recollected with sorrow and regret as misfortunes past and gone. And indeed the Odyses deserve no other title than that of an epilogue to the Iliads:

> Here the feirce Ajax, there Achilles lies,
> Here the divine Patroclus groans and dies,
> There my belove'd Antilochus

[170v] And tis upon this account that the Iliads being wrot { ... } the efforts of a mature and sprightly fancie are fully garnisht with life and vigour and seem but one continued scene of action, whereas the Odyses are stufft only with fulsom relations which agree exactly with the humour of a talkative old age. So that Homer in respect of this last of his composures may aptly be compard to the setting sun which makes indeed as big an appearance but is really shrunk from its former heat and splendour. For in this last he keeps not up to the same strain with that in his Iliads: his fancie that soard in the one seems inspid and weakly fluttring in the other. He daubs where before he drew lively stroaks, he is not neer so happy in representing any passion but is grown awkward and clumsy in the dressing up any thought or fancie. In a word his witt seems shrunk to a shallowness of ebb falling back from those higher bounds it before came up to, like the recoiling ocean which at a falling tide deserts those banks it so lately oreflow'd. In this censure on the Odysses I have respect to the unnaturall description of tempests, to the story of the Cyclops, and some other passages therein contain'd: and this is it which even in stories I justly tak for dotage, nay dare roundly term it the dotage of Homer, there being through all his forementioned Odyses more of fabulous narration than of brisquer life & action. I have made this digression as I before hinted to shew that lofty and aspiring fancies after a declining from their former pitch doe often fall in to a sordid trifling dullness. Instances whereof are the poor stories of Aeolus's barrling up the winds, of Ulyses's companions by the enchantments of Circe metamorphos'd into swine, whome Zoilus archly enough calls litle weeping grunters, of Iupiters being fed by doves as a young pidgeon, of the hardships of Ulysees undergoing after shipwrack the pennance of ten daies fast, and lastly the thick absurdities in relating the murder of Penelope's suitors, all which odd conceits are but a better sort of enthusiastick dreams. The cheif inducement of my making these remarques on the Odysses is to convince you the more strongly that the most elevated orators and poets by a graduall decay of spiritts fall from the rellish of lofty & pathetick and corrupt into the dross of dull insipid trumperie. For thus the account that Homer gives in his Odyses of the behaviour of Penelope's lovers in the house of absent Ulyses seems all but a kind of farce or sluttish comedy. [171r]

8

Let us now consider what other methods may be made use of to promote & advance this loftiness in speech. And since in all subjects of discourse there be such and such circumstances which are necessary parts and appendages of the whole, to cull out of these the most pat and materiall, and to range them to such a regular advantage as to make one connected body of all the particular members is the best and aptest improvement of sublime. For by the proper choice of circumstances, and the delightfull variety of the circumstances so chose, doe without doubt very much affect an understanding auditory. As for example when Sappho would describe those extravagancies which naturally attend the madness of lovers shee reckons up all those severall accidents they are most subject to, and this shee does very happily in this following citation where shee recounts and joyns together all the cheif affections of love:

> That Man may with the Gods for grandeur vie
> Who reaps the sweets of your bless'd companie,
> Devoutly listens to your tunefull song
> And owne the magick of your charming tongue,
> Who while his wonder does his joys enhance
> Can feeds on smiles and surfeits on a glance.
>
> When you appear unto my longing sight
> My bloud grows chilld from the surprizing fright,
> My heart recoils in starting leaps to show
> That all her forces are dischargd on you,
> My tongue does in a silent arc confess
> My joys too great for scanty words t' express;
>
> My high colour'd looks my feavrish ills proclaime
> And boyling veins betray their inward flame,
> My eyes as if encountring with the light
> Of noon daies sun sink in to blackest night,
> My ears in boistrous ravishments are drownd
> And only catch at undistinguisht sound.
>
> An aguish sweat ladens my clammy skin
> While outward Symptoms speak my state within,
> My joints their steady posture keep no more
> But trembling seizes all my body ore,
> My lips make short & quick returns of breath
> And all seem grapling with the pangs of death.
>
> And yet I still must fatally pursue,
> Bold wretch, the threatning harms &c.

[171v] Can you without a pleasing wonder observe how shee compacts into one description the motions of soul, body, hearing, speech, looks, &c as if they were all severall parties just perishing in the same engagement: see how by fitts and turns shee is now cold then burns, now raves then seemingly recovers her lost reason ore while distracted with fear, soon after labouring under the very agonies of death, so that in a word shee seems not to combat with the assault of any one single passion, but with the generall conflict of them all. And this indeed is the exact case of all that love. Well then, the being copious in

circumstances and discreat in the application of them (as before mentioned) is a very great advancement to the loftiness of speech. Thus when Homer would dwell on the description of a tempest he recounts all the most ghastly accidents that can be supposd to attend it. The author indeed of the poem entitled Arimaspia mistook these flourishes for noble thoughts:

> What madness this, that men should quit their ease
> On safer shore for tumbling on the seas,
> They'r wretches all and weakly undergoe
> Those toils that serve but to augment their woe,
> Their eyes on heaven, & their thoughts on th' flouds,
> They stretch their hands to th' unregarding gods
> And pray with no return &c.

There is none I beleive but will agree that this has more of daubure and specious varnish then of true and lively beauty. Observe how much better Homer acquitts himself on the same subject, as among many other this one instance may suffice to shew:

> So waves assault the tottring walle of wood
> And loudly roar their scorn to be withstood,
> The sullen clouds wrapt up in angry frown
> In rustling storms pour all their vengeance down,
> Sails grapling with the wind are soon orecome
> And the boyling billows cast up frosty foam,
> While th' reeling seamen doe with horrour spie
> Each wave a summons to praepare to die

Aratus attempted to improve this latter part of the fancie by adding:

> Twixt them and death no greater distance was
> Than one thin plank.

But this indeed is but mean and ordinary instead of great and terrible, for he puts as it were bounds and limits to the danger by saying

> Twixt them and death &c.

And so seemingly deferrs what he should have made more imminent and pressing. Whereas Homer allows no distance at all from the threatned ruine, but gives the most lively draught imaginable of a tempest, making each minute the utmost date of life and every wave the harbinger of shipwrack. [172r] Nay beside the excellence of fancye his phrase and periods are so apt and suitable that his very words seem the naturall colours of a storm in effigie. Archilochus was as happy in his description of a shipwrack, and Demosthenes upon information of the taking of Helice and the tumultuary disorders thereby occasioned in the city of Athens beginning thus: It was somewhat late in the evening &c. Both these having discreetly made choice of the most pertinent circumstances and passd by whatever might seem trifling or paedantick, which when foisted in are but like botches in architecture which sully the lustre and spoil the symmetry of the whole building.

9

Among the forementioned methods for attainment of loftiness of speech may be reckoned that which they call amplification. For when the nature of our subject and scope of argument so require that we should be more copious in expression and extend or enlarge our periods, we may so contrive it that the heights and falls of sentences may sett off each other with the greater grace and elegancie. And this may be done either upon the longer handling of any topique, upon the reinforcing any argument, in a narrative of any remarquable actions, or giving the most agreeable idea of any passion: for amplification admitts of severall parts & degrees, though an oratour ought to be sensible that no one of em can be duly perfect and complete without the joint concurrence of what is lofty or sublime, except in moving of stile, or extenua[3]

---

[3] The translation ends mid-word.

Works Cited

I. Manuscripts and Adversaria

Amsterdam, Amsterdam University Library
Remonstrant collection III C 4, fol. 336r–336v: *Excerpta theologica* of Grotius

Austin, Harry Ransom Center, University of Texas
HRC 127: Latin prose theme and poems attributed to Milton

Cambridge, Cambridge University Library
Adv.d.4.4: Bartholomew Dodington's annotated copy of Portus 1569/70
Ely.a.272: Milton's copy of Chrysostom 1604
KK.VI.34: Greek MS of Longinus' *Peri hupsous*
P*.14.30(F): Bishop John Hacket's annotated copy of Portus 1569/70
UA Luard 187: Letters patent of Elizabeth I dispatching a new code of laws or statutes to the University of Cambridge

Cambridge, Parker Library, Corpus Christi College
MS 355: John Colet, *Epistolae beati Pauli ad Romanos expositio, Geneseos expositio ad Radulphum*

Cambridge, Trinity College Library
MS O.10.22: *The Constant Method of Teaching in St. Pauls Schoole London*
MS R.3.4: Manuscript of Milton's early writings ("Trinity manuscript")

Cambridge (Massachusetts), Harvard University Library
MS Eng. 739: Verse inscription from Thomas Farnaby to Alexander Gil the Younger
*OGC.P653.620 (B): Copy of Pindar 1620 with annotations previously attributed to Milton

Dublin, Marsh's Library
[Shelfmark unlisted]: Copy of Hall 1652 in the collection of Edward Stillingfleet
[Shelfmark unlisted]: Copy of Le Fèvre 1663 in the collection of Edward Stillingfleet

Dublin, Trinity College Dublin
Press B.4.16: Volume of Milton's tracts with the author's dedication to Patrick Young

Durham, Durham University Library
Bamburgh L.6.52: Copy of Langbaine 1636 with autograph of Samuel Cholmley
Cosin W.5.15: Bishop John Cosin's annotated copy of Langbaine 1638

Florence, Biblioteca Nazionale Centrale di Firenze
MS Aut. Palat. IV.56: Letter from Lucas Holstenius to Leopoldo de' Medici, (January 30, 1649)
MS Magl. VI.33: Giovanni di Niccolò da Falgano, *Libro della altezza del dire di Dionysio Longino rhetore tradotto dalla greca nella toscana lingua*

London, British Library
1088.m.2: Isaac Casaubon's annotated copy of Robortello 1554
1089.e.7: Sir Henry Cuffe's copy of Portus 1569/1570
Add. MS 4464: Extracts from Robert Sidney's commonplace book
Add. MS 32310: Milton family Bible
Add. MS 34362: Danvers anthology of political poetry
C.59.i.8: Uncensored copy of Marvell 1681
C.60.1.7: Milton's annotated copy of Aratus 1559
C.134.h.1: Benjamin Stillingfleet's annotated copy of Bentley 1732
E.50(12): George Thomason's dated copy of Milton's *Of Education*
E.1294.(2.): George Thomason's annotated copy of Hall 1652
Evelyn MSS 33, 34, 34a: John Evelyn's translation of and commentary on Lucretius
Loan MS 76: Bridgewater manuscript of *Maske*
MS Lansdowne 1045, fols. 166–172: *Of Sublimity of Stile Or The Raptures of Eloquence From Dionysius Longinus Περὶ Ὕψους Done from the Greek in to English For the Improvement of Oratory*

London, Lambeth Palace Library
C11/AP4 02: Sir Robert Coke's copy of de Petra 1612

London, National Archives
SP 9/61: Manuscript of Milton's *De Doctrina Christiana*
SP 18/155, fol. 131: Letter from Thomas Smith to Joseph Williamson, 22 June 1657

Modena, Biblioteca Estense
Campori App. 432 (Γ S 3.18): Franciscus Portus' commentary on Longinus

Naples, Biblioteca Nazionale di Napoli
Papyri Herculanenses 831: Demetrius of Laconia, *Peri meteōrismou*

New Haven, Yale University Library
GfL29 b636ba: Richard Byfield's annotated copy of Langbaine 1638

New York, Morgan Library and Museum
MA 307: Manuscript of *Paradise Lost* Book I

New York, New York Public Library
*KB 1529: Sammelband containing Dante 1529, della Casa 1563, and Varchi 1555, with annotations in several hands, including Milton's

Nottingham, Nottingham University Library
Mi LM 15/1: Francis Willughby's commonplace book

Oxford, Bodleian Library
8° St.Amand 152: Edward Pococke's copy of Langbaine 1638
8° St.Amand 438: Edward Pococke's copy of Langbaine 1636
8° W 30 Med.Seld: Abiel Borfet's annotated copy of Langbaine 1636
Arch. A f.145: Milton's copy of Boccaccio 1544

Don.d.27-28: Milton's annotated copy of Euripides 1602
MS Casaubon 1: Papers of Isaac Casaubon
MS Casaubon 51: Papers of Isaac Casaubon
MS Rawl. D.314: Anonymous prose translation of Lucretius
MS Wood E. 2(70), fol. 39: Catalogue of Anthony Wood's library
MS Wood F. 39, fol. 372r: Letter from John Aubrey to Anthony Wood (May 24, 1684)
O 2.26 Art.Seld: Dean Wren's copy of Thomas Browne's *Pseudodoxia Epidemica*

Oxford, Wadham College Library

[Shelfmark unlisted]: Sir William Godolphin's copy of Hall 1652

Paris, Bibliothèque nationale de France

Codex Parisinus Graecus 1741: Greek MS of Demetrius' *Peri hermēneias*
Codex Parisinus Graecus 2036: Greek MS of Longinus' *Peri hupsous*
Codex Parisinus Graecus 2974: Greek MS of Longinus' *Peri hupsous*
MS Italien 2028, fols. 127-158: *De la sublimité du discours*
X.3074: Denys Lambin's annotated copy of Robortello 1554

Philadelphia, Free Library of Philadelphia

RBD EL SH15M 1623: Shakespeare First Folio with annotations (possibly Milton's)

Rome, Biblioteca Vallicelliana

MS Allacci XXIX.1-8: Autograph and manuscript copies of Allatius' Latin translation of Longinus and commentary

San Marino, Huntington Library

79660: Uncensored copy of Marvell 1681

Sheffield, Sheffield University Library

Hartlib Papers 28/2/27-44: *Ephemerides* 1652
Hartlib Papers 31/22: *Ephemerides* 1648
Hartlib Papers 38/7: *Compendium Oratorium Totam Dicendi Artem Methodice & Dilucide exponens*
Hartlib Papers 60/14: Letters from John Hall to Samuel Hartlib

Stamford, Lincolnshire, Burghley House

Muniments Drawer 49/5/2: List of books donated by William Cecil, 1st Baron Burghley

Stanford, Stanford University Libraries

RBC KB1570.A6: Sir Henry Wotton's annotated copy of Portus 1569/70

Urbana, University of Illinois Library

881 L71601 copy 1: Milton's copy of Lycophron 1601
X881 H215 1544: Milton's copy of Heraclides Ponticus 1544

Vatican City, Bibliotheca Apostolica Vaticana

MS Barb. Gr. 190, fols. IIIr.-21r: Allatius' commentary on Longinus
MS Barb. Lat. 2181, fols. 57r-58v: Milton's letter to Lucas Holstenius

MS Vat. Lat. 3441, fols. 12r–31r: *Dionysii Longini de altitudine et granditate orationis*
Stamp. Barb. JJJ.VI.67: Cardinal Francesco Barberini's copy of Ronconi 1639

Venice, Biblioteca Nazionale Marciana
MS Marcianus Graecus 522: Greek MS of Longinus

II. Editions of Milton's Works

Bentley, R. (ed.). 1732. *Milton's Paradise Lost. A New Edition*. London.
Callander, J. (ed.). 1750. *Milton's Paradise Lost Book I*. Glasgow.
Darbishire, H. (ed.). 1931. *The Manuscript of Milton's Paradise Lost Book I*. Oxford.
Darbishire, H. (ed.). 1952–5. *The Poetical Works of John Milton*. Oxford.
Flannagan, R. (ed.). 1998. *The Riverside Milton*. New York.
Fowler, A. (ed.). 2007. *Paradise Lost*. Abingdon.
Haan, E. (ed.). 2019. *John Milton: Epistolarum Familiarium Liber Unus and Uncollected Letters*. Leuven.
Hale, J. K. and J. D. Cullington (eds.). 2012. *The Complete Works of John Milton Volume VIII: De Doctrina Christiana*. 2 vols. Oxford.
Hughes, M. Y. (ed.). 1957. *Complete Poems and Major Prose*. New York.
Keeble, N. H. and N. McDowell (eds.). 2013. *The Complete Works of John Milton Volume VI: Vernacular Regicide and Republican Writings*. Oxford.
Kerrigan, W. et al. (eds.). 2007. *The Complete Poetry and Essential Prose of John Milton*. New York.
Knoppers, L. L. (ed.). 2008. *The Complete Works of John Milton Volume II: The 1671 Poems: Paradise Regain'd and Samson Agonistes*. Oxford.
Lewalski, B. K. (ed.). 2007. *Paradise Lost*. Oxford.
Lewalski, B. K. and E. Haan (eds.). 2012. *The Complete Works of John Milton Volume III: The Shorter Poems*. Oxford.
Masson, D. (ed.). 1874. *The Poetical Works of John Milton*. 3 Vols. London.
Milton, J. 1667. *Paradise Lost. A Poem Written in Ten Books*. London.
Milton, J. 1674a. *Paradise Lost. A Poem in Twelve Books*. London.
Milton, J. 1674b. *Epistolarum Familiarium Liber Unus: quibus Accesserunt, Eiusdem, iam olim in Collegio Adolescentis, Prolusiones Quaedam Oratoriae*. London.
Newton, T. (ed.). 1749. *Paradise Lost*. 2 vols. London.
Patterson, F. A. (gen. ed.). 1923–40. *The Works of John Milton*. 20 vols. New York.
Poole, W. (ed.). 2019. *The Complete Works of John Milton Volume XI: Manuscript Writings*. Oxford.
Sumner, C. R. (trans.). 1825. *A Treatise of Christian Doctrine*. Cambridge.
Tillyard, P. B. (trans.). 1932. *Private Correspondence and Academic Exercises*. Cambridge.
Warton, T. (ed.). 1785. *Poems Upon Several Occasions*. London.
Wolfe, D. M. (gen. ed.). 1953–82. *Complete Prose Works of John Milton*. 8 vols. New Haven.

III. Editions and Translations of Longinus

[Anon.]. 1698. *An Essay Upon Sublime, Translated from the Greek of Dionysius Longinus Cassius the Rhetorician, Compared with the French of the Sieur Despréaux Boileau*. Oxford.

Aromatari, G. 1643. "Liber de Grandi, sive Sublimi Dicendi Genere Orationis." *Degli autori del ben parlare, opere diverse. Degli stili, et eloquenza. Tomo quinto*, Venice: 451–86.

Boileau, N. 1674. *Oeuvres Diverses du Sieur D***, avec le Traité du Sublime ou du Merveilleux dans le Discours, Traduit du Grec de Longin.* Paris.

Le Fèvre, T. 1663. *Dionysii Longini Philosophi et Rhetoris Περὶ ὕψους Libellus.* Saumur.

Fyfe, W. H. and D. A. Russell. 1999. "On the Sublime." In Halliwell et al. 1999: 143–305.

Gilby, E. 2006. *De la sublimité du discours: traduction inédite du XVIIe siècle.* Paris.

Hall, J. 1652. *Περὶ ὕψους, or Dionysius Longinus of the Height of Eloquence. Rendered out of the Original by J. H. Esq.* London.

Halliwell, S. 2022. *Pseudo-Longinus: On the Sublime.* Oxford.

Langbaine, G. 1636. *Dionysii Longini rhetoris praestantissimi liber De grandi loquentia sive sublimi dicendi genere, Latine redditus.* Oxford.

Langbaine, G. 1638. *Dionysii Longini rhetoris praestantissimi liber De grandi loquentia sive sublimi dicendi genere, Latine redditus.* Oxford.

Langbaine, G. 1650. *Dionysii Longini rhetoris præstantissimi liber De grandi loquentia sive sublimi dicendi genere.* Oxford.

Manolessi, C. 1644. *Dionysii Longini Cassii Graeci Rhetoris De Sublime Genere Dicendi Libellus.* Bologna.

Manutius, P. 1555. *Dionysii Longini: De sublimi genere dicendi.* Venice.

Mazzucchi, C. M. 1992. *Dionisio Longino: Del sublime.* Milan.

Pagano, P. 1572. *De sublimi dicendi genere.* Venice.

Pearce, Z. 1733a. *Dionysii Longini de sublimitate commentarius [....] Accessit F. Porti in Longinum commentaries integer.* 3rd Edition. Amsterdam.

de Petra, G. 1612. *Dionysii Longini Liber de grandi, sive sublimi genere orationis.* Geneva.

Pinelli, N. 1639. *Dell'altezza del dire.* Padua.

Pizzimenti, D. 1566. *Liber de grandi orationis genere.* Naples.

Portus, F. 1569/70. *Aphthonius, Hermogenes et Dionysius Longinus, Praestantissimi Artis Rhetorices Magistri.* Geneva.

Pulteney, J. 1680. *A Treatise of the Loftiness or Elegancy of Speech. Written Originally in Greek by Longin and now Translated out of French by Mr. J. Pulteney.* London.

Robortello, F. 1554. *Dionysii Longini rhetoris praestantissimi liber de grandi sive sublimi orationis genere.* Basel.

Russell, D. A. 1964. *On the Sublime.* Oxford.

IV. Seventeenth-Century Book and Manuscript Catalogues

Cooper, W. 1676. *Catalogus Variorum & Insignium Librorum Instructissimae Bibliothecae Clarissimi Doctissimique Viri Lazari Seaman, S.T.D.* London.

Cooper, W. 1678a. *Catalogus variorum & insignium librorum instructissimae bibliothecae clarissimi doctissimiq; Viri Thomae Manton, S.T.D.* London.

Cooper, W. 1678b. *Catalogus Variorum & Insignium Librorum Instructissimarum Bibliothecarum Doctiss. Clarissimorumq; Virorum D. Johannis Godolphin, J.U.D. et D. Oweni Phillips, A.M.* London.

Cooper, W. 1679. *Catalogus Librorum In plurimis Linguis Maxime Insignium Bibliothecarum Viri Eruditi Stephani Watkins, D. Doctoris Thomæ Sherley, atque alterius cujusdam hominis docti dudum decessi, &c.* London.

Cooper, W. 1680. *Catalogus Librorum Bibliothecae Reverend. & Eruditi Viri D. Samuelis Brooke.* London.

Cooper, W. 1681. *Catalogus Librorum Bibliothecae Viri Cujusdam Literati.* London.
Cooper, W. 1685. *Catalogus Librorum Theologicorum, Philologicorum, Mathematicorum, &c. Dris. Stokes & aliorum.* London.
Cooper, W. 1686. *Catalogus Librorum Bibliothecae Viri Cujusdam Literati.* London.
Dunmore, J. 1680. *Bibliotheca Bissaeana: Sive Catalogus Librorum In omni Arte & Lingua praestantissimorum.* London.
Dunmore, J. and R. Chiswell. 1678. *Catalogus Librorum in Quavis Lingua & Facultate insignium Instructissimarum Bibliothecarum Tum Clarissimi Doctissimique Viri D. Doctoris Benjaminis Worsley.* London.
London, W. 1657. *A Catalogue of the Most Vendible Books in England.* London.
Millington, E. 1680a. *Bibliotheca Charnockiana Sive Catalogus Librorum Selectissimae Bibliothecae Clarissimi, Doctissimiq; Viri Domini Steph. Charnock, S.T.B.* London.
Millington, E. 1680b. *Catalogus Librorum Bibliothecae Selectissimae Edoardi Palmer Armigeri.* London.
Millington, E. 1680c. *Catalogus Variorum Librorum Instructissimae Bibliothecae Doctissimi Viri D. Thomae Watson.* London.
Millington, E. 1681a. *Catalogus Variorum Librorum Selectissimarum Bibliothecarum Doctissimi Viri D. Thom. Jessop.* London.
Millington, E. 1681b. *Catalogus Librorum Bibliothecis Selectissimis Doctissimorum Virorum Viz. D. Radulphus Button... D. Thankfull Owen.* London.
Millington, E. 1684. *Bibliotheca Oweniana, sive Catalogus Librorum Plurimis Facultatibus Insignium, Instructissimae Bibliotheca Rev. Doct. Vir. D. Joan. Oweni.* London.
Millington, E. 1686. *Catalogus Variorum Librorum Instructissimae Bibliothecae. Rev. Jac. Chamberlaine.* London.
Millington, E. 1687a. *Bibliotheca Jacombiana, sive Catalogus Variorum Librorum Plurimis Facultatibus Insignium Instructissimae Bibliothecae Rev. Doct. Thomae Jacomb, S.T.D.* London.
Millington, E. 1687b. *Catalogus Variorum Librorum Bibliothecarum Selectissimarum Rev. D. D. Sill.... Doct. Vir. D. Cornel. Callow.* London.
Philipps, T. 1686. *Bibliotheca Angleseiana, sive Catalogus Variorum Librorum In Quavis Lingua, & Facultate Insignium.* London.
Ranew, N. 1678. *Catalogus Librorum Ex Bibliotheca Nobilis Cujusdam Angli... Accesserunt Libri Eximii Theologi, D. Gabrielis Sangar.* London.
Rookes, T. 1667. [*The late conflagration consumed my own, together with the Stock of Books (as it were) of the Company of Stationers, London....*]. [London].
Rouse, J. 1635. *Appendix ad catalogum librorum in Bibliotheca Bodleiana, qui prodiit anno Domini 1620.* Oxford.
Spencer, J. 1650. *Catalogus Universalis Librorum Omnium in Bibliotheca Collegii Sionii.* London.

V. Miscellaneous Printed Primary Sources

Addison, J. 1970. *Critical Essays from The Spectator.* Ed. D. F. Bond. Oxford.
Allatius, L. 1635. *De erroribus magnorum virorum in dicendo.* Rome.
Allatius, L. 1638. *Sallustii Philosophi de Diis et Mundo.* Rome.
[Anon.]. 1560. *The Bible and Holy Scriptures Conteyned in the Olde and Newe Testament.* Geneva.
Anyan, T. 1615. *A Sermon Preached at Saint Marie Spittle.* Oxford.

Aratus. 1559. *Phaenomena & Diosemeia*. Paris.
Ascham, R. 1570. *The Scholemaster*. London.
Aubert, H. et al. 1980. *Correspondance de Théodore de Bèze Tome X: 1569*. Geneva.
Aubrey, J. 2015. *Brief Lives with An Apparatus for the Lives of Our English Mathematical Writers*. 2 vols. Ed. K. Bennett. Oxford.
Bembo, P. 1496. *De Aetna dialogus*. Venice.
Blount, T. 1654. *The Academie of Eloquence*. London.
Blount, T. 1656. *Glossographia*. London.
Blount, T. 1660. *Boscobel: or, The History of His Sacred Majesties Most miraculous Preservation After the Battle of Worcester, 3. Sept. 1651*. London.
Boccaccio, G. 1544. *Vita di Dante*. Rome.
Boccaccio, G. 2011. *Genealogy of the Pagan Gods. Volume I: Books I-V*. Trans. J. Solomon. Cambridge, MA.
Boughton, J. 1623. *God and Man. A Treatise Catechisticall*. London.
Boyle, R. 1661. *Some Considerations Touching the Style of the H. Scriptures*. London.
Brinsley, J. 1612. *Ludus Literarius: or, The Grammar Schoole*. London.
Browne, T. 1981. *Pseudodoxia Epidemica*. 2 vols. Ed. R. Robbins. Oxford.
Bruno, G. 1879. "Oratio Valedictoria a Jordano Bruno Nolano D. Habita, ad amplissimos et clarissimos professores, atque auditores in Academia Witebergensi anno MDLXXXVIII. VIII Martii." *Opera latine conscripta* I.1, ed. F. Fiorentino, Naples: 1–25.
Burgess, T. 1829. *Milton Not the Author of the Lately-Discovered Arian Work De Doctrina Christiana*. London.
Burmann, P. 1727. *Sylloges Epistolarum*. 5 vols. Leiden.
Burrough, J. 1648. *Jacobs Seed. Or The Generation of Seekers. And Davids Delight: Or The Excellent on Earth*. Cambridge.
Burton, R. 1989–94. *The Anatomy of Melancholy*. 3 vols. Eds. R. L. Blair et al. Oxford.
Calvin, J. 1559. *Institutio Christianae Religionis*. Geneva.
Capaccio, G. C. 1607. *La vera antichita di Pozzuolo*. Naples.
della Casa, G. 1563. *Rime et prose*. Venice.
Casaubon, I. 1603. *Historiae Augustae Scriptores Sex*. Paris.
Casaubon, I. 1605. *C. Suetonii Tranquilli de XIII Caesaribus libri VIII*. Geneva.
Casaubon, I. 2018. *The Correspondence of Isaac Casaubon in England*. 4 vols. Eds. P. Botley and M. Vince. Geneva.
Casaubon, M. 1646. *A Discourse concerning Christ His Incarnation, and Exinanition*. London.
Casaubon, M. 1655. *A Treatise Concerning Enthusiasme, As it is an Effect of Nature: but is Mistaken by Many for either Divine Inspiration, or Diabolical Possession*. London.
Chaloner, E. 1625. *Credo Ecclesiam Sanctam Catholicam*. London.
Chamier, D. 1626–30. *Panstratiae Catholicae*. 4 vols. Geneva.
Chapman, G. 1614. *Homers Odysses*. London.
Chaucer, G. 2008. *The Riverside Chaucer*. Ed. C. Cannon. Oxford.
Chrysostom, D. 1604. *Orationes LXXX*. Paris.
Cocceius, J. 1662. *Judaicarum Responsionum & Quaestionum Consideratio*. Amsterdam.
Coleridge, S. T. 1995. *Shorter Works and Fragments I*. Eds. H. J. Jackson and J. R. de J. Jackson. Princeton.
Colet, J. 1876. *Letters to Radulphus on the Mosaic Account of the Creation, Together with Other Treatises*. Trans. J. H. Lupton. London.
Colet, J. 2013. *John Colet on the Ecclesiastical Hierarchy of Dionysius*. Eds. D. T. Lochman and D. J. Nodes. Leiden.

Conti, N. 1602. *Mythologiae, sive Explicationis Fabularum, Libri decem.* Geneva.

Cowley, A. 1660. *The Visions and Prophecies Concerning England, Scotland, and Ireland, of Ezekiel Grebner.* London.

Cowley, A. 1661. *A Proposition for the Advancement of Experimental Philosophy.* London.

Cromwell, O. 1937–47. *The Writings and Speeches of Oliver Cromwell.* 4 vols. Ed. W. C. Abbott. Cambridge, MA.

Dante. 1529. *L'Amoroso Convivio di Dante.* Venice.

Darbishire, H. (ed.). 1965. *The Early Lives of Milton.* New York.

Davidson, P. (ed.). 1998. *Poetry and Revolution: An Anthology of British and Irish Verse 1625–1660.* Oxford.

Dennis, J. 1696. *Remarks On a Book Entituled, Prince Arthur, an Heroick Poem.* London.

Dennis, J. 1721. *Proposals for Printing by Subscription, In Two Volumes in Octavo, The following Miscellaneous Tracts.* London.

Dering, E. 1644. *A Discourse of Proper Sacrifice.* Cambridge.

Dickson, D. 1664. *Therapeutica Sacra.* Edinburgh.

Diels, H. (ed.). 1882–1909. *Commentaria in Aristotelem Graeca.* 23 vols. Berlin.

Diodati, G. 1643. *Pious Annotations Upon the Holy Bible.* London.

Dudith, A. 1560. *Dionysii Halicarnassei de Thucydides Historia Iudicium.* Venice.

Elizabeth. 1852. "Statuta Reginae Elizabethae anno duodecimo regni sui edita." *Documents Relating to the University and Colleges of Cambridge*, 3 vols., London: I 454–95.

Erasmus, D. 1528. *Dialogus Ciceronianus: sive De optimo genere dicendi.* Leiden.

Erasmus, D. 1535. *In Novum Testamentum Annotationes.* Basel.

Erasmus, D. 2004. *Novum Testamentum ab Erasmo Recognitum III: Epistolae Apostolicae (Prima Pars).* Ed. A. J. Brown. Amsterdam.

Essenius, A. 1665. *Systematis Dogmatici Tomus Tertius, & Ultimus.* Amsterdam.

Estienne, H. 1587. *De criticis vet[eris] Gr[aecis] et Latinis.* Paris.

Euripides. 1602. *Tragoediae quae extant.* Geneva.

Evelyn, J. 1656. *An Essay on the First Book of T. Lucretius Carus De rerum natura.* London.

Evelyn, J. 1955. *The Diary of John Evelyn.* 6 vols. Ed. E. S. de Beer. Oxford.

Evelyn, J. 2000. *John Evelyn's Translation of Titus Lucretius Carus, De rerum natura: An Old-Spelling Critical Edition.* Ed. M. M. Repetzki. Frankfurt am Main.

Fairclough, R. 1650. *The Prisoners Praises for their Deliverance from their Long Imprisonment in Colchester.* London.

Farindon, A. 1647. *XXX. Sermons Lately Preached Of Saint Mary Magdalen Milkstreet.* London.

Farnaby, T. 1625. *Index Rhetoricus.* London.

Ferguson, A. S. 1920. "Paradise Lost, IV, 977–1015." *Modern Language Review* 15.2: 168–70.

Ferrand, J. 1640. *Erotomania or A Treatise Discoursing of the Essence, Causes, Symptomes, Prognosticks, and Cure of Love, or Erotique Melancholy.* Oxford.

Fontenelle, B. Le B. de. 1686. *Entretiens sur la pluralité des mondes.* Paris.

Gale, T. 1669. *The Court of the Gentiles.* Oxford.

Galileo, G. 1610. *Sidereus Nuncius.* Venice.

Galileo, G. 1632. *Dialogo.* Florence.

Galileo, G. 1635. *Dialogus de Systemate Mundi.* Strasbourg.

Geminus. 1590. *Elementa Astronomiae.* Ed. E. Hildericus. Altdorf.

Geminus. 2006. *Geminos's Introduction to the Phenomena.* Trans. J. Evans and J. L. Berggren. Princeton.

Gessner, C. 1545. *Bibliotheca Universalis, sive Catalogus omnium scriptorum locupletissimus.* Zurich.

Gil [the Elder], A. 1619. *Logonomia Anglica, qua gentis sermo facilius addiscitur*. London.
Gil [the Younger], A. 1632. *Parerga*. London.
Giacomini, L. 1597. *Orationi e discorsi*. Florence.
Goodwin, J. 1648. *The Divine Authority of the Scriptures Asserted*. London.
Goodwin, J. 1649. Ὑβριστοδίκαι. *The Obstructours of Justice. Or a Defence of the Honourable Sentence passed upon the late King, by the High Court of Justice*. London.
Greaves, J. 1646. *Pyramidographia, or a Description of the Pyramids in Aegypt*. London.
Gregory, J. 1646. *Notes and Observations upon Some Passages of Scripture*. Oxford.
Grotius, H. 1601. *Sacra in quibus Adamus exul tragoedia*. The Hague.
Grotius, H. 1627. *Pro veritate religionis Christianae*. Leiden.
Grotius, H. 1641. *Annotationes in Libros Evangeliorum*. Amsterdam.
Grotius, H. 1644. *Annotata ad Vetus Testamentum*. 3 vols. Paris.
Grotius, H. 1646. *Annotationum in Novum Testamentum Tomus Secundus*. Paris.
Grotius, H. 1988. *Meletius sive de iis quae inter Christianos conveniunt Epistola*. Ed. G. H. M. Posthumus Meyjes. Leiden.
Hacket, J. 1692. *Scrinia Reserata: A Memorial Offer'd to the Great Deservings of John Williams, D.D*. London.
Hackluyt, J. 1648. *The Parliament Arraigned, Convicted; Wants nothing but Execution*. [London?].
Hall, J. 1646. *Poems*. Cambridge.
Hall, J. 1648. *Mercurius Britanicus Alive Again*. London.
Hall, J. 1649. *An Humble Motion to the Parliament of England Concerning the Advancement of Learning: And Reformation of the Universities*. London.
Hall, J. 1656. *Hierocles upon the Golden Verses of Pythagoras; Teaching a Vertuous and Worthy Life*. London.
Hall, J. 1679. *Contemplations upon the Remarkable Passages in the Life of the Holy Jesus*. London.
Halliwell, S. et al. 1999. *Aristotle: Poetics. Longinus: On the Sublime. Demetrius: On Style*. Cambridge, MA.
Hammond, H. 1659. *A Paraphrase and Annotations Upon the Books of the Psalms*. London.
Heinsius, D. 1627. *Aristarchus Sacer, sive ad Nonni in Iohannem Metaphrasin Exercitationes*. Leiden.
Henry, P. 1882. *Diaries and Letters of Philip Henry*. Ed. M. H. Lee. London.
Heraclides Ponticus. 1544. *Allegoriae in Homeri fabulas de dijs*. Basel.
Hobbes, T. 1651. *Leviathan, or The Matter, Forme, & Power of a Common-wealth Ecclesiasticall and Civill*. London.
Holstenius, L. 1630. *Porphyrii vita Pythagorae*. Rome.
Holstenius, L. 1638. *Demophili Democratis et Secundi veterum philosophorum sententiae morales*. Rome.
Hooke, R. 1705. *The Posthumous Works of Robert Hooke*. London.
Hughes, G. 1647. *Vae-Euge-Tuba. Or, The Wo-Ioy-Trumpet*. London.
Hume, P. 1695. *Annotations on Milton's Paradise Lost*. London.
Hutchinson, L. 2001. *Order and Disorder*. Ed. D. Norbrook. Oxford.
Hutchinson, L. 2011. *The Works of Lucy Hutchinson Vol. 1: The Translation of Lucretius*. Eds. R. Barbour et al. Oxford.
Innes, D. C. 1999. "Demetrius: *On Style*." Halliwell et al. 1999: 307–521.
James, J. 1820. *Sketches of Travels in Sicily, Italy, and France*. Albany, NY.
Jocelyn, H. D. 1969. *The Tragedies of Ennius*. Cambridge.
Junius, F. 1637. *De Pictura Veterum*. Amsterdam.

Junius, F. 1638. *The Painting of the Ancients, in Three Bookes: Declaring by Historicall Observations and Examples, the Beginning, Progresse, and Consummation of That Most Noble Art.* London.
Junius, F. 1641. *De Schilder-konst der Oude begrepen in drie boecken.* Middelburg.
King, J. 1608. *A Sermon Preached at White-Hall the 5. Day of November ann. 1608.* Oxford.
Kircher, A. 1664–5. *Mundus Subterraneus.* 2 vols. Amsterdam.
Kircher, A. 1671. *Latium.* Amsterdam.
Leigh, E. 1646. *A Treatise of Divinity Consisting of Three Bookes.* London.
Leslie, C. 1698. *The History of Sin and Heresie.* London.
Lilburne, J. 1652. *As You Were.* Amsterdam.
Lindsay, W. M. (ed.). 1913. *Sexti Pompei Festi De Verborum Significatu Quae Supersunt cum Pauli Epitome.* Leipzig.
Lorich, R. 1542. *Aphthonii Sophistae Progymnasmata.* Marburg.
Lowth, R. 1753. *De Sacra Poesi Hebraeorum Praelectiones Academicae.* Oxford.
Lycophron. 1601. *Lycophronis Alexandra.* Geneva.
Manso, G. B. 1634. *Vita di Torquato Tasso.* Rome.
Manutius, A. 1508. *Rhetores in hoc volumine habentur hi. Aphthonii sophistae Progymnasmata. Hermogenis Ars rhetorica. Aristotelis Rhetoricorum ad Theodecten libri tres. Eiusdem Rhetorice ad Alexandrum. Eiusdem Ars poetica.* Venice.
Marston, J. 1606. *Parasitaster, or The Favvne.* London.
Marvell, A. 1681. *Miscellaneous Poems.* London.
Marvell, A. 1971. *The Poems and Letters of Andrew Marvell.* 2 vols. Eds. H. M. Margoliouth and P. Legouis. Oxford.
Montaigne, M. 1588. *Essais de Michel Seigneur de Montaigne.* Paris.
More, H. 1656. *Enthusiasmus Triumphatus, or a Discourse of the Nature, Causes, Kinds, and Cure of Enthusiasme.* London.
Morland, S. 1666. *A New Method of Cryptography.* London.
Morland, S. 1695. *The Urim of Conscience.* London.
Muretus, M. A. 1554. *Catullus, et in eum commentarius M. Antonii Mureti.* Venice.
[Nedham, M.]. 1648. *The Second part of Crafty Crumwell or Oliver in his Glory as King. A Trage Commedie.* London.
Newton, I. 1687. *Philosophiae Naturalis Principia Mathematica.* London.
Newton, T. 1581. *Seneca His Tenne Tragedies, Translated into Englysh.* London.
Norden, E. (ed.). 1957. *P. Vergilius Maro Aeneis Buch VI.* Stuttgart.
Oldenburg, H. (ed.). 1665a. "Of the *Mundus Subterraneus* of Athanasius Kircher." *Philosophical Transactions of the Royal Society* 1.6: 109–17.
Oldenburg, H. (ed.). 1665b. "An Experiment of a way of preparing a Liquor, that shall sink into, and colour the whole Body of *Marble*, causing a *Picture*, drawn on a surface, to appear also in the inmost parts of the Stone." *Philosophical Transactions of the Royal Society* 1.7: 125–7.
Oldenburg, H. (ed.). 1669. "A Chronological Accompt of the Several *Incendium's* or Fires of Mount *Aetna.*" *Philosophical Transactions of the Royal Society* 4.48: 967–9.
Owen, J. 1682. *A Short and Plain Answer to Two Questions.* London.
Paleario, A. 1992. *Aonii Palearii Verulani De animorum immortalitate libri III: Introduction and Text.* Ed. D. Sacré. Brussels.
Palingenius, M. 1548. *Zodiacus Vitae.* Basel.
Parisetti, L. 1541a. *De immortalitate animae.* Reggio Emilia.
Parisetti, L. 1541b. *Epistolae.* Reggio Emilia.
Parker, M. 1567. *The Whole Psalter Translated into English Metre.* London.

Patillon, M. (ed.). 2012. *Corpus rhetoricum Tome IV. Prolégomènes au De Ideis. Hermogène: Les catégories stylistiques su discours (De Ideis). Synopse des exposés sur les Ideai.* Paris.
Patrizi, F. 1969-71. *Della Poetica.* 3 vols. Ed. D. Aguzzi Barbagli. Florence.
Peiper, R. (ed.). 1961. *Alcimi Ecdicii Aviti Viennensis Episcopi Opera Quae Supersunt.* Berlin.
Pearce, Z. 1733b. *A Review of the Text of Paradise Lost.* London.
Pemberton, W. 1613. *The Godly Merchant, or The Great Gaine.* London.
Phillips, E. 1658a. *The Mysteries of Love & Eloquence.* London.
Phillips, E. 1658b. *The New World of English Words.* London.
Phillips, E. (ed.). 1669. *Sacrarum Profanarumque Phrasium Poeticarum Thesaurus.* London.
Phillips, E. 1675. *Theatrum Poetarum, or A Compleat Collection of the Poets.* London.
Phillips, E. (ed.). 1694. *Letters of State, Written by Mr. John Milton.* London.
Phillips, E. 1699. *The Beau's Academy.* London.
Pierce, T. 1649. *Caroli τοῦ μακαρίτου Παλιγγενεσία.* London.
Pindar. 1620. *Pindarou periodos. Pindari Olympia, Pythia, Nemea, Isthmia.* Saumur.
Polanus, A. 1609-10. *Syntagma Theologiae Christianae.* 2 vols. Hanau.
Pontano, G. 1943. *Dialoghi.* Ed. C. Previtera. Florence.
Poole, J. 1657. *The English Parnassus: Or, A Helpe to English Poesie.* London.
Pope, A. 1938-68. *The Twickenham Edition of the Poems of Alexander Pope.* 11 vols. Ed. J. Butt. London.
Purchas, S. 1626. *Purchas His Pilgrimage. Or Relations of the World and the Religions Observed in all Ages and places Discovered, from the Creation unto this Present.* London.
Puteanus, E. 1608. *Comus, sive Phagesiposia Cimmeria. Somnium.* Leuven.
Rainolds, J. 1619. *Orationes Duodecim.* London.
Reinhold, E. 1551. *Prutenicae Tabulae Coelestium Motuum.* Tübingen.
Reynolds, E. 1657. *Sions Praises.* London.
Ribbeck, O. (ed.). 1897-8. *Scaenicae Romanorum Poesis Fragmenta.* 2 vols. Leipzig.
Robortello, F. 1552. *De militaribus ordinibus instituendis more Greacorum liber a Francisco Robortello Utinensi in Latinum sermonem versus.* Venice.
Robortello, F. 1975. *Francisci Robortelli Utinensis de arte sive ratione corrigendi antiquorum libros disputatio.* Ed. G. Pompella. Naples.
Ronconi, F. (ed.). [1639]. *Applausi poetici alle glorie della Signora Leonora Baroni.* [Rome].
Ross, A. 1653. *Pansebeia, or, A View of all Religions in the World.* London.
Sandys, G. 1615. *A Relation of Iourney begun An: Dom: 1610.* London.
Sandys, G. 1632. *Ovid's Metamorphosis. Englished, Mythologiz'd, And Represented in Figures.* London.
Scaliger, J. 1577. *Catulli, Tibulli, Properti nova editio. Iosephus Scaliger Iul. Caesaris f. recensuit. Eiusdem in eosdem Castigationum liber.* Paris.
Scaliger, J. 1600. *Castigationes et Notae in M. Manili Astronomicon.* Leiden.
Schauer, M. (ed.). 2012. *Tragicorum Romanorum Fragmenta, Vol. 1: Livius Andronicus, Naevius, Tragici minores, Fragmenta adespota.* Göttingen.
Selden, J. 1617. *De Diis Syris.* London.
Shakespeare, W. 1623. *Mr. William Shakespeares Comedies, Histories, & Tragedies.* London.
Skinner, S. 1671. *Etymologicon Linguae Anglicanae.* London.
Skutsch, O. 1985. *The Annals of Quintus Ennius.* Oxford.
Snell, B. et al. 1971-2004. *Tragicorum Graecorum Fragmenta.* Göttingen.
Spencer, J. 1665. *A Discourse Concerning Vulgar Prophecies.* London.
Spinoza, B. 1925. *Spinoza Opera.* 4 vols. Ed. C. Gebhardt. Heidelberg.

Spinoza, B. 1985–2016. *The Collected Works of Spinoza*. 2 vols. Ed. E. Curley. Princeton.
Stillingfleet, E. 1662. *Origines Sacrae*. London.
Stoughton, J. 1640. *XI. Choice Sermons Preached Upon Selected Occasions, in Cambridge*. London.
Sweeney, R. D. (ed.). 1997. *Lactantii Placidi in Statii Thebaida Commentum: Volumen I*. Stuttgart.
Sylvester, J. 1605. *Bartas: His Devine Weekes and Workes Translated*. London.
Tasso, T. 1594. *Discorsi del poema eroico*. Naples.
Tasso, T. 1823. *Discorsi di Torquato Tasso. Tomo I*. Ed. G. Rosini. Pisa.
Tasso, T. 1973. *Discourses on the Heroic Poem*. Trans. M. Cavalchini and I. Samuel. Oxford.
Taverner, R. (trans.). 1536. *The Confessyon of the Fayth of the Germaynes [...]. To which is Added the Apologie of Melancthon*. London.
Taylor, J. 1644. *Crop-Eare Curried, or, Tom Nash His Ghost*. Oxford.
Thorne, W. 1592. *Ducente Deo. Willelmi Thorni Tullius seu Rhetor in tria stromata divisus*. Oxford.
Toland, J. 1699. *The Life of John Milton*. London.
Tombes, J. 1667. *Theodulia*. London.
Tyson, E. 1699. *Orang-Outang, sive Homo Sylvestris: or, the Anatomy of a Pygmie compared with that of a Monkey, an Ape, and a Man*. London.
Vadian, J. 1518. *De Poetica et Carminis Ratione, Liber ad Melchiorem Vadianum fratrem*. Vienna.
Varchi, B. 1555. *I Sonetti di M. Benedetto Varchi*. Venice.
Vettori, P. 1562. *Commentarii in Librum Demetrii Phalerei de elocutione*. Florence.
Vielmi, G. 1575. *De Sex Diebus Conditi Orbis Liber*. Venice.
Vossius, G. 1630. *Commentariorum Rhetoricorum, sive Oratoriarum Institutionum Libri Sex*. 2 vols. Leiden.
Walker, J. 1799. *Historical Memoir on Italian Tragedy*. London.
Wall, J. 1627. *Alae Seraphicae*. London.
Walz, C. (ed.). 1832–6. *Rhetores Graeci*. 9 vols. Stuttgart.
Weinberg, B. (ed.). 1972. *Trattati di poetica e retorica del Cinquecento*. 4 vols. Bari.
Wilkes, W. 1608. *A Second Memento for Magistrates*. London.
Wilkins, J. 1640. *A Discourse Concerning a New World and Another Planet*. London.
Wilkins, J. 1675. *Of the Principles and Duties of Natural Religion*. London.
Wollebius, J. 1655. *Compendium Theologiae Christianae*. Oxford.
Wollstonecraft, M. 1787. *Thoughts on the Education of Daughters*. London.
Wood, A. 1691–2. *Athenae Oxonienses*. 2 vols. London.
Wotton, H. 1672. *Reliquiae Wottonianae*. London.

VI. Secondary Sources

The following abbreviations are used for periodicals:

AJP	*American Journal of Philology*
ANRW	*Aufstieg und Niedergang der römischen Welt*
AS	*Annals of Science*
BHR	*Bibliothèque d'Humanisme et Renaissance*
BLR	*Bodleian Library Record*
CP	*Classical Philology*

CR	Classical Review
EJP	European Journal of Philosophy
ELH	English Literary History
ELN	English Language Notes
ELR	English Literary Renaissance
HL	Humanistica Lovaniensia
HLQ	Huntington Library Quarterly
IJCT	International Journal of the Classical Tradition
JEGP	Journal of English and Germanic Philology
JHI	Journal of the History of Ideas
Libr.	The Library
LRB	London Review of Books
MLN	Modern Language Notes
MLQ	Modern Language Quarterly
MLR	Modern Language Review
Mnem.	Mnemosyne
MP	Modern Philology
MS	Milton Studies
MQ	Milton Quarterly
NQ	Notes & Queries
PBSA	Papers of the Bibliographical Society of America
PMLA	Publications of the Modern Language Association
PQ	Philological Quarterly
PS	Prose Studies
RES	Review of English Studies
RHLF	Revue d'Histoire littéraire de la France
RQ	Renaissance Quarterly
RR	Renaissance and Reformation/Renaissance et Réforme
SC	The Seventeenth Century
SEL	Studies in English Literature 1500–1900
SP	Studies in Philology
TLS	Times Literary Supplement
UTQ	University of Toronto Quarterly

Achinstein, S. 1994. *Milton and the Revolutionary Reader*. Princeton.
Achinstein, S. 1996. "Milton's Spectre in the Restoration: Marvell, Dryden, and Literary Enthusiasm." *HLQ* 59.1: 1–29.
Achinstein, S. 2003. *Literature and Dissent in Milton's England*. Cambridge.
Achinstein, S. 2015. "Did Milton Read Selden?" In Jones 2015: 266–93.
Achinstein, S. and E. Sauer (eds.). 2007. *Milton and Toleration*. Oxford.
Adams, B. S. 1983. "Miltonic Metaphor and Ramist 'Invention': The Imagery of the Nativity Ode." *MS* 18: 85–102.

WORKS CITED

Adams, R. M. 1954. "The Text of *Paradise Lost*: Emphatic and Unemphatic Spellings." *MP* 52.2: 84–91.
Adams, R. M. 1955. *Ikon: John Milton and the Modern Critics*. Ithaca.
Ademollo, A. 1888. *I teatri di Roma nel secolo decimosettimo*. Rome.
Adlington, H. 2015. "'Formed on ye Gr. Language': Benjamin Stillingfleet Reads *Paradise Lost*, 1745–46." *MQ* 49.4: 217–242.
Ainsworth, D. 2013. "Getting Past the Ellipsis: The Spirit and Urania in *Paradise Lost*." In *Renaissance Papers 2012*, eds. A. Shifflett and E. Gieskes, Rochester: 117–25.
Allen, G. 2013. *The Cooke Sisters: Education, Piety, and Politics in Early Modern England*. Manchester.
Allen, M. J. B. 1984. *The Platonism of Marsilio Ficino: A Study of His Phaedrus Commentary, Its Sources and Genesis*. Berkeley.
Anderson, J. 2008. *Reading the Allegorical Intertext: Chaucer, Spenser, Shakespeare, Milton*. New York.
Armitage, D. et al. (eds.). 1995. *Milton and Republicanism*. Cambridge.
Ayala, L. 2014. "Cosmology after Copernicus: Decentralisation of the Sun and the Plurality of Worlds in French Engravings." In *The Making of Copernicus: Early Modern Transformations of a Scientist and his Science*, eds. W. Neuber et al., Leiden: 201–26.
Bailey, J. 1915. *Milton*. New York.
Barker, A. 1937. "Milton's Schoolmasters." *MLR* 32.4: 517–36.
Barlow, R. G. 1973. "Infinite Worlds: Robert Burton's Cosmic Voyage." *JHI* 34.2: 291–302.
Bauman, M. 1987. *Milton's Arianism*. Frankfurt.
Barbour, R. 2010. "Anonymous Lucretius." *BLR* 23.1: 105–11.
Barnes, D. 2016. *Epistolary Community in Print, 1580–1664*. Abingdon.
Barton, W. M. 2017. *Mountain Aesthetics in Early Modern Latin Literature*. London.
Beekes, R. 2010. *Etymological Dictionary of Greek*. 2 vols. Leiden.
Bevir, M. 2008. "What is Genealogy?" *Journal of the Philosophy of History* 2: 263–75.
Binns, J. W. 1990. *Intellectual Culture in Elizabethan and Jacobean England: The Latin Writings of the Age*. Leeds.
Binski, P. 2010. "Reflections on the 'Wonderful Height and Size' of Gothic Great Churches and the Medieval Sublime." In Jaeger 2010a: 129–56.
Birrell, T. A. 1980. "The Reconstruction of the Library of Isaac Casaubon." In *Hellinga Festschrift/Feestbundel/Mélanges*, eds. A. R. A. Croiset van Uchelen, Amsterdam: 59–68.
Birrell, T. A. 2013. *Aspects of Book Culture in Early Modern England*. Ed. J. Blom. London.
Blackwell, M. 2004. "The Subterranean Wind of Allusion: Milton, Dryden, Shadwell, and Mock-Epic Modernity." *Restoration* 28.1: 15–36.
Blissett, W. 1957. "Caesar and Satan." *JHI* 18.2: 221–32.
Blom, F. J. M. 1984. "Lucas Holstenius (1596–1661) and England." In *Studies in Seventeenth-Century English Literature, History and Bibliography*, eds. G. A. M. Janssens and F. G. A. M. Aarts, Amsterdam: 25–39.
Boitani, P. 1989. *The Tragic and the Sublime in Medieval Literature*. Cambridge.
de Bolla, P. 1989. *The Discourse of the Sublime: Readings in History, Aesthetics, and the Subject*. Oxford.
Bolt, T. J. 2019. "Theomachy in Greek and Roman Epic." In *Structures of Epic Poetry*, 4 vols, eds. C. Reitz and S. Finkmann, Berlin: II 283–316.
Boot, P. 1980. "The Place of Longinus' *De Sublimitate* C. 44." *Mnem.* 33.3/4: 299–306.
Bottkol, J. M. 1953. "The Holograph of Milton's Letter to Holstenius." *PMLA* 68.3: 617–27.
Bourne, C. 2018. "*Vide Supplementum*: Early Modern Collation as Play-Reading in the First Folio." In *Early Modern English Marginalia*, ed. K. Acheson, London: 195–233.

Bourne, C. and J. Scott-Warren. 2023. "'thy unvalued Booke': John Milton's Copy of the Shakespeare First Folio." *MQ* 56.1-2: 1-85.
Boutcher, W. 2017. *The School of Montaigne in Early Modern Europe*. 2 vols. Oxford.
Bowden, C. 2005. "The Library of Mildred Cooke Cecil, Lady Burghley." *Libr.* 7th ser. 6.1: 3-29.
Brady, M. 2005. "Galileo in Action: The 'Telescope' in *Paradise Lost*." *MS* 44: 129-52.
Brady, M. 2007. "Space and Persistence of Place in *Paradise Lost*." *MQ* 41.3: 167-82.
Broadbent, J. B. 1967. *Some Graver Subject: An Essay on Paradise Lost*. London.
Broadbent, J. B. 1972. *Paradise Lost: Introduction*. Cambridge.
Brody, J. 1958. *Boileau and Longinus*. Geneva.
Brown, A. 2010. *The Return of Lucretius to Renaissance Florence*. Cambridge, MA.
Brown, C. C. 1985. *John Milton's Aristocratic Entertainments*. Cambridge.
Brown, C. C. 1995. "Great Senates and Godly Education: Politics and Cultural Renewal in Some Pre- and Post-revolutionary Texts of Milton." In Armitage et al. 1995: 43-60.
Brown, P. A. 2015. "The Mirror and the Cage: Queens and Dwarfs at the Early Modern Court." In *Historical Affects and the Early Modern Stage*, eds. R. Arab et al., New York: 137-51.
Budick, S. 2010. *Kant and Milton*. Cambridge, MA.
Bullard, P. 2012. "Edmund Burke Among the Poets: Milton, Lucretius, and the *Philosophical Enquiry*." In *The Science of Sensibility: Reading Burke's Philosophical Enquiry*, eds. K. Vermeir and M. F. Deckard, Dordrecht: 247-64.
Burnett, A. N. 2006. *Teaching the Reformation: Ministers and Their Message in Basel, 1529-1629*. Oxford.
Burrow, C. 1999. "Combative Criticism: Jonson, Milton, and Classical Literary Criticism in England." In Norton 1999: 487-99.
Bussels, S. 2016. "Theories of the Sublime in the Dutch Golden Age: Franciscus Junius, Joost van den Vondel and Petrus Wittewrongel." *History of European Ideas* 42.7: 882-92.
Butler, G. F. 1998. "Giants and Fallen Angels in Dante and Milton: The *Commedia* and the Gigantomachy in *Paradise Lost*." *MP* 95.3: 352-63.
Butler, G. F. 2003. "Boccaccio and Milton's 'Manlike' Eve: The *Genealogia Deorum Gentilium Libri* and *Paradise Lost*." *MQ* 37.3: 166-71.
Butler, G. F. 2005. "Milton's Meeting with Galileo: A Reconsideration." *MQ* 39.3: 132-9.
Cable, L. 1995. *Carnal Rhetoric: Milton's Iconoclasm and the Poetics of Desire*. Durham, NC.
Calloway, K. 2009. "Milton's Lucretian Anxiety Revisited." *RR* 32.3: 79-97.
Cambers, A. 2011. *Godly Reading: Print, Manuscript and Puritanism in England, 1580-1720*. Cambridge.
Campbell, G. 1977. "Milton's *Index Theologicus* and Bellarmine's *Disputationes De Controversiis Christianae Fidei Adversus Huius Temporis Haereticos*." *MQ* 11.1: 12-16.
Campbell, G. 1987. "Milton and the Septuagint: The Problem of Chrysolite." *Journal of Theological Studies* 38.2: 441-3.
Campbell, G. 1997. *A Milton Chronology*. Basingstoke.
Campbell, G. and T. N. Corns. 2008. *John Milton: Life, Work, and Thought*. Oxford.
Campbell, G. et al. 1997. "The Provenance of *De Doctrina Christiana*." *MQ* 31.3: 67-117, 119-21.
Campbell, G. et al. 2007. *Milton and the Manuscript of De Doctrina Christiana*. Oxford.
Capizzi, A. 1983. "Mente elevata e mente profonda: *Hypsos* e *bathos* dal concreto alla metafora." In *Il Sublime: Contributi per la storia di un'idea*, eds. G. Casertano and G. Martano. Naples, 55-75.
Cardillo, A. 2010. "Giovanni da Falgano, *Libro della altezza del dire* (Per l'edizione del volgarizzamento del *Perí hýpsus* di Ps. Longino)." In *Macramé: Studi sulla letteratura e le arti*, 2 vols., eds. R. Giulio et al., Naples: 1.91-135.

Carruthers, M. 2014. "Terror, Horror and the Fear of God, or, Why There Is No Medieval Sublime." In *'Truthe is the beste': A Festschrift in Honour of A. V. C. Schmidt*, eds. N. Jacobs and G. Morgan, Bern: 17–36.

Cawley, R. R. 1951. *Milton and the Literature of Travel*. Princeton.

di Cesare, M. A. (ed.). 1991. *Milton in Italy: Contexts, Images, Contradictions*. Binghampton.

Cefalu, P. 2016. "Incarnational *Apophatic*: Rethinking Divine Accommodation in John Milton's *Paradise Lost*." *SP* 113.1: 198–228.

Chaudhuri, P. 2014. *The War with God: Theomachy in Roman Imperial Poetry*. Oxford.

Cheney, P. 2009a. *Marlowe's Republican Authorship: Lucan, Liberty, and the Sublime*. London.

Cheney, P. 2009b. "Milton, Marlowe, and Lucan: The English Authorship of Republican Liberty." *MS* 49: 1–19.

Cheney, P. 2011. "'The forms of things unknown': English Authorship and the Early Modern Sublime." In *Medieval and Early Modern Authorship*, eds. G. Bolens and L. Erne, Tübingen: 137–60.

Cheney, P. 2018a. "The Sublime." In *A Companion to Renaissance Poetry*, ed. C. Bates, Oxford: 611–27.

Cheney, P. 2018b. *English Authorship and the Early Modern Sublime: Fictions of Transport in Spenser, Marlowe, Jonson, and Shakespeare*. Cambridge.

Chernaik, W. 2017. *Milton and the Burden of Freedom*. Cambridge.

Chiron, P. 1993. *Démétrios: Du style*. Paris.

Clark, A. F. B. 1925. *Boileau and the French Classical Critics in England*. Paris.

Clark, D. L. 1946. "Milton's Schoolmasters: Alexander Gil and His Son Alexander." *HLQ* 9.2: 121–47.

Clark, D. L. 1953. "John Milton and 'the fitted stile of lofty, mean, or lowly.'" *Seventeenth-Century News* 9.4: 5–9.

Clark, D. L. 1964. *John Milton at St. Paul's School: A Study of Ancient Rhetoric in English Renaissance Education*. New York.

Cocco, S. 2007. *Antiquity Recovered: The Legacy of Pompeii and Herculaneum*. Los Angeles.

Cocco, S. 2013. *Watching Vesuvius: A History of Science and Culture in Early Modern Italy*. Chicago.

Coffey, J. 2006. *John Goodwin and the Puritan Revolution: Religion and Intellectual Change in Seventeenth-Century England*. Woodbridge.

Coiro, A. B. 2008. "Milton & Sons: The Family Business." *MS* 48: 13–37.

Cokayne, G. E. 1887–98. *Complete Peerage of England, Scotland, Ireland, Great Britain, and the United Kingdom*. 8 vols. London.

Colclough, D. 2005. *Freedom of Speech in Early Stuart England*. Cambridge.

Coleman, D. G. 1985. "Montaigne and Longinus." *BHR* 47: 405–13.

Colie, R. L. 1960. "Dean Wren's Marginalia and Early Science at Oxford." *BLR* 6: 541–51.

Conklin, G. N. 1949. *Biblical Criticism and Heresy in Milton*. New York.

Connor, J. T. 2006. "Milton's *Art of Logic* and the Force of Conviction." *MS* 45: 187–209.

Connor, W. R. 2011. "The Pygmies in the Cage: The Function of the Sublime in Longinus." In *Literary Study, Measurement, and the Sublime: Disciplinary Assessment*, eds. D. Heiland and L. J. Rosenthal, New York: 97–114.

Conte, G. B. 1966. "*Hypsos* e diatriba nello stile di Lucrezio: *De Rer. Nat.* II 1–61." *Maia* 18: 338–68.

Conte, G. B. 1994. *Genres and Readers: Lucretius, Love Elegy, Pliny's Encyclopedia*. Trans. G. W. Most. Baltimore.

Cook, A. K. 1917. *About Winchester College*. London.
Corns, T. N. 1984. "The *Complete Prose Works of John Milton* in Retrospect." *PS* 7.2: 179–86.
Corns, T. N. 1994. *Regaining Paradise Lost*. London.
Corns, T. N. (ed.). 2012a. *The Milton Encyclopedia*. New Haven.
Corns, T. N. 2012b. "The Early Lives of John Milton." In *Writing Lives: Biography and Textuality, Identity and Representation in Early Modern England*, eds. K. Sharpe and S. N. Zwicker, Oxford: 75–90.
Corns, T. N. (ed.). 2016. *A New Companion to Milton*. Oxford.
Costa, G. 1984a. "Paolo Manuzio e lo Pseudo-Longino." *Giornale storico della letteratura italiana* 161: 60–77.
Costa, G. 1984b. "Appunti sulla fortuna dello Pseudo-Longino nel Seicento: Alessandro Tassoni e Paganino Gaudenzio." *Studi secenteschi* 25: 123–43.
Costa, G. 1985. "The Latin Translations of Longinus' *Peri Hypsous* in Renaissance Italy." In *Acta Conventus Neo-Latini Bononiensis*, ed. R. J. Schoeck, Binghamton, NY: 224–38.
Costa, G. 1987a. "Un annoso problema: Tasso e il Sublime." *Rivista di Estetica* 27: 49–63.
Costa, G. 1987b. "Pietro Vettori, Ugolino Martelli e lo Pseudo Longino." In *Da Longino a Longino: I luoghi del Sublime*, ed. L. Russo, Palermo: 65–79.
Costa, G. 1994. *Il sublime e la magia. Da Dante a Tasso*. Naples.
Costa, G. 2003. "Storia del Sublime e storia ecclesiastica." *Aevum Antiquum* 3: 319–50.
Costelloe, T. M. (ed.). 2012. *The Sublime: From Antiquity to the Present*. Cambridge.
Costil, P. 1935. *André Dudith Humaniste Hongrois 1533–1589*. Paris.
Crane, D. 1986. "Marvell and Milton on Cromwell." *NQ* 33.4: 464.
Crawford, J. 2011. *Raising Milton's Ghost: John Milton and the Sublime of Terror in the Early Romantic Period*. London.
Creaser, J. 1983. "Editorial Problems in Milton." *RES* 34.135: 279–303.
Creaser, J. 1984. "Editorial Problems in Milton (*Concluded*)." *RES* 35.137: 45–60.
Cronk, N. 2002. *The Classical Sublime: French Neoclassicism and the Language of Literature*. Charlottesville.
Crossett, J. M. and J. A. Arieti. 1975. *The Dating of Longinus*. University Park, PA.
Curtius, E. R. 2013. *European Literature and the Latin Middle Ages*. Trans. W. R. Trask. Princeton.
D'Angour, A. 2006. "Conquering Love: Sappho 31 and Catullus 51." *Classical Quarterly* 56.1: 297–300.
D'Angour, A. 2013. "Love's Battlefield: Rethinking Sappho Fragment 31." In *Erôs in Ancient Greece*, eds. E. Sanders et al., Oxford: 59–71.
Dahlø, R. 1979. "The Date of Milton's *Artis Logicae* and the Development of the Idea of Definition in Milton's Works." *HLQ* 43.1: 25–36.
Danielson, D. 1982. *Milton's Good God: A Study in Literary Theodicy*. Cambridge.
Danielson, D. (ed.) 1999. *The Cambridge Companion to Milton*. 2nd Edition. Cambridge.
Danielson, D. 2010. "Astronomy." In *Milton in Context*, ed. S. B. Dobranski, Cambridge: 213–25.
Danielson, D. 2014. *Paradise Lost and the Cosmological Revolution*. Cambridge.
Darbishire, H. 1933. "The Chronology of Milton's Handwriting." *Libr.* 4th ser. 14.2: 229–35.
Dasen, V. 1988. "Dwarfism in Egypt and Classical Antiquity: Iconography and Medical History." *Medical History* 32: 253–76.
Davis, P. 2015. "Addison's Forgotten Poetic Response to *Paradise Lost*: 'Milton's Stile Imitated, in a Translation of a Story out of the Third *Aeneid*' (1704): An Edited Text with Annotation and Commentary." *MQ* 49.4: 243–74.

Delehanty, A. T. 2007. "Mapping the Aesthetic Mind: John Dennis and Nicolas Boileau." *JHI* 68.2: 233-53.

Dietz, M. 1997. "'Thus Sang the Uncouth Swain': Pastoral, Prophecy, and Historicism in *Lycidas*." *MS* 35: 42-72.

Dixon, D. 1951. *Alexander Gil's Logonomia Anglica Edition of 1621 Translated with an Introduction and Critical and Explanatory Notes*. University of Southern California PhD thesis.

Dobbins, A. C. 1975. *Milton and the Book of Revelation: The Heavenly Cycle*. Tuscaloosa.

Dobranski, S. B. 1999. *Milton, Authorship, and the Book Trade*. Cambridge.

Dobranski, S. B. 2015. *Milton's Visual Imagination: Imagery in Paradise Lost*. Cambridge.

Dodds, L. 2008. "Milton's Other Worlds." In *Uncircumscribed Mind: Reading Milton Deeply*, eds. C. W. Durham and K. A. Pruitt, Selinsgrove: 164-82.

Doran, R. 2015. *The Theory of the Sublime from Longinus to Kant*. Cambridge.

Dubrow, H. 2008. *The Challenges of Orpheus: Lyric Poetry and Early Modern England*. Baltimore.

Duhamel, P. A. 1952. "Milton's Alleged Ramism." *PMLA* 67.7: 1035-53.

Duran, A. 2003. "The Sexual Mathematics of *Paradise Lost*." *MQ* 37.2: 55-76.

Duran, A. 2007. *The Age of Milton and the Scientific Revolution*. Pittsburgh.

DuRocher, R. J. 2001. *Milton Among the Romans: The Pedagogy and Influence of Milton's Latin Curriculum*. Pittsburgh.

Dzelzainis, M. 1997. "Milton and the Limits of Ciceronian Rhetoric." In *English Renaissance Prose: History, Language, and Politics*, ed. N. Rhodes, Tempe: 203-26.

Dzelzainis, M. 2007. "Milton and Antitrinitarianism." In Achinstein and Sauer 2007: 171-85.

Dzelzainis, M. 2012. "Milton, Foucault, and the New Historicism." In *Rethinking Historicism from Shakespeare to Milton*, eds. A. B. Coiro and T. Fulton, Cambridge: 209-33.

Earle, P. 2020. "'Till Body Up to Spirit Work': Maimonidean Prophecy and Monistic Sublimation in *Paradise Regained*." *MS* 62.1: 159-89.

van Eck, C. 2012. "Figuring the Sublime in English Church Architecture 1640-1730." In van Eck et al. 2012: 221-45.

van Eck, C. et al. (eds.). 2012. *Translations of the Sublime: The Early Modern Reception and Dissemination of Longinus' Peri Hupsous in Rhetoric, the Visual Arts, Architecture and the Theatre*. Leiden.

Edwards, K. L. 1995. "Comenius, Milton, and the Temptation to Ease." *MS* 32: 23-43.

Edwards, K. L. 2003. "Inspiration and Melancholy in *Samson Agonistes*." In *Milton and the Ends of Time*, ed. J. Cummins, Cambridge: 224-40.

Edwards, K. L. 2005. *Milton and the Natural World: Science and Poetry in Paradise Lost*. Cambridge.

Edwards, K. L. 2006. "Milton's Reformed Animals: An Early Modern Bestiary D-F." *MQ* 40.2: 99-187.

Edwards, K. L. 2008. "Engaging with Pygmies: Thomas Browne and John Milton." In *Sir Thomas Browne: The World Proposed*, eds. R. Barbour and C. Preston, Oxford: 100-17.

Edwards, K. L. 2014. "Cosmology." In Schwartz 2014: 109-22.

Ehwald, R. 1892. "Ad historiam carminum Ovidianorum recensionemque symbolae." *Programm des Herzoglichen Gymnasium Ernestinum zu Gotha*, Gotha: 1-22.

Elliott, E. 1974. "Milton's Biblical Style in *Paradise Regained*." *MS* 6: 227-41.

Ellison, J. 2002. *George Sandys: Travel, Colonialism, and Tolerance in the Seventeenth Century*. Cambridge.

Empson, W. 1965. *Milton's God*. London.

Ernout, A. and A. Meillet. 2001. *Dictionnaire étymologique de la langue latine.* Paris.
Ettenhuber, K. 2021. "Milton's Logic: The Early Years." *SC* 36.2: 187–212.
Evans, J. M. 1968. *Paradise Lost and the Genesis Tradition.* Oxford.
Falkeid, U. 2015. "The Sublime Realism of Gaspara Stampa." In Falkeid and Feng 2015: 39–54.
Falkeid, U. and A. A. Feng (eds.). 2015. *Rethinking Gaspara Stampa in the Canon of Renaissance Poetry.* Aldershot.
Fallon, R. T. 1984. *Captain or Colonel: The Soldier in Milton's Life and Art.* Columbia, MO.
Fallon, S. M. 1991. *Milton among the Philosophers: Poetry and Materialism in Seventeenth-Century England.* Ithaca.
Fallon, S. M. 2007. *Milton's Peculiar Grace: Self-Representation and Authority.* Ithaca.
Farrell, A. 1943. "Joshua Poole and Milton's Minor Poems." *MLN* 58.3: 198–200.
Feingold, M. 1997. "The Humanities." In *The History of the University of Oxford: Volume IV Seventeenth-Century Oxford*, ed. N. Tyacke, Oxford: 211–357.
Feingold, M. et al. (eds.). 2001. *The Influence of Petrus Ramus: Studies in Sixteenth- and Seventeenth-Century Philosophy and Sciences.* Basel.
Feinstein, S. 1998. "Milton's Devilish Sublime." *Ben Jonson Journal* 5: 149–66.
Festa, T. 2004. "Repairing the Ruins: Milton as Reader and Educator." *MS* 43: 35–63.
Festa, T. 2006. *The End of Learning: Milton and Education.* London.
Fisch, H. 1967. "Hebraic Style and Motifs in *Paradise Lost.*" In *Language and Style in Milton: A Symposium in Honor of the Tercentenary of Paradise Lost*, eds. R. D. Emma and J. T. Shawcross, New York: 30–64.
Fish, S. 1997. *Surprised by Sin: The Reader in Paradise Lost.* 2nd Edition. Cambridge, MA.
Flannagan, R. 1986. "Art, Artists, Galileo and Concordances." *MQ* 20.3: 103–5.
Fletcher, A. 1971. *The Transcendental Masque: An Essay on Milton's Comus.* Ithaca.
Fletcher, H. F. 1948. "Milton's Copy of Gesner's Heraclides, 1544." *JEGP* 47.2: 182–7.
Fletcher, H. F. 1956–61. *The Intellectual Development of John Milton.* 2 vols. Urbana.
Fletcher, H. F. 1958. "Milton's Demogorgon: *Prolusion I* and *Paradise Lost*, II, 960–65." *JEGP* 57.4: 684–9.
Fletcher, H. F. 1989. "John Milton's Copy of Lycophron's *Alexandra* in the Library of the University of Illinois." *MQ* 23: 129–58.
Flinker, N. 1980. "Father–Daughter Incest in *Paradise Lost.*" *MQ* 14.4: 116–22.
Forsyth, N. 2003. *The Satanic Epic.* Princeton.
Fortescue, G. K. 1908. *Catalogue of the Pamphlets, Books, Newspapers, and Manuscripts Relating to the Civil War, Commonwealth, and Restoration, Collected by George Thomason, 1640–1661.* 2 vols. London.
Foster, J. 1888–91. *Alumni Oxonienses: The Members of the University of Oxford, 1500–1714.* 4 vols. Oxford.
Foucault, M. 1977. "Nietzsche, Genealogy, History." In *Language, Counter-Memory, Practice: Selected Essays and Interviews*, ed. D. F. Bouchard, Ithaca: 139–164.
Foucault, M. 1995. *Discipline and Punish: The Birth of the Prison.* Trans. A. Sheridan. New York.
Francis, J. 1994. "The Kedermister Library: An Account of Its Origins and a Reconstruction of Its Contents and Arrangement." *Records of Buckinghamshire* 36: 62–85.
Freeman, J. A. 1980. *Milton and the Martial Muse: Paradise Lost and European Traditions of War.* Princeton.
Friedman, D. 1991. "Galileo and the Art of Seeing." In di Cesare 1991: 159–74.
Fritz, M. 2011. *Vom Erhabenen: Der Traktat Peri Hypsous und seine ästhetisch-religiöse Renaissance im 18. Jahrhundert.* Tübingen.

Fumaroli, M. 1986. "Rhétorique d'école et rhétorique adulte: Remarques sur la réception européenne du traité *Du Sublime* au XVIe et au XVIIe siècle." *RHLF* 86: 33–51.

Fumaroli, M. 2002. *L'Âge de l'éloquence: Rhétorique et «res literaria» de la Renaissance au seuil de l'époque classique*. Geneva.

Fulton, T. 2010. *Historical Milton: Manuscript, Print, and Political Culture in Revolutionary England*. Amherst.

Gabe, D. 1991. "Denys Lambin's Own Copy of Longinus' «*Peri Hupsous*.»" *BHR* 53.3: 743–8.

Gadd, I. 2013. "The University and the Oxford Book Trade." In *The History of Oxford University Press. Volume I: Beginnings to 1780*, ed. I. Gadd, Oxford: 549–600.

Garland, R. 2010. *The Eye of the Beholder: Deformity and Disability in the Graeco-Roman World*. 2nd Edition. London.

Gay, D. 1995. "'Rapt Spirits': 2 Corinthians 12.2-5 and the Language of Milton's *Comus*." *MQ* 29.3: 76–86.

Gelber, M. W. 2002. *The Just and the Lively: The Literary Criticism of John Dryden*. Manchester.

Geuss, R. 1994. "Nietzsche and Genealogy." *EJP* 2.3: 274–92.

Geuss, R. 2002. "Genealogy as Critique." *EJP* 10.2: 209–15.

Gigante, D. 2016. "Milton's Spots: Addison on *Paradise Lost*." In Hoxby and Coiro 2016: 7–21.

Gilbert, A. H. 1922. "Milton and Galileo." *SP* 19.2: 152–85.

Gilbert, A. H. 1923. "Milton's Textbook of Astronomy." *PMLA* 38.2: 297–307.

Gilbert, A. H. 1942. "The Theological Basis of Satan's Rebellion and the Function of Abdiel in *Paradise Lost*." *MP* 40.1: 19–42.

Gilby, E. 2006. *Sublime Worlds: Early Modern French Literature*. London.

Gilby, E. 2016. "Where to Draw the Line?: Longinus, Goulu, and Balzac's *Lettres*." In van Oostveldt et al. 2016: 225–40.

Godefroy, F. 1902. *Dictionnaire de l'ancienne langue française et de tous ses dialectes du IXe siècle au XVe siècle. Tome Dixième: Complément Inaccoutumé—Zoophyte*. Paris.

Goldstein, R. J. 2017. *The English Lyric Tradition: Reading Poetic Masterpieces of the Middle Ages and Renaissance*. Jefferson.

Goode, J. 1930. "Milton and Longinus." *TLS* 22 August 1930: 668.

Goold, G. P. 1961. "A Greek Professorial Circle at Rome." *Transactions and Proceedings of the American Philological Association* 92: 168–92.

Gorecki, J. 1976. "Milton's Similitudes for Satan and the Traditional Implications of Their Imagery." *MQ* 10.4: 101–8.

Goyet, F. 1996. *Le sublime du «lieu commun»: L'invention rhétorique dans l'Antiquité et à la Renaissance*. Paris.

Grafton, A. and J. Weinberg. 2011. *"I Have Always Loved the Holy Tongue": Isaac Casaubon, the Jews, and a Forgotten Chapter in Renaissance Scholarship*. Cambridge, MA.

Graziani, F. 1996. "Le miracle de l'art: le Tasse et la poétique de la meraviglia." *Revue des Études Italiennes* 42: 117–40.

Greengrass, M. et al. (eds.). 2002. *Samuel Hartlib and Universal Reformation: Studies in Intellectual Communication*. Cambridge.

Gregory, T. 2006. *From Many Gods to One: Divine Action in Renaissance Epic*. Chicago.

Gregory, T. 2010. "Murmur and Reply: Rereading Milton's Sonnet 19." *MS* 51: 21–43, 254–7.

Gregory, T. 2015. "Milton and Cromwell: Another Look at the Evidence." *Journal of British Studies* 54.1: 44–62.

Greteman, B. 2016. "'To Secure Our Freedom': How *A Mask Presented at Ludlow-Castle* Became *Milton's Comus*." In Hoxby and Coiro 2016: 143–8.

Grose, C. 1971. "Milton on Ramist Similitude." In *Seventeenth Century Imagery*, ed. E. Miner, Berkeley: 103–16.

Grube, G. M. A. 1957. "Notes on the Περὶ ὕψους." *AJP* 78.4: 355–74.

Grube, G. M. A. 1961. *A Greek Critic: Demetrius on Style*. Toronto.

Grube, G. M. A. 1965. *The Greek and Roman Critics*. Toronto.

Guillory, J. 1993. *Cultural Capital: The Problem of Literary Canon Formation*. Chicago.

Haan, E. 1992. Milton's *In Quintum Novembris* and the Anglo-Latin Gunpowder Epic." *HL* 41: 221–95.

Haan, E. 1998. *From Academia to Amicitia: Milton's Latin Writings and the Italian Academies*. Philadelphia.

Haan, E. 2003. "From Neo-Latin to Vernacular: Celestial Warfare in Vida and Milton." In *Hommages à Carl Deroux V - Christianisme et Moyen Âge: Néo-Latin et Survivance de la latinité*, ed. P. Defosse, Brussels: 408–19.

Haan, E. 2012. *Both English and Latin: Bilingualism and Biculturalism in Milton's Neo-Latin Writings*. Philadelphia.

Haffter, H. 1935. "Sublimis." *Glotta* 23.3/4: 251–61.

Hale, J. K. 1991. "Milton's Euripides Marginalia: Their Significance for Milton Studies." *MS* 27: 23–35.

Hale, J. K. 1995. "*Paradise Lost*: A Poem in Twelve Books, or Ten?" *PQ* 74: 131–49.

Hale, J. K. 1997a. "Voicing Milton's God." *Journal of the Australasian Universities Language and Literature Association* 88.1: 59–70.

Hale, J. K. 1997b. *Milton's Languages: The Impact of Multilingualism on Style*. Cambridge.

Hale, J. K. 2005. *Milton's Cambridge Latin: Performing in the Genres 1625–1632*. Tempe.

Hale, J. K. 2010. "The Problems and Opportunities of Editing *De Doctrina Christiana*." *MQ* 44.1: 38–46.

Hale, J. K. 2014. "Points of Departure: Studies in Milton's Use of Wollebius." *Reformation* 19.1: 69–82.

Hale, J. K. 2015. "Young Milton in His Letters." In Jones 2015: 66–86.

Hale, J. K. 2016a. "A Study of Milton's Greek." *MS* 57: 187–210.

Hale, J. K. 2016b. "The Classical Literary Tradition." In *A New Companion to Milton*, ed. T. N. Corns, Chichester: 22–36.

Hale, J. K. 2019. *Milton's Scriptural Theology: Confronting De Doctrina Christiana*. Leeds.

Hale, J. K. 2022. "Longinus and Milton: "Tis the *hupsos* I looke after.'" *Milton Studies* 64.2: 153–72.

Hamlett, L. 2012. "The Longinian Sublime, Effect and Affect in 'Baroque' British Visual Culture." In van Eck et al. 2012: 187–219.

Hamlett, L. 2013. "Longinus and the Baroque Sublime in Britain." In Llewellyn and Riding 2013, URL=<https://www.tate.org.uk/art/research-publications/the-sublime/lydia-hamlett-longinus-and-the-baroque-sublime-in-britain-r1108498>.

Hammond, F. 1994. *Music and Spectacle in Baroque Rome: Barberini Patronage under Urban VIII*. New Haven.

Hammond, P. 2013. Review of Lewalski and Haan 2012. *SC* 28:2: 239–44.

Hammond, P. 2019. Review of Poole 2019. *SC* 34.5: 671–5.

Hardie, P. 2009. *Lucretian Receptions: History, The Sublime, Knowledge*. Cambridge.

Hardie, P. 2012. *Rumour and Renown: Representations of Fama in Western Literature.* Cambridge.

Harding, D. P. 1946. *Milton and the Renaissance Ovid.* Urbana.

Harding, D. P. 1962. *The Club of Hercules: Studies in the Classical Background of Paradise Lost.* Urbana.

Hardy, N. 2016. "Is the *De rerum natura* a Work of Natural Theology? Some Ancient, Modern, and Early Modern Perspectives." In Norbrook et al. 2016: 200–21.

Hardy, N. 2017. *Criticism and Confession: The Bible in the Seventeenth Century Republic of Letters.* Oxford.

Harper, D. 2019. "The First Annotator of *Paradise Lost* and the Makings of English Literary Criticism." *SEL* 59.3: 507–30.

Harris, N. 1985. "Galileo as Symbol: The 'Tuscan Artist' in *Paradise Lost*." *Annali dell'Istituto e Museo di storia della scienza di Firenza* 10: 3–29.

Hartman, G. 1958. "Milton's Counterplot." *ELH* 25.1: 1–12.

Hartmann, A.-M. 2018. *English Mythography in Its European Context, 1500–1650.* Oxford.

Hartwell, K. E. 1929. *Lactantius and Milton.* Cambridge, MA.

Haskell, Y. 1998. "Renaissance Latin Didactic Poetry on the Stars: Wonder, Myth, and Science." *Renaissance Studies* 12.4: 495–522.

Haskell, Y. 2016. "Poetic Flights or Retreats? Latin Lucretian Poems in Sixteenth-Century Italy." In Norbrook et al. 2016: 91–121.

Hathaway, B. 1962. *The Age of Criticism: The Late Renaissance in Italy.* Ithaca.

Häublein, E. 1975. "Milton's Paraphrase of Genesis: A Stylistic Reading of *Paradise Lost*, Book VII." *MS* 7: 101–25.

Hawes, C. 1996. *Mania and Literary Style: The Rhetoric of Enthusiasm from the Ranters to Christopher Smart.* Cambridge.

Heath, M. 1999. "Longinus, *On Sublimity.*" *Cambridge Classical Journal* 45: 43–74.

Heath, M. 2012a. "Longinus and the Ancient Sublime." In Costelloe 2012: 11–23.

Heath, M. 2012b. *Ancient Philosophical Poetics.* Cambridge.

Henderson, F. 2017. "Taking the Moon Seriously: John Wilkins's *Discovery of a World in the Moone* (1638) and *Discourse Concerning a New World and Another Planet* (1640)." In Poole 2017b: 129–57.

Hendrix, H. 2005. "Renaissance Roots of the Sublime: Ugliness, Horror and Pleasure in Early Modern Italian Debates on Literature and Art." In Pieters and Vandenabeele 2005: 13–22.

Herman, P. C. 2003. "*Paradise Lost*, the Miltonic "Or," and the Poetics of Incertitude." *SEL* 43.1: 181–211.

Herman, P. C. 2015. Review of Lewalski and Haan 2012. *RQ* 68.4: 1546–9.

Herz, J. S. 1978. "Milton and Marvell: The Poet as Fit Reader." *MLQ* 39.3: 239–63.

Herz, J. S. 1988. "*Paradise Lost* VIII: Adam, Hamlet, and the Anxiety of Narrative." *English Studies in Canada* 14.3: 259–69.

Herz, J. S. 1991. "'For whom this glorious sight?': Dante, Milton and the Galileo Question." In di Cesare 1991: 147–57.

Heubi, W. 1916. *L'Académie de Lausanne à la fin du XVIme siècle: Étude sur quelques professeurs d'après des documents inédits.* Lausanne.

Heyd, M. 1995. *"Be Sober and Reasonable": The Critique of Enthusiasm in the Seventeenth and Early Eighteenth Centuries.* Leiden.

Hill, C. 1977. *Milton and the English Revolution.* London.

Hill, C. 1994. "Professor William B. Hunter, Bishop Burgess, and John Milton." *SEL* 34.1: 165–93.

Hinds, S. 1987. *The Metamorphosis of Persephone: Ovid and the Self-Conscious Muse.* Cambridge.
Hirst, D. 1990. "The Politics of Literature in the English Republic." *SC* 5.2: 133–55.
Hotson, H. 2007. *Commonplace Learning: Ramism and Its German Ramifications, 1543–1630.* Oxford.
Howarth, R. G. 1959. "Edward Phillips's *Compendiosa Enumeratio Poetarum.*" *MLR* 54.3: 321–8.
Hoxby, B. 2016. "'In the Dun Air Sublime': Milton, the Richardsons, and the Invention of Aesthetic Categories." In Hoxby and Coiro 2016: 69–96.
Hoxby, B. and A. B. Coiro (eds.). 2016. *Milton in the Long Restoration.* Oxford.
Hughes, M. Y. 1965. *Ten Perspectives on Milton.* New Haven.
Huguelet, T. L. 1974. "The Rule of Charity in Milton's Divorce Tracts." *MS* 6: 199–214.
Hunter, W. B. 1992. "The Provenance of the *Christian Doctrine.*" *SEL* 32.1: 129–42.
Hunter, W. B. 1993. "The Provenance of the *Christian Doctrine*: Addenda from the Bishop of Salisbury." *SEL* 33.1: 191–207.
Hunter, W. B. 1994. "Animadversions upon the Remonstrants' Defenses against Burgess and Hunter." *SEL* 34.1: 195–203.
Hunter, W. B. 1998. *Visitation Unimplor'd: Milton and the Authorship of De Doctrina Christiana.* Pittsburgh.
Hunter, W. B. et al. 1971. *Bright Essence: Studies in Milton's Theology.* Salt Lake City.
Huntley, F. L. 1947. "Dryden's Discovery of Boileau." *MP* 45.2: 112–17.
Inglis, E. 2003. "Gothic Architecture and a Scholastic: Jean de Jandun's *Tractatus de laudibus Parisius* (1323)." *Gesta* 42.1: 63–85.
Innes, D. C. 2002. "Longinus and Caecilius: Models of the Sublime." *Mnem.* 55.3: 259–84.
Jaeger, C. S. (ed.). 2010a. *Magnificence and the Sublime in Medieval Aesthetics: Art, Architecture, Literature, Music.* New York.
Jaeger, C. S. 2010b. "Richard of St. Victor and the Medieval Sublime." In Jaeger 2010a: 157–78.
Janowitz, A. 2010. "The Sublime Plurality of Worlds: Lucretius in the Eighteenth Century." In Llewellyn and Riding 2013, URL=<https://www.tate.org.uk/art/research-publications/the-sublime/anne-janowitz-the-sublime-plurality-of-worlds-lucretius-in-thesup-supeighteenth-century-r1138670>.
Jansen, W. L. 2016. "Defending the Poet: The Reception of *On the Sublime* in Daniel Heinsius' *Prolegomena on Hesiod.*" In van Oostveldt et al. 2016: 199–223.
Jansen, W. L. 2019. *Appropriating Peri hypsous: Interpretations and Creative Adaptations of Longinus' Treatise On the Sublime in Early Modern Dutch Scholarship.* Leiden University PhD thesis.
Johnson, F. R. 1943. "Two Renaissance Textbooks of Rhetoric: Aphthonius' *Progymnasmata* and Rainolde's *A booke called the Foundacion of Rhetorike.*" *HLQ* 6.4: 427–44.
Johnson, C. D. 2010. *Hyperboles: The Rhetoric of Excess in Baroque Literature and Thought.* Cambridge, MA.
Johnson, J. and S. Gibson. 1946. *Print and Privilege at Oxford to the Year 1700.* Oxford.
Jones, E. 2002. "'Filling in a Blank in the Canvas': Milton, Horton, and the Kedermister Library." *RES* 53: 31–60.
Jones, E. (ed.). 2012a. *Young Milton: The Emerging Author, 1620–1642.* Oxford.
Jones, E. 2012b. "The Archival Landscape of Milton's Youth, University Years, and Pre-London Residencies." In Jones 2012a: 3–20.
Jones, E. (ed.). 2015. *A Concise Companion to the Study of Manuscripts, Printed Books, and the Production of Early Modern Texts.* Oxford.

de Jonge, C. C. 2009. Review of Marini 2007. *Bryn Mawr Classical Review* 2009.08.12. URL=<https://bmcr.brynmawr.edu/2009/2009.08.12>.

de Jonge, C. C. 2012. "Dionysius and Longinus on the Sublime: Rhetoric and Religious Language." *AJP* 133.2: 271–300.

de Jonge, C. C. 2014. "The Attic Muse and the Asian Harlot: Classicizing Allegories in Dionysius and Longinus." In *Valuing the Past in the Greco-Roman World*, eds. J. Ker and C. Pieper, Leiden: 388–409.

Kahn, V. 1992. "Allegory and the Sublime in *Paradise Lost*." In *John Milton*, ed. A. Patterson, London: 185–201.

Kamesar, A. 2016. "Philo and Ps.-Longinus: A Case of Sublimity in Genesis 4." *Studia Philonica Annual* 28: 229–38.

Kaoukji, N. and N. Jardine. 2010. "'A frontispiece in any sense they please'? On the significance of the engraved title-page of John Wilkins's *A Discourse concerning A NEW world & Another Planet*, 1640." *Word & Image* 26.4: 429–47.

Kelley, M. 1935. "Milton's Debt to Wolleb's *Compendium Theologiae Christianae*." *PMLA* 50.1: 156–65.

Kelley, M. 1941. *This Great Argument: A Study of Milton's De Doctrina Christiana as a Gloss upon Paradise Lost*. Princeton.

Kelley, M. 1959. "Grammar School Latin and John Milton." *Classical World* 52.5: 133–36, 138.

Kelley, M. 1962. "Milton's Dante-Della Casa-Varchi Volume." *Bulletin of the New York Public Library* 66: 499–504.

Kelley, M. 1967. "The Composition of Milton's *De Doctrina Christiana*—The First Stage." In *Th'Upright Heart and Pure: Essays on John Milton Commemorating the Tercentenary of the Publication of Paradise Lost*, ed. A. P. Fiore, Pittsburgh: 35–44.

Kelley, M. 1994. "The Provenance of John Milton's *Christian Doctrine*: A Reply to William B. Hunter." *SEL* 34.1: 153–63.

Kelley, M. and S. D. Atkins. 1955. "Milton's Annotations of Aratus." *PMLA* 70.5: 1090–106.

Kelley, M. and S. D. Atkins. 1961. "Milton's Annotations of Euripides." *JEGP* 60.4: 680–7.

Kelley, M. and S. D. Atkins. 1964. "Milton and the Harvard Pindar." *Studies in Bibliography* 17: 77–82.

Kerr, J. A. 2015. "Milton and the Anonymous Authority of *De Doctrina Christiana*." *MQ* 49.1: 23–43.

Kerrigan, W. 1974. *The Prophetic Milton*. Charlottesville.

Kiessling, N. K. 2002. *The Library of Anthony Wood*. Oxford.

Kilgour, M. 2008. "Satan and the Wrath of Juno." *ELH* 75.3: 653–71.

Killeen, K. 2013. "Immethodical, Incoherent, Unadorned: Style and the Early Modern Bible." In *The Oxford Handbook of English Prose 1500–1640*, ed. A. Hadfield, Oxford: 505–21.

Knapp, S. 1985. *Personification and the Sublime: Milton to Coleridge*. Cambridge, MA.

Knight, S. 2011. "Milton's Forced Themes." *MQ* 45.3: 145–60.

Knott, J. R. 1980. *The Sword of the Spirit: Puritan Responses to the Bible*. Chicago.

Knox, R. A. 1950. *Enthusiasm: A Chapter in the History of Religion with Special Reference to the XVII and XVIII Centuries*. Oxford.

Konečný, L. 1974. "Young Milton and the Telescope." *Journal of the Warburg and Courtauld Institutes* 37: 368–73.

Koslow, J. 2008. "'Not a Bow for Every Man to Shoot': Milton's *Of Education*, between Hartlib and Humanism." *MS* 47: 24–53.

Kramnick, J. B. 1999. *Making the English Canon: Print-Capitalism and the Cultural Past, 1700–1770*. Cambridge.

Kranidas, T. 1965. *The Fierce Equation: A Study of Milton's Decorum.* The Hague.
Labriola, A. C. 1978. "The Titans and the Giants: *Paradise Lost* and the Tradition of the Renaissance Ovid." *MQ* 12.1: 9-16.
Landi, C. 1930. *Demogorgone.* Palermo.
Langdon. H. 2012. "The Demosthenes of Painting: Salvator Rosa and the 17th Century Sublime." In van Eck et al. 2012: 163-85.
Langdon, H. et al. 2010. *Salvator Rosa.* London.
Lares, J. 2001. *Milton and the Preaching Arts.* Cambridge.
Laskowsky, H. J. 1981. "A Pinnacle of the Sublime: Christ's Victory of Style in *Paradise Regained.*" *MQ* 15.1: 10-13.
Lazarus, M. 2021. "Sublimity by Fiat: New Light on the English Longinus." In *The Places of Early Modern Criticism*, eds. G. Alexander et al., Oxford: 191-205.
Leasure, R. 2002. "Milton's Queer Choice: Comus at Castlehaven." *MQ* 36.2: 63-86.
Le Comte, E. 1982. "Dubious Battle: Saving the Appearances." *ELN* 19.3: 177-93.
Leedham-Green, E. 1986. *Books in Cambridge Inventories.* 2 vols. Cambridge.
Leedham-Green, E. 2004. "The Book and the Books." In *L'Europa del libro nell'età dell'Umanesimo*, ed. L. S. Tarugi, Florence: 611-20.
Lefèvre, E. (ed.). 1973. *Die Römische Komödie: Plautus und Terenz.* Darmstadt.
Lehnhof, K. R. 2007. "Scatology and the Sacred in Milton's *Paradise Lost.*" *ELR* 37.3: 429-49.
Lehtonen, K. 2016. "*Peri Hypsous* in Translation: The Sublime in Sixteenth-Century Epic Theory." *PQ* 95.3-4: 449-65.
Lehtonen, K. 2019. "The Satanic Sublime in *Paradise Lost*: Tasso, Charisma, Abjection." *MP* 116.3: 211-34.
Leng, T. 2008. *Benjamin Worsley (1618-1677): Trade, Interest and the Spirit in Revolutionary England.* Woodbridge.
Leonard, J. 2000. "Milton, Lucretius, and 'the Void Profound of Unessential Night.'" In Pruitt and Durham 2000: 198-217.
Lehtonen, K. 2009. "The Troubled, Quiet Endings of Milton's English Sonnets." In McDowell and Smith 2009: 136-52.
Lehtonen, K. 2013. *Faithful Labourers: A Reception History of 'Paradise Lost', 1667-1970.* 2 vols. Oxford.
Lehtonen, K. 2016a. *The Value of Milton.* Cambridge.
Lehtonen, K. 2016b. "Milton, the Long Restoration, and Pope's *Iliad.*" In Hoxby and Coiro 2016: 447-64.
Lehtonen, K. 2020. "'Or' in *Paradise Lost*: The Poetics of Incertitude Reconsidered." *RES* 71.302: 896-920.
Letham, R. 1990. "Amandus Polanus: A Neglected Theologian?" *Sixteenth Century Journal* 21.3: 463-76.
Lewalski, B. 1966. *Milton's Brief Epic: The Genre, Meaning, and Art of Paradise Regained.* Providence.
Lewalski, B. 1985. *Paradise Lost and the Rhetoric of Literary Forms.* Princeton.
Lewalski, B. 1994. "Milton and the Hartlib Circle: Educational Projects and Epic Paideia." In *Literary Milton: Text, Pretext, Context*, eds. D. Benet and M. Lieb. Pittsburgh: 202-19.
Lewalski, B. 2003. "Milton and Idolatry." *SEL* 43.1: 213-32.
Lewalski, B. 2013. "Milton: The Muses, the Prophets, the Spirit, and Prophetic Poetry." *MS* 54: 59-78.
Lewalski, B. et al. 1992. "Forum: Milton's *Christian Doctrine.*" *SEL* 32.1: 143-66.
Lewis, C. S. 1943. *A Preface to Paradise Lost.* London.

Lewis, C. S. 1964. *The Discarded Image: An Introduction to Medieval and Renaissance Literature.* Cambridge.
Lieb, M. 1970. *The Dialectics of Creation: Patterns of Birth and Regeneration in Paradise Lost.* Amherst.
Lieb, M. 1978. "Further Thoughts on Satan's Journey Through Chaos." *MQ* 12.4: 126-33.
Lieb, M. 1981. *Poetics of the Holy: A Reading of Paradise Lost.* Chapel Hill.
Lieb, M. 1985. "S. B.'s *In Paradisum Amissam*: Sublime Commentary." *MQ* 19.3: 71-3, 75-8.
Lieb, M. 1994. *Milton and the Culture of Violence.* Ithaca.
Lieb, M. 2006. *Theological Milton: Deity, Discourse and Heresy in the Miltonic Canon.* Pittsburgh.
Lieb, M. 2009. "John Milton." In *The Oxford Handbook of English Literature and Theology,* eds. A. Hass et al., Oxford: 413-30.
Lieb, M. and J. T. Shawcross (eds.). 1974. *Achievements of the Left Hand: Essays on the Prose of John Milton.* Amherst.
Liljegren, S. B. 1918. *Studies in Milton.* Lund.
Lindberg, G. 1997. "Hermogenes of Tarsus." *ANRW* 34.3: 1978-2063.
Llewellyn, N. and C. Riding (eds.). 2013. *The Art of the Sublime.* URL=<https://www.tate.org.uk/art/research-publications/the-sublime>.
Loewenstein, D. 1990. *Milton and the Drama of History: Historical Vision, Iconoclasm, and the Literary Imagination.* Cambridge.
Loewenstein, D. 1996. "The Revenge of the Saint: Radical Religion and Politics in *Samson Agonistes.*" *MS* 33: 159-80.
Loewenstein, D. 2001. "Milton among the Religious Radicals and Sects: Polemical Engagements and Silences." *MS* 40: 222-47.
Logan, J. L. 1983. "Montaigne et Longin: une nouvelle hypothèse." *RHLF* 83.3: 355-70.
Logan, J. L. 1999. "Longinus and the Sublime." In Norton 1999: 529-39.
Love, H. 1998. *The Culture and Commerce of Texts: Scribal Publication in Seventeenth-century England.* Amherst.
Lovejoy, A. 1962. "Milton's Dialogue on Astronomy." In *Reason and the Imagination: Studies in the History of Ideas 1600-1800*, ed. J. A. Mazzeo, New York: 129-42.
Low, A. 1984. "*Mansus*: In Its Context." *MS* 19: 105-26.
Lummus, D. 2012. "Boccaccio's Poetic Anthropology: Allegories of History in the *Genealogie deorum gentilium libri.*" *Speculum* 87.3: 724-65.
Lyle, J. 2000. "Architecture and Idolatry in Paradise Lost." *SEL* 40.1: 139-55.
MacCallum, H. R. 1962. "Milton and Figurative Interpretation of the Bible." *UTQ* 31.4: 397-415.
Machacek, G. 2011. *Milton and Homer: "Written to Aftertimes."* University Park, PA.
Mack, P. 2011. *A History of Renaissance Rhetoric, 1380-1620.* Oxford.
Malcolm, N. 2002. *Aspects of Hobbes.* Oxford.
von Maltzahn, N. 1991. *Milton's History of Britain: Republican Historiography in the English Revolution.* Oxford.
von Maltzahn, N. 1994. "Wood, Allam, and the Oxford Milton." *MS* 31: 155-77.
von Maltzahn, N. 1995. "'I admire Thee': Samuel Barrow, Doctor and Poet." *MQ* 29.1: 25-28.
von Maltzahn, N. 2001. "The War in Heaven and the Miltonic Sublime." In *A Nation Transformed: England after the Restoration*, eds. A. Houston and S. Pincus, Cambridge: 154-79.
von Maltzahn, N. 2008. "L'Estrange's Milton." In *Roger L'Estrange and the Making of Restoration Culture*, eds. A. Dunan-Page and B. Lynch, Aldershot: 27-52.

von Maltzahn, N. 2016. "Milton and the Restoration *Literae.*" In Hoxby and Coiro 2016: 302–18.
Marjara, H. S. 1992. *Contemplation of Created Things: Science in Paradise Lost.* Toronto.
Marini, N. 2007. *Demetrio: Lo Stile.* Rome.
Martano, G. 1984. "Il 'Saggio sul Sublime'. Una interessante pagina di retorica e di estetica dell'antichità." *ANRW* 32.1: 364–403.
Martin, C. G. 1996. "'Boundless the Deep': Milton, Pascal, and the Theology of Relative Space." *ELH* 63.1: 45–78.
Martin, C. G. 2001. "'What if the Sun Be Centre to the World?': Milton's Epistemology, Cosmology, and Paradise of Fools Reconsidered." *MP* 99.2: 231–65.
Martin, C. G. 2017. *Milton's Italy: Anglo-Italian Literature, Travel, and Religion in Seventeenth-Century England.* London.
Martin, C. G. (ed.). 2019. *Milton and the New Scientific Age: Poetry, Science, Fiction.* London.
Martin, É. M. 2012. "The 'Prehistory' of the Sublime in Early Modern France: An Interdisciplinary Perspective." In Costelloe 2012: 77–101.
Martindale, C. 1986. *John Milton and the Transformation of Ancient Epic.* London.
Martindale, C. 2012a. "Milton's Classicism." In *The Oxford History of Classical Reception in English Literature Vol. III: 1660–1790,* eds. D. Hopkins and C. Martindale, Oxford: 53–90.
Martindale, C. 2012b. Review of Machacek 2011. *RES* 63.262: 853–5.
Martinez, A. A. 2016. "Giordano Bruno and the Heresy of Many Worlds." *AS* 73.4: 345–74.
Martz, L. L. 1995. "Milton's Prophetic Voice: Moving Toward Paradise." In *Of Poetry and Politics: New Essays on Milton and His World,* ed. P. G. Stanwood, Binghamton, NY: 1–16.
Matthews, A. G. 1934. *Calamy Revised: Being a Revision of Edmund Calamy's Account of the Ministers and Others Ejected and Silenced, 1660–2.* Oxford.
Matthews, A. G. 1948. *Walker Revised: Being a Revision of John Walker's Sufferings of the Clergy during the Grand Rebellion, 1642–1660.* Oxford.
Mazzucchi, C. M. 1989. "La tradizione manoscritta del *Peri Ypsous.*" *Italia medioevale e umanistica* 32: 205–26.
Mazzucchi, C. M. 1990. "Longino in Giovanni di Sicilia: con un inedito di storia, epigrafia e toponomastica di Cosma Manasse dal Cod. Laurenziano LVII.5." *Aevum* 64.2: 183–98.
McBride, K. B. and J. C. Ulreich. 2001. "Answerable Styles: Biblical Poetics and Biblical Politics in the Poetry of Lanyer and Milton." *JEGP* 100.3: 333–54.
McCluskey, P. M. 1997. "Milton and the Winds of Folly." In *Arenas of Conflict: Milton and the Unfettered Mind,* eds. K. P. McColgan and C. W. Durham, Selinsgrove: 227–38.
McColley, G. 1932. "The Theory of a Plurality of Worlds as a Factor in Milton's Attitude Toward the Copernican Hypothesis." *MLN* 47.5: 319–25.
McColley, G. 1936. "The Second Edition of *The Discovery of a World in the Moone.*" *AS* 1.3: 330–4.
McColley, G. 1937. "Milton's Dialogue on Astronomy: The Principal Immediate Sources." *PMLA* 52.3: 728–62.
McDowell, N. 2003. *The English Radical Imagination: Culture, Religion, and Revolution, 1630–1660.* Oxford.
McDowell, N. 2008. *Poetry and Allegiance in the English Civil Wars: Marvell and the Cause of Wit.* Oxford.
McDowell, N. 2016. "Milton's Euripides and the Superior Rationality of the Heathen." *SC* 31.2: 215–37.

McDowell, N. 2019. "Refining the Sublime: Edward Phillips, a Miltonic Education and the Sublimity of *Paradise Lost*." *MS* 61.2: 239–60.
McDowell, N. 2020. *Poet of Revolution: The Making of John Milton*. Princeton.
McDowell, N. and N. Smith (eds.). 2009. *The Oxford Handbook of Milton*. Oxford.
McKitterick, D. 2006. "Libraries and the Organization of Knowledge." In *The Cambridge History of Libraries in Britain and Ireland Volume 1: To 1640*, eds. E. Leedham-Green and T. Webber, Cambridge: 592–615.
McMurray, P. 1998. "Aristotle on the Pinnacle: *Paradise Regained* and the Limits of Theory." *MQ* 32.1: 7–14.
McRae, C. 2015. "Direct Address in *Paradise Lost*." *MS* 56: 17–43.
Meister, K. 1925. *Die Hausschwelle in Sprache und Religion der Römer*. Heidelberg.
Melzer, A. 2014. *Philosophy Between the Lines: The Lost History of Esoteric Writing*. Chicago.
van Miert, D. 2017. "The Janus Face of Scaliger's Philological Heritage: The Biblical Annotations of Heinsius and Grotius." In *Scriptural Authority and Biblical Criticism in the Dutch Golden Age: God's Word Questioned*, eds. D. van Miert et al, Oxford: 91–108.
Miller, J. A. 2011. "Reconstructing Milton's Lost *Index Theologicus*: The Genesis and Usage of an Anti-Bellarmine, Theological Commonplace Book." *MS* 52: 187–219.
Miller, L. 1971. "The Italian Imprimaturs in Milton's *Areopagitica*." *PBSA* 65.4: 345–55.
Miller, L. 1972. "Milton Edits Freigius' 'Life of Ramus'." *RR* 8.3: 112–14.
Miller, L. 1976. "Milton's Portraits: An *Impartial* Inquiry into their Authentication." *MQ* Special Issue: 1–43.
Miller, L. 1980. "Milton's Clash with Chappell: A Suggested Reconstruction." *MQ* 14.3: 77–87.
Miller, L. 1984. "Some Inferences from Milton's Hebrew." *MQ* 18.2: 41–6.
Miller, L. 1990. "On Some of the Verses by Alexander Gil Which John Milton Read." *MQ* 24.1: 22–5.
Miller, L. 1991. "Milton and Holstenius Reconsidered: An Exercise in Scholarly Practice." In di Cesare 1991: 573–87.
Mills, R. J. W. 2016. "Alexander Ross's *Pansebeia* (1653), Religious Compendia and the Seventeenth-Century Study of Religious Diversity." *SC* 31.3: 285–310.
Miner, E. (ed.). 2004. *Paradise Lost, 1668-1968: Three Centuries of Commentary*. Lewisburg.
de Miranda, G. 2000. *Una quiete operosa: Forma e pratiche dell'Accademia napoletana degli Oziosi, 1611-1645*. Naples.
Mirto, A. 1999. *Lucas Holstenius e la corte medicea: Carteggio (1629–1660)*. Florence.
Mish, C. C. 1967. "*Comus* and Bryce Blair's *Vision of Theodorus Verax*." *Milton Newsletter* 1.3: 39–40.
Miyoshi, K. 2017. *The First Century of English Monolingual Lexicography*. Newcastle upon Tyne.
Mohamed, F. G. 2005. "Confronting Religious Violence: Milton's *Samson Agonistes*." *PMLA* 120.2: 327–40.
Mohamed, F. G. 2011. *Milton and the Post-Secular Present: Ethics, Politics, Terrorism*. Stanford.
Monk, S. H. 1935. *The Sublime: A Study of Critical Theories in XVIII-Century England*. New York.
Moore, L. 1990. *Beautiful Sublime: The Making of Paradise Lost, 1701-1734*. Stanford.
Moore, W. G. 1967. "Lucretius and Montaigne." *Yale French Studies* 38: 109–14.
Morris, D. B. 1972. *The Religious Sublime: Christian Poetry and Critical Tradition in 18th-Century England*. Lexington.

Moshenska, G. 2013. "The Duke of Sussex's Library and the First Debates on the Authorship of *De Doctrina Christiana*." *MQ* 47.1: 1–12.
Mulryan, J. 1996. *"Through a Glass Darkly": Milton's Reinvention of the Mythological Tradition*. Pittsburgh.
Munby, A. N. L. and L. Coral. 1977. *British Book Sale Catalogues, 1676–1800*. London.
Murray, S. and A. H. A. Rushdy. 1994. "On the Margins of an Unnoted Annotator of Milton: William Hayley's Dialogue with Richard Bentley." *MS* 31: 197–242.
Murrin, M. 1980. *The Allegorical Epic: Essays in Its Rise and Decline*. Chicago.
Myers, R. et al. (eds.). 2001. *Under the Hammer: Book Auctions since the Seventeenth Century*. London.
Nativel, C. 2016. "Lectures du *Traité du sublime* par Franciscus Junius F.F." In van Oostveldt et al. 2016: 263–79.
Nelson, J. G. 1963. *The Sublime Puritan: Milton and the Victorians*. Madison.
Nicholls, C. 2016. "Body Out of Spirit: Medical Science and the Creation of Living Soul in *Paradise Lost*." *MS* 57: 119–53.
Nicholls, C. 2019. "'By Gradual Scale Sublimed': Chymical Medicine and Monist Human Physiology in John Milton's *Paradise Lost*." In Martin 2019: 167–91.
Nicolson, M. H. 1935. "Milton and the Telescope." *ELH* 2.1: 1–32.
Nicolson, M. H. 1938. "Milton's Hell and the Phlegraean Fields." *UTQ* 7.4: 500–13.
Nicolson, M. H. 1963. *Mountain Gloom and Mountain Glory: The Development of the Aesthetics of the Infinite*. New York.
Nietzsche, F. 2006. *On the Genealogy of Morality*. Ed. K. Ansell-Pearson. Trans. C. Diethe. Cambridge.
Noggle, J. 2001. *The Skeptical Sublime: Aesthetic Ideology in Pope and the Tory Satirists*. Oxford.
de Nolhac, P. 1887. *La bibliothèque de Fulvio Orsini: contributions à l'histoire des collections d'Italie et à l'étude de la Renaissance*. Paris.
Nonnoi, G. 2003. "Images, Models and Symbols in Copernican Propaganda." In *The Power of Images in Early Modern Science*, eds. W. Lefèvre et al., Basel: 227–50.
Norbrook, D. 1990. "Marvell's 'Horatian Ode' and the Politics of Genre." In *Literature and the English Civil War*, eds. T. Healy and J. Sawday, Cambridge: 147–69.
Norbrook, D. 1999. *Writing the English Republic: Poetry, Rhetoric and Politics, 1627–1660*. Cambridge.
Norbrook, D. 2013. "Milton, Lucy Hutchinson, and the Lucretian Sublime." In Llewellyn and Riding 2013, URL=<https://www.tate.org.uk/art/research-publications/the-sublime/david-norbrook-milton-lucy-hutchinson-and-the-lucretian-sublime-r1138669>.
Norbrook, D. et al. (eds.). 2016. *Lucretius and the Early Modern*. Oxford.
Norton, G. P. (ed.). 1999. *The Cambridge History of Literary Criticism Vol. III: The Renaissance*. Cambridge.
Ong, W. J. 1958. *Ramus, Method, and the Decay of Dialogue*. Cambridge, MA.
van Oostveldt, B. and S. Bussels (eds.). 2016. "The Sublime and Seventeenth-Century Netherlandish Art." Special Issue, *Journal of Historians of Netherlandish Art* 8.2. URL=<https://jhna.org/issues/vol-8-2-2016/>.
van Oostveldt, B. et al. (eds.). 2016. "The Sublime in Early Modern Theories of Art and Literature." Special Issue, *Lias* 43.2: 191–296.
Orgel, S. 2003. "The Case for Comus." *Representations* 81.1: 31–45.
Ossa-Richardson, A. 2014. "Sublimity as Resistance to Form in the Early Modern Bible." In *The Edinburgh Companion to the Bible and the Arts*, ed. S. Prickett, Edinburgh: 69–87.

Pade, M. 1997. "The Fragments of Theodontius in Boccaccio's *Genealogie Deorum Gentilium Libri*." In *Avignon & Naples: Italy in France, France in Italy in the Fourteenth Century*, eds. M. Pade et al., Rome: 149-82.
Paleit, E. 2013. *War, Liberty, and Caesar: Responses to Lucan's Bellum Ciuile, ca. 1580-1650*. Oxford.
Pallister, W. 2008. *Between Worlds: The Rhetorical Universe of Paradise Lost*. Toronto.
Palmer, A. 2014. *Reading Lucretius in the Renaissance*. Cambridge, MA.
Papaioannou, S. 2013. *Michael Psellos: Rhetoric and Authorship in Byzantium*. Cambridge.
Park, Y. 2000. *Milton and Isaiah: A Journey through the Drama of Salvation in Paradise Lost*. New York.
Parker, R. 2017. *Greek Gods Abroad: Names, Natures, and Transformations*. Berkeley.
Parker, W. R. 1958. "Wood's Life of Milton: Its Sources and Significance." *PBSA* 52.1: 1-22.
Parker, W. R. 1968. *Milton: A Biography*. 2 vols. Oxford.
Parry, G. and J. Raymond (eds.). 2002. *Milton and the Terms of Liberty*. Cambridge.
Passannante, G. 2011. *The Lucretian Renaissance: Philology and the Afterlife of Tradition*. Chicago.
Patterson, A. 1970. *Hermogenes and the Renaissance: Seven Ideas of Style*. Princeton.
Patterson, A. 1993. *Reading Between the Lines*. Madison.
Patterson, A. 1997. *Early Modern Liberalism*. Cambridge.
Patterson, A. 2009. *Milton's Words*. Oxford.
Pearce, E. H. 1913. *Sion College and Library*. Cambridge.
Pearson, D. 2010. "Patterns of Book Ownership in Late Seventeenth Century England." *Libr.* 7th ser. 11.2: 139-67.
Pearson, D. 2012. "The English Private Library in the Seventeenth Century." *Libr.* 7th ser. 13.4: 379-99.
Pearson, D. 2021. *Book Ownership in Stuart England*. Oxford.
Pennington, L. E. 1997. "Samuel Purchas: His Reputation and the Uses of His Works." In *The Purchas Handbook Volume I*, ed. L. E. Pennington, London: 3-118.
Pfeiffer, R. H. 1955. "The Fear of God." *Israel Exploration Journal* 5.1: 41-8.
Pieters, J. and B. Vandenabeele (eds.). 2005. *Histories of the Sublime*. Brussels.
Pitman, J. H. 1925. "Milton and the Physiologus." *MLN* 40: 439-40.
Platt, P. G. 1992. "'Not Before Either Known or Dreamt of': Francesco Patrizi and the Power of Wonder in Renaissance Poetics." *RES* 43: 387-94.
Poole, W. 2004. "Milton and Science: A Caveat." *MQ* 38.1: 18-34.
Poole, W. 2005. *Milton and the Idea of the Fall*. Cambridge.
Poole, W. 2007. "Out of His Furrow." *LRB* 29.3: 16-17.
Poole, W. 2009. "The Genres of Milton's Commonplace Book." In McDowell and Smith 2009: 367-81.
Poole, W. 2012. "'The Armes of Studious Retirement'? Milton's Scholarship, 1632-1641." In Jones 2012a: 21-47.
Poole, W. 2013. "Down and Out in Leiden and London: The Later Careers of Venceslaus Clemens (1589-1637), and Jan Sictor (1593-1652), Bohemian Exiles and Failing Poets." *SC* 28.2: 163-85.
Poole, W. 2014. "John Milton and Giovanni Boccaccio's *Vita di Dante*." *MQ* 48.3: 139-70.
Poole, W. 2015. "Analysing a Private Library, with a Shelflist Attributable to John Hales of Eton, c.1624." In Jones 2015: 41-65.
Poole, W. 2017a. *Milton and the Making of Paradise Lost*. Cambridge, MA.
Poole, W. (ed.). 2017b. *John Wilkins (1614-1672): New Essays*. Leiden.
Poole, W. 2018. "The Literary Remains of Alexander Gil the Elder (1565-1635) and Younger (1596/7-1642?)." *MQ* 51.3: 163-91.

Poole, W. 2019. "More Light on the Literary Remains of Alexander Gil the Younger (1596/7-1644)." *MQ* 53.4: 215-21.
Porter, J. I. 2003. "Lucretius and the Poetics of Void." In *Le jardin romain: Épicurisme et poésie à Rome*, ed. A. Monet, Villeneuve d'Ascq. 197-226.
Porter, J. I. 2007. "Lucretius and the Sublime." In *The Cambridge Companion to Lucretius*, eds. S. Gillespie and P. Hardie, Cambridge: 167-84.
Porter, J. I. 2010. *The Origins of Aesthetic Thought in Ancient Greece: Matter, Sensation, and Experience*. Cambridge.
Porter, J. I. 2016. *The Sublime in Antiquity*. Cambridge.
Posthumus Meyjes, G. H. M. 1994. "Some Remarks on Grotius' *Excerpta Theologica*, Especially Concerning his *Meletius*." In *Hugo Grotius, Theologian*, eds. H. J. M. Nellen and E. Rabbie, Leiden: 1-17.
Prawdzik, B. 2017. *Theatrical Milton: Politics and Poetics of the Staged Body*. Edinburgh.
Prickett, S. 2016. "Robert Lowth's Biblical Poetics and Romantic Theory." In *Interpreting Scriptures in Judaism, Christianity and Islam: Overlapping Inquiries*, eds. M. Z. Cohen and A. Berlin, Cambridge: 309-25.
Prince, F. T. 1962. *The Italian Element in Milton's Verse*. Oxford.
Prins, J. 2014. *Echoes of an Invisible World: Marsilio Ficino and Francesco Patrizi on Cosmic Order and Music Theory*. Leiden.
Pruitt, K. A. and C. W. Durham (eds.). 2000. *Living Texts: Interpreting Milton*. Selinsgrove.
Quint, D. 1975. "Epic Tradition and *Inferno* IX." *Dante Studies* 93: 201-7.
Quint, D. 2004. "Fear of Falling: Icarus, Phaethon, and Lucretius in *Paradise Lost*." *RQ* 57.3: 847-81.
Quint, D. 2007. "Milton's Book of Numbers: Book 1 of *Paradise Lost* and Its Catalogue." *IJCT* 13.4: 528-49.
Radzinowicz, M. A. 1976. Review of Kerrigan 1974. *RQ* 29.3: 458-61.
Radzinowicz, M. A. 1978. *Toward Samson Agonistes: The Growth of Milton's Mind*. Princeton.
Radzinowicz, M. A. 1989. *Milton's Epics and the Book of Psalms*. Princeton.
Rahe, P. A. 2004. "The Classical Republicanism of John Milton." *History of Political Thought* 25.2: 243-75.
Rajan, B. 1945. "Simple, Sensuous, and Passionate." *RES* 21.84: 289-301.
Ramminger, J. (ed.). 2020. *Neulateinisches Wortliste: Ein Wörterbuch des Lateinischen von Petrarca bis 1700*. URL=<http://nlw.renaessancestudier.org/>.
Rankin, S. 2010. "*Terribilis est locus iste*: The Pantheon in 609." In *Rhetoric Beyond Words*, ed. M. Carruthers, Cambridge: 281-310.
Rappaport, R. 1986. "Hooke on Earthquakes: Lectures, Strategy and Audience." *British Journal for the History of Science* 19.2: 129-46.
Raylor, T. 1993. "New Light on Milton and Hartlib." *MQ* 27.1: 19-31.
Raylor, T. 2009. "Milton, the Hartlib Circle, and the Education of the Aristocracy." In McDowell and Smith 2009: 382-406.
Raymond, J. 2005. *The Invention of the Newspaper: English Newsbooks 1641-1649*. Oxford.
Raynouard, M. 1843. *Lexique roman ou Dictionnaire de la langue des troubadours. Tome Cinquième: Q.-Z.* Paris.
Rebora, P. 1953. "Milton a Firenze." *Nuova Antologia* 88: 147-63.
Refini, E. 2012. "Longinus and Poetic Imagination in Late Renaissance Literary Theory." In van Eck et al. 2012: 33-51.
Refini, E. 2016. "*Soni fiunt suaviores*: Musical Implications in the Early Modern Reception of Longinus' *On the Sublime*." In van Oostveldt et al. 2016: 241-62.

Reid, S. J. and E. A. Wilson (eds.). 2011. *Ramus, Pedagogy, and the Liberal Arts: Ramism in Britain and the Wider World*. Farnham.
Reisner, N. 2004. "The Prophet's Conundrum: Poetic Soaring in Milton's 'Nativity Ode' and 'The Passion.'" *PQ* 83.4: 371–87.
Reisner, N. 2009. *Milton and the Ineffable*. Oxford.
Reisner, N. 2011. *John Milton's Paradise Lost: A Reading Guide*. Edinburgh.
Remmert, V. 2005. *Widmung, Welterklärung und Wissenschaftslegitimierung: Titelbilder und ihre Funktionen in der Wissenschaftlichen Revolution*. Wiesbaden.
Revard, S. P. 1980. *The War in Heaven: Paradise Lost and the Tradition of Satan's Rebellion*. Ithaca.
Rhys Roberts, W. 1897. "The Quotation from *Genesis* in the *De Sublimitate* (IX. 9)." *CR* 11.9: 431–6.
Rhys Roberts, W. 1898. "Notes on a Cambridge Manuscript of the *De Sublimitate*." *CR* 12.6: 299–301.
Ribard, D. 2008. "Le «petit maître de Saumur»: Tanneguy Le Fèvre et la socialisation de l'érudition protestante." *Bulletin de la Société de l'Histoire du Protestantisme Français* 154: 41–59.
Ricks, C. 1963. *Milton's Grand Style*. Oxford.
Rietbergen, P. 2006. *Power and Religion in Baroque Rome: Barberini Cultural Policies*. Leiden.
Riggs, W. G. 1992. "Poetry and Method in Milton's *Of Education*." *SP* 89.4: 445–69.
Rigolot, F. 1997. *Louise Labé Lyonnaise ou la Renaissance au féminin*. Paris.
Ringler, W. 1938. "An Early Reference to Longinus." *MLN* 53: 23–4.
Rogers, J. H. 1996. *The Matter of Revolution: Science, Poetry, and Politics in the Age of Milton*. Ithaca.
Roilos, P. 2018. "Ancient Greek Rhetorical Theory and Byzantine Discursive Politics: John Sikeliotes on Hermogenes." In *Reading in the Byzantine Empire and Beyond*, eds. T. Shawcross and I. Toth, Cambridge: 159–84.
Rosenblatt, J. P. 1975. "'Audacious Neighborhood': Idolatry in Paradise Lost, Book I." *PQ* 54.3: 553–68.
Rosenblatt, J. P. 1982. "Sir Edward Dering's Milton." *MP* 79.4: 376–85.
Rosenblatt, J. P. 2006. *Renaissance England's Chief Rabbi: John Selden*. Oxford.
Rosenblatt, J. P. 2007. "Milton, Natural Law, and Toleration." In Achinstein and Sauer 2007: 126–43.
Rosenblatt, J. P. 2021. *John Selden: Scholar, Statesman, Advocate for Milton's Muse*. Oxford.
Ross, T. 1998. *The Making of the English Literary Canon: From the Middle Ages to the Late Eighteenth Century*. Montreal.
Rousseau, P. 1998. "Procopius' *Buildings* and Justinian's Pride." *Byzantion* 68.1: 121–30.
Rumrich, J. P. 1996. *Milton Unbound: Controversy and Reinterpretation*. Cambridge.
Rumrich, J. P. 1998. "Milton's Arianism: Why It Matters." In *Milton and Heresy*, eds. S. Dobranski and J. P. Rumrich, Cambridge: 75–92.
Rumrich, J. P. 2000. "Of Chaos and Nightingales." In Pruitt and Durham 2000: 218–27.
Russell, D. A. 1981. *Criticism in Antiquity*. Berkeley.
Russell, D. A. 1990. "Greek Criticism of the Empire." In *The Cambridge History of Literary Criticism Vol. I: Classical Criticism*, ed. G. A. Kennedy, Cambridge: 297–329.
Samuel, I. 1957. "The Dialogue in Heaven: A Reconsideration of *Paradise Lost*, III. 1-417." *PMLA* 72.4: 601–11.
Samuel, I. 1966. *Dante and Milton: The Commedia and Paradise Lost*. Ithaca.
Sarkar, M. 2012. *Cosmos and Character in Paradise Lost*. Basingstoke.

Schibille, N. 2014. *Hagia Sophia and the Byzantine Aesthetic Experience.* Farnham.
Schlueter, K. 1995. "Milton's Heroical Sonnets." *SEL* 35.1: 123–36.
Schwartz, L. (ed.). 2014. *The Cambridge Companion to Paradise Lost.* Cambridge.
Schwartz, R. M. 1988. *Remembering and Repeating: Biblical Creation in Paradise Lost.* Cambridge.
Scott-Craig, T. S. K. 1940. "Milton's Use of Wolleb and Ames." *MLN* 55.6: 403–7.
Seaford, R. 2009. "The Fluttering Soul." In *Antike Mythen: Medien, Transformationen und Konstruktionen*, eds. U. Dill and C. Walde, Berlin: 406–14.
Sedley, D. L. 2005. *Sublimity and Skepticism in Montaigne and Milton.* Ann Arbor.
Sedley, D. N. 1998. *Lucretius and the Transformation of Greek Wisdom.* Cambridge.
Segal, C. P. 1959. "ὕψος and the Problem of Cultural Decline in the *De Sublimate*." *Harvard Studies in Classical Philology* 64: 121–46.
Serjeantson, R. W. 2009. "*Samson Agonistes* and 'Single Rebellion.'" In McDowell and Smith 2009: 613–31.
Serjeantson, R. W. 2016. "The Education of Francis Willughby." In *Virtuoso by Nature: The Scientific Worlds of Francis Willughby FRS (1635-1672)*, ed. T. Birkhead, Leiden: 44–98.
Sewell, A. 1939. *A Study in Milton's Christian Doctrine.* Oxford.
Shaheen, N. 1974. "Milton's Muse and the *De Doctrina*." *MQ* 8.3: 72–6.
Shaw, C. 2019. *Isabella d'Este: A Renaissance Princess.* Abingdon.
Shaw, P. 2006. *The Sublime.* London.
Shaw, P. 2017. *The Sublime.* 2nd Edition. London.
Shawcross, J. 1965. "The Dating of Certain Poems, Letters, and Prolusions Written by Milton." *ELN* 2: 261–6.
Shawcross, J. 2004. *The Arms of the Family: The Significance of John Milton's Relatives and Associates.* Lexington.
Shore, D. 2009. "Things Unattempted...Yet Once More." *MQ* 43.3: 195–200.
Shore, D. 2012. *Milton and the Art of Rhetoric.* Cambridge.
Shore, D. 2014. "Milton and Kant?" *MQ* 48.1: 26–38.
Shoulson, J. 2008. "Milton and Enthusiasm: Radical Religion and the Poetics of *Paradise Regained*." *MS* 47: 219–57.
Shoulson, J. 2013. *Fictions of Conversion: Jews, Christians, and Cultures of Change in Early Modern England.* Philadelphia.
Shuger, D. K. 1988. *Sacred Rhetoric: The Christian Grand Style in the English Renaissance.* Princeton.
Shullenberger, W. 2008. *Lady in the Labyrinth: Milton's Comus as Initiation.* Teaneck, NJ.
Singleton, R. H. 1943. "Milton's *Comus* and the *Comus* of Erycius Puteanus." *PMLA* 58.4: 949–57.
Skelton, K. 2009. "Reading as a Gentleman and an Architect: Sir Roger Pratt's Library." *Transactions of the Ancient Monuments Society* 53: 15–50.
Skerpan-Wheeler, E. 1999. "Authorship and Authority: John Milton, William Marshall, and the Two Frontispieces of *Poems* 1645." *MQ* 33.4: 105–14.
Skerpan-Wheeler, E. 2013. "The Logical Poetics of *Paradise Regained*." *HLQ* 76.1: 35–58.
Skinner, Q. 1998. *Liberty before Liberalism.* Cambridge.
Skinner, Q. 2002. *Visions of Politics.* 3 vols. Cambridge.
Skinner, Q. 2008. "What does it mean to be a free person?" *LRB* 30.10: 16–18.
Skinner, Q. 2018. *From Humanism to Hobbes: Studies in Rhetoric and Politics.* Cambridge.
Smart, J. S. 1913. "Milton in Rome." *MLR* 8.1: 91–2.
Smart, J. S. 1921. *The Sonnets of Milton.* Glasgow.
Smith, N. 1994. *Literature and Revolution in England, 1640-1660.* New Haven.

Solomon, J. 2012. "Boccaccio and the Ineffable, Aniconic God Demogorgon." *IJCT* 19: 31-62.
Spencer, T. J. B. 1957. "Longinus in English Criticism: Influences before Milton." *RES* 8.30: 137-43.
Stang, C. M. 2012. *Apophasis and Pseudonymity in Dionysius the Areopagite*. Oxford.
Stark, R. J. 2003. "Cold Styles: On Milton's Critiques of Frigid Rhetoric in *Paradise Lost*." *MQ* 37.1: 21-30.
Stark, R. J. 2009. *Rhetoric, Science, and Magic in Seventeenth-Century England*. Washington, D.C.
Stein, A. 1953. *Answerable Style: Essays on Paradise Lost*. Minneapolis.
Steppich, C. J. 2006. "Inspiration through *imitatio / mimesis* in *On the Sublime* of 'Longinus' and in Joachim Vadian's *De poetica et carminis ratione* (Vienna, 1518)." *HL* 55: 37-70.
Strauss, L. 1988. *Persecution and the Art of Writing*. Chicago.
Sugimura, N. K. 2009. *"Matter of Glorious Trial": Spiritual and Material Substance in Paradise Lost*. New Haven.
Sugimura, N. K. 2014a. "Eve's Reflection and the Passion of Wonder in *Paradise Lost*." *Essays in Criticism* 64.1: 1-28.
Sugimura, N. K. 2014b. "Milton and Matter." In *Oxford Handbooks Online*. URL=<https://doi.org/10.1093/oxfordhb/9780199935338.013.11>.
Sugimura, N. K. 2021. "Benjamin Stillingfleet's Notes on *Paradise Lost*, Lost and Found." *RES* 72.307: 900-32.
Sullivan, F. A. 1972. "Volcanoes and Volcanic Characters in Virgil." *CP* 67.3: 186-91.
Svendsen, K. 1956. *Milton and Science*. Cambridge, MA.
Taylor, G. C. 1934. *Milton's Use of Du Bartas*. Cambridge, MA.
Teague, F. 1986. "Milton and the Pygmies." *MQ* 20.1: 31-2.
Terry, R. 2001. *Poetry and the Making of the English Literary Past 1660-1781*. Oxford.
Teskey, G. 2015. *The Poetry of John Milton*. Cambridge, MA.
Tessier, A. 2015. *Réseaux diplomatiques et République des Lettres: Les correspondants de Sir Joseph Williamson (1660-1680)*. Paris.
Thom, J. C. (ed.). 2014. *Cosmic Order and Divine Power: Pseudo-Aristotle, On the Cosmos*. Tübingen.
Thomas, C. 2006. "Chaste Bodies and Poisonous Desires in Milton's *Mask*." *SEL* 46.2: 435-59.
Thrush, A. and J. P. Ferris (eds.). 2010. *The History of Parliament: The House of Commons 1604-1629*. 6 vols. Cambridge.
Till, D. 2012. "The Sublime and the Bible: Longinus, Protestant Dogmatics, and the 'Sublime Style.'" In van Eck et al. 2012: 55-64.
Tillyard, E. M. W. 1930. "Milton and Longinus." *TLS* 29 August 1930: 684.
Tisch, J. H. 1968. "Milton and the German Mind in the Eighteenth Century." In *Studies in the Eighteenth Century*, ed. R. F. Brissenden, Canberra: 205-29.
Too, Y. L. 1998. *The Idea of Ancient Literary Criticism*. Oxford.
Toomer, G. J. 2009. *John Selden: A Life in Scholarship*. 2 vols. Oxford.
Toorn, K. van der. et al. (eds.) 1999. *Dictionary of Deities and Demons in the Bible*. Leiden.
Tournu, C. and N. Forsyth (eds.). 2007. *Milton, Rights and Liberties*. Bern.
Trentin, L. 2011. "Deformity in the Roman Imperial Court." *Greece & Rome* 58.2: 195-208.
Trentman, J. A. 1978. "The Authorship of *Directions for a Student in the Universitie*." *Transactions of the Cambridge Bibliographical Society* 7.2: 170-83.
Trubowitz, R. 2017. "Reading Milton and Newton in the Radical Reformation: Poetry, Mathematics, and Religion." *ELH* 84.1: 33-62.

Tucker, S. 1972. *Enthusiasm: A Study in Semantic Change*. Cambridge.
Turnbull, G. H. 1953. "John Hall's Letters to Samuel Hartlib." *RES* 4.15: 221–33.
Tylus, J. 2015. "Naming Sappho: Gaspara Stampa and the Recovery of the Sublime in Early Modern Europe." In Falkeid and Feng 2015: 15–38.
Ulreich, J. C. 1983. "'And by Occasion Fortells': The Prophetic Voice in *Lycidas*." *MS* 18: 3–23.
Usher, M. D. 2007. "Theomachy, Creation, and the Poetics of Quotation in Longinus Chapter 9." *CP* 102.3: 292–303.
de Vaan, Michiel. 2008. *Etymological Dictionary of Latin and the other Italic Languages*. Leiden.
Venn, J. and J. A. Venn. 1922–7. *Alumni Cantabrigienses*. 4 vols. Cambridge.
Vozar, T. M. 2019. "Sir Henry Wotton's Copy of Portus' *Aphthonius, Hermogenes, & Dionysius Longinus*." *NQ* 66.3: 473–4.
Vozar, T. M. 2020. "An English Translation of Longinus in the Lansdowne Collection at the British Library." *SC* 35.5: 625–50.
Vozar, T. M. 2021a. "*Timor Dei* and *Timor Idololatricus* from Reformed Theology to Milton." *Reformation* 26.1: 62–72.
Vozar, T. M. 2021b. "Henry Oldenburg and a Brief Notice of Milton's *Of Education* in the *Philosophical Transactions*." *Milton Quarterly* 55.1: 63–6.
Vozar, T. M. 2022. "Milton, Sublime Style, and the Problem of Enthusiasm." In *Milton in Strasbourg: A Collection of IMS12 Essays*, eds. Christophe Tournu, Neil Forsyth, and John K. Hale, Bern: 137–60.
Vozar, T. M. Forthcoming. Ps.-Longinus, Dionysius Cassius. Addenda et Corrigenda." In *Catalogus Translationum et Commentariorum: Mediaeval and Renaissance Latin Translations and Commentaries*, eds. Greti Dinkova-Bruun, Julia Haig Gaisser, and James Hankins, Toronto.
Walsh, G. B. 1988. "Sublime Method: Longinus on Language and Imitation." *Classical Antiquity* 7.2: 252–69.
Warkentin, G. et al. 2013. *The Library of the Sidneys of Penshurst Place circa 1665*. Toronto.
Webber, J. 1979. *Milton and His Epic Tradition*. Seattle.
Weber, C. 2019. "*Mollis* and Its Stylistic Resonance in Vergil." *Vergilius* 65: 33–41.
Webster, C. 2002. *The Great Instauration: Science, Medicine, and Reform, 1626–1660*. Bern.
Webster, E. 2015. "Milton's Pandaemonium and the Infinitesimal Calculus." *ELR* 45.3: 425–58.
Weinberg, B. 1950. "Translations and Commentaries of Longinus *On the Sublime* to 1600: A Bibliography." *MP* 47.3: 145–51.
Weinberg, B. 1961. *History of Literary Criticism in the Italian Renaissance*. 2 vols. Chicago.
Weinberg, B. 1962. "Une traduction française du *Sublime* de Longin vers 1645." *MP* 59.3: 159–201.
Weinberg, B. 1971. "Ps. Longinus, Dionysius Cassius." In *Catalogus Translationum et Commentariorum: Mediaeval and Renaissance Latin Translations and Commentaries*, vol. 2, eds. P. O. Kristeller and F. E. Cranz, Washington, D.C.: 193–8.
Welch, A. 2016. "*Paradise Lost* and English Mock Heroic." In Hoxby and Coiro 2016: 465–82.
West, J. 2018. *Dryden and Enthusiasm: Literature, Religion, and Politics in Restoration England*. Oxford.
West, M. L. 1995. "'Longinus' and the Grandeur of God." In *Ethics and Rhetoric: Classical Essays for Donald Russell on his Seventy-Fifth Birthday*, eds. D. Innes et al., Oxford: 335–42.

West, M. L. 1997. *The East Face of Helicon: West Asiatic Elements in Greek Poetry.* Oxford.
West, R. H. 1955. *Milton and the Angels.* Athens, Georgia.
Whaler, J. 1931a. "Compounding and Distribution of Similes in *Paradise Lost.*" *MP* 28.3: 313–27.
Whaler, J. 1931b. "Grammatical Nexus of the Miltonic Simile." *JEGP* 30.3: 327–34.
Whaler, J. 1931c. "The Miltonic Simile." *PMLA* 46.4: 1034–74.
Whaler, J. 1932. "Animal Simile in *Paradise Lost.*" *PMLA* 47.2: 534–53.
Wilding, M. 1986. "Milton's *Areopagitica*: Liberty for the Sects." *PS* 9.2: 7–38.
Williams, A. 1948. *The Common Expositor: An Account of the Commentaries on Genesis 1527–1633.* Chapel Hill.
Williams, A. 2005. *Poetry and the Creation of a Whig Literary Culture 1681–1714.* Oxford.
Williams, C. 1950. "An Introduction to Milton's Poems (1940)." In *Milton Criticism: Selections from Four Centuries,* ed. J. Thorpe, London: 252–66.
Williams, G. 2016. *The Cosmic Viewpoint: A Study of Seneca's Natural Questions.* Oxford.
Williams, G. 2017. *Pietro Bembo on Etna: The Ascent of a Venetian Humanist.* Oxford.
Wilson, E. A. 2010. "The Art of Reasoning Well: Ramist Logic at Work in *Paradise Lost.*" *RES* 61.248: 55–71.
Wittreich, J. A. (ed.). 1974. "'The Crown of Eloquence': The Figure of the Orator in Milton's Prose Works." In Lieb and Shawcross 1974: 3–54.
Wittreich, J. A. 1979. "From Pastoral to Prophecy: The Genres of *Lycidas.*" *MS* 13: 59–80.
Wolfe, J. 2015. *Homer and the Question of Strife from Erasmus to Hobbes.* Toronto.
Wood, D. N. C. 2001. "Milton and Galileo." *MQ* 35.1: 50–2.
Woolrych, A. 1974. "Milton and Cromwell: 'A short but scandalous night of interruption.'" In Lieb and Shawcross 1974: 185–218.
Worden, B. 1991. "Milton's republicanism and the tyranny of heaven." In *Machiavelli and Republicanism,* eds. G. Bock et al., Cambridge: 225–46.
Worden, B. 2009. *Literature and Politics in Cromwellian England.* Oxford.
Wright, B. A. 1933. "The Alleged Falsehoods in Milton's Account of His Continental Tour." *MLR* 28.3: 308–14.
Wright, B. A. 1947. "Note on *Paradise Lost,* I. 230." *RES* 23.90: 146–7.
Wright, B. A. 1962. *Milton's Paradise Lost.* London.
Wright, M. 2012. *The Comedian as Critic: Greek Old Comedy and Poetics.* London.
Wright, M. 2016–18. *The Lost Plays of Greek Tragedy.* 2 vols. London.

Index

Note: Tables and figures are indicated by an italic "*t*" and "*f*", respectively, following the page number. For the benefit of digital users, indexed terms that span two pages (e.g., 52–53) may, on occasion, appear on only one of those pages.

Accius 5
Achinstein, Sharon 67, 96
Acts of the Apostles 133–4
Addison, Joseph 10, 90–1, 126–7, 129–32, 148
Aesop 44–5
Aetna 34–5, 91 n.19; *see also* Etna
Aldrovandi, Ulisse 99–100
Allacci, Leone, *see* Allatius
Allatius 25*t*, 48–9
Anabaptists 64, 68–9; *see also* enthusiasm
Annesley, Arthur 152–3
antitrinitarianism 137–41; *see also* Socinianism
Aphthonius 23–6, 28–30, 29*f*, 44–5, 149–51, 153–4
Aratus 44–5, 49 n.34, 108–9
Aristophanes 19–20
Aristotle
 in Cambridge curriculum 108–9
 in Galileo iconography 104–5*f*
 on imitation 21–2
 Milton's *At a Vacation Exercise* features categories of 85
 on rhetoric cited by Milton, *see* Milton, John, *Of Education*
 on rhetoric printed by Aldine press 23–4
 on oratorical enthusiasm 15, 19–20
 treatise *Peri kosmou* attributed to 34–5
Aromatari, Giuseppe 27*t*
Ascham, Roger 28–30, 44–5
astronomy, *see* science; space
Aubrey, John 11, 52–3, 76–9, 148
Augustine 39–40, 83–4
Avitus of Vienne 6

Baal 39, 143–4; *see also* Chemos
Barberini, Francesco 47–9
Barberini, Maffeo, *see* Pope Urban VIII
Baroni, Leonora 48–9
Barrow, Samuel 10, 129–31, 148
Baylie, Richard 78–9
Du Bartas, Guillaume de Salluste 59–62, 64–5
Bembo, Pietro 35–6

Benci, Francesco 26–8
Bernegger, Matthias 102–6
Bessarion 23–4
Beza, Theodore 24–6, 137–9
Blount, Thomas 79
Boccaccio, Giovanni 49 n.34, 144–5
Boileau, Nicolas
 L'Art poétique 126–7, 129–31
 Discours au roi 78–9
 Longinus translation by 1–2, 10, 24–8, 30–2, 78–9, 147–9, 152–4
Bonaventure 39–40
Borfet, Abiel 151–2
Boughton, Robert 54–5
Boyle, Robert 54–5
Bracciolini, Poggio 35–6
Brahe, Tycho 110–11, 113 n.103
Brooke, Samuel 152–3
Brown, Cedric 99–100, 124–5
Browne, Thomas 99–100, 106–8
Bruno, Giordano 35–6, 113–14
Buchlerus, Joannes 52–3
Burke, Edmund 1–2
Burton, Robert 97–8, 113–14
Button, Ralph 152–3
Byfield, Richard 151–2
Bysshe, Edward 152–3

Cable, Lana 142–3
Caecilius of Calacte 7–8, 13–18, 37–8
Callimachus 121
Callow, Cornelius 152–3
Calvin, John 24–6, 41, 123
Cambers, Andrew 152–3
Capaccio, Giulio Cesare 92–3
Cardonnel, Peter 149–51
Catholicism, *see* idolatry
Casaubon, Isaac
 on eloquence under Roman emperors according to Longinus 73
 calls Longinus "semi-Christian," 41–2
 cites Longinus on pygmification 100–1

Casaubon, Isaac (*cont.*)
  copy of Robortello's Longinus annotated by 26–8, 30–2, 43–4, 46–7, 149–51
  on the sublimity of the Bible 11, 54–5
Casaubon, Meric 11, 66–7, 72
Castelvetro, Lodovico 50–1
Cato, *Distichs* of 44–5
Cato the Elder 52–3
Cefalu, Paul 134
censorship 77–8, 109–10
Charles I 30–2, 57–8, 68–9, 75–6, 78–80
Charles II 68–9, 71–4, 78–9, 151–3
Chaloner, Edward 57–8
Chamberlaine, James 152–3
Chamier, Daniel 12, 123–5, 133
Chapman, George 28–30, 135–6
Charnock, Stephen 152–3
chastity, *see* virginity
Chaucer, Geoffrey 6–7
Chemos 142–6
Cheney, Patrick 4, 28–30
Cholmley, Samuel 151–2
Chrysostom, Dio 49 n.34
Cicero
  and Demosthenes 19–20, 82
  Renaissance vogue of as context for printing Longinus 24
  on rhetoric cited by Milton, *see* Milton, John, *Of Education*
  on sublime style cited by Tasso 26–8
  taught at St Paul's School and Cambridge 44–6
Cocceius, Johannes 41
Coke, Robert 151–2
Coleridge, Samuel Taylor 1
Colet, John 12, 132–4
Columella 6, 52–3
Conti, Natale 88–90
Copernicus, Nicolaus 102–6, 103–5*f*, 109–10, 113–14
Cosin, John 151–2
Cowley, Abraham 73–4, 78–9
Crespin, Jean 24–6, 27*t*, 149
Cromwell, Oliver 57–8, 73–80, 82–4
Cuffe, Henry 149–51
Culmann, Leonhard 44–5
Curtius, Ernst Robert 39–40
Cyrenaic philosophy 121–2

Danielson, Dennis 114
Dante 6, 49 n.34, 122
Davies, John 73–4
Della Bella, Stefano 102–6
Della Casa, Giovanni 49 n.34
Delphi, Oracle of, *see* Pythia

Demetrius Phalereus 2, 16, 18, 20–1, 26–8, 50–1
democracy 22–3, 56–7, 72–3, 82; *see also* republicanism
Democritus 33–4
Demogorgon 144–5
Demosthenes 17–20, 44–5, 66, 82
Dennis, John 10, 129–31, 148
Denys, John 149–51
Dering, Edward 51–2
Diodati, Charles 54–5, 60–2
Diodati, Giovanni 54–5
Dionysius the Areopagite, *see* Pseudo-Dionysius the Areopagite
Dionysius of Halicarnassus 13–14, 16–20
Dionysius Periegetes 44–5
Dodington, Bartholomew 28–30, 45–6, 149–51
Doran, Robert 1–2
Downame, George 94
Dryden, John 10, 67
dwarfs, *see* pygmies
Dudith, Andreas 24–6

Edwards, Karen 99–100
Egerton family 120–1
Ehwald, Rudolf 5
emotion, *see* pathos
Empedocles, *see* Etna
Empson, William 135
Ennius 5
enthusiasm
  Aristotle on 15
  Meric Casaubon on Longinus and, *see* Casaubon, Meric
  Dionysius of Halicarnassus on 17–18
  early modern understanding of 64–7
  Longinus on 8–9, 20–2, 26–30, 51–2, 72–3, 78–9, 83–4
  Milton and 11, 43, 64–72
Epicurus 33–4, 124–5
Erasmus 24, 41, 44–5
Erizzo, Benedetto 24–6
Erizzo, Francesco 24–6
Ernout-Meillet, etymological dictionary by 4
d'Este, Isabella 100–1
Estienne, Henri 26–8
Etna 11–12, 33–6, 85–94, 98
Eunapius 24–6
Euripides 49 n.34, 55, 60, 108–9, 125
Evelyn, John 36–7, 76, 116–17
Exodus, Book of 135–7, 139

Fairfax, Thomas 73–4, 76–8
da Falgano, Giovanni di Niccolò 7–8, 25*t*
Fallon, Stephen 85

Farnaby, Thomas 28–30, 43–4
fear of God 12, 39, 124–5, 140–7
Festus 4
Fletcher, Harris 144–5
Forsyth, Neil 136–7
Le Fèvre, Tanneguy 24–6, 27t, 31 n.77, 149, 152–4
fiat lux, *see* Genesis, Book of
Ficino, Marsilio 26–8
Fifth Monarchy Men 68–9
Fish, Stanley 95–6
de Fontenelle, Bernard le Bovier 113–14, 115f
freedom, *see* liberty
fulmen eloquentiae, *see* sublimity, thunderbolt as emblem of
Fumaroli, Marc 24
furor poeticus, *see* enthusiasm

Gale, Theophilus 54–5
Gale, Thomas 44–5
Galileo
    John Hall on 108–9
    iconography of 102–8, 103–5f, 107f
    Milton on 11–12, 85, 95–7, 109–10
Gellius, Aulus 90–1
Geminus 108–9
Genesis, Book of
    Augustine on the Spirit of God in 39–40
    John Colet on, *see* Colet, John
    Longinus on, *see* Longinus, on Genesis
    cited by Milton in *De Doctrina Christiana* 140–1
    imitated by Milton in *Paradise Lost* 58–9
    Philo of Alexandria on, *see* Philo of Alexandria
genre 50–4, 77–8, 121
Gessner, Conrad 23–4
Giacomini, Lorenzo 26–8
Gil the Elder, Alexander 43–4, 46–7
Gil the Younger, Alexander 43–4, 46–7
Godolphin, John 152–3
Godolphin, William 78–9, 151–2
Goodwin, John 41–2
Gorgias 15
Greaves, John 118–19
Gregory, Tobias 142–3
Greville, Robert 152–3
Griffith, Matthew 68–9
Grotius, Hugo 11, 55–9
Gunpowder Plot 88, 129

Hacket, John 149–51
Hall, John
    first English translation of Longinus in print by 24–6, 27t
    on Galileo 108–9
    An Humble Motion to the Parliament of England 76
    Milton acquainted with 74–5
    Lansdowne Longinus compared with translation by 30–2, 78–9
    private owners of Longinus translation by 73–4, 149, 151–4
    royalist readers of Longinus translation by 79
    republicanism and Longinus by 24–6, 73–5, 78–80
Hardie, Philip 33–4
Harrington, James 77–8
Hartlib, Samuel 9, 50, 73–5, 153
Haug, Ralph 120
Heinsius, Daniel 26–8
Henrietta Maria 78–9, 100–1
Henry, Philip 76
Heraclides Ponticus 49 n.34
Hermogenes
    taught at Cambridge 45–6
    early editions of 23–6, 28–30, 149–51, 153–4
    cited by Milton, *see* Milton, John, *Of Education*
    on physical and theological sublimity 32
    on rhetorical sublimity 18, 26–8, 51–2
Hesiod 89, 127
Hill, Christopher 83–4
Historia Augusta 73
Hobbes, Thomas 64
Holdsworth, Richard 92–3
Holstenius, Lucas 47–9
Homer
    Iliad 32, 37–8, 66–7, 77–8, 95–6, 98–101, 125–32
    Odyssey 28–30, 65–6, 86–8, 95–7, 135–6
    taught at St Paul's School 44–5
Hooke, Robert 85–6
Horace 44–5, 50–1, 73–4, 76–8, 82–3, 124–5, 135–6
Hudson, Jeffrey 100–1
Hume, Peter 59, 89–91, 118–19, 129–31, 143–6
hupsos, *see* sublimity
Hutchinson, Lucy 36–7, 116–17

iconography 102–8, 110–11
idolatry 12, 141–6
Iliad, *see* Homer
imitation
    of biblical style by Milton 58–9
    of Galileo iconography by William Marshall 106–8
    of God by pagan idols 143–5
    of Homer by Milton 95–6, 98, 125–32
    of Horace by Milton 124–5, 135–6

imitation (cont.)
   of Lucan by Milton 127–8
   of Milton on heavenly battle refused by
     Samuel Morland 129–31
   of pagans by Catholics 141–2
   as a source of the sublime according to
     Longinus 21–2
   of Vergil on Etna avoided by Milton 90–1
Inquisition 96, 109–10, 113–14
inspiration, *see* enthusiasm; *Paradise Lost*,
   divinely inspired
Isaiah 54–5, 60–2, 139
Isocrates 17–18

Jacomb, Thomas 152–3
James I 43–4, 149–51
Jardine, Nicholas 102–6
Jean de Jandun 39–40
Jessop, Thomas 152–3
Job, Book of 112–13
Jocelyn, H. D. 5
John, Gospel of 100–1, 123, 134 n.66
John of Sicily 23–4
Jonson, Ben 121–2
Jordan, Thomas 79–80
Judges, Book of 139
Junius, Franciscus 43–4
Justin 44–5
Juvenal 44–5

Kant, Immanuel 1–2
Kaoukji, Natalie 102–6
Kepler, Johannes 102–6, 103*f*
King, John 129
Kircher, Athanasius 10–12, 35–6, 86, 87*f*, 91–3

Labé, Louise 77–8
Lactantius 137
Lambin, Denys 26–8
Langbaine, Gerard
   first English edition of Longinus by 27*t*, 30–2
   lent Robortello's Longinus by Patrick
     Young 30–2, 43–4
   Milton's potential use of Longinus edition
     by 49–53, 74–5
   de Petra's preface reprinted in Longinus
     edition by 73–5, 80–1
   private owners of Longinus edition by 49–50,
     147–9, 151–4
   royalist politics of 78–9
   title page of Longinus edition by, *see* Marshall,
     William
Lansdowne Longinus, *see* Longinus, Lansdowne
   translation of

Lascaris, Janus 23–4
Laud, William 78–9, 142–4, 146
Lawes, Henry 120
Leonard, John 113–14, 116–17, 131–2
Leslie, Charles 129–31
Lewis, C. S. 99, 117, 134–5, 144
Lieb, Michael 140–1
Lilburne, John 67–8
liberty 22–3, 72–84, 113–14
Livy 5
Logan, John 24–6
London, William 149
Longinus
   ascription of *Peri hupsous* to 1–2, 13–14
   Byzantine manuscript of 13–14, 23–4
   dating of 13–14, 17–18
   on democracy and letters 22–3, 72–3,
     80–2, 100
   editio princeps of, *see* Robortello, Francesco
   early editions and translations of 24–6, 25–7*t*
   on Genesis 23–4, 37–8, 41–2, 51–2, 55–9, 120,
     124, 133, 136–7, 152
   Greek rhetorical theory as context for 13–23
   Lansdowne translation of 12, 25*t*, 30–2, 65–6,
     72, 78–9, 147–8, 155–68
   cited by Milton, *see* Milton, John, *Of Education*
   in private libraries 12, 28–30, 49–50, 78–9,
     147–54
   Renaissance reception of 23–32
   see also sublimity
Longinus, Cassius 1 n.3, 13–14, 18, 24–6, 73
Lorich, Reinhard 44–5
Louis XIV 78–9
Lowth, Robert 54–5
Lucan 55, 82–3, 125, 127–8
Lucretius
   Adam in *Paradise Lost* echoes 133
   Denys Lambin as editor of 26–8
   in Milton's *Of Education* 108–9
   the phrase *sublime volans* in 5
   and physical sublimity 10–11, 33–7, 85–6,
     91, 113–14
   Renaissance reception of 35–7
   and space in *Paradise Lost* 113–14, 116–17
Lycophron 49 n.34
Lysias 16–17

Manilius 108–9
Manolessi, Carlo 27*t*, 149, 151–4
Manso, Giovanni Battista 92–3
Manton, Thomas 152–3
Manuel, Albert 24–6
Manutius the Elder, Aldus 23–6, 35–6
Manutius the Younger, Aldus 24–6

Manutius, Paulus 24, 27t, 37–8, 149–51
Marino, Giambattista 92–3
Marsh, Narcissus 152
Marshall, William 60, 61f, 102–8, 103f, 106–7f, 110–11
Marston, John 64–5
Martelli, Francesco 35–6
Martial 44–5
Marvell, Andrew
  confronted Milton's enthusiasm 67
  Horatian Ode upon Cromwel's Return from Ireland 73–80, 82–3
  praised Milton's *Defensio Secunda* as sublime 74–5
  praised *Paradise Lost* as sublime 10, 85, 129–31, 148
Matthew, Gospel of 55–6, 58–9
Mazzoni, Jacopo 50–1
Mazzucchi, Carlo 7–8
McDowell, Nicholas 53–4, 79
Mede, Joseph 108–9
Melanchthon, Philip 64–5
Mendoza, Diego Hurtado de 23–4
Milton, John
  Animadversions 60–2
  Apology for Smectymnuus (*Apology for a Pamphlet*) 45–6, 122
  Areopagitica 69–70, 96, 109–10
  Artis Logicae Plenior Instituto 94–6
  Brief Notes upon a Late Sermon 68–9
  commonplace book of 80–1, 83–4, 137, 142–3
  Defensio pro Populo Anglicano 67–8
  Defensio Secunda 67–8, 74–5, 117–18
  De Doctrina Christiana 12, 56, 62–3, 116–17, 120, 133, 137–43, 147
  Doctrine and Discipline of Divorce 68–9
  education of 43–7
  Of Education 2, 9, 11, 30–2, 44–5, 50–4, 59–60, 76, 108–9
  epigrams addressed to Leonora Baroni by 48–9
  Epistolae Familiares 46–50, 60–2
  History of Britain 81
  in Italy 47–50, 92–3, 96
  Letters of State 52–3, 77–8
  Likeliest Means to Remove Hirelings 82–3
  Lycidas 67–8
  Mansus 92–3
  Maske Presented at Ludlow Castle 12, 120–5, 135–6, 147
  Nativity Ode 60–2
  Paradise Lost, see *Paradise Lost*
  Paradise Regain'd 56–60, 96
  Il Penseroso 67–8, 72
  1645 Poems 46–7, 121
  Prolusiones 45–6, 89–90, 92–3, 144
  Readie and Easie Way to Establish a Free Commonwealth 71–2, 82–3
  Reason of Church-Government 43–4, 59–62, 68–9, 118–20
  Of Reformation 57–8, 142–4
  reputation for sublimity of 1–2, 10, 52–4, 129–31
  Samson Agonistes 12, 58–9, 68–9, 145–6
  sonnets addressed to Cromwell, Fairfax, and Vane by 76–8, 80–1
  Tenure of Kings and Magistrates 41–2, 75–6, 80–1
  Tetrachordon 56, 123
  theme on early rising by 44–5
  In Quintum Novembris 11–12, 88–9
  At a Vacation Exercise 85
Minshull, Elizabeth 62–3
Mocenigo, Alvise I 24–6
Mommsen, Theodor 37–8
Monk, Samuel 2
Montaigne, Michel de 26–8
Moore, Leslie 2, 129–31, 148
More, Henry 64–5
Morland, Samuel 129–31
Moses, see Longinus, on Genesis
mountains 35–6, 86–8, 91, 97–8, 127, 129–31, 135–6; see also Etna
Muretus 24, 26–8

Naevius 5
natural philosophy, see science
Nedham, Marchamont 79–80
newsbooks 73–4, 79–80
Newton, Isaac 117–18
Newton, Thomas, eighteenth-century Milton scholar 62–4
Newton, Thomas, Elizabethan translator of Seneca 28–30
Norbrook, David 3–4, 11, 73–4
Numbers, Book of 143–4

Odyssey, see Homer
Oldenburg, Henry 86
d'Olivar, Juan 113–14, 115f
Oporinus, Johannes 24, 27t, 149
Orsini, Fulvio 24, 25t
Ovid 6, 17–18, 33–4, 44–5, 59–60, 88–9, 106–8, 122
Owen, John 57–8, 152–3
Owen, Thankful 152–3

Pagano, Pietro 24–8, 27t
Paleario, Aonio 35–6

Palingenius, Marcellus 35–6
Palmer, Edward 152–3
Paradise Lost
   Adam in 59, 80–1, 108–14, 116, 125–6, 133
   astronomical dialogue in 110–14
   Chaos in 12, 63–4, 114–19, 127–8, 144, 147
   the Creation in 58–9, 116–17, 133
   Demogorgon in, *see* Demogorgon
   divinely inspired 62–4, 67, 69–72; *see also* enthusiasm
   Eve in 59, 81–2
   God in 12, 58–9, 82–4, 111–14, 116–17, 128–9, 132–46
   Michael in 80–1, 125–8, 131–2
   the Muse in 59–64, 67, 69–72
   Raphael in 58–60, 109–14, 125–6, 133
   early reception of 10, 52–4, 67, 85, 126–7, 129–31, 148
   Satan as cosmic traveler in 114–19
   Satan as exemplar of false sublimity in 11, 81–4
   Satan fights angels in, *see* theomachy
   Satan hateful in 137
   Satan as republican orator in 11, 81–4, 147
   Satan in similes in, *see* similes
   Satan warned of God's wrath in 140–1
   similes in, *see* similes
   the Son in 58–9, 131–2
   style of 10, 43, 52–4, 58–63, 67, 69–72
   war in heaven in, *see* theomachy
Parisetti, Lodovico 35–6
Parker, Matthew 6–7
passion, *see* pathos
pathos
   Dionysius of Halicarnassus on 17
   as an emendation of *bathos* in Longinus 7–8
   enslaves according to Longinus 22–3, 72–3
   enslaves according to Milton 80–1
   of God according to Milton 137
   as a source of the sublime according to Longinus 15, 20–2, 28–30, 65–6, 78–9
   Lucretius on 33–4
   of poetry according to Milton 50–2
   Satan enslaved by 11, 82–4
   sublimity without 86–7, 97
Patrizi, Francesco 26–8
Patterson, Annabel 3–4, 73–4
Pauline Epistles 41, 56, 133–4, 137–41
Pearce, Zachary 116
Peor, *see* Chemos
Peri hupsous, *see* Longinus
Pericles 19–20, 56–7
Persius 44–5
Petrarch 122

de Petra, Gabriel
   Geneva edition of Longinus by 24–6, 27t
   Langbaine's reuse of Longinus edition by 30–2, 49–50, 73–5, 80–1
   private owners of Longinus edition by 149, 151–4
   on the republicanism of Longinus 73–5, 78–81
Phillips, Edward
   Compendiosa Enumeratio Poetarum 10, 52–4
   educated under Milton 11, 50, 52–4, 108–9
   introduced to Longinus by Milton 11, 50, 52–4
   Mysteries of Love & Eloquence 79
   New World of English Words 52–3, 110–11
   on the sublimity of *Paradise Lost* 10, 52–4, 148
   Theatrum Poetarum 52–3, 69–70
   published political sonnets by Milton 77–8
   on Wollebius 140–1
Phillips, John 50
Phillips, Owen 152–3
Philo of Alexandria 10–11, 39
Philosophical Transactions 86
Philostratus 121–2
Pindar 49 n.34
Pinelli, Niccolò 24–6, 27t
Pizzimenti, Domenico 24–6, 27t
Plato
   Demogorgon a misinterpretation of the demiurge of 144
   Dionysius of Halicarnassus on the sublimity of 17–18
   on eyes being suited for astronomy 106–8
   on the flight of the soul 60–2
   on *furor poeticus* 19–20, 26–8, 72
   on imitation 21–2
   on rhetoric cited by Milton, *see* Milton, John, *Of Education*
   on the tetrahedral shape of fire 118–19
Pliny the Elder 108–9
Plutarch 19–20, 100–1
Pococke, Edward 152
Polanus, Amandus 12, 141–3
Pontano, Giovanni 35–6
Poole, Josua 97–8
Poole, William 63–4
Pope, Alexander 131–2
Pope Clement IX 47–8
Pope Urban VIII 47–8
Porphyrion 124
Porphyry 24–6, 47–8
Porter, James 2–3, 7, 13

Portus, Franciscus
  Isaac Casaubon studied Greek under 26–8
  commentary on Longinus by 26–8, 37–8
  early edition of Longinus by 24–6, 27t
  manuscript of Longinus annotated by 30–2
  Milton as possible reader of Longinus edition
    by 45–7, 49–50
  on Longinus' paraphrase of Genesis 37–8
  private owners of Longinus edition by 28–30,
    149–54
possession, see enthusiasm
Presocratics 34–5
Pratt, Roger 151–2
Procopius 39–40
Proverbs, Book of 41, 84
Psalms 44–5, 111–12, 131, 139–41, 144–5
Psellos, Michael 23–4, 131–2
Pseudo-Apollodorus 44–5
Pseudo-Dionysius the Areopagite 12, 133–5
Pseudo-Longinus, see Longinus
Ptolemy 104–5f, 108–11, 114
Purchas, Samuel 97–8
Puteanus, Erycius 121–2
pygmies 11–12, 98–101, 118–19
pyramids 118–19
Pythagoras 47–8
Pythia 21–2, 26–8, 65–6

Quintilian 15, 45–6

Rabelais, François 91
Rainolds, John 28–30
Ramus, Petrus 94–5
Refini, Eugenio 26–8
regicide 30–2, 67, 71–2, 75–6, 80
Reinhold, Erasmus 109–10
republicanism 3–4, 11, 22–6, 28–30, 43,
    72–84, 147
Revard, Stella 128–9
Revelation, Book of 60–2, 88–9, 125, 129–31,
    133–4
Reynolds, Edward 41
Rhetorica ad Herennium 16
Richard of St. Victor 39–40
Richardson, Jonathan 148
Ricks, Christopher 43, 99
Robortello, Francesco
  Isaac Casaubon's copy of Longinus edition
    by 26–8, 43–4, 46–7, 149–51, 153–4
  editio princeps of Longinus by 2–3, 24, 27t
  on *furor* in Longinus 26–8, 65
  Patrick Young lent Langbaine Longinus
    edition by 30–2, 43–4
Rookes, Thomas 151–2

Rosa, Salvator 35–6
Ross, Alexander 102–6, 146
Rospigliosi, Giulio, see Pope Clement IX
Rouse, John 46–7
Royal Society 86, 101, 108–9, 153
Russell, D. A. 8–9

de Sacrobosco, Johannes 108–9
Sallust 44–5
Sallustius 48–9
Salmasius, Claudius 67–8
Sandys, George 88–9, 92–3
Sangar, Gabriel 152–3
Sappho 77–8, 121
Scaliger, Joseph 26–8, 108–9
scatological imagery 91–2
science 6–7, 11–12, 34–5, 85, 147
Scory, Edmund 97–8
Seaman, Lazarus 152–3
Selden, John 143–4
Seneca the Elder 22–3, 82
Seneca the Younger 28–30, 34–5, 91
Septuagint 37–9, 60–2, 133, 139
Servetus, Michael 137–9
Shakespeare, William 1–2, 49 n.34, 99, 110–11
Sherley, Thomas 152–3
Shore, Daniel 145
Shuger, Debora 26–8
Sidney, Robert 151–2
Sill, William 152–3
similes 11–12, 70–1, 81–5, 88–101,
    118–19, 147
Skinner, Quentin 80–1
slavery 11–12, 22–3, 45–6, 72–3, 80–1, 83–4,
    99–101
Smith, Nigel 73–4
Smith, Thomas 30–2
Socinianism 24–6; *see also* antitrinitarianism
space 11–12, 32–6, 85, 101–19
Spencer, John 11, 64–6
Spenser, Edmund 144–5
Spinoza 86
Stampa, Gaspara 77–8
Statius 144
Stein, Arnold 126–7, 129–31
Stillingfleet, Benjamin 134–5
Stillingfleet, Edward 152
Stobaeus 55
Stoicism 22–3, 121–2
Stokes, David 78–9, 151–2
Stoughton, John 41–2
Sturler, Abraham 24–6
sublime, the, *see* sublimity
On the Sublime, *see* Longinus

sublimity
  of the Bible 37–42, 54–64, 69–70, 120, 123–4
  definitions of 4, 10, 18–20
  eagle as emblem of 60–2, 102–8, 106–7f
  failures at achieving 15, 20–1, 81–4
  as perilous flight 59–60, 69–71, 79–80
  historiography of 1–4, 7
  medieval conception of 39–40
  philology of 4–10
  physical or natural-philosophical species of 10–13, 32–7, 85, 127, 147
  politics of 3–4, 11, 18–19, 22–3, 28–30, 43, 72–84, 147
  rhetorical species of 10–11, 13–32, 43, 147
  sources of according to Longinus 20–2
  theological species of 10–13, 32, 36–42, 120, 147
  thunderbolt as emblem of 19–20, 39–40, 56–7, 123
Suda 37–8
Suetonius 100–1
Sugimura, N. K. 134
Sylvester, Josuah 59–60, 64–5

Tacitus 22–3, 82
Tasso, Torquato 26–8, 50–1, 76, 88–9, 92–3, 144–5
Taverner, Richard 64–5
Taylor, John 79–80
theomachy 12, 37–8, 78–9, 125–33, 147
Theophrastus 15
Thomason, George 151–2
Timaeus 15
timor Dei, *see* fear of God
timor idololatricus, *see* idolatry
translation, *see* Longinus, early editions and translations of
Typhon (Typhoeus) 88–91, 93–4
Tyson, Edward 99–100

de Vaan, Michiel 4
Vadian, Joachim 24 n.39

Vane, Henry 77–8
Varchi, Benedetto 49 n.34
Varro 6, 52–3
Venner, Thomas 68–9
Vergil 5, 26–8, 44–5, 60, 90–1, 97–8, 129–31
Vettori, Pietro 26–8
Vida, Marco Girolamo 125–7
virginity 12, 120–5
volcanos, *see* Etna
Voltaire 126–7
Vossius, Gerardus 9, 26–8
Vossius, Isaac 43–4

Wallis, John 117–18
war in heaven, *see* theomachy
Warton, Thomas 124
Watkins, Stephen 152–3
Watson, Thomas 152–3
West, John 67
Wethereld, Thomas 30–2
Whaler, James 93–6
Whitelocke, Bulstrode 24–6, 73–4
Wilkins, John 11–12, 102–8, 103f, 107f, 110–11, 113–14
Williams, Charles 121–2
Willughby, Francis 108–9
Wollebius, Johannes 12, 140–2
Wollstonecraft, Mary 1–2
Wood, Anthony 46–7, 76, 152–3
Worden, Blair 135
Worsley, Benjamin 152–3
Wotton, Henry 12, 28–30, 29–30f, 121, 149–51
wrath 12, 67–8, 124–5, 135–7, 140–1, 144–5, 147
Wren, Christopher, Dean of Windsor 108

Young, Patrick 30–2, 43–4, 46–8
Young, Thomas 43–4

Zeno of Verona 39–40